The Commands
of the Apostles

PRACTICAL NEW TESTAMENT FOUNDATIONS FOR VIBRANT
PERSONAL GROWTH AND INFLUENTIAL CHURCH LIFE

ASSEMBLED AND WITH NOTES BY MICHAEL PHILLIPS

This edition of *The Commands of the Apostles* is published by Sunrise Books, Publishers. Additional quantities are available through FatherOfTheInklings.com.

It may be my reader will desire me to say *how* the Lord will deliver him from his sins. That is like the lawyer's "Who is my neighbour?" The spirit of such a mode of receiving the offer of the Lord's deliverance is the root of all the horrors of a corrupt theology, so acceptable to those who love weak and beggarly hornbooks of religion. Such questions spring from the passion for the fruit of the tree of knowledge, not the fruit of the tree of life. Men would understand: they do not care to *obey*;—understand where it is impossible they should understand save by obeying. They would search into the work of the Lord instead of doing their part in it—thus making it impossible both for the Lord to go on with his work, and for themselves to become capable of seeing and understanding what he does. Instead of immediately obeying the Lord of life, the one condition upon which he can help them, and in itself the beginning of their deliverance, they set themselves to question their unenlightened intellects as to his plans for their deliverance...They would bind their Samson until they have scanned his limbs and thews. Incapable of understanding the first motions of freedom in themselves, they proceed to interpret the riches of his divine soul in terms of their own beggarly notions, to paraphrase his glorious verse into their own paltry commercial prose; and then, in the growing presumption of imagined success, to insist upon their neighbours' acceptance of their distorted shadows of "the plan of salvation" as the truth of him in whom is no darkness, and the one condition of their acceptance with him. They delay setting their foot on the stair which alone can lead them to the house of wisdom, until they shall have determined the material and mode of its construction. For the sake of knowing, they postpone that which alone can enable them to know, and substitute for the true understanding which lies beyond, a false persuasion that they already understand. They will not accept, that is, act upon, their highest privilege, that of obeying the Son of God. It is on them that do his will, that the day dawns; to them the day-star arises in their hearts. Obedience is the soul of knowledge...

God forbid I should seem to despise understanding. The New Testament is full of urgings to understand. Our whole life, to be life at all, must be a growth in understanding. What I cry out upon is the misunderstanding that comes of man's endeavour to understand while not obeying. Upon obedience our energy must be spent; understanding will follow. Not anxious to know our duty, or knowing it and not doing it, how shall we understand that which only a true heart and a clean soul can ever understand...Until a man begins to obey, the light that is in him is darkness...

The sum of the whole matter is this: The Son has come from the Father to set the children free from their sins; the children must hear and obey him.

George MacDonald, *The Hope of the Gospel*, 1892 "Salvation From Sin"

A small abridged version of this book, *The Pocket Commands of the Apostles*, is available through FatherOfTheInkling.com.

© 2014 by Michael and Judy Phillips

The Commands of the Apostles: Practical New Testament foundations for vibrant personal growth and influential church life

ISBN 978-0940652279

CONTENTS

THE APOSTOLIC COMMANDS

1. JERUSALEM
Pursue Godliness

1   Yield yourself to God.
2   Present yourself as a daily living sacrifice to God.
3   Choose to be transformed by the renewal of mind.
4   Seek to grow in righteousness.
5   Train yourself in Godliness.
6   Be constant in prayer.
7   Abide in Jesus.
8   Lead a virtuous life.
9   Set your thoughts on high things.
10 Serve God and live for his glory.

2. ANTIOCH
Nurture Personal Spirituality

11 Obey the Lord's commands.
12 Be a doer of the word, not a hearer only.
13 Take your faith seriously.
14 Take heed to yourself.
15 Do not envy.
16 Do not be afraid or lose heart.
17 Keep watchful and alert.
18 Stand firm and courageous in God.
19 Be thankful in all circumstances.
20 Don't worry.

3. GALATIA
Grow the Fruits of the Spirit

21 Walk by the Spirit.
22 Make love your aim.
23 Rejoice in all circumstances, especially in your trials.
24 Walk in peace.
25 Respond with patience.
26 Be kind.
27 Do good, love good, be good.
28 Walk faithfully by faith, not by sight.
29 Be a gentle person.
30 Exercise self-control.

4. CORINTH
Turn From Sin

31 Repent.
32 Do not be conformed to the world.
33 Hate evil.
34 Sin no more—do not yield to sin.
35 Do not participate in the sins of others.
36 Do not associate with immorality.
37 Avoid worldly-minded believers.
38 Revere no idols.
39 Confess your sins.
40 Keep your conscience clear.

5. THESSALONICA
Live God's Priorities at Home

41 Christian leaders, live exemplary lives.
42 Honor marriage.
43 Husbands, love, honor and serve your wives.
44 Wives, respect and submit to your husbands.
45 Children, obey and honor your parents.
46 Practice hospitality.
47 Manage your households well.
48 Raise your children in the wisdom of the Lord.
49 Train young men to be self-controlled, young women to be chaste and domestic.
50 Care for widows and orphans.

7. ATHENS
Develop Wise and Gracious Habits

61 Conduct yourself becomingly.
62 Be courteous and full of grace toward all.
63 Do not insist on your own way.
64 Don't be suspicious. (Don't yield to or allow suspicions to fester)
65 Live without guile.
66 Do not be irritable or resentful.
67 Do not be foolish.
68 Mind your own business.
69 Give generously.
70 Owe no one anything.

6. LAODICEA
Show Respect in Relationships

51 Show honor and respect to all.
52 Seek the good of others.
53 Put others first.
54 Be merciful and full of sympathy.
55 Harbor no grievances or animosities.
56 Avoid the shallow and hypocritical who do not live their faith.
57 Control anger.
58 Don't judge.
59 Associate with the lowly. Show no partiality to the rich and powerful.
60 Place no stumbling blocks in the way of another's faith.

8. CAESSAREA
Speak With Grace

71 Speak graciously.
72 Control your tongue.
73 Be quick to listen, slow to speak.
74 Say what you mean.
75 Do not grumble, complain, or speak against others.
76 Do not gossip, slander, or lie.
77 Do not swear.
78 Do not quarrel.
79 Speak to edify, encourage, and bless one another.
80 Speak not to flatter, impress, or please men.

9. PHILIPPI
Reflect Christlikeness of Character

81 Put on the character of Christ.
82 Seek God's will and live by it.
83 Pray for wisdom and walk in wisdom.
84 Be pure.
85 See through God's eyes by developing the mind of Christ.
86 Do not be covetous, greedy, or a lover of money.
87 Clothe yourself with humility.
88 Eagerly rejoice in right and goodness.
89 Endure suffering with faith, fortitude, grace, and courage.
90 Wage vigorous spiritual warfare.

10. COLOSSAE
Build Mature Beliefs

91 Be mature in your thinking and wise in doctrine.
92 Increase your knowledge of God.
93 Build on a foundation of Jesus Christ.
94 Love truth.
95 Do not be ruled by legalisms.
96 Do not be shallow of belief.
97 Walk with discernment.
98 Do not dispute over doctrine.
99 Do not be deceived.
100 Equip yourselves for fitness to teach spiritual completeness.

11. EPHESUS
Exemplify Unity and Servanthood in Church Life

101 Do not be anxious to teach or place the immature in leadership.
102 Older men and women, teach younger men and women.
103 Pursue and emphasize what builds up the body of Christ.
104 Encourage one another.
105 Be sensitive to the weak in faith.
106 Use your gifts wisely.
107 Do all things decently and in order.
108 Deal with body conflicts in the church.
109 Don't neglect fellowship with your brothers and sisters.
110 Maintain unity.

12. ROME
Evidence Discipleship in the World

111 Live quiet peaceable lives.
112 Live in harmony with all.
113 Honor and submit to authority.
114 Honor, respect, and give your best to your masters and employers.
115 Be modest in dress, manners, and demeanor.
116 Aim at what is honorable in men's eyes as well as God's.
117 Work diligently and do not be slothful or idle.
118 Live your faith with zeal, good cheer, and steadfastness.
119 Consider your witness.
120 Recognize yourselves as a people set apart.

INTRODUCTION

Doctrine and Theology vs. Character and Conduct:
Which is Capable of Validating Truth and Bringing the World to Christ?

This book is a companion to "The Commands of Jesus," which was entitled simply *The Commands*. In the Introduction to that earlier volume, I explained the priorities undergirding our discussion of the Commands. Those same priorities apply to *The Commands of the Apostles*. Rather than repeating everything here, I refer you to that introduction. It will provide the best preparation for what we will be seeking to do here.

Similar though the two volumes appear, there exists an enormous difference in the raw material from which each set of commands has been drawn. Jesus' commands are almost universally addressed to *individuals*. Not so the commands and instructions of the Apostles. Many of their instructions are directed toward "the church" at large, or to specific church groups, to factions within a church, to various functions of the church, and to issues that arise in a church setting. Some of these are intended to be universally applicable to all Christians. Some are not. It can be difficult to discern the difference.

THE *IDEAS* OF CHRISTIANITY VS. THE *DO* OF THE GOSPEL

A hindrance to a straightforward grouping of the Apostolic commands is the heavy "spiritual" tone of the epistles. Anyone who has read the post-gospel writings of the New Testament recognizes immediately that they are primarily theological documents. As important as theology is to *understand* the Christian faith, it is not particularly helpful in assisting us to *do* the Christian faith. Both elements are vital. We are commanded to think and understand. We are also commanded to *live* the practical tenets of Christianity. In 1 Corinthians 14:20, Paul writes, *In understanding be men* (KJV), or, as the RSV has it, *In thinking be mature*. But on the other side of it, we are all familiar with James' words, *Faith without works is dead.*

Most studies and commentaries on the epistles of the New Testament emphasize the *ideas* of their authors, especially the theology of Paul. This little book will be different. We will focus mostly on the *do*—on the practical commands and instructions given us by the Apostolic writers. This is not because the ideas are unimportant. But books and studies too numerous to count are already available dissecting every doctrinal nuance of every book of the New Testament. Writings that challenge and exhort toward obedience are rare, and thus perhaps more urgently needed. Such will be our emphasis.

Discovering the practical challenges to obedience in the writings of the Apostles is a daunting task precisely because those men were largely preoccupied with the theology of a new faith (call it a new "religion" if you like) that the life and teachings of Jesus Christ had set in motion. Everything was new. They were grappling with ideas and principles no one had heard before. They were *formulating* a doctrine of Christianity even as they were desperately trying to understand the complexities of exactly what the Lord's life, death, and resurrection signified. They were trying both to escape the confines of Judaism while at the same time figure out what Judaism had been intended to mean all along. This was essentially a *theological* struggle. Every one of the New Testament writers was involved on the front lines of that tussle and debate about Christianity's *ideas*. Therefore, much in their writings is more theological than practical. *Christ died for your sins* is a great truth, one of Christianity's most pivotal truths. But it is not something you can go out and *do* in the next ten minutes. There is not an immediately visible component of obedience attached to the truth until other commands are brought alongside it.

THEOLOGICAL VS. PRACTICAL COMMANDS

Therefore, turning from the relatively straightforward Commands of Jesus to the commands and instructions of the Apostles, we face the dilemma of how to balance a complex mix of diverse instructions—those theologic instructions aimed toward our *understanding*, and those aimed at *character and conduct*. In other words, those that target the *ideas* of faith, and those that target *obedience*.

A few brief examples will illustrate the distinction clearly.

The Apostles command us:

> *Consider yourselves dead to sin and alive to God.* (Romans 6:11)
> *Understand this mystery: a hardening has come upon part of Israel, until the full number of Gentiles come in.* (Romans 11:25-26)
> *Be rooted and built up in Jesus and established in the faith.* (Colossians 2:7)
> *Work out your own salvation with fear and trembling.* (Philippians 2:12)
> *Show earnestness in realizing the full assurance of hope until the end.* (Hebrews 6:11)
> *Go forth to Jesus outside the camp.* (Hebrews 13:13)
> *Conduct yourself with fear throughout the time of your exile.* (1 Peter 1:17)
> *Count the forbearance of our Lord as salvation.* (2 Peter 3:15)

Though truth is represented here, practicality is more difficult to lay hold of. The writers are speaking to our understanding, not to the obedience of our behavior.

They also command us:

> *Practice hospitality.*
> *Love the brethren.*
> *Build one another up.*
> *Speak graciously.*
> *Do not be a drunkard.*
> *Rejoice in your trials.*
> *Ask God for wisdom.*
> *Edify your neighbor.*
> *Do not associate with the immoral.*
> *Live peaceably with all.*

The difference is obvious. These are all things we as individual Christian men and women can DO. We don't do them only in church, we do them where we live. Most of them are things we can do in the next ten minutes.

HOW TRUTH IS VALIDATED AND THE WORLD BROUGHT TO CHRIST

An even more important distinction exists between these various kinds of instructions and commands we find in the New Testament. Only one of the two above types of commands is capable of validating the truth of Christianity and bringing the world to a knowledge of Christ. On the surface it might seem that convincing the world of the truth of Jesus' claims would require a massive dissemination of the *ideas* of Christianity.

This is one of the great dichotomies of the faith Jesus brought to the world. It is not, in fact, transmitted by *ideas*, but by living *example*.

Counterintuitive as it seems, all the ideas, all the expositions, all the knowledge, all the understanding, all the apologetics, all the proofs, all the persuasive scriptural arguments in the world are *incapable* of validating Christianity's truth on a widespread scale that will bring the world to a knowledge of Christ. Isolated cases certainly exist where conversions occur solely on the basis of a persuasive apologetic of ideas. God can use anything to convict of truth—including ideas and theology. But conversions based on pure theological persuasion are rare.

It is in the *practical commands of personal character and Christlikeness* where one discovers the power to influence the world. Theology and doctrine are fine...but they must be seen as *sidelights* to the living essence of gospel truth. The reason that the down-to-earth, practical, conduct-and-character commands are what most powerfully validate the truths of Christianity comes straight from Jesus himself. He says in no uncertain terms. *People will believe in me, not from your theology, but because of how you live.* That's why Jesus didn't teach primarily with theological treatises. He taught and commanded his listeners in conduct, behavior, and character.

Therefore, our emphasis in this book will be on the second type of commands, those that address daily life. Some will be phrased more spiritually and theologically than others. Some may be addressed to the church, yet will still be a matter of *individual* obedience. But *all* the commands and instructions we will consider have some element of practical obedience that is demanded of us.

This distinction between theology and practicality also highlights why, in compiling this book, I have found myself occasionally writing rather more personally than was the case when discussing the Commands of Jesus. Though I have tried to avoid overuse of personal anecdote, because the commands of the Apostles are more subject to such wide diversity of personal application, I often found that I could not help speaking of my own response to these commands. Whether this will be a help or a hindrance to readers, I suppose that will be a matter of very personal response as well. Appendix 1 explains in more detail the methods used in determining which commands we will consider out of the multitude of diverse instructions found in the post-gospel New Testament.

WHAT IS SPIRITUAL MATURITY?

One of the important commands from the epistles is found in Hebrews 6:1-2. It is a lengthy and predominately "theological" command. But its essence can be boiled down to this: *Let us go on to maturity.*

This raises the obvious question—What comprises spiritual maturity? Christians are fond of talking about spiritual "growth." What is it we are growing into?

Many earnest Christians assume that growth means increasing one's knowledge and understanding of the theology and ideas of Christianity. By this view, maturity is an intellectual exercise. Those of this perspective pore over their Bibles. They read books and attend Bible studies and listen to sermons and take notes...increasing their store of information about Christ, his work, the church, the Bible, the atonement, the Trinity, sanctification, and so on. Scriptures and proof-texts are memorized to bolster various doctrines. In time all this study creates walking encyclopedias of spiritual knowledge. This they call "growing" in faith.

Alongside these, we might consider the man or woman who has never read the New Testament through, who is not interested in the various theories of the atonement, for whom the book of *Romans* would be incomprehensible, and who has never taken a sermon note in his or her life. Yet among these "theologically unenlightened" souls may be some who for thirty, forty, fifty years or more have lived the Commands of Jesus with sacrificial selflessness, and whose character has thus over the decades slowly come to reflect the Christlikeness that must be the objective of every Christian.

Where is the real "growth" into maturity?

Surely maturity in the Christian faith must be measured by Christlikeness of character and conduct, not an encyclopedic knowledge of doctrines and their proof texts. There is no *true* "understanding" of spiritual principles without the obedience that leads to Christlikeness. That is precisely why I called theology a "sidelight." No theology or doctrine ever produced a Christlike man or woman. Doctrine and theology are among Christianity's hobbies. Some people like to pursue them. Others don't. But they do not represent the essence of what Christianity actually *is*.

In his sermon "Justice," George MacDonald perceptively puts this dichotomy into crystal-clear perspective: "Our business is not to think correctly, but to live truly; then first will there be a possibility of our thinking correctly."

THE TWELVE CITIES

Organizing the commands that follow into groupings according to twelve New Testament cities merely provides a means to help us gain an appreciation for the setting and historical milieu which produced the apostolic writings. In the same way that the villages, hills, and seashores of Galilee produced the Commands of Jesus, the development of the church as it moved outward from Jerusalem and ultimately to Rome gives us the raw material out of which the Apostolic commands emerged.

More important than the city headings, however, may be the sub-titles for each group. These give us profound insight into the breadth and extent of the commands the apostles laid upon the Christians of the first century. The apostolic commands touched every facet of life. The demand they made upon attitude, lifestyle, conduct, and character was stringent, uncompromising, and total. These were no commands for the faint-hearted, for Sunday-only Christians. Paul went so far as to command having nothing to do with Christians who played at religion but whose character and conduct were no different than people of the world. These commands represent graduate level Christian living.

It might behoove us as we set out, therefore, to ponder with prayerful sobriety the progression of the apostolic commands as we will encounter them:

PURSUE GODLINESS—*A holy foundation of spiritual intimacy upon which to build a church.*
NURTURE PERSONAL SPIRITUALITY—*Qualities of individual obedience that produce maturity.*
GROW THE FRUITS OF THE SPIRIT—*Qualities of personal behavior, attitude, and character that exemplify the fruit of the Christ-life.*
TURN FROM SIN—*Leaving the past behind by renouncing the priorities of the world.*
LIVE GOD'S PRIORITIES AT HOME—*Christian maturity and leadership begin in the family.*
SHOW RESPECT IN RELATIONSHIPS—*How we treat others reflects our love for Christ.*
DEVELOP WISE AND GRACIOUS HABITS—*Daily habits that reveal inner character.*
SPEAK WITH GRACE—*The grace of Christ begins with the tongue, mirror of the soul.*
REFLECT CHRISTLIKENESS OF CHARACTER—*The ultimate life goal for Christians.*
BUILD MATURE BELIEFS—*Developing rigorous intellectual foundations for faith.*
EXEMPLIFY UNITY AND SERVANTHOOD IN CHURCH LIFE—*Serving and becoming one with the brethren.*
EVIDENCE DISCIPLESHIP IN THE WORLD—*The world will know the truth by our BE and DO, not our SAY.*

In the Introduction to *The Commands of Jesus,* I wrote the following.

"Christianity *is* a code of attitude and behavior. It is what we do and how we think. It is a *code of personal character.* Jesus laid out very succinctly and specifically what that code is. To summarize, he told his listeners, 'If you want to be my follower, if you want to be called my disciple, if you want to be identified with my name, do these things. Live by these principles. Think by these patterns. Behave in these ways. You cannot be my follower any other way than by adopting this code of conduct and character. To be *my* follower, you must live the Commands. Do so, and you will become like me, and the

7

world will know that I came from the Father.'"

The true gold of the epistles is not found in its theology. Let us leave the elementary doctrines of Christ and go on to maturity.

The Commands.

Pursue Godliness

A HOLY FOUNDATION OF SPIRITUAL INTIMACY
UPON WHICH TO BUILD A CHURCH

JERUSALEM—GROUND ZERO OF THE CHRISTIAN MOVEMENT

The worldwide movement called "Christianity" began in earnest fifty days after the resurrection of Jesus, on the Day of Pentecost. On that day, as recounted in the second chapter of the book of *Acts*, Peter preached the first spell-binding evangelistic sermon of Christianity.

At first the movement called "the Way" was merely a sect within Judaism. None of Jesus' followers dreamed of starting a new and separate religious faith. They were loyal and dedicated Jews. They believed Jesus to be the prophesied Messiah of the Jews. They intended to remain faithful Jews. The last thing on any of their minds was breaking from Judaism. In fact, early Christian worship was conducted in the Jewish Temple.

But this soon changed. Jewish officialdom considered the followers of Jesus dangerous heretics who had to be silenced at any cost.

Christianity spread at first, as we see both in Jesus' teaching and Peter's first sermon, *orally*. The most obvious reason for this was that literacy was much lower in the first century. Yet *writing* was an integral part of Jewish culture as well. It was only natural, then, that the new movement within Judaism would gradually develop and accumulate its own writings to supplement those from Judaism's storied past. Again, none of the first Christians intended or would have dreamed of adding a "new testament" to the existing Scriptures of Judaism any more than they thought of themselves as the progenitors of a *new* religion. The Christian writings of the first century were an informal means to supplement and reinforce what was primarily a *spoken* witness about Jesus Christ and his life and teachings.

We can easily deduce how Christianity's first writings came about. Exciting things were happening in the young movement. The most natural thing in the world was to tell people about it. When the Day of Pentecost came, Peter jumped up and said, "Let me tell you what's going on!" In the same way, letters no doubt circulated throughout Palestine as friends told friends about Jesus and his teachings. Yet these earliest Christian writings did not survive. Few people other than their recipients ever knew about them.

Eventually, however, letters also began to be written by some of Christianity's notable leaders. That's when the writings of early Christianity began to take on more import. People began gradually thinking, "Maybe we ought to pass this around to be read by others...maybe we ought to make copies of this letter...we need to save this." We really have no way of knowing what the first of such letters were or who wrote them. All we can do is study with interest those letters that history *has* preserved for us, and use them to try to understand the times and circumstances in which they were written.

Another form of writing was also taking place in the first years of the Christian movement. Various brief pithy teachings and sayings were being written down and collected. We might envision them as a *Wit and Wisdom of Jesus* collection. Such sayings, which were later expanded with narrative, formed the raw material from which the gospels were produced.

These two types of writing, then—*letters*, and *sayings collections*—formed the basic foundation of what became the New Testament.

As we consider the writings that helped spawn the worldwide movement of Christianity, it is unfortunate to realize that we do not have in our possession the very first writings. We have to wait over fifteen years—from the year 30 until sometime after the year 45—before we encounter the first Christian document that history has preserved.

That document, fittingly, comes from a member of Jesus' own family. It is the letter of *James*, written by the Lord's brother. Even though it appears toward the end of the New Testament, this was the *first* Christian document which has survived through the centuries. After the disciples began to travel throughout Judea and Palestine sharing the gospel, James became the acknowledged leader of the church in Jerusalem, where "the Way" remained centered and focused for the first fifteen years of its existence.

A HOLY FOUNDATION OF SPIRITUAL INTIMACY UPON WHICH TO BUILD A CHURCH

1. Yield yourself to God.

2. Present yourself as a daily living sacrifice to God.

3. Choose to be transformed by the renewal of your mind.

4. Seek to grow in righteousness.

5. Train yourself in Godliness.

6. Be constant in prayer.

7. Abide in Jesus.

8. Lead a virtuous life.

9. Set your mind and heart on high things.

10. Serve God and live for his glory.

1. Yield Yourself to God

Having acknowledged God's existence, it can truly be said that the foundational appropriate response of any human being to God is to yield to him. This is not to say that humanity *does* yield to him. But such is the response that *ought* to characterize our recognition of who God is and how we stand in relation to him.

The verb *yield* is pregnant with meaning. It is a word full of truth in defining the intended human half of the relational equation between created and Creator. That it does not usually define that relationship is the reason for humankind's grief upon the earth. All happiness, fulfillment, and contentment emerge from a heart and a life *yielded*, and thus in proper relation, to the God and Father of its origin.

Humanity, however, hates the idea of yielding to anyone or anything. To "yield" is to submit, defer, relinquish, capitulate, surrender, admit defeat. We hate the very idea of it. We will do anything to avoid it. We fight and squirm and strut and argue and bluster and fuss and defend and justify ourselves...*anything* rather than give in.

The highway sign that reads "Yield" in the U.S. reads "Give Way" in the U.K. The dynamic of those two signs, and their commands upon drivers, truly points the way to life. We are commanded to let *Another* go ahead of us, to give *Another* the right of way, to let *Another* lead while we follow. To "yield" is to *give way*.

Francis Schaeffer calls such yielding "lifting the empty hands of faith." C.S. Lewis speaks of "laying down our arms." The descriptions of both men reveal two aspects of what it means to *yield to God*. The first may occur once in life, when we acknowledge that God is God, that he has a claim on our lives, when we thus confess our belief in him and our desire to live as his child. C.S. Lewis's autobiography *Surprised By Joy* chronicles Lewis's inner struggle against this admission, and the yielding that he recognized was part of it. He describes the conclusion of this inner war as a battle coming to an end: "I unbuckled my armor...I gave in, and admitted that God was God...perhaps, that night, the most dejected and reluctant convert in all England...I surrendered." It is little wonder, after such an experience, that he later spoke in *Mere Christianity* of the "laying down of arms."

Once having yielded in this way, another form of yielding to God takes over. This new yielding becomes a daily, moment-by-moment way of life. It is Schaeffer's "lifting of the empty hands of faith," not once, but *continually*. This daily ongoing yielding becomes the mindset, the outlook, the entire life's perspective of the Christian committed to seeing and doing things God's way. It is the yielding of one who chooses to sit in the back seat of the car rather than the driver's seat.

The sad fact is that many Christians yield in the first way but not the second, They yield once. They acknowledge belief and join a church. Yet they are not taught to yield as a continual, moment-by-moment way of life. They do not learn what Thomas Kelly calls the life of "the second half."

It is in second-half Christianity that God renews, remakes, and transforms his sons and daughters according to the truth of Romans 12:2. The "new nature" of Christ comes alive, not by studying spiritual ideas, doctrines, and theologies, nor in worship at church, but by heeding the all-important signpost of the Christian walk. Every time our hands tingle to take control of life's steering wheel, the habitual, daily, moment-by-moment, internal response reminds us: *Yield...Give Way.*

"It is just this astonishing life which is willing to follow Him the other half, sincerely to disown itself, this life which intends *complete* obedience, without *any* reservations, that I would propose to you...in all boldness, in all seriousness—commit your lives in unreserved obedience to Him." (Thomas Kelly, *A Testament of Devotion,* p. 52)

Do not yield your members to sin...but yield yourselves to God. (Romans 6:13)
Submit yourselves therefore to God. (James 4:7)

2. Present Yourself as a Daily Living Sacrifice to God

The next two apostolic commands come to us most succinctly in Romans 12:1-2. These verses represent one of the New Testament's foundational challenges in Christian discipleship. It is not an exaggeration to call this one of the most significant passages to come to us from Paul's pen. As familiar as these verses are, however, their huge import is not quickly unraveled. Paul presents us here with a complex train of thought.

Six factors are involved:

Presenting ourselves a living sacrifice.
Spiritual worship.
Conformity to the world.
Personal transformation.
Renewal of the mind.
Proving the will of God.

The first two come to us in verse one. Paul says that our worship of God is manifested as we present ourselves as a living, holy, and acceptable sacrifice to him.

Steeped and trained in the tradition of Judaism, and as himself a devout Pharisee, Paul seeks to explain most of the theology of the Christian faith through the lens of Judaism. Paul wears *"Jewish* glasses" to illuminate *Christian* truth. Here he calls upon the Old Testament sacrifice to reveal the dynamic of a correct working relationship between man and God.

But the new sacrifice is altogether different than the old sacrifice. No more does the Christian bring an offering of grain, dove, goat, bull, or lamb to lay on the altar. It is not something *else* we offer to God. The Christian comes to the altar of sacrifice empty-handed.

The worship at the altar has entirely changed. *We* are now the sacrifice. The most astonishing aspect of this new sacrifice is that it must be *chosen.* It is a *self-willed* sacrifice. On the face of it, the thing is patently ridiculous. Who in his right mind willingly *chooses* to be slain on an altar of sacrifice? Yet this is the heart of Christianity—the suicide of the will—the self-chosen suicide of our right to dictate our own way. This sacrifice of self reveals the ultimate *yielding,* the completest "submission" possible to God in this life. Commands 1 and 2 illuminate the same command. And *this,* says Paul, not anything we do in church, represents true worship. We must reemphasize the imperative point: True *worship* does not take place in church.

The self-chosen sacrifice of the Christian is distinct in a far more important way. It is no yearly, monthly, nor weekly "service" of worship. It is an *ongoing* and *continual* sacrifice. Paul calls it a *living* sacrifice. Again, on the surface of it the words are absurd. Sacrifice implies death. Who ever heard of a "living sacrifice" before Paul coined the term? Yet in these two words—mutually exclusive in the world's eyes—Paul probes to the heart of what new life in Christ is and how it works.

It functions by an ongoing, daily, moment-by-moment yielding of my will into God's will. It is a *living* "death." My life as a Christian, as a follower of Jesus, is not built on a foundation of doctrinal belief. It is based on a continual sacrifice of my self. It is founded on the suiciding of *my* wishes, priorities, and desires into God's.

I appeal to you brethren...to present your bodies as a living sacrifice, holy and acceptable to God, which is your spiritual worship. (Romans 12:1)

Let us cleanse ourselves from every defilement of body and spirit. (2 Corinthians 7:1)

Walk...as Christ...gave himself up for us, a fragrant offering and sacrifice to God. (Ephesians 5:2)

Let us offer to God acceptable worship. (Hebrews 12:28)

Draw near to God and he will draw near to you. (James 4:8)

As he who called you is holy, be holy yourselves. (1 Peter 1:15)

---

3. Choose to Be Transformed by the Renewal of Your Mind

The intricate progression of Paul's thought in Romans 12:1-2 continues. Verse 1 is highlighted by the chosen "living sacrifice" which characterizes the moment-by-moment life of the Christian in relation to God. It is nothing more nor less than the "Christ life"—the kind of life Jesus lived with his Father. In verse 2, Paul illuminates what is the intended result of this daily, living sacrifice—a transformation of the way we think.

God's intent is that we learn to think in the same way he thinks. Jesus came to show us how his Father thinks. Therefore, to think like God is to think like *Jesus*.

The balance between spiritual and corporeal, eternal and temporal, is a tension in all religions. Christendom has suffered much from the failure of its advocates to live that even-keeled symmetry of lifestyle and personal character as it is exemplified in the gospels. Paul understood that balance. His writings are suffused with eternal ideas and daily practicality. These two opposite strands provide the strengthening warp and woof upon which he interweaves the tapestry of the Christian life.

Both threads are visible. It is beautiful to behold Paul's brain at work, and the precision of his insightful elocution. He speaks of offering our *bodies* as a living sacrifice, then follows with the command to be transformed in our *minds*. This is always Paul's balance. Living the Christ life brings *all* aspects of being into harmony. Discipleship requires commitment of the *whole* man—mind, body, spirit.

So Paul now explains what the yielding of ourselves in living sacrifice to God achieves—nothing less than a transformation of the whole man, highlighted by a *renewal of the mind*. In other words, learning to think like God thinks. Thus we are enabled—because we are learning to think like God thinks—to know God's will.

The will of God is no longer a closed book. Transformed and renewed of mind, our inner spiritual eyes are opened to perceive and behold God's priorities, purposes, objectives, and methods. By obedience we are able to fall in with them.

All this proceeds as cause and effect out of the yielding, daily, ongoing living sacrifice of our wills into his. But notice, Paul does not phrase this renewal as *automatic* cause and effect. Paul phrases both halves of the equation as commands.

Present your bodies as a living sacrifice. *Command.*

Be transformed by the renewal of your mind. *Command.*

Thus, you will prove (know) the will of God. This is the outflowing result of obeying the two commands. We control the outcome of the cause and effect. We have to take our own share in the process or this transformation will not take place. We must *allow* it. We must *want* it. We must *choose* it. We must *dedicate* ourselves to it. As *we* obey the commands, God effects the transforming renewal of the whole man. It won't happen just because we are Christians. That's why there are transformed Christians and *un*transformed Christians. Not all Christians walk in the living reality of Romans 12:1-2. We might paraphrase the command to read: Be renewed in your mind in all ways so that your outlook and priorities are no longer your own but God's.

This, of course, highlights the third major component in Paul's progressive choice-equation of transformed Christlikeness. It is the third imperative command found in Romans 12:1-2.

This is the familiar injunction: *Do not be conformed to this world.*

This chosen hinge-point of Christian transformation is too vital to be passed over lightly, and will be considered in more depth later.

Be transformed by the renewal of your mind, that you may prove what is the will of God, what is good and acceptable and perfect. (Romans 12:2)

Be renewed in the spirit of your minds. (Ephesians 4:23)

Put on the new nature, which is being renewed in knowledge after the image of its creator. (Colossians 3:10)

---

4. Seek to Grow in Righteousness

Many are the injunctions from the mouth of Jesus and the other New Testament writers toward righteousness. This command will not surprise anyone. Indeed, the entire message of Scripture can be summarized as a call to righteous living. *Be righteous* is one of the Bible's clearest, focused, and most repeated commands. *Live a righteous life* frames the foundation and essence of the teaching of both Judaism and Christianity.

Yet the Devil lurks in the details. More disputes, judgments, divisions, and hypocrisies have been generated by the debate over what comprises a righteous life than nearly any other Christian doctrine. It may be that the command, *Be righteous* has given the Devil more footholds to *prevent* true righteousness than any other.

The problem is twofold. One, the command toward righteousness lends itself to legalism. History is full of lists designed to achieve the pretence of righteousness in the absence of *true* righteousness. Judaism's entire history can be written from the perspective of such lists. Catholicism, Calvinism, and most branches of Christendom have all stumbled over the precipice into this alluring deception. The greater the attempt to *define* righteousness, the greater becomes *self*-righteousness, and the further away is heart righteousness. External legalisms cannot by their very nature lead to righteousness.

The second more penetrating difficulty lies closer to home. It hits us between the eyes the instant we wake up in the morning. It confronts us the moment we walk out the door and try to live in the world as people set apart from the world. It remains with us as a glaring microscope into our souls every waking moment until we fall asleep at night. This is simply the *impossibility* of the command.

We are commanded to be righteous. We want to be righteous. But we *aren't* righteous. The thing seems hopeless. It appears that we are commanded to do the impossible, to be something no mortal can ever be.

Yet neither Jesus nor Paul nor any other biblical writer issues impossible commands. We are only told to do what we *can* do. So how do we find the "can do" in, *Be righteous?*

The answer may lie in a simple rewording of the command as presented above. We unlock the do-ability of the command by changing the passive verb "be" to the active "grow." I know what I *am*. I am *not* righteous. Confronted on the street by the question, "Are you a righteous man?" I would not hesitate to answer, "Of course not...not by a long shot." But if the question came, "Are you *growing* in righteousnes?" suddenly the dynamic shifts. Now I can truthfully answer, "I am trying to. I believe that with God's help I am growing *into* righteousness. Such is my goal, my hope. I pray with all my heart, even with all my daily failings, that I am moving toward and *growing* in righteousness."

All at once I am faced with a command I can obey. I can *seek* righteousness. I can *grow* in righteousness. Nothing more is required than desire, will, and obedience. My imperfection is built into the equation. Knowing myself unrighteous, I *desire* (seek) to be righteous, and thus I am committed to the obedience that leads to growth into righteous.

I thus wake every morning with fresh hope. I can walk into the world with enthusiasm. I know that the day will present me with challenges to *grow* in righteousness. And I can end the day by looking in the mirror and saying to myself, "Not there yet! Long way to go. But with Jesus at my side, we are moving together toward the goal!"

Put on the new nature, created after the likeness of God in true righteousness. (Ephesians 4:24)
Put on the breastplate of righteousness. (Ephesians 6:14)
Aim at righteousness. (1 Timothy 6:11, 2 Timothy 2:22)
Sow peace and reap a harvest of righteousness. (James 3:18)
As he who called you is holy, be holy yourselves in all your conduct. (1 Peter 1:15)
Be persons of holiness and godliness. (2 Peter 3:11)
He who does right is righteous, as he is righteous. (1 John 3:7)

---

5. Train Yourself in Godliness

Again we confront the dichotomy between who we *are* and who we *want* to be. Simply told, "*Be* holy...*be* Godly...*be* righteous," we sigh and say, "Who can possibly be these?" Then we realize what is expected of us—not perfection of eternal *result*, but movement, progress, growth *toward* the heavenly objective. Desire, will, and obedience move us with daily baby steps in the direction of Christlikeness.

Many of the New Testament's commands are phrased with an eye on the goal, as Paul would say—on the high calling, the eternal prize. They look not to the reality of now but to the hope of eternity. Whenever we confront such a *Be* command (Be strong, be patient, be watchful, be kind, be pure, be at peace, be gentle), we can instantly translate them in our minds, substituting active "growing" verbs for the passive "to be." The beautiful moment-by-moment progressive practicality of the Bible instantly focuses:

Train yourself to be strong, *practice* patience, *learn* watchfulness, *show* kindness, *grow* in purity, *walk* in peace, *speak* with gentleness.

Today's command is almost identical to the previous. However, we now take it a step further. Not only do we have to *seek* it, we have to *train* ourselves in righteous living. Developing Godly habits is hard work. This fitness training begins by deciding if we really *want* it. Or do we actually want to preserve some worldliness in our lifestyle? After all, we rationalize, we don't want to get fanatical about it. A little religion mixed with a little worldliness makes for a pleasant, balanced, happy life without too many demands on character.

Those who teach that "accepting" and "trusting" Christ according to right belief will result in righteousness automatically being developed in the believer, as if by some magic power of the cross, have led thousands of gullible Christians astray. Wrongly taught about spiritual "fitness," these unsuspecting men and women never fortify the spiritual muscles necessary to walk in vigorous Christlike faith. Expecting God to accomplish righteousness for them, they spend their entire lives as spiritual toddlers.

Paul often uses the phrase "walk in" to focus the progressive, developmental, imperative of the commands. No one walks perfectly with his first step. It is a learned skill that is achieved over time. Practice hardens the muscles required to walk with dexterity. "Walking" as a Christian is matured the same way. It is a seasoned skill requiring the mastery of a new set of internal muscles of will. We develop the ability to live by our new nature, to walk in Godliness, in the way any new skill is reinforced—by ceaseless *training*. This is why, speaking in Philippians of the high calling and the eternal prize, Paul says clearly, "Not that I have obtained this or am already perfect; but I *press on* to make it my own." (Philippians 3:12) The words "press on" describe Paul's ceaseless strengthening regimen. He was constantly "exercising" his Godliness muscles.

C.S. Lewis explains this training by building on the phrase, "Put on your new nature," and calls it "dressing up" as Christ. I have called it donning "the cloak of Christlikeness." Lewis likens it to "pretending" to be like Christ in the same way that a child pretends to be grown up. Lewis says that something very significant happens as a result. The child learns and practices and "grows into" adulthood by such training. This is also how we develop our spiritual muscles that enable us to walk, gradually with steadier step as we mature, in Christlikeness.

No miracle will turn us into saints. We become strong "fit" Christians by ceaseless discipline in the habit patterns that lead to Godliness.

Train yourself in godliness by putting on, living by, and walking in your new nature.

Put on the new nature, created after the likeness of God in true righteousness. (Eph. 4:24)
Put on the new nature, which is being renewed...after the image of its creator. (Colossians 3:10)
Train yourself in godliness. (1 Timothy 4:7)
Aim at godliness. (1 Timothy 6:11)

6. Be Constant in Prayer

In *The Commands* of Jesus, we discussed the frequency with which Jesus issued certain commands. We found this telling component clarifying where our own priorities ought to lie. This was obviously not the only indicator, but was an important factor in illuminating what the Lord wanted to emphasize. How *often* did he lay various commands upon his disciples? If he said something a *lot*, we had better be paying close attention. We found that his most frequently given injunctions were not always what we might have expected.

One injunction we discovered in the top tier was the command to pray. This was no surprise. Pointing his disciples toward prayer represented one of Jesus' expected and most persistent priorities. Whether he was teaching them *how* to pray (*When you pray, pray like this...*), telling them how *not* to pray (*And when you pray, do not be like the hypocrites...*), instructing them in the necessity of prayer in a variety of circumstances (*This kind only comes out by prayer and fasting...*), demonstrating prayer by his own example (*Sit here, while I go and pray...*), or warning them about the trials coming to them (*Watch and pray that you may not enter into temptation...*), Jesus used nearly every situation that came up as a reminder to his disciples to pray.

We find the injunction to prayer also among the most frequent of the apostolic commands. The words *pray* and *prayer* occur everywhere one looks. This emphasis is heightened when one considers the incident-specific commands. Paul begs the readers of his letters, *Pray for us.* He asks them to pray for such-and-such an individual or church, and reminds them of *Pray for the brethren.*

From the pen of Paul, however, this command takes a fascinating twist. Paul elevates the dynamic of prayer to a lofty new level of intimacy. He commands not an occasional exercise, not an object of special times of worship, but *constant, continual,* and *ongoing* prayer. "Pray without ceasing," are the familiar words of 1 Thessalonians 5:17.

Encountering this command for the first time, we throw up our hands in despair. But then we see that Paul is not counseling us to become Trappist monks. He is revealing a high truth: True prayer is no mere *exercise of devotion.* It is not a *litany of requests* placed before God, nor even a *cry for help* in an hour of darkness. It may include all these, but the prayer commanded by Jesus and the apostles is far more. It is a *state of consciousness.* Being "constant in prayer" describes an orientation of heart. It is a life-synchronization of submitted, humble attentive childness toward our Father—listening moment-by-moment to what he would have us do and say, how he would have us think. The whispered *words* that come from our lips are but invisible butterflies winging heavenward, birthed by the deeper condition of being in which our hearts and minds live. The true home of our existence dwells in a realm of obedient childness in the heart of Fatherness. Prayer is the oxygen of that inner dwelling place. It speaks of an energy of spirit-conversance in which our spiritual lungs inhale and exhale in sympathetic responsiveness to the One who loves, rules, speaks, guides, and in all ways IS our life.

George MacDonald calls it the air of eternal Fatherhood. Thomas Kelly describes this ongoing exchange between Father and child, "a gentle receptiveness to divine breathings." It is this, I believe, that Paul means when he says, "Be constant in prayer."

Be constant in prayer. (Romans 12:2)

Pray at all times in the Spirit, with all prayer and supplication. (Ephesians 6:18)

In everything by prayer and supplication with thanksgiving let your requests be made known to God. (Philippians 4:6)

Continue steadfastly in prayer. Be watchful in prayer...pray also for us. (Colossians 4:2-3)

Pray constantly. (1 Thessalonians 5:17)

I urge that...prayers, intercessions, and thanksgivings be made for all men. (1 Timothy 2:1)

Men should pray in every place. (1 Timothy 2:8)

7. Abide in Jesus

Among my favorite passages of Scripture are the Upper Room chapters of John 13-17. This poignantly intimate final dialog between the Lord and his disciples is rich with significance on so many levels it is impossible to enumerate them briefly.

Pivotal in this preparatory pre-crucifixion exchange are Jesus' commands in the 15th chapter to *abide* in him. It is this revolutionary and unique relationship (*My Father is the vinedresser...I am the vine, you are the branches*) between God the Father, Jesus, and his disciples that establishes and will carry the spirit-life of Christ throughout the world for all time. It is the abiding life of John 15 that links the love commanded in chapters 13 and 14 with the Lord's high prayer for unity of John 17. As we *abide* in him, *love* between the brethren results, and the *unity* of Father and Son is fulfilled in their followers.

I cannot be the only lover of the gospels who finds the tone of *Acts* and Paul's epistles occasionally abrupt, jarring, and filled with what seem like entirely shifted priorities from those emphasized by Jesus. Signs, wonders, speaking in tongues, theology, and doctrinal bickering seem quickly to have replaced practical teachings of daily lifestyle.

In my journey through the New Testament, therefore, when I come to 1 John, written at the close of the first century, and again encounter exhortations to love, abide, and keep the Lord's commandments, a wave of peace washes over me. The doctrines and disputes of the first century church fade. The force of the gospel story returns with fresh power and simplicity. Over sixty years have passed since that night in the Upper Room. Yet for John the Lord's words are ever present in his heart. His first letter serves as a wonderful expansion of what he began in the 15th chapter of his gospel—illuminating yet more specifically the Lord's command, *Abide in me, and I will abide in you.*

With John's words, and the Lord's in our minds, we are reminded that in the midst of his theological treatises, Paul pointed toward the same foundation. His words to the Ephesians and Colossians unveil with clarity the "memory miracle" that enabled the beloved disciple John to record that Upper Room discourse with such precision and power.

Paul writes: *Allow Christ to dwell in your heart.* (Ephesians 3:17) And, *Let the word of Christ dwell in you richly. (*Colossians 3:16) Peter adds: *Reverence Christ as Lord in your heart.* (1 Peter 3:15)

This John did. The words of Jesus dwelt richly in John's heart. They *abided* in him. What John heard that night so long ago *abided* in him, and thus *remained* with him. We gain great insight, as well as down-to-earth practical help, in understanding what it means to "abide" in Jesus simply by doing what John did—allowing the *words* of Jesus to *dwell* in us, reverencing them, holding fast to them. Whether this involves memorizing his words, reading the gospels with regularity, or studying and reflecting on the Lord's Commands, each will discover his or her own personal means and methods.

However we practicalize this command, let us commit ourselves to *some* daily form of heeding Paul's exhortation and following John's example—allowing Christ's words to dwell in us richly, and thus allowing Jesus to *abide* in us, and we in him.

"Let what you heard from the beginning abide in you, and you will abide in the Son and in the Father." (I John 2:24)

Allow Christ to dwell in your heart through faith. (Ephesians 3:17)
Hold fast to the word of life. (Philippians 2:16)
Let the word of Christ dwell in you richly. (Colossians 3:16)
Reverence Christ as Lord in your heart. (1 Peter 3:15)
Abide in him. (1 John 2:28)
Keep his commandments and abide in him. (1 John 3:24)
Keep yourselves in the love of God. (Jude 21)

---

8. Lead a Virtuous Life

It is a good practice to keep aware of one's spiritual rudders. These are the priorities and perspectives that keep life's ship on course, moving straight and true, impervious to changes of weather and winds and waves of circumstance. What are our *deepest* foundations? What principles and truths set the tone for our entire life's outlook?

We are all lazy. The world pressures us unseen. We drift from our foundations. We need to look in the mirror periodically and ask if our hand is keeping the rudder steady. Am I moving in the direction I want to go? Am I becoming the kind of person I want to be? Is God *pleased* with the way I am steering my ship? What example am I setting?

It is easy for Christians to deflect the personal imperative of such questions with generalizations. But spiritualizations don't grow us into Christlike men and women. Even in reflecting on the Bible's commands, it is fearfully easy to get distracted by discussion and analysis. But what are the "rudder-commands," those that influence how we conduct ourselves every day...even every *moment* of every day? If you had to take this book and pull out two or three of its injunctions and say, "These will order my life...these fundamental commands represent my life's rudder," what commands would you choose?

That's why a Command such as, *Do and think toward others as you would have them behave toward you,* is so fundamental to one's focus. It cuts through all spiritualization, all doctrine, all churchiness, all dogma, all dispute, and shines a piercing light on personal conduct and character. How do I treat people through the day? Do I speak, behave, and think toward them as *I* want to be treated? The Golden Rule is profoundly a rudder-command. It orients all the Commands of Jesus with brilliantly focused precision. *Do as you would be done by* is ALL "do." It is a command impossible to spiritualize. We can ignore it. But we cannot spiritualize it. The words leave us no place to hide.

Such is the command before us today. We here encounter, in a sense, the "golden rule" of the Apostolic Commands—the preeminent command toward which all others point: *Lead a virtuous life.* It is ALL do. No spiritualization is possible. Virtue is virtue. It is goodness, kindness, generosity, selflessness, graciousness, mercy, forgiveness, gentleness, patience, grace, tolerance, humility, self-control, courtesy, sincerity, encouragement, cheerfulness, self-discipline, sensitivity, maturity, purity, wisdom.

Virtue is more than sexual, moral, and ethical purity, though these are key elements of it. True virtue, however, encompasses the complete scope of character. It is surprising to learn that the primary meaning of virtue is *strength*—a strength similar to that of gravitational pull. Webster's Dictionary of 1828 describes *Virtue* as: "Strength; that substance or quality of physical bodies by which they act and produce effects on other bodies." What an amazing thing! Virtue primarily acts as an influence on others. Virtue is the gravitational pull of goodness! Following this definition, Webster adds, "Bravery; valor...Moral goodness; the practice of moral duties and the abstaining from vice..."

What is virtue but the embodiment of love? What is virtue but Christlikeness?

We are commanded, not primarily to be spiritual men and women, but to live virtuous lives. We are commanded, not primarily to study our Bibles, but to live virtuous lives. We are commanded, not primarily to believe certain truths, but to live virtuous lives. We are commanded, not primarily to share the gospel, but to live such that those around us observe and say, "There is a life of virtue—a life well-lived."

This is the rudder of all the commands—*Live a virtuous life.*

Let your manner of life be worthy of the gospel of Christ. (Philippians 1:27)
Lead a life worthy of God. (1 Thessalonians 2:12)
Live sober, upright, godly lives in this world. (Titus 2:12)
Maintain good conduct. (1 Peter 2:12)
Supplement your faith with virtue. (2 Peter 1:5)

9. Set Your Mind and Heart on High Things

We have spoken about *growing* in righteousness and the corresponding *training* that goes with it. One of the foundational components of such "fitness training" is so simple it takes no extra time at all. It may be practiced throughout the day, anywhere, anytime, in any setting or circumstance. Yet the impact upon our spiritual development may be more profound than anything else we do.

Consider the phrase "Set the mind." What do those words mean? We tend to think of our thoughts as coming and going in our brains without being able to control them. To a certain extent, of course, this is true. However, the mind is like any muscle, whether of body or character. The hand doesn't wave, clench, swing a hammer, or caress a cheek unless we tell it to, unless we *choose* to do so. Our hands do what our brains tell them.

The mind is certainly more complex than the hand. But it still does what we tell it. That's why the command, *Set the mind,* is so vital to spiritual growth. *Set* is an active not a passive verb. It is something we do. We must *choose,* then we must actively take action to *point* or "set" the mind in certain directions. The mind will focus on what we tell it to focus on. In order to lay hold of the vigorous, chosen, active, powerful, force of this command, consider these synonyms: *Position* your mind, *fix* your mind, *orient* your mind, *direct* your mind, *exhort* your mind, *turn toward* and *resolve* your mind to think good thoughts. These patterns are not random or accidental. We *choose* what directions our minds go. When they stray off the mark, we have to bring them back.

So Paul commands us to focus on high things, good things, pure things, noble things...to look at life and people and situations and circumstances through "God eyes."

These are choices we make countless times a day. How do we respond to what we see and hear? Do we drift along in the low mental currents of those around us with rude, pointless, unseemly, joking, critical, gossipy, self-centered chatter? Or do we exert ourselves *against* the downward lure of the world's current? Are we setting the course of our own mental rivers to think *nobly, thankfully, pleasantly* about what *edifies* rather than what mocks, belittles, and tears down? Is *goodness* the orientation of our thought-rudder?

It is a matter of what focus we *decide* (actively, determinedly, vigorously, forcefully) to think about. As our mind moves in either high or low channels, the heart follows.

We are reminded of Jesus' command to *Abide.* The words are synonymous—*abide* in goodness, *remain* in goodness, *dwell* in goodness. Jesus' disciples were able to dwell and abide and remain because they were "steeped" in the Lord's words. His outlook and priorities were infused into them. This "infusion" comes as we also steep our hearts and minds in goodness...or as we might term it, in *God-ness.*

In eight crisp words, Paul illuminates this infusion outlook. We steep ourselves in it by *setting* our minds and hearts on what is true, honorable, just, pure, lovely, gracious, excellent, and praiseworthy. Philippians 4:8 is positively remarkable . Stop and seriously reflect on the implications of this verse. It contradicts every imaginable perspective the world takes for granted as the acceptable norm. The world would have us blame, criticize, grumble, ridicule, discredit, complain, demean...expose wrong, point out error, withhold praise, disdain weakness, deprecate strength, laugh at vulgarity, excuse laziness, accept mediocrity, fudge truth, delight in sin. All these low habits of the Old Man Paul wipes off the face of the map for the Christian man or woman who would steep himself or herself in the priorities of the gospel: "Set your mind and heart on *high* things."

Think about goodness.

Finally, brethren, whatever is true, whatever is honorable, whatever is just, whatever is pure, whatever is lovely, whatever is gracious, if there is any excellence, if there is anything worthy of praise, think about these things. (Philippians 4:8)

Set your hearts on things above...set your minds on things above, not on earthly things. (Colossians 3:1-2, NIV)

10. Serve God and Live For His Glory

In emphasizing the practicality of the New Testament, we occasionally encounter a command where the "do" is more difficult to lay hold of than *Do as you would be done by*. Such is the command before us today. When you and I walk out the door into the world, how do we actually give glory to God? What does it mean when I am at the wheel of my car or walking the aisles of the grocery store or standing in line at Starbucks to "serve" him? Does it mean I should be praying and thinking about God, that I should have a smile on my face, that I should talking about God, that I should act reverent so that people will look and say, *Whoa, who is that!*, that I should go about humming or singing spiritual songs, that I should sprinkle my conversation with Scripture and spiritual jargon and *Praise the Lords* so that everyone will know I am a Christian?

What does it mean to *you*, in the next five minutes, to serve God and give him glory?

These are difficult personal questions. This is a hard command to lay hold of. Of course, we think, our pastor "serves" God. Billy Graham served God. Missionaries serve God. It's different for *them*. They glorify God in their vocations. But what does it mean for *me* to "serve" God and "live for his glory?"

Do we glorify God in prayer and song and by "talking up" spirituality with outward manifestations? Do these bring God the kind of "glory" Paul is talking about? Or is something deeper and more intimately personal involved?

Most resolve this dichotomy by falling into the fatal mistake of defining the parameters of this command in the context of church. Anything connected with the so-called "ministry" of their church becomes imbued with greater significance than those activities may deserve. This grievous error miscolors the focus of many by equating what is commonly called "worship" with *glorifying* God. The expressive musical displays and liturgical ceremonies that take place in thousands of churches every Sunday may be many things, but they are not what Paul was speaking of when he said, "Do all to the glory of God." The tiny word *all* tells us that Paul meant something far more whole-life encompassing than what takes place in church, or that has anything to do with church.

As he often does, George MacDonald unlocks the high truth of what gives God glory. He likens the "glory" of anything to that which it was made for, its blossom, the fulfilling of the purpose for which it was created. In the sermon "The Truth," MacDonald explains: "The truth then, is the blossom of it, the thing it is made for...and wherever, in anything that God has made, in the glory of it...we see the glory of God, there a true imagination is beholding a truth of God."

To give God glory is simply to become what we were made to become, to grow into the human blossoms we were made to grow into, to be the people he intended us to be.

We do not glorify God in church any more than we do in the grocery store or at Starbucks. We glorify God by being the men and women he created us to be. What is the blossom he created *you* to be and express? It will be a different flower, with distinct nuances of color and fragrance, perhaps blooming at different times and ways than the blossom of my flower. Some flowers blossom in sunlight, others bloom in shade. Some give off subtle earthy aromas, others are rich with sweet perfume. We are each created to fulfill our *own* unique blossoming personhood. But all the blooms of God's garden are intended to radiate and reflect and exude the perfume of his being.

We are God's flowers. We glorify him by blossoming into the full creative, colorful, fragrant, expressive manifestation of his character, nature, and eternal purposes.

Serve the Lord. (Romans 12:11)
In whatever you do, do all to the glory of God. (1 Cor. 10:31)
Whatever you do, in word or deed, do everything in the name of the Lord Jesus. (Col. 3:17)
Live as servants of God. (1 Peter 2:16)

Nurture Personal Spirituality

QUALITIES OF INDIVIDUAL OBEDIENCE THAT PRODUCE MATURITY

ANTIOCH — EXPANSION AND CONFLICT COMES TO THE CHURCH

Two chief forces on the church during the years of its infancy in the 30s and 40s were seeming opposites—violent persecution of the "Jesus movement," and the explosive expansion of that movement. The more Jewish officialdom tried to stamp out the new sect, the more it grew. Since the persecution was largely centered in Jerusalem, Christian leaders, led by the original Apostles, began traveling away from Judea. Eventually their travels took them south into Egypt and Africa, and north and west around the Mediterranean. They spread news of Jesus and his teaching wherever they went, and gained converts rapidly everywhere.

Between the years 38 and 43, the Christian movement in Antioch began to take center stage. It soon became a vibrant center for growing Christianity. But Syria in the north represented an entirely different environment in which for Christianity to take root. Antioch was cosmopolitan, Greek, and Roman. The work of the Christian leaders there was different than anything they had faced before. The cultural shift between Jewish Jerusalem and Gentile Antioch eventually precipitated the first major controversy in the young church. It arose as the budding faith tried to figure out its own identity—was it a sect *within* Judaism, or did it represent a complete *break* with the past?

From our vantage point today it is difficult to appreciate the historical context of the pivotal twenty years between 30 and 50 A.D. for the fledgling Christian movement. Nearly all the first followers of Jesus considered themselves faithful Jews. They had no intent nor desire to break with Judaism. They saw their discipleship to Jesus as *fulfilled* Judaism, not *non*-Judaism. As more and more Gentile converts accepted the Christian faith, however, accelerated by official Judaism's violent repudiation of *The Way*, this self-perception began to change.

The fact that Gentiles in *The Way* gradually began to outnumber Jews raised enormous theological questions. Were Gentile converts required to adhere to *Jewish* law? Specifically, did they have to be circumcised and follow Jewish eating regulations to be Christians? The entire future of Christianity depended on the answer to a fundamental question: Was Christianity Jewish, and thus were Christians also bound by Jewish law...or was Christianity altogether new, and thus completely free from Jewish law?

When word exploded through the church that Christianity's arch-enemy and persecutor, the Pharisee Saul of Tarsus had had a vision of Jesus on the Damascus road, most were understandably suspicious. But the leader of the Antioch church, a man called Barnabas, believed in Saul, took him personally to meet the disciples, and then mentored Saul in his new Christian faith.

None loved the legalisms of Jewish tradition more than the Pharisees. Surprisingly, however, the change in Christianity's perception of itself was articulated in the coming years by the forceful personality of this very man Saul, eventually known as Paul.

Contrasting Christianity with the legalism of Judaism's past, the former Pharisee argued passionately through the following decades, and with theological brilliance, intellectual precision, unbounded personal confidence, and a keen understanding of Scripture, that Christians were completely free from the ordinances of Judaism. In no way whatever were they subject to the Law of Moses. Paul laid out his new theology, what he called "his" gospel, through a series of letters to the churches around the Mediterranean. Circumcision, food regulations, and all the rest of the Law, contended Paul, were not to be placed as obligations upon new believers.

Not all Christian leaders agreed. A great controversy developed within the church between the two vehemently opposing camps. Over the years, however, the force of Paul's theological and scriptural logic carried the day. It became clear that faith in Jesus represented more than a mere extension of Judaism, but an entirely *new* faith.

Paul's letters laying out the doctrinal underpinnings of Christianity as separate and distinct from Old Testament Judaism eventually helped form a specifically Christian "*new* Testament" of Scripture.

QUALITIES OF INDIVIDUAL OBEDIENCE THAT PRODUCE MATURITY

11. Obey the Lord's commands.

12. Be a doer of the word, not a hearer only.

13. Take your faith seriously.

14. Take heed to yourself.

15. Do not envy.

16. Do not be afraid or lose heart.

17. Keep watchful and alert.

18. Stand firm and courageous in God.

19. Be thankful in all circumstances.

20. Don't worry.

11. Obey the Lord's Commands

The companion volume to this, *The Commands*, opened with the command from Jesus: *Obey my commands*. This same exhortation is urged by the apostles in a hundred different ways. Everything they say is suffused with this imperative. It is the unspoken life and energy of *all* the commands. It is the entire basis for the Christian faith. There is nothing else.

The nature of a command requires obedience. A "command" is not a "suggestion." A command is a *command*. Obedience is compulsory. Even so, there remains such a thing as *dis*obedience. The Bible highlights the two divergent paths from beginning to end—clarifying that the difference between them lies within the will of the human mind and heart. We *choose* whether to obey or disobey, we *choose* whether to live by God's principles or disregard them, we *choose* whether to exalt ourselves or deny ourselves. We make that choice dozens of times every day.

Perhaps this is why Jesus often commands obedience in the context of the tiny but eternally significant word *If*. The apostles, too, recognized that there are always two paths—obedience and disobedience. Jesus commands obedience. But many will *not* obey. Paul, James, Peter, John all focus this distinction, comparing those who follow with their whole hearts and those who turn away from the stringency of discipleship.

Jesus often phrased his command to obedience, not as a *direct* command, but as a natural outgrowth of love, again with the all-important *if* as the hinge-point linking love and obedience.

If you love me you will keep my commandments. (John 14:15)

If a man loves me, he will keep my word. (John 14:23)

You are my friends if you do what I command you. (John 15:14)

Jesus wants none to mistake what it means to be his follower. Many will claim to love him. Many will talk about loving him. Many will analyze what it means to love him.

But there exists only one validating sign. A Christian is distinguished and defined by that one, and *only* that one, validating proof of love. The progression is clear. *If you love me you will obey my commands. This is my commandment, that you love one another as I have loved you.*

John follows in his first epistle with a series of similarly worded injunctions. The theme runs from the gospels straight through to the end of the New Testament. Obedience to the Commands is a moment-by-moment choice. We make it over and over. We are *continually* making it. It is an ongoing choice that defines obedience to all the Commands. It defines what it means to love Jesus and be his follower.

"What is faith in him?" I answer, The leaving of your way, your objects, your self, and the taking of his and him; the leaving of your trust in men, in money, in opinion, in character, in atonement itself, and doing as he tells you. I can find no words strong enough to serve for the weight of this necessity—this obedience. It is the one terrible heresy of the church, that it has always been presenting something else than obedience as faith in Christ. (George MacDonald, *Unspoken Sermons, Second Series*, "The Truth in Jesus.")

Obey God rather than men. (Acts 5:29)

Be obedient. (Titus 3:1)

Purify your souls by obedience. (1 Peter 1:22)

Be sure that you know him by keeping his commandments. (1 John 2:3)

Keep his commandments and do what pleases him. (1 John 3:22)

Keep his commandments and abide in him. (1 John 3:24)

This command...we have from him...he who loves God should love his brother also. (1 Jn 4:21)

This is the love of God, that we obey his commandments. (1 John 5:3)

This is love, that we follow his commandments. (2 John 6)

---

12. Be a Doer of the Word, Not a Hearer Only

As the church expanded and the hub of its missionary outreach shifted north to cosmopolitan Antioch, one church leader remained in Jerusalem. That man was James, the Lord's brother. He was viewed as an Apostle and eventually came to be considered head of the Jerusalem church, at the highest level of leadership with Peter himself. When a major council was held (Acts 15) to discuss the question whether adherence to Jewish law was required for Gentile converts, it was James who presided over the meeting of church leaders. It was also James who rendered the final decision.

Appropriately, then, the first surviving document from those early days of the church is the letter of *James*. Some scholars believe that the "letter" was actually written down in the late 40s as a composite from several of James' spoken sermons, and then compiled into a single document which was sent around to the churches. Because *James* is found near the end of the New Testament, its historical and spiritual importance is often overlooked. Not theological enough to suit his tastes, Martin Luther called it "an epistle of straw." Luther went so far as to omit *James* from his edition of the New Testament.

But is *James* really a lightweight document? How might we value it if it appeared in its proper historical sequence as the first of the epistles right after *Acts*? A prayerful reading brings a much different perspective into focus. Indeed, the clarion message from James' mouth may provide the clearest articulation of the practicality of the gospel since Jesus' own parables. We should hardly be surprised, after initial doubts, that Jesus' own brother should know his heart as well as any other. How fitting that James and Peter were the church's first two leaders! They *knew* Jesus with an intimacy we can scarcely fathom.

The marvelous down-to-earth *practicality* of this wonderful letter reveals that James learned from his brother well. The gospels are entirely practical. Everything in Jesus' teaching always focuses the DO with pinpoint and personal precision. Every word that fell from Jesus' lips reduced in the end to nothing more nor less than what was to be *done*. After the parable of the Good Samaritan, Jesus' words are unmistakable: *Go and DO the same*. Concluding the Sermon on the Mount, Jesus says, *Every one then who hears these words of mine and DOES them will be like a wise man.*

James takes up this same theme. It resounds through every word of his letter. He will leave theology to Paul. Using practical examples and succinct language, James focuses his hearers instead on what it means to *live* practically as a Christian. It is the daily, down-to-earth life of one who dwells in the home of obedience to the commands of his brother. James' single message is summed up simply: DO the word.

All religions are full of *hearers*. Christianity is full of hearers. The first century church was full of hearers. The hills where Jesus preached were full of hearers. Jerusalem during the last week of Jesus' life was full of hearers. Your church every Sunday is full of hearers. All around us are hearers. Hearing is easy. Who are the DO-ers?

No ten words so succinctly capture the essence of practical Christian living, and the essence of the gospel of Jesus Christ, as the words, *Be a doer of the word, not a hearer only*. These ten words represent James' signature tune, the single command upon which his entire message is founded. Everything else he says proceeds out of this: *DO the word.*

"Doing the word" implies more than simply absorbing the teaching. It is doing what Jesus said: *Obey the Lord's commands*. John lifts the "Word" (Logos) to an even more exalted level by calling Jesus himself *the Word*.

If we may phrase it thus, and elevate James' command into this same lofty realm, the Lord's brother is commanding us: *Be a doer of Jesus...Do as Jesus did...Do Jesus.*

Be doers of the word, not hearers only...Do not deceive yourselves—one who is a hearer of the word and not a doer is like a man who looks in the mirror and quickly forgets what he has seen...Do not pretend to have faith without works. (James 1:22, 23-24, 2:17)

Do not merely love in word and speech, but in deed and in truth. (1 John 3:18)

---

13. Take Your Faith Seriously

One of the helpful benefits in focusing on the Commands is that it immediately shatters our preconceptions about spirituality. The Commands act as a giant screen to weed out superficiality and false priorities. The Commands reduce spirituality to its essentials, to first causes, to the lowest common denominators of Christian discipleship. Doctrine and theology, churchiness and legalisms, all fall away in the blinding light of the probing DO of the Commands. We have said before, the Commands leave us nowhere to hide. They strip us naked before the mirror of motive and practicality. To DO or *not* to do, that is the only question the Commands leave on the table.

This command before us would not cause the Christians of the first three centuries of the church to double-take as it no doubt will many today. This would have been among the *first* commands, assumed, obvious, and imperative. Taking upon yourself the label "Christian" put a death threat on your head that would follow you the rest of the days of your life. The church was no club you joined for "fellowship."

That's all changed now. The cancer of entertainment and fun, blessing and celebration, has infected the modern church with the mentality of what has been dubbed "hot tub" Christianity. The churches who want to "attract" people have reinvented themselves into country clubs whose *social* rather than *spiritual* fabric represents the face and character they present to the world. To entice young people, they have turned worship services into rock concerts. In this environment, "Take your faith seriously" will ring with dissonance. How will we get people through our doors *that* way?

How incongruous to modernism, then, are Paul's qualifications for church leadership. What do we make of his injunction toward sober-mindedness, when he commands it of elders and deacons, men and women, the young and the old. Paul commanded sobriety of *everyone*! Why did he place such importance on dignified, sensible Christian solemnity?

The answer is as close as our Bibles. Christianity has a very serious side.

We all know, of course, that hardships are indigenous to life's training ground. But we tend to view them as the exception rather than the rule. Rejoice in your trials...BUT *joy* comes in the morning. Yet here a sense of serious import is commanded of us, not merely *until* joy returns, but as a permanent component of our carriage and demeanor, intrinsic to the *normal* countenance with which a Christian is intended to walk.

We are *supposed* to be cool-headed, sensible, equanimous, and thoughtful. Joy *and* sober-mindedness are to walk hand in hand. *Both* are to characterize our outlook. Because of joy, we know that such earnest serenity does not mean we are to be gloomy sourpusses. Because of sobriety, we know that neither are we to be frivolous and superficial. This command fuses contrasting character qualities into a Christlike harmony of countenance such as is not often witnessed in the world—serious joyfulness...peaceful sobriety...the poised, calm, level-headed, composure of maturity. Here we meet the self-assurance of contented grace exuded by one who knows who he is in God, knows what he is about, and recognizes the import and magnitude of what it means to be a Christian.

In our day the world associates Christians with the mirror opposite of what this command should imply. Christians are viewed as lightweights. This is our own fault. We have not apprehended the *weight* of faith, that we are called to walk in the world with what is called *gravitas*—the solemn, dignified, quiet demeanor of wisdom.

A bishop must be sensible, dignified....a deacon must be serious. (1 Timothy 3:2, 8)
Women must be serious. (1 Timothy 3:11)
Bid older men to be serious, sensible, sound...steadfast... (Titus 2:2)
Bid older women to be reverent...[and] to teach younger women to be sensible. (Titus 2:3, 5)
In your teaching show...gravity...Live sober, upright, and godly lives in the world.(Titus 2:7, 12)
Be sober minded...Keep sane and sober for your prayers. (1 Peter 1:13; 4:7)

---

14. Take Heed to Yourself

In one way or another, all the commands hit us between the eyes. If we are paying attention. That is their design. Jesus never left his listeners neutral. He looked people straight in the eye. When he and the rich young ruler faced one another in their poignant exchange, we *feel* their eyes locking before the young man turned away. When Jesus spun around to rebuke Peter, we sense the same dramatic tension of challenge—the Lord's piercing eyes drilling straight into Peter's with, *Get behind me, Satan!* Every parable and every command, stated or implied, carries the same eyeball to eyeball charge with which the Lord ended the story of the Good Samaritan: *Go and do the same.*

This command before us today goes yet further. We are here commanded to look *ourselves* in the eye. What Jesus often finds it necessary to do, we must regularly do to ourselves. The mirror of spirituality is an inner magnifying glass into character and motive. The Lord could not say it more clearly: "Take heed to yourselves." (Luke 17:3)

In an era of self-esteem and *I'm-okay-you're-okay,* the mastery of probing, self-examination and introspection has fallen on hard times. When was the last time your minister or priest urged prayerful heart-analysis and soul searching? In these feel-good days, people want to be told that they are fine and dandy as they are. Mirror, mirror on the wall, who's the fairest of them all? ME! shouts modernism. That's also the message of today's church. We've forgotten how to use the inner magnifying glass to root out weaknesses of character in order to submit them to the transforming power of obedience.

Jesus approached personhood a little differently. He made the mirror the primary tool of discipleship, not a piece of self-esteem furniture to see if our hair is looking good, and to insure that our vanity is unruffled and our self-satisfaction remains happy and content.

A mirror is a fascinating device. We cannot see *others* in a mirror without turning it sideways. Though it is not what it is intended for, we love using the mirror this way. Focusing on *others* is one of life's favorite pastimes. Addressing this desire to fix everyone else, Jesus used another parable—the speck and the log. But his message was clear: "The flaws in other people's characters are none of your business. The tool I want *you* to use is the mirror, and not turned sideways trying to look at others. I want you turning it on yourself."

Neglecting the all-important mirror commands is death to spiritual development. The New Testament reveals the result—*drift* and *laziness*. Spiritual self-satisfaction becomes an unseen, numbing, growth-killing tolerance that eats away from the inside. *Take care lest you drift...test your work...examine yourselves*—we ignore these words at our peril.

Yet modernism arms us with an arsenal of excuses and justifications. Brainwashed by a narcissistic culture and a self-pleased church, we gullibly believe the great lie—that we are "okay" *without* having to submit to the scalpel, *without* the altar, that we can be "good Christians" *without* following the Lord into Gethsemane. No mirrors required.

Modernism has turned the magnifying glass of the Lord's probing eyes into Snow White's mirror of self-smug blindness. The church sees in its reflection a fair image of beauty. In truth it is standing in the ugly nakedness of weak and complacent self-worship.

Take heed to yourselves and to all the flock... (Acts 20:28)
Examine yourselves to see whether you are holding to your faith. (2 Cor. 13:5)
Test yourselves. (2 Cor. 13:5)
Look to yourselves, lest you too be tempted. (Galatians 6:1)
Let each one test his own work. (Galatians 6:4)
Look carefully how you walk. (Ephesians 5:15)
Take heed to yourself and to your teaching. (1 Timothy 4:16)
Take care lest there be an evil unbelieving heart in any of you. (Hebrews 3:12)
Look to yourselves, that you not lose what you have worked for. (2 John 8)

15. Do Not Envy

Envy represents one of life's most lethal personal cancers. It corrupts, spoils, ruins, and eventually kills. Envy kills at every level of personhood—spiritually, emotionally, psychologically, relationally, even perhaps vocationally. When we lay hold of this eye-opening truth, envy is seen for what it is—a deadly instrument of destruction that taints every good in life. It is especially sinister because it is a sword we use on ourselves.

To understand envy's infectious corrosiveness, envision not a double-edged sword, but a double-*tipped* sword. Two razor sharp points at both ends are laced with deadly venom. Envy poisons twice, in opposite directions, inwardly and outwardly.

The sword takes advantage of our wants, desires, even our goals, ambitions, and dreams—all good things in themselves. It is natural and healthy to be driven forward in life by what we want to do and have and achieve and become. Desire has been implanted in us by God as a healthy component of personhood. Without desire, there is no growth.

But when desire crosses the line of wanting what we are not *supposed* to have, then envy sets in. Wanting what we don't have, and what we are not intended to have, we become dissatisfied with what we *do* have. That's when the sword digs into our souls and infects us with its invisible malignancy. Puncturing the outer layers of personhood, the poison pierces deeper and deeper. The seeds of dissatisfaction sprout and send down roots. They breed the desire for *more*, for *else*, for *other*. Malaise and disquiet replace peace, contentment, and gratefulness.

As this is taking place *within*, the other end of the sword is probing silently in the opposite direction. It is *outwardly* pillaging relationships with family, friends, neighbors, acquaintances, remarkably even with those we don't know. The lethal poison of envy has no boundaries. The focus of invisible *I-wish* thoughts takes a thousand forms. It is not limited to money and possessions. It may be looks, intelligence, job, health, reputation. We may be envious of personality, opportunities, of another family, of where someone lives. It can be as irrational as begrudging one standing ahead of us in a check-out line. That inner tension is a cancer that destroys both personhood and relationship.

These, then, are the two poison tips of envy's lance—dissatisfaction and jealousy. They poison one's health *inwardly*, and relationships *outwardly*. That's why we have to ruthlessly root out dissatisfaction in all its forms. Even responses that many would justify as "natural" and seemingly harmless, such as coveting George MacDonald's spiritual insight, C.S. Lewis's intelligence, James Michener's command of history, or another author's sales figures—*anything* that makes me wish (even subtly) that I were gifted differently or that circumstances in *my* life were more like those of someone *else's*—can send down roots of unthankfulness, discontent, and envy. Dissatisfaction will poison me, and my relationships, if I do not crush its seeds before they germinate.

Envy thus poisons the most basic commodity in life everyone wants—happiness. What is happiness but contentment in the moment? Contentment in the *now*. Envy undoes all that. Dissatisfaction robs today's minutes and hours of their essential *life*. It takes from the *now* the goodness today's now has for us to enjoy, give thanks for, and grow from.

When the apostles command, *Do not envy,* they strike at the very core of the human condition. They are exhorting us to lay hold of the secret of life itself—gratitude and contentment with the eternal now of the present...with who we are, what we possess, with those around us, and with the circumstances in which we find ourselves.

Love is not jealous. (1 Corinthians 13:4)
The work of the flesh is jealousy...envy...Let us have no envy of one another. (Gal. 5:20, 21, 26)
Put to death covetousness, which is idolatry. (Colossians 3:5)
Avoid envy. (1 Timothy 6:4)....Be content with what you have. (Hebrews 13:5)
Do not...be false to the truth if you have bitter jealousy...in your heart. (James 13:14)
Put away all envy. (1 Peter 2:1)

16. Do Not Be Afraid or Lose Heart

An old-fashioned phrase perfectly expresses the emotion toward which this command is directed. "His heart *failed him*...her heart *failed her*." It is that sinking feeling that comes when we realize that all hope is gone. We have reached the end of the line. All options are exhausted. Help will not arrive. The Marines are not coming. We are alone...hopeless...helpless. There is nowhere to turn. The nightmare is not a dream.

We've all experienced it. Indeed it literally feels like emotional "heart failure." Our heart (as expressing hope, vision, optimism, courage, the very motivation to go on breathing) simply wilts, gives up, and fails us.

Such a season came upon me recently. I sat a few moments ago staring at the words I had typed: *Do not be afraid or lose heart.* My mind was blank. I simply sat and stared. I had nothing to say. No words of prayer came to my lips. I was completely empty. The words on the page described *me*. I had lost heart. I was discouraged into hopelessness. Everything within me wanted to give up the fight, give up this project, give up writing...just *give up*. Honestly, I wanted to give up life itself.

Perhaps "fear" is an intrinsic component of such emotional and spiritual heart failure. That is why in Scripture the words, *Take heart, take courage, do not be afraid* are inextricably linked. The discouraged, fearing, failing heart are all symptoms of a common malady. They strike when we forget our Father...when we think we are alone.

We are not alone. Such desperate moments challenge us to seize upon the reality of a mighty theological truth. We speak of God's *omnipresence* in lofty abstract tones. Yet is this the most down-to-earth reality in the entire lexicon of our theological belief system? God is omni-*present*. He is present *everywhere*. He in this room at this moment. Not merely in the room, he is *beside* me. He is *with* me. He invites me into his lap.

That's what omnipresence means—that I may climb up onto my Father's lap. He is *present* with me, and in me, and I in him. He quietly whispers, "As your Mommy or Daddy held you and bandaged your skinned knee and soothed your tears, now you are in *my* lap. I am holding your bruised heart in my hand, my son. I will care for it. You may trust me because I am your good and loving Father. I love you more than you know."

Even realizing this great truth, however, it is easier said than done to *Take heart* when everything about us shouts, *Give up*. It is hard to hear the Father's gentle Voice. It is hard to feel the comfort of his invisible caress. No simple answers cure a failing heart. No spiritual "heart transplant" miraculously prevents fear and discouragement.

We must thus devise methods for heart health, ways to keep the spiritual hearts we have fit. I exercise daily to keep my physical heart in shape. My wife and I eat carefully to supplement exercise with good nutrition. Similarly, we must discover methods for keeping our hearts *spiritually* and *emotionally* fit. Prayer, Scripture reading, and devotional books obviously form a foundation to that regimen. To these we each add our individual heart therapies. Simple things like fresh air can help clear the brain and boost the heart physically and emotionally. I started reading a book this week to stimulate my sagging prayer life. I am hoping it will give my failing heart some badly needed nutrition. Contrary as it seems, even talking with a friend who is also discouraged—or who is *not* discouraged and whose optimism can buoy me up—provides a great tonic. So occasionally I pick up the phone and call my sister or my friend in Indiana or another in Ireland...just to talk and laugh and pour out a few of my troubles to a listening ear whom I know loves me. I invariably set down the phone feeling better...encouraged...not feeling alone...not fearful of the future...more aware of the Father's loving family encompassed about me...and my heart no longer failing.

I bid you to take heart...take heart, men. (Acts 27:22, 25)
Do not lose heart...we are always of good courage. (2 Corinthians 4:16; 5: 6)
Have no fear...nor be troubled. (1 Peter 3:14)

17. Keep Watchful and Alert

In considering the Commands of Jesus, we discovered that the Lord's most frequently given injunctions in the gospels were not what we would perhaps consider the most "spiritual." Three groups topped the list: *Watchfulness, Fearlessness, and Mental diligence.* We considered them as six distinct commands.

It is not surprising, in now considering the commands of the Apostles, that we find these same commands urged upon us. The apostles were focusing Christians of the first century, and we who follow, toward the teachings of Jesus himself. Their commands reflect *his* commands. They often used precisely the same language he did.

Heading this vital series of "surprising" commands is watchfulness, the opposite of mental sloth and laziness. Jesus and the apostles urge watchfulness with such regularity because spiritual health *requires* it. Attentiveness is intrinsic to the "good soil" that produces growth and fruitfulness.

When one's eyes are opened to this frequently given command, we suddenly see it wherever we turn in our Bibles. The specific words may vary, but it is the same charge: The call to *attentiveness* in all aspects of life—to pay attention, to consider implications and consequences, to keep the heart and brain alert, to examine motives, to be observant and shrewd, insightful and wise, vigilant in matters within oneself and in the world.

The Command to watchfulness has deep but often overlooked consequences. Counterfeits creep in to distract us when we let our spiritual guards down. How easily the world's priorities lure our eyes off the bull's eye of God's purpose. We observe this drift with the twelve. Every time they became distracted by peripheral tangents, Jesus yanked them back to foundational priorities with some variation of, "You lost your focus…now pay attention." Perhaps this is why the apostles later urged watchfulness on the first century Christians. They knew from personal experience what was at stake.

The all-important question, however, is what kind of watchfulness is being urged on us—internal or external? In which direction are the Christian's alert and watchful eyes supposed to be looking? Many take this command as a basis for cultural awareness and involvement. They read the command in the familiar context of the phrase "political *watch*dog group." Others imbue the words with prophetic overtones—that we are to be alert and *watching* for Christ's return. Nothing, however, could have been further from Jesus' mind. He was instructing his disciples in the use of the mirror. He was speaking primarily of *internal* watchfulness.

We know this because Jesus always links watchfulness not merely to his return, but to hypocrisy. He says, *Beware of the leaven of the Pharisees and Sadducees.* Luke includes the telling addition, *which is hypocrisy.* (Luke 12:1) *This* is the leaven Jesus warns against. Hypocrisy always creeps in unseen. The hypocrite is blind to his own hypocrisy. To keep hypocrisy at bay requires constant self-examination and prayerful self-regulation. Alert internal watchfulness is our primary weapon to slay hypocrisy.

Jesus points to the same truth in Luke 11:35: *Be careful lest what you think is light within you is actually darkness.* This is the classic definition of spiritual blindness, thinking you are what you are not, thinking you know what you do not know, thinking you are spiritual when self-righteousness is festering within you, thinking you are full of light when your motives and attitudes are a breeding ground for seeds of hypocrisy.

Jesus encapsulates this pivotal requirement of attentive watchfulness in Luke 17:3 that we looked at a few days ago—*Take heed to yourselves.*

Therefore, be alert. (Acts 20:31)
Be watchful. (1 Corinthians 16:13)
Keep alert with perseverance. (Ephesians 6:18)
Be watchful in prayer. (Colossians 4:2)
Be watchful. (1 Peter 5:8)

18. Stand Strong and Courageous in God

Many kinds of courage have been required of Jesus' followers at distinct seasons in the history of Christendom. More physical bravery was demanded of those men and women who faced the lions den and burning at the stake in former times than any level of courage required of you and me today. The men whose commands we are considering lived in an era when to admit, "I am a Christian" carried consequences not unlike proclaiming, "I am a Jew" in Nazi Germany. If placing a potential death sentence on one's head was required for church membership, how many 10,000 member mega-churches do you suppose would exist today? We can only humbly honor those of our brothers and sisters in times and places more terrifying than our own whose courage truly makes us wonder what mettle we would display in similar circumstances. Such times may come again, perhaps sooner than we think. The perils of progressivism, and the threat to western civilization of Islamic domination are rolling silently into our lives and culture with the power of an unseen tsunami. Our grandchildren and great-grandchildren may indeed live in times that witness widespread religious executions when the courage to say, *I am a Christian* will mean something much different than it means today.

Yet we must live the lives that God marks out for us, in the circumstances in which we find ourselves. That you and I do not walk out our doors wondering whether we will be arrested does not allow us to ignore this command. God requires different kinds of courage from us, and that we take *different* stands than ones that threaten our lives.

Courage cannot be quantitatively measured. Even less can the courage of one be ranked alongside the courage of another. Many of us are perhaps more courageous than we give ourselves credit for. With life and death suddenly staring us in the face, most would probably rise to the occasion and display what others would call "courage."

We are *not* very courageous, however, when it comes to ideas and ethics. In these subtle arenas of life, we are cowards. We might find it easier to face a mortal crisis than a moral one—take a stand, speak up, refuse to go along, and say, "No, this is wrong." So we smile with everyone else at the joke, the put-down, the subtle ridicule of the black sheep. We participate in the gossip. We allow untruth, social tolerance, ethical laxity, and careless talk to infect our habits and outlook. We tacitly endorse the world's values. We string along with the crowd at work, at school, in whatever might be the "group" where we find ourselves. We are afraid of being labeled prudish, old-fashioned, "religious."

Christians are also notable cowards doctrinally. In no other sphere do millions of Christians daily *disobey* the command to stand strong and be courageous than in their doctrinal conformity to ideas about God. They would rise with more courage to face a lions den than they demonstrate in their churches and Bible studies when the most egregious doctrines are perpetuated about the Father of Jesus Christ. They sit in silence rather than say, "This is not worthy of Jesus' Father."

The words *Take heart, take courage* point toward an internal boldness in the spiritual realm to stand, not against mortal enemies, but invisible ones. It is a charge to stand strong with personal fortitude and inner strength. Be strong and courageous of *character*. Bravely gird up your loins and take heart to believe *truly* about God. The prayer, *Make me like Jesus,* is a prayer reserved for the most courageous men and women on the planet.

Be watchful, stand firm in your faith, be courageous, be strong. (1 Corinthians 16:13)
Stand against the wiles of the devil. (Ephesians 6:11) Stand firm in the Lord. (Philippians 4:1)
Continue in the faith, stable and steadfast. (Colossians 1:23)
Be steadfast in faith. (2 Thessalonians 1:4) Let steadfastness have its full effect, that you may be perfect and complete and lacking in nothing. (James 1:4)
Stand fast in the true grace of God. (1 Peter 5:12)

---

19. Be Thankful in All Circumstances

I'm sure you've had the experience of rediscovering a treasure from former times, or one thought to be lost. I often find this happening with ideas as well as possessions. A thought, the solution to a problem, an insight, a scriptural insight flashes upon the brain...then just as suddenly vanishes into thin air. When these ideas are rediscovered, perhaps prompted by a new set of circumstances, it is indeed like finding a buried treasure. Even now, a *new* idea, a previously *unthought* insight, for me is pure gold.

I also periodically experience the rediscovery of a formerly loved book or author. What a joy it is to reconnect with a set of ideas that were influential at some former time that can be read anew from a more mature vantage point. Such a rediscovery came this week of an author whose books were pivotal in the early deepening of my walk with God. One of the important truths I am reconnecting with through him is the great truth of gratitude—especially in *small* things, *hard* things...thankfulness in *disappointments* and *discouragements*, thankfulness in *weakness* and *suffering*. When I was full of youthful enthusiasm for God, it was easy to be thankful for vision, for high goals, for great insights and dreams of accomplishment. Reading the same words from this author now, from the other side of life's mountain—no longer climbing up toward visionary peaks but realizing that I am descending toward the sunset and that life's great visions are behind me—I must face an entirely different question. Am I also willing to be thankful for *unfulfilled* visions, *lost* dreams, *disappointed* hopes, and *painful* realizations?

I was helped by this man's thought-provoking insight into the life of Jesus. He identified Jesus' outlook on all of life as a parable—as a *continual* parable—of our hidden life with God. Jesus framed so many of his teachings as parables because for him all of life was a parable that revealed secrets about life with God.

"Jesus' attitude toward life," he wrote, *"was one of converting everything He saw and touched to parables. He stood on this earth as a symbol of a greater world. He gripped the issues of life as...symbols of eternal and heavenly Realities. Petty problems and sorrows and disasters He converted into beautiful symbols of eternal and infinite goodness. Thus nothing was petty, nothing was trivial, nothing was without meaning in Jesus' world, for all things combined to reveal the Kingdom—the Kingdom of Heaven...*

"To me this was the greatest discovery of my life...For in Jesus' parabolic interpretation of life actually lay the secret of...His healing and teaching ministry...Jesus looked at Reality through the lens of the divine imagination. By means of that fact troubles vanished around Him, obstacles fell away...The imagination is the power we all possess of seeing harmonies, unities, and beauties in things where the non-imaginative mind sees nothing but discords, separations, and ugliness. It is the tool of the mind with which we build our affirmations...It brings us into a condition of continuous prayer...which is conducive above all else, to bringing into our life those larger harmonies and unities..." (The Soul's Sincere Desire, Glenn Clark, pp. 21-23)

This principle explodes open a great truth—we really can give thanks in ALL circumstances because everything in life is tinged with hidden eternal significance. What something *looks* like may not be its real meaning. The *outer* shell of circumstance is a parable of deeper *internal* truth. I can only step into those realities by recognizing that I am walking inside a living eternal parable. That's why Jesus' teachings are so powerful—we have the opportunity to live inside them and participate in those parables ourselves.

And this, I realized, is the root of thankfulness in all things—recognizing every situation, every encounter, every blessing, every trial, every happiness, every pain...every *moment* as imbued with the purposeful radiance of eternity.

Always and for everything give thanks. (Ephesians 5:20) Be thankful...Give thanks to God. (Colossians 3:15, 17) Give thanks in all circumstances. (1 Thessalonians 5:18) Continually offer up a sacrifice of praise. (Hebrews 13:15)

20. Don't Worry

The command not to worry—both from Jesus' lips and from the pens of James, Paul, Peter, and John—is probably the single most difficult biblical command for me to lay hold of and simply *obey*.

I cannot say how it is for others, but for me anxiety is *involuntary*. I can't help it. I can't prevent it. Worry comes unbidden, uninvited, unwelcome. It wakes me at night and literally at times consumes me.

Most of the commands are clearly practical. They speak to duties and habits we can get up from our chairs, walk through our doors...and DO. *Speak graciously, don't swear, be kind, honor your parents, don't associate with immoral people, don't spread gossip*—there's no mystery here. We can obey whether we feel like it or not. These are things that we can do fairly simply every day...or not do. There is a choice involved and we decide which side of the choice we will come down on. We can obediently DO our duty.

There exists another class of commands, however, that targets attitude, perspective, outlook, and far more ethereal regions within us. These commands are less tangible. They seem to rely on feelings that we cannot always control. In my life, *Don't worry* heads this list of very difficult feelings-commands. When anxiety sweeps over me, it is like a tidal wave I cannot stop.

Sharing his similar struggle with this command, a friend recently pointed out an insight from Psalm 37. In a threefold progression, David first links "fretting" to envy, which we considered a few days ago, then makes the somewhat astonishing assertion that envy leads to evil.

Do not fret...do not be envious of wrongdoers. (37:1)
Do not fret over those who prosper...over those who carry out evil devices. (37:7)
Do not fret—it leads only to evil. (37:8, all NRSV)

More may be at stake from worry and fretting than we realize.

Where, then, does simple *obedience* come in? How am I to obey in an area where I seemingly have no control? I don't *choose* to worry. I don't *want* to worry. It just comes. Difficult circumstances overwhelm me. I toss and turn through the long hours of night's blackness plagued by a thousand imaginary *What ifs*. The tidal wave sweeps in.

So how do I obey this command? I have been wrestling with this conundrum for more than forty years of walking with God. This is a command I approach at the outset sort of assuming my own failure. I know I am going to worry. Perhaps that sounds defeatist. But I am trying to be realistic. Then I reaffirm the truths that form the basis for my life—God is good, the Father is with me, he knows my circumstances, he is in control, he is a good Father, I can give thanks in spite of my anxieties, and so on. These are eternal truths. I believe them. Thus, I can affirm them in spite of the fact that my thoughts and emotions may be going off the rails into worry. I simply ask the Holy Spirit to send the reality of these truths deeper into my being than my anxieties...and then I go on with life. If I am anxious, I don't worry about it. As long as I am affirming the anti-worry truths with God's loving Fatherhood at the center of them, I don't worry about worrying. I know it will subside in time. Obviously this perspective can only be adopted toward *involuntary* attitudes. We cannot rationalize *chosen* disobedience by saying, "I can't help lying, gossiping, or my sexual sin so I'm not going to worry about it."

My answer to the dilemma, then, is this: I may worry, but I don't worry about it. That is my method. Not very spiritual I admit. But we have to find ways to walk in obedience to the commands while recognizing that we're not very good at it. Obedience is a constant skirmish against invisible enemies. Most of mine seem to exist in my own mind.

Be free from anxieties. (1 Corinthians 7:32)
Have no anxiety about anything. (Ephesians 4:6)
Cast all your anxieties on him, for he cares about you. (1 Peter 5:7)

"THE GALATIA COMMANDS"

Grow the Fruits of the Spirit

QUALITIES OF PERSONAL BEHAVIOR,
ATTITUDE, AND CHARACTER THAT
EXEMPLIFY THE FRUIT OF THE CHRIST-LIFE

GALATIA—CONFLICT, THEOLOGICAL DISPUTE, AND FACTIONALISM INFILTRATE THE CHURCH

From Antioch, which became the hub and center of missionary activity in the mid to late-40s, Christianity exploded west around the entire Mediterranean. This expansion resulted chiefly from and can be traced to a series of "missionary journeys" through the region by the apostles and other Christian leaders. Most of the disciples were traveling and spreading the good news about Jesus in every direction outward from Jerusalem. The book of *Acts* chronicles some of this early missionary zeal in the church. Most of what is known of this expansion follows the four missionary trips of Paul and his companions during an approximately fifteen year period between the late 40s and early 60s. Paul was not the only Christian teacher and evangelist spreading the gospel through the Roman world. In his case, however, we have the accounts of *Acts* written by Luke that recount Paul's movements and give us a clear picture of this dramatic epic in the burgeoning life of the Christian movement.

The missionary travels of Paul in particular began in the late 40s. The church in Antioch commissioned its leader Barnabas to undertake a trip into the western region of Pamphylia, Galatia, and Cilicia—through what is today Turkey—to preach the gospel of Jesus Christ. Barnabas took with him his assistant Saul and his young nephew John Mark. This trip lasted about a year and is chronicled in Acts 13-14. By the end of the trip, Luke has changed from speaking of Barnabas and Saul to *Paul and Barnabas*. Saul has changed his name and has become the leader of the duo.

Most memorable about this trip for the development of the church concerns what happened later, after Barnabas and Paul returned to Syria. Two sets of circumstances arose that greatly troubled Paul. First, reports began coming back to him about teachings spreading through the new churches of Galatia that went against what he and Barnabas had taught them. These teachings emphasized the importance of Jewish Law and insisted that Gentile Christians must be circumcised and adhere to other points of that Law. About the same time some Jewish Christians arrived in Antioch from the Jerusalem church. When Peter and Barnabas partook in meals with these visitors, Paul interpreted their action as representing an endorsement of the "Judaizers"—those who taught that the church was still subject to the Jewish Law. In full view of the Antioch church, Paul publicly rebuked Peter and Barnabas for what he perceived as their hypocrisy.

Both these situations prompted Paul in about the year 49 to write a letter to be read in the churches of Galatia. This letter was the first of Paul's "epistles" that became so foundational in the unfolding of the New Testament writings. It is of course the book we know as Paul's *Letter to the Galatians*. In it Paul addressed the "Judaizing" teaching being spread through Galatia. Additionally, he used the incident at Antioch with Peter as a springboard to outline what he called "*his* gospel" of freedom from Jewish Law.

Not only is *Galatians* thus the first of Paul's letters, it is one of Christianity's important foundational documents. It set many patterns in motion—both theological and historical, some good, some bad. In spite of the conflict inherent in the circumstances of its writing, the letter of *Galatians* also brings us one of the most succinct portraits of the Christian life. In his first letter, Paul's genius is clearly evident as he captures the essence of that life, blending theology and practice, lofty ideas with daily character. This harmonized insight of wisdom and practicality reveals why Paul was the church's leading written communicator, and became the voice and image of first century Christianity.

In a few brief words—Galatians 5:22-23—Paul brings the full power of his practical wisdom to bear on a lovely and succinct nine-fold portrayal of Christlikeness. These nine qualities, Paul says, will evidence the "character-fruit" that Christians will grow in their lives when they are "walking in the Spirit." This new concept, and this phrase coined for the first time by Paul in *Galatians*, provides a focused "bull's eye" of what comprises the pragmatic, daily, moment-by-moment essence of the Christian life.

SERIES THREE

QUALITIES OF PERSONAL BEHAVIOR, ATTITUDE, AND CHARACTER THAT EXEMPLIFY THE FRUIT OF THE CHRIST-LIFE

21. Walk by the Spirit.

22. Make love your aim.

23. Rejoice in all circumstances, especially in your trials.

24. Walk in peace.

25. Respond with patience.

26. Be kind.

27. Do good, love good, be good.

28. Walk faithfully by faith, not by sight.

29. Be a gentle person.

30. Exercise self-control.

21. Walk by the Spirit

The familiar passage in *Galatians* that underlies the ten "Galatia" commands of this section emerges out of an extensive study in contrasts presented by Paul throughout this entire epistle. These contrasts reach their climax in the second half of chapter 5.

Paul compares himself with Peter, the Law with Freedom, the Old Covenant with the New, slaves with sons, and Hagar with Sarah. Now he reaches the pinnacle of contrasts with the brutally insightful distinction that slams every Christian between the eyes—the contrast between two ways of "walking" as a disciple of Christ, two ways of ordering our lives, two ways of setting our priorities, two ways of going about our affairs, two ways of making decisions, two ways of regulating attitudes, two ways of relating to people, two ways of responding to circumstances. That is the contrast between the *flesh* and the *Spirit*.

The contrast between Hagar and Sarah may be interesting theologically. But it does not intersect very closely with a dispute with my neighbor, my response to disappointing news, my attitude toward one who has wronged me, or a visit to the hardware store this afternoon. The battle between flesh and spirit, on the other hand, is waged every minute of my life. Paul's use of the verb "walk" to characterize which of the two paths I choose highlights that the choice is active, moving, ongoing, continual. This is a dynamic, breathing, palpably *real* contrast. It touches me right now!

Our moment-by-moment choices (in line with either the flesh or the spirit) take us somewhere. They move us forward on life's journey toward very different results of character. *Walk* is not merely a verb of motion. One can walk in place, I suppose, but true "walking" leads somewhere. That *destination* is what Paul is talking about. Moving in one direction or the other produces results. Paul calls those fruits. They are fruits that grow on the tree of character depending on how we are growing, depending on whether we allow the "sap of the flesh" or the "sap of the Spirit" to flow within us.

We're mixing our metaphors here, a writer's cardinal sin. Yet Paul fuses both images in his explanation—*walking* and *growing*. In a sense, then, we have to intermingle two related analogies to illuminate the essence of the Spirit-life. We can look at this process through the eyes of either—either as the *destination* of a walking journey, or as the *fruit* of growth, the fruit growing on our life's tree. Both analogies basically speak the same truth: Identifiable results will be visible in our characters depending on how we live. Paul is essentially telling us: *Walk and grow* according to these principles of character.

Those two different sets of character-fruits are enumerated in Galatians 5:19-21 and 5:22-23. Both walking and growing are intrinsic to each. As I rebuke anger and jealousy and respond with gentleness and kindness (obediently choosing how to *walk*), the fruit of kindness and gentleness will *grow* within me. The two images work simultaneously within my character. The growth does not take place without the walking choice.

Perhaps the most fascinating element of Paul's flesh-Spirit contrast is found in the shockingly commonplace (tolerated, justified, and easily excused) "sins" of the flesh we discover in the first list. Anger is listed alongside drunkenness, selfishness and jealousy alongside sexual impurity. Tolerated and acceptable sins such as anger, strife, envy, and that mentality so common in the church, "party spirit," will prevent the fruits of the Spirit growing within us exactly as will immorality and drunkenness.

Walk by the Spirit...the fruit of the Spirit is love, joy, peace, patience, kindness, goodness, faithfulness, gentleness, self-control...if we live by the Spirit, let us also walk by the Spirit. (Galatians 5:16, 22-23, 25)

Demonstrate the fruit of light, which is found in all that is good and right and true...Look carefully how you walk. (Ephesians 5:9, 15)

May your love abound...so that you may...[be] filled with the fruits of righteousness. (Philippians 1:9-11)

Show God's wisdom by demonstrating good fruit. (Hebrews 3:17)

22. Make Love Your Aim

It comes as no surprise that the first "fruit of the Spirit" Paul lists in Galatians 5:22 is love. Love is the topmost fruit of the Christ-life, the first and highest commandment, the summation and apex of all the Law and the Prophets and the Gospel of Jesus Christ.

In *The Commands* we noted: *The command to Love—all men, all women, all people, all children, all life, all truth, the very creation itself and everything in it—and the love demonstrated and exampled by his own life and sacrificial death, is truly the single fact, the single teaching, the single Command, the single life-power, that distinguishes Jesus Christ from all other teachers. It is his love that separates Jesus from all other human beings that have ever walked this planet. That single command is intended to set apart and differentiate his followers from the world and everything in it. Love is thus intended to be the visible mark and characteristic which Christians wear, which exudes from their very being. It is LOVE which will result in the transformation of the world, and the transformation of individual human character into the Christlikeness which is the image of Jesus himself, a reflection of God the Father, the Creator of heaven and earth.*

Only love has the power to accomplish these mighty purposes of God, which Jesus came among men to make possible in the lives of those who came after him. For LOVE is the creative power of God himself, the essence of his nature and being. All love in the universe flows out of that infinite and eternal well of God's being-ness. When we love, we touch others and ourselves with God himself...

The difficulty is obviously in the details. We don't know how to love God and love man very well in the moment-by-moment minutes and hours of life. That's why Jesus gave us the rest of the Commands. They are nothing more than the specific ways and means and methods of carrying out these two greatest Commands which include all the rest within them. The two "greatest" commandments—LOVE GOD, LOVE MAN—represent the overarching blueprint for life...for eternal life. The rest of the Commands tell us how practically to live the days of our lives according to that blueprint."

Practically speaking, then, what is love? The Beatles sang, "All you need is love." But did they have any notion what true "Love" really was? What is meant by this topmost fruit on the Spirit's character-tree to which we give the exalted name of *love*?

I would suggest that Paul gives us a focused image of crystalline clarity right here. These verses combine with his equally powerful exposition in 1 Corinthians 13:4-7 to tell us exactly what love is. We need be in no doubt whether we are "walking" in love. The evidences and symptoms and fruits of love and unlove are too clear to mistake.

We walk in *unlove* when we are selfish, impure, envious, angry, jealous, immoral... when there is animosity, strife, argumentation, or dissension in our relationships. We *love* when we are patient, kind, good, peaceful, joyful, faithful, gentle, and self-controlled. It's not rocket science. These are choices we make a hundred times a day.

Let love be genuine. (Romans 12:9)
Love your neighbor as yourself. (Romans 13:9)
Make love your aim...Let all you do be done in love. (1 Corinthians 14:1; 16:14)
Walk by the Spirit...the fruit of the Spirit is love. (Galatians 5:16, 22)
Walk in love. (Ephesians 5:2)
Above all things, put on love. (Colossians 3:14)
Abound in love to one another...Love one another...Love the brethren more and more. (1 Thessalonians 3:12; 4:9, 10)
Aim at love. (1 Timothy 6:11; 2 Timothy 2:22)
Love one another earnestly from the heart. (1 Peter 1:22)
Hold unfailing your love for one another. (1 Peter 4:8)
Love your brother and walk in the light...Love one another...lay your lives down for the brethren...This is the love of God, that we obey his commandments. (1 John 2:10; 3:11, 16; 5:3)

---

23. Rejoice in All Circumstances, Especially in Your Trials

The secret to understanding the Bible is really quite simple. The formula for unlocking Genesis 1 is the same as that needed to penetrate the mysteries of Revelation 22...and everything between. That powerful key is: *Converting principle to command.*

When the Bible's history, theology, poetry, and teaching is transformed into practical, living, obedient, selfless *doing* of the principles embedded in that history, theology, poetry, and teaching, their hidden meanings will unfold themselves into our hearts, minds, and spirits. Converting principle to command places the key in our hand. *Doing* the commands turns the key and opens the door of *understanding.*

The outer courts of the Temple may be stormed by study and analysis. The Holy of Holies can be penetrated only by transforming truth into obedience.

It is to point us continually and oft to the imperative of this transformation process—Principle, Command, Obedience—that these volumes of commands are being written. We are seeking to penetrate the Bible's deepest truths, the scriptural Holy of Holies. We can only enter that sacred chamber through command and obedience.

We discover an example of that imperative here. Second among the fruits of the Spirit we find joy: *The fruit of the spirit is...joy.* This is a scriptural principle which Paul has set forth. If we are walking by the Spirit, joy will result. Simple cause and effect.

But thus far it is only a principle. At this point its truth may remain abstract, theoretical, an ideal to gaze upon and analyze. Perfect sermon material. The principle has not yet become *live* truth breaking in upon our deepest understanding. It may even rise from principle to the outer edges of the *realm* of truth. But it is not yet itself truth in our inward parts. As yet it is only knocking on truth's door. It is not yet a *living* Truth.

To cross that threshold and pass into that inner holy region of vibrant, moment-by-moment Life, the transformation must be made—turning the *principle* into *command.* This is the key that unlocks the understanding that brings Life. It is the key of DO.

Therefore, we take the principle Paul has opened, and we search further. We discover the intimate relationship between the *noun-joy* of the principle, and the *verb-rejoice* of the command. We dig deep into the mineshafts of the Bible's joy-rejoice veins to discover Paul's command to rejoice in our *sufferings,* which he penned in prison not a mountaintop. We read James and Peter exhorting us to rejoice in our *trials,* exactly as Paul did when he wrote *Philippians.* Peter adds that we will share the *sufferings* of Christ. Unpleasant images suddenly become apparent that live on the other side of joy's coin.

We discover the high principle that the joy produced by spirit-walking comes with a price. It is a *costly joy,* for it requires a sacrificial and other-worldly response to life's difficulties and heartbreaks and disappointments. It is joy with strings attached. It is a joy that to enter into requires a rejoicing that may be the very opposite of joyful.

We fall on our knees. Quietly we whisper, "Thank you, Father...I rejoice for this heartache that is pressing the very life out of me. I rejoice though I feel no joy. I give you thanks for this season of despair. I know you are a good Father."

We rise, with tears in our eyes it may be. Tears that sting with the anguish of unfaith, the despondency of *unfelt joy,* rather that what the world calls rejoicing. We have converted the principle into the living truth of which James spoke. It feels like the opposite of joy. Yet in obedient faith, we say, *Thank you...I choose to rejoice.*

Truth comes. Understanding opens into the deep places. With tears, we have walked through the door into the Holy Place where joy and rejoice merge in obedience.

Rejoice in your sufferings, knowing that suffering produces endurance, and endurance produces character. (Romans 5:3-4) Walk by the Spirit...the fruit of the Spirit is...joy. (Galatians 5:16, 22)
Rejoice in the Lord...Rejoice in the Lord always; again I say rejoice. (Philippians 3:1; 4:4)
Count it all joy when you meet various trials. (James 1:2)
Rejoice...though now for a little while you may have to suffer various trials. (1 Peter 1:6)
Rejoice when you share Christ's sufferings. (1 Peter 4:13)

24. Walk in Peace

Peace is one of those evanescent felt singularities in life for which we hunger yet experience all too seldom. Its moments are fleeting and transitory, mere hints that something greater lies beyond the horizon if only we could lay hold of it. Jesus' words, *Peace I leave with you, my peace I give to you,* fill our hearts with more longing than reality. We yearn for constancy. We want more than brief tastes. We desire to abide in the peace of the Upper Room. We want peace to nourish our souls. But peace eludes us.

How, then, do we enter into this high state of harmony with ourselves, God, and others, this inner dwelling place of tranquility, quietude, and contentment? This raises the question: What are the characteristics of the fruit of peace that Paul said would grow on the character-tree of one who "walks in the Spirit?" Are our expectations accurate?

We have had frequent occasion to examine the cause and effect relationship between the Bible's commands and the fruits of obedience to those commands. There are, however, less tangible components of discipleship that cannot always predictably be gotten at through the front door of obedience. Some of the fruits enter through side doors unseen. It may be that we encounter one of those invisible side-door fruits of the spirit here. For have we not all experienced the peace of God stealing upon us unbidden, delicious moments in the midst of life's pace. These come, as far we know, from nothing we have done to deserve it. Peace just *comes.* In these brief seasons, cares and anxieties fall away. A hush descends. We are quietly at rest, serene, content in the eternal moment.

Perhaps here we begin to lay hold of a great truth. What is peace but *contentment in the eternal moment?* Not wishing the moment, or the circumstances of the moment, or myself as I stand at the heart of the moment, to be other than they are?

Turning the peace-coin over to gaze at its other side, I discover a host of familiar impediments to the very contentment that lies at the heart of peace. Suddenly from within—shockingly unexpected!—rise the very "works of the flesh" that Paul warns will prevent the Spirit-fruits from ripening on my life's vine: Selfishness, envy, and jealousy. What are all three but the latent desire that the moment be somehow *other* than it is? My wanting what is *not* brings selfishness, envy, and jealousy crashing with dissonance into the eternal now of the present. I selfishly wish for something *else.* I am jealous for *another* now. I envy a *different* set of circumstances. I thus murder my own contentment.

Peace is rooted in thankfulness for what *is,* in gratitude for *this* moment. Contentment is born in the simple words, *Thank you,* addressed to our Father. *Thank you that THIS moment is what it is. Thank you that though my circumstances may be hard, you are in the midst of them. I rest content in your arms. This is your now, and I am in it with you.*

Perhaps we cannot always walk with peace in our hearts. Perhaps we cannot summon peace at will. Perhaps we cannot say, "If I obey such-and-such a command, I will always feel peace." Perhaps we will never abide continually in the "peace that passes understanding." Perhaps in this life peace will always be fleeting.

We can, however, abide in *the prayer of thankfulness.* Our lips can murmur continual whispers of gratitude for the present moment. We can invite contentment for this eternal now by simple thankfulness. As we do, in its own time...peace will come.

Walk by the Spirit...the fruit of the Spirit is...peace. (Galatians 5:16, 22)

Fit your feet with the gospel of peace. (Ephesians 6:15)

Be at peace among yourselves. (1 Thessalonians 5:13)

Live a quiet and peaceable life, godly and respectfully in every way. (1 Timothy 2:2)

Aim at peace. (2 Timothy 2:22)

Show God's wisdom by being peaceable...Sow peace and reap a harvest of righteousness. (James 3:17, 18)

Seek peace and pursue it. (1 Peter 3:12)

25. Respond With Patience

Our response to patience all depends on how we phrase the command. *Be* patient may sound impossible. Few of us would make the claim, "I am a patient person."

Turning it around, however, we can transform the principle into a command that we *can* obey in the midst of what may in reality be the very opposite of patience: *Exercise* patience...*choose* patience...*respond* with patience. Suddenly the command is do-able.

I may not like it. Inside I may be stewing with *im*patience. But I still have the opportunity to *respond with patience.*

I continually find it remarkable in enumerating God's character traits (Love=God) in 1 Corinthians 13, that Paul leads with patience. He is essentially saying that patience is one of God's first and most divine qualities of character. What about the great spiritual attributes—sovereign, almighty, omniscient, omnipotent, holy? Surely these rank higher in the catalog of divine attributes than such a commonplace trait as patience.

How different would our theologies be if for two thousand years Christians had been telling the world above all else that God was patient and kind! How much farther along toward its ultimate redemption might the world be now if God's people had known the Father of Jesus Christ *truly*, and had communicated that nature to the world. Alas, we will never know. Thus, we are still playing catch-up—having to overcome nearly two thousand years of misplaced teaching that has done more to alienate the unbelieving world than draw it to the Father of Jesus.

Patience—that wonderfully down-to-earth quality none of us possesses by nature, which is so easily upset by the most trivial of circumstances, which always seems to elude us when we need it most...yet which can be practiced in the small moments a hundred times a day. Surely this is one of the most practical of all the virtues! But not so commonplace a virtue as it seems. For we discover holiness here. When we respond with patience (whether feeling patient or not), we touch the essence of God himself.

Patience is so...down-to-earth. It takes no heightened wisdom...or spiritual insight to be patient. Atheists and heathens can be patient just as well as Christians...

God did not create the world in a moment. He took his time about it...aeons of creating "days."...His purposes are never rushed. God is never in a hurry.

Thus when Jesus commands patience, he is commanding nothing more nor less than for us to be like God, to wait with a graceful heart...

The impatience of modern Christendom must be heartbreaking to God. Everywhere there is rush, hurry, and freneticism. We are in a hurry for our prayers to be answered, in a hurry to do and become all we want to do and be, in a hurry to serve God, in a hurry to save the world. We are impatient in traffic, frustrated in lines, importune in conversation, demanding in business, more intent to be heard than to listen...eager, interrupting, pushy, vocal, hasty, impulsive, insistent...

Slow down. Be calm. Relax. Wait. Take the eternal perspective. Display God's nature to the world. (From *The Commands of Jesus,* p. 25)

Be a patient person. Patiently endure stressful circumstances. Take a few deep breaths, then graciously persevere through the adversity and injustice confronting you.

Be patient in tribulation. (Romans 12:12)
Love is patient. (1 Corinthians 13:4)
Commend yourself by forbearance. (2 Corinthians 6:6)
Walk by the Spirit...the fruit of the Spirit is...patience. (Galatians 5:16, 22)
Live with patience. (Ephesians 4:2)
Put on patience. (Colossians 3:12)
Be patient with all. (1 Thessalonians 5:14)
Be patient like a farmer awaiting the precious fruit from the earth. (Hebrews 5:7-8)
Endure pain and injustice patiently. (1 Peter 2:19-20)

---

26. Be Kind

The more down-to-earth one makes the teachings of the Bible, the more certain intellectual spiritualists resent the absence of doctrine, theology, and analysis. The practicality of the gospel is too much for them. One wonders, if they met him face to face, if Jesus himself would be *spiritual* enough for them.

It is always simplistic to reduce spiritual principles to formula. But we will risk it here, hopefully with good result. If we had to boil the enormous complexities of the New Testament down into a single principle or teaching, a single command...even a single *word*, how would you and I choose to summarize God's charge to humankind?

Would we select for our one-term encapsulization a "spiritual" term of *theological* import: Salvation, Propitiation, Sanctification, Eternal Life?

Would we choose a high word of lofty *divine* characteristic: Sovereignty, Love, Fatherhood, Sonship, Sacrifice, Truth.

Or would it be a practical virtue capable of regulating *personal* human attitude and behavior, conduct and character: Goodness, Humility, Servanthood, Discipleship.

All these, of course, reveal important facets of the complex diamond of Truth. But if I had to choose one, the word that to my mind epitomizes and compresses the Gospel into a single radiant eternal entity expressive of Jesus' life among men and his command to men, I would choose KINDNESS. It may not be spiritual enough for some. But I stand by it. Kindness represents the apex of Gospel practicality. In all the thousand forms by which it can be lived and manifested in the small moments of every day between the men and women of God's creation, kindness demonstrates God's living Love to the world as nothing else is capable of. In simple *kindness* to others of our kind, we become God's hands, his mouth, his feet, his heart to a kindness-starved world.

The entire Gospel is infused with kindness from beginning to end. In this larger sense, every word, every gesture, every prayer of Jesus speaks of kindness. Love, kindness, and goodness provide the underlying life-pulsating air of the gospel. Jesus hardly needed to say, "Love, be kind, be good." Every teaching, every parable, every exhortation positively shouted, "Love, be kind, be good."...

It has been said that the teaching of Jesus, in its simplest form, can be expressed as, "Be nice and treat people with kindness."...When Paul spelled out the components of love...he begins with two towering attributes that ought to be the first character-clothes we put on every morning: Love is patient and kind...Every kindness we show, however large or small—a cup of cold water, a kind word, a smile, a gracious gesture—is a visible expression of the face of God smiling into humanity, the hand of the Creator reaching into his world to touch the brother and sister, made in his image, beside us...

"Have you ever noticed how much of Christ's life was spent in doing kind things—in merely doing kind things?...He spent a great proportion of His time simply in making people happy, in doing good turns to people. There is only one thing greater...and that is holiness; and it is not in our keeping; but what God has put in our power is the happiness of those about us, and that is largely to be secured by our being kind to them.

"'The greatest thing,' says someone, 'a man can do for his Heavenly Father is to be kind to some of His other children.'" (From *The Commands of Jesus,* p. 69; final quote from Henry Drummond, *The Greatest Thing in the World.*)

Lose no opportunity to show kindness. Define your character by kindness.

Love is kind. (1 Corinthians 13:4)
Commend yourself by kindness. (2 Corinthians 6:6)
Walk by the Spirit...the fruit of the Spirit is...kindness. (Galatians 5:16, 22)
Be kind to one another. (Ephesians 4:32)
Bid older women to teach younger women to be kind...Show yourself in all respects a model of good deeds...Let our people learn to apply themselves to good deeds. (Titus 2:5, 7; 3:14)

27. Do Good, Love Good, Be Good

Many may be the lingering objections from yesterday's examination of kindness. It is admittedly bold to identify a principle of behavior and conduct as surpassing theology to epitomize the foundation of the gospel message. How can we possibly identify the archetype of Christian behavior as a quality of conduct that atheists can demonstrate as readily as believers? Where is the scriptural basis for such a claim? In answer I would reply that we need look no farther than the red letters in our Bibles.

However, I understand the objection. And I admit to overstatement in order to drive home the imperative point that practicality must trump theology or everything in our religion is vain. Christianity is clearly more complex than being nice. All the high principles of Fatherhood, salvation, eternal life, sacrifice, servanthood, and the entire scope of scriptural teaching combine and flow together, drawing the practicality of daily kindness up into the realm of the Eternal.

Continuing to amplify on similar themes (and again risking overstatement to make a vital point) we now identify an equally imperative practical virtue to stand alongside *kindness* and *love*. Together they form a threefold foundational strength upon which the entire edifice of the Christian life is built. That of course is GOODNESS.

Again the down-to-earth simplicity of goodness may disarm the theologically minded. Is goodness *too* simple? Consider the Genesis 1 foundation upon which Creation is based. God established the entire Creation on goodness. It is the life-tree from which all the Life of the universe sent down roots and grew. Not "spiritual" enough? *Goodness* is the core and essence of *all* spirituality. It is the core and essence of God himself.

The objection is never far from the minds of pietists that "goodness is not enough and won't get you into heaven." Perhaps they are right. However, we don't know exactly how the entry requirements for heaven work. All we can do, therefore, is ask, "What do we know about God?" Then we must make that our *enough*. God's Fatherhood is the central and originating truth of his being. You and I are commanded to reflect God's Genesis 1 nature in the simplicity of daily life through *goodness*. As God's children we are called to be *good* people, and then to live by and manifest goodness in a thousand ways.

This obviously begins simply by *doing* good. *Loving* good is more difficult. This requires serious soul searching. Do we even really *want* to love good? Or do we want to retain some worldliness in the shadows. Pure goodness seems a bit much. We flatter ourselves that we can be "good Christians" while preserving our favorite vices. *Hey, I'm not perfect,* we say. God doesn't expect it. He loves me as I am. So we try to *do* good, but keep *love* for goodness topped off at about 70% or 80%. We figure that's enough.

The final progression of goodness—goodness of *be*-ing—becomes the result of a lifetime not merely doing but also *loving* good. When the fruit of the Spirit truly comes alive within us, the Christlikeness of true goodness—the character of God himself, the goodness of Creation, the goodness which resounded through Eden and across the vault of the heavens—blossoms and bears fruit within you and me! Genesis 1:31 is thus linked with Galatians 5:22 in an unbroken and glorious span of eternal purpose.

Hold fast to what is good...Overcome evil with good. (Romans 12:9, 21)
Do what is good...Be wise as to what is good. (Romans 13:3; 16:9)
Let no one seek his own good, but the good of his neighbor. (1 Corinthians 10:24)
Love rejoices in the right. (1 Corinthians 13:6)
Walk by the Spirit...the fruit of the Spirit is...goodness. (Galatians 5:16, 22)
As we have opportunity, let us do good to all men. (Galatians 6:10)
Always seek to do good to all. (1 Thessalonians 5:15). Be rich in good deeds. (1 Timothy 6:18)
A bishop must be a lover of goodness...Bid older women to teach what is good. (Titus 1:8; 2:3)
Stir one another up to love and good works...Do not neglect to do good. (Hebrews 10:24; 13:16)
By your good life, show works in the meekness of wisdom. (James 3:13)

---

28. Walk Faithfully by Faith, Not by Sight

The Spirit-fruit Paul defines as "faithfulness" clearly derives from, though may not be exactly the same as, that quality of mind and heart we call "faith." Though originating out of the same root, the two clearly carry distinct attributes.

Faith implies the capacity to believe in what we cannot see. *Faithfulness* adds an additional range of character qualities—diligence, responsibility, perseverance, loyalty, dependability, trustworthiness, truthfulness, virtue, conscientiousness, and so on. All these are qualities of character observed less and less in the world. But they *are* to be observed in Christians. Obviously the fruit Paul is speaking of is multi-dimensional. Does he imply that *all* such virtues of the "faithful" life will emerge from walking in the Spirit?

I believe so. When we convert the principle to command, unifying *faith* and *faithfulness* into a harmonized lifestyle of obediently walking by faith not by sight, and living according to the principles of faithfulness, the twin fruits of faith and faithfulness will indeed grow as blossoms on our character tree.

The "great cloud of witnesses" in Hebrews 11 reprises the "faith" of a series of God's "faithful" men and women. The two concepts are not always interchangeable but in Hebrews 11 they are. Without altering the meaning , the author might well have written, "In faithfulness Enoch...in faithfulness Noah...in faithfulness Abraham...in faithfulness Moses..." By *faith*, these men acted in faithfulness. In *faithfulness*, they lived their faith.

In introducing these saints of faith, therefore, Hebrews 11:1 stands as the great scriptural pillar for the defining of faith: "Now faith is the substance of things hoped for, the evidence of things not seen. (KJV) It joins with Galatians 5:23, "...the fruit of the Spirit is...faithfulness..." and 2 Corinthians 5:7, "For we walk by faith, not by sight," to give us a threefold portrait of the high thing of *faithful faith*. Transforming principle into command, the three merge as one: *Walk faithfully by faith, not by sight.*

This does not merely mean to *believe* that God will answer our prayers though we don't *see* the answering fruit of those prayers. That's often the construction we give it. And occasionally it may mean exactly that. Walking faithfully by faith, however, draws all life into it, not just one's prayer life. We are to live by the principles of faithfulness, even though perhaps we do not *see* the fruit of our labors, though we *see* no reason to be trustworthy and faithful, loyal and dependable, virtuous and high-principled, diligent and responsible, persevering and truthful. We continue to live faithfully anyway. We're not merely speaking of prayer. Faithfulness is an all-life virtue.

The fruit of faithfulness may remain unseen. Live faithfully anyway. The fruit is God's to grow, not ours to force into fruition in a hothouse of spiritual haste. For "the fruit of the spirit is...faithfulness."

Faithfulness is its own fruit. We need look for no reward for faithfulness. Becoming a faithful man or woman *is* the reward.

Look not to the things that are seen, but to the things that are not seen...for the things that are unseen are eternal. (2 Corinthians 4:18)

Walk by the Spirit...the fruit of the Spirit is...faithfulness. (Galatians 5:16, 22)

Continue in the faith, stable and steadfast. (Colossians 1:23)

Put on the breastplate of faith. (1 Thessalonians 5:8)

Occupy yourself with the divine training that is faith. (1 Timothy 1:4)

The aim of our charge is love that issues from a pure heart and a good conscience and sincere faith...holding faith and a good conscience....Aim at faith. (1 Timothy 1:5, 19; 6:11)

Fight the good fight of faith. (1 Timothy 6:12)

Bid older men to be sound in faith. (Titus 2:2)

Supplement your faith with virtue. (2 Peter 1:5)

Build yourself up in your holy faith. (Jude 20)

---

29. Be a Gentle Person

The final two fruits of the Spirit listed by Paul in Galatians 5:23 are positively astounding. If we are paying attention, they stagger the world of our spiritual preconceptions. Take a deep breath. Whisper a silent prayer for insight and wisdom. May these two fruit-commands help us grasp the enormity and simplicity of Spirit-life.

Has Paul saved the best for last? Or has he tacked on these last two fruits as an afterthought, knowing that they do not rise to the level of those listed earlier? I believe Paul knew exactly what he was doing. It may be that he wanted to climax his list with two of the most important fruits of all.

It is not difficult to recognize the overarching importance of love, goodness, faith, joy, and peace. We encounter them in the Beatitudes the moment we open the Gospels. None of the fruits that have come before are a surprise. When we read them from Paul's pen, in a sense they are completely expected. Now suddenly we are doused in the face with two buckets of cold water. We have spoken of the down-to-earth nature of kindness and goodness. That practicality now becomes nothing short of incredible.

Think of the implications if this character fruit is really true. Is Paul actually implying that the highest thing in the world—walking through life with God's Spirit ruling character, conduct, attitude, and behavior—can be partially defined simply by being a gentleman or gentle woman? Is Paul equating being gentle and gracious with godliness of character? The idea of *spirituality* defined by *politeness* is astounding.

Where are the pious attributes of those we admire as spiritual gurus? Where is belief, faith, prayer? Where is theology? Where is salvation? Where is doctrinal correctness? Where is orthodoxy? Where is biblical knowledge? Where is Christian ministry?

When we really grasp what Paul is saying, it turns external religious piety on its ear. What is "gentleness" but grace in relationships—the practiced skill to put others at their ease? We might employ the word *seemly* to help us lay hold of this high yet everyday virtue—decent, discreet, inoffensive, unobtrusive, in good taste, decorous...speaking and interacting with soft edges of character. On the other hand, loud, forceful, argumentative, hard edges are nowhere to be found in the demeanor of a *gentle* man or woman.

We are left to draw the astonishing conclusion that Paul seems to be defining a Spirit-led life with God by what we might call good etiquette!

Look around in a crowd. The gentle people are not hard to find. Their demeanor is distinct, their expression calm, their words soft and measured, their carriage full of grace.

"The fifth ingredient [of love] is...Courtesy. This is Love in society, Love in relation to etiquette. 'Love doth not behave itself unseemly.' Politeness has been defined as love in trifles. Courtesy is said to be love in little things. And the one secret of politeness is to love. Love cannot behave itself unseemly. You can put the most untutored person into the highest society, and if they have a reservoir of love in their heart, they will not behave themselves unseemly. They simply cannot do it...

"You know the meaning of the word "gentleman". It means a gentle man—a man who does things gently, with love. And that is the whole art and mystery of it. The gentle man cannot in the nature of things do an ungentle, an ungentlemanly thing. The ungentle soul, the inconsiderate, unsympathetic nature cannot do anything else. 'Love doth not behave itself unseemly.'" (Henry Drummond, *The Greatest Thing in the World.*)

Let us conduct ourselves becomingly. (Romans 13:13)
Walk by the Spirit...the fruit of the Spirit is...gentleness. (Galatians 5:16, 23)
If a man is overtaken in any sin...restore him in a spirit of gentleness. (Galatians 6:1)
A bishop must be gentle...Aim at gentleness. (1 Timothy 3:3; 6:11)
The Lord's servant must correct his opponents with gentleness. (2 Timothy 2:25)
Be gentle. (Titus 3:2).
Show God's wisdom by being gentle. (Hebrews 3:17)

30. Exercise Self-Control

Self-control and patience are closely linked, but contain intrinsic differences. Though patience is more familiar, it is also elusive. Self-control is more powerful. As a "principle" it needs no conversion. By its nature self-control is a *command*. The words cannot be read except as a command—*self*-control means controlling oneself. It is something one *does*. It cannot be spiritualized. When I am late and rushed, my impulse is to hurry. Self-control would have me regulate and harness that impulse, then relax and proceed with calm. If I am not feeling anxious, then patience is no virtue. It is when I *am* pressured, and I *control* the impulse to haste, that the fruit of self-control has the opportunity to grow. When I *control* my impulses, I step into harmony and concert with God's Spirit. What an amazing truth, a positively remarkable trait of spiritual maturity.

There exist clear and obvious areas where lack of self-control has ruinous consequences—overeating, gambling, drinking, spending. But self-control reveals itself also in more subtle ways. As much as in any other aspect of character, self-control manifests itself in speech. Most people simply talk too much. The talkative person is not a self-controlled person. The loquacious man or woman in love with the sound of his or her own voice, who leaps into every conversational gap with a comment or tangential anecdote, is one who, whatever his or her other virtues, is not walking by the Spirit.

When gossip circulates, the impulse is to join in. When an idea pops into the head, the impulse is to speak. It is so pleasing to tell stories, regale others with humor, and share insights about life and the world. Self-control, however, would have us regulate and channel those urges and allow silence to reign in our demeanor. Others may dominate discussions and add fuel to the rumor mills. The man or woman of self-control leaves noisy prattle to others. It is no mystery why James uses the term "*bridle* the tongue."

Not only is self-control twinned with patience, it is inextricably linked to humility. Self-control is an *invisible* virtue. With fearful ease we allow others to notice us. We can even subtly "show off" the fruits of the Spirit. Self-control, however, hides in the recesses of the will. No one *sees* self-control deep inside regulating will, choice, and behavior.

Not only is self-control invisible, it is largely a lost virtue. Who measures maturity by such commonplace strength of will as self-control? Who are assumed to be most spiritually knowledgeable—those whose responses are measured, who exercise the restraint *not* to say everything they are thinking...or one who blabs every thought that comes to mind? Who in your church are those sought for leadership—those eager to be seen and heard...or those restrained individuals who dwell hidden from the limelight? To whom do you go for perspective and counsel—the charismatic pastor or teacher, or youth leader who makes a show of his vast insights, or one who lives in the gentleness of a quiet spirit, whose life demonstrates the peace of self-control?

As we thus reach the climax of Paul's list of Spirit fruits with these two unexpected qualities of spiritual maturity, I leave you with this word: Though it may be difficult to discover those in your fellowships walking invisibly in these strengths of character, seek them out as treasures! You will have to look where the spotlights don't shine. In all likelihood you will not find examples of quietude and humility on the music team.

But if you search diligently, you will discover such mentors of the Spirit-life. Then learn from their example. Become such a one yourself, that when the day comes when another seeks *you* out in the quiet places, and asks, "Whence comes that look of peace in your eyes," you can smile and reply: *The fruit of the spirit is gentleness and self-control.*

Walk by the Spirit...the fruit of the Spirit is...self-control...if we live by the Spirit, let us also walk by the Spirit. (Galatians 5:16, 23, 25)

A bishop must be temperate, sensible, dignified...self-controlled. (1 Timothy 3:2; Titus 1:8).

Urge younger men to control themselves. (Titus 2:6).

Supplement knowledge with self-control. (2 Peter 1:6)

Turn From Sin

LEAVING THE PAST BEHIND BY RENOUNCING
THE PRIORITIES OF THE WORLD

CORINTH—A HOTBED OF SIN, A LABORATORY
FOR PERSONAL TRANSFORMATION

In the early 50s Paul set out again from Antioch on what is called his "second missionary journey." An unfortunate footnote rears its head at this point. The conflict alluded to earlier between Paul, Peter, and Barnabas was apparently not thoroughly healed. For in contemplating a second trip, a heated disagreement broke out between Barnabas and Paul over whether Barnabas' nephew John Mark, the future gospelist, should accompany them. Paul's refusal resulted in a breakup of the partnership. Barnabas and Mark embarked on their own missionary journey, and Paul set out with Silas instead.

Paul's travels this time were more extensive than those through Galatia earlier. They lasted two to three years, roughly between 50-52 A.D., and extended all the way to Macedonia, or Greece, around the Aegean Sea, and to many cities familiar to us. The trip took Paul and his companions to Lystra, then to Troas, Philippi, Thessalonica, Athens, Corinth, and Ephesus. There they sailed again homeward for Caesarea and Antioch.

During these years, for the first time, the ideas of Christianity confronted the intellectualism of ancient Greece. This voyage laid the foundation for the majority of Paul's writings. Many of the churches established during these years of the early 50s later received letters from Paul. The Thessalonian and Corinthian epistles came first. Several years later they were followed by *Philippians* and *Ephesians*, as well as other letters.

The chronology of Paul's writings are uncertain. Many theories surround his first five epistles—the letters to Galatia, Corinth, and Thessalonica. This uncertainty is heightened by the fact that scholars generally believe there actually to have been *four* separate letters to the Corinthians. Without trying to unravel this sequence, we will consider the next grouping of apostolic commands as the "Corinth" commands for several reasons. First, however many letters Paul actually wrote to Corinth, what is beyond dispute is that we possess more of Paul's instructions to this single church than to any other. This alone places the Corinthian correspondence in a position of preeminence in the Pauline corpus.

A second more compelling reason concerns the content of the Corinthian letters. That subject matter is sin. The church at Corinth was a mess. Having looked at the contrast in *Galatians* between the works of the flesh and the fruits of the Spirit, Paul's letters to Corinth put the sinful life of the flesh into perspective in no uncertain terms.

Corinth was a religious center of the Roman world. Its location attracted immigrants from all over the Empire. It boasted twelve temples to a variety of Greek gods and goddesses. A more thorough mix of cultures and races was found in Corinth than in any Mediterranean city other than Rome. Immorality was rife, encouraged by bizarre religious practices. The cult of Aphrodite is estimated to have housed a thousand temple priestess-prostitutes in its Corinthian temple. Sexual immorality was thus Corinth's trademark. The city was a breeding ground for sin of every kind. The sexual depravity of Corinth was so widely known throughout the Greek world that the term *corinthianize* was synonymous with sexual immorality.

A sizeable Jewish community already existed in Corinth when Paul arrived and began to preach in their homes and synagogues. After eighteen months in Corinth, Paul sailed for Antioch. He did not spend much time back in Syria. Within a year he set out again, this time on his "third missionary journey." While at Ephesus between the years 53 and 55, disturbing reports came to Paul about the church at Corinth—marriages in shambles, rampant divorce, lawsuits between Christians, factionalism, cliques, and disunity. In a dozen different ways the young Corinthian church was being pulled and tested in the crucible of an immoral, godless city whose influence was all about them.

At the center of this firestorm of immorality and controversy was a man, perhaps one of the church's leaders, who was involved in an affair with his stepmother.

Paul immediately began an intense correspondence with the Corinthian church to address these problems. His overriding message was unambiguous: *Turn from sin.*

SERIES FOUR

LEAVING THE PAST BEHIND BY RENOUNCING THE PRIORITIES OF THE WORLD

31. Repent.

32. Do not be conformed to the world.

33. Hate evil.

34. Sin no more—do not yield to sin.

35. Do not participate in the sin of others.

36. Do not associate with immorality.

37. Avoid worldly-minded believers.

38. Revere no idols.

39. Confess your sins.

40. Keep your conscience clear.

31. Repent

Christians and non-Christians alike almost universally associate "repentance" with an eye-opening revelation that takes place at a critical turning point of life, an overwhelming sense of contrition for sin, a decisive and pivotal juncture when everything changes. Conversion, salvation, and dedication of one's life to Christ or the church or to a new and different lifestyle usually follows. Many terms identify such experiences—being *saved* or *born again, accepting* Christ, *trusting* in Jesus for salvation, *repenting* of one's sins, etc. Obviously the specifics vary widely—of the *process* of repentance, of *changed outlook* and lifestyle, and of the *church affiliation* and involvement that result. These range from the experiential manifestations of Pentecostalism to the liturgical orientation of Catholicism and Orthodoxy...and everywhere between.

As divergent as these outward forms are, a universal perspective throughout most of Christendom nevertheless views repentance as an act or experience or revelation that, except occasionally, takes place *once*. The meaning of the word "repentance"—to *turn around*, to turn from sin—would seem to validate this once-in-life perspective.

This is true enough, as far as it goes. But it only goes so far. It serves as an indication of one's *entry* into the Christian life, but not necessarily as offering much ongoing daily insight into how one then *lives* the Christian life.

We embark on this series of ten commands enjoining us to "Turn from sin" reminding ourselves of the contrast Paul lays out in Galatians 5 between the *works of the flesh* and the *fruits of the Spirit*. In our discussion of the fruits, we repeatedly emphasized the daily, ongoing nature of the Spirit-life by Paul's use of the active verb *walk*. We may be baptized *once*...but we have to walk in the Spirit *every day*, every moment

From the vantage point of those fruits, casting our gaze back over the *Galatians* list to the unholy evidences that undermine and spoil them, which Paul calls "the works of the flesh," it may be helpful to ask if these, too, are also continual and ongoing. If Paul was contrasting "Spirit-fruit" with "fleshly-works," can the *walking* parallel be applied to both? Is it also possible to "*walk* in the flesh?"

Clearly the answer is yes. What, then, is the remedy? Obviously repentance—turning from one kind of walking to another. Standing in the gap between Spirit-walking and flesh-walking, "repentance" must be *ongoing* as well. Just like Spirit-walking, flesh-walking is made up of daily, moment-by-moment choices.

The conclusion is obvious: There are two kinds of repentance—*one-time* repentance, and ongoing *daily* repentance. The one has salvationary implications, the other has lifestyle implications. Foreign though the concept may be to many, *repentance-walking* thus becomes one of the keys to vigorous Christlikeness. We repent over and over.

This truth reveals why *Repent* is such a relevant and powerful command. It is not directed only to unbelievers, but equally toward lifelong Christians. You and I are under the same injunction as the murderer, prostitute, or drug dealer: *Repent*. The prayers of repentance may differ dramatically. The repentant sinner in the one case may fall on his or her knees in tears and cry out, "God, be merciful to me a sinner!" The mature Christian may breathe the silent prayer, "I'm sorry, Lord, I realize I blew it. Forgive my short-sightedness. Help me get back on the right path and resume Spirit-walking."

The ongoing, daily dynamic of salvation has repeatedly been emphasized—that salvation is no mere one-time act but an ongoing process of *being* saved from our sins. We now see repentance illuminated with that same light of understanding. Salvation and repentance are intrinsically linked as twin door-openers (*beginning* the life of faith) and fitness-strengtheners (to mature, empower, and grow the fruitful daily *walk* of faith.)

Repent and be baptized in the name of Jesus. (Acts 2:38)
Repent and turn. (Acts 3:19)
Turn from evil and do right. (1 Peter 3:11)

---

32. Do Not Be Conformed to the World

We return to the pivotal passage of Romans 12:1-2, the all-important undergirding foundation of the Commands. Jesus said: *My kingdom is not of this world.* In becoming his followers, we make ourselves citizens of a different world than that existing around us. We have emigrated to a new kingdom. We have relinquished former allegiances. Our citizenship is now elsewhere. We still live *in* the former world, but we are no longer *of* it. Therefore, the apostles also uniformly command: *Do not be conformed to the world.*

We opened this book by asserting the principles of Romans 12:1-2 as the hinge upon which swings the transformation process in which God is engaged in our lives. This is the pivot point both of sacrifice and renewal. It reveals the *how* of Commands 2 and 3—presenting ourselves as a *living sacrifice*, then allowing God to *renew our minds.*

Moving on to the ten "Corinth commands," repentance begins by "turning" from the world. The world's values are in the air around us. *Sin* is the world's oxygen. We are steeped in it from the moment of birth. We flow comfortably along in the world's wind, or we refuse to allow its priorities and outlook to dictate our own. There is no middle ground. We either conform to the prevailing breezes, the wind at our backs, or we battle against it by relinquishing, rebuking, rejecting, and renouncing the direction it is blowing.

God's purposes, priorities, and eternal plan are *completely* contrary in every way to the world's. It is impossible to look in two opposite directions. The wind is at our backs or in our faces. This explains why there exist transformed Christians and *un*transformed Christians. Therefore, harsh as it seems, Paul tells us to stay away from worldly Christians. They pull us into the world's values. "Christians" perhaps in belief, they have not dedicated themselves to an other-worldly life of Christlikeness. They are floating with the wind. They will thus subtly oppose our efforts to fight against it.

Lest we point the finger too quickly at what we consider the obvious worldliness in others, the probing mirror reveals a far more penetrating truth. You and I are conflicted in our priorities too. We have not entirely relinquished our former citizenship either.

That's what makes this command so devilishly difficult to obey. I *like* too much about the world. The world is fun, cool, hip. The world flatters, pampers, and indulges. And the church is positively in *love* with the world. It has adopted the world's outlook and methods in everything it does...on behalf of the kingdom, of course. This is the evil seduction, that the church can use the world's methods to advance God's kingdom. Could ever a more devious lie exist? Its cancer is at work everywhere. You will be immersed in it this very Sunday. Beware—it is a subtly invisible but lethally *contagious* cancer.

We are easily tempted to define non-conformity by external escapism—circling the wagons, building fences around our lives, keeping the world *out*. It may be that the Amish do not conform to the world by outward appearance. However, it takes no scriptural genius to see that Jesus and Paul were speaking of something much different. No externals regulate non-conformity of the heart. The challenge is not to escape, but to discover the balance between *in* the world but not *of* the world. Are we learning to view life, others, and ourselves with *God's* eyes? Paul thus compares non-conformity with "renewal of our minds." An Amish man or woman may be no less filled with pride, lust, envy, selfishness, and unforgiveness as a ruthless unbelieving corporate executive. Paul is contrasting *Christlikeness of character and outlook* with *worldliness of character and outlook*. No externals mark the difference. Getting off the grid won't grow Christlikeness.

J.B. Phillips has captured the essence of this command with his exquisite probing translation of Rom. 12:2: *Don't let the world around you squeeze you into its own mold.*

Do not be conformed to this world but be transformed by the renewal of your mind. (Rom. 12:2)
Keep yourself unstained from the world. (James 1:27)
Do not be a friend of the world or you make yourself an enemy of God. (James 4:4)
Do not love the world or the things of the world. (1 John 2:15)

33. Hate Evil

We suddenly crash headlong into a command whose reality may be difficult to penetrate at first glance. You may have turned the page and feel like you rounded a corner and collided with a stranger.

Many may read the words, *Hate evil* with that reaction—Where did *this* come from! The words jar us. Inoculated by the world's culture of tolerance, the idea of *hating* evil sends shock waves through the system. What about being kind, gentle, and accepting? In response, I would ask: How does one nicely and gently take a meat cleaver to an enemy that must be ruthlessly killed?

Yet our objection persists. *Hate evil* is such an unyielding, in-your-face command. Surely there is some kinder gentler way to convey the same idea. A sandwich-board prophet has suddenly barged in on our refined sensitivities. We're not supposed to hate anything these days. Tolerance reigns. The most disgusting, degrading, and degenerate examples of man's depravity are excused, accepted, and justified. Modernity's only intolerance is toward Christians who take seriously the command to hate evil.

Maybe it's time for a douse of cold water in the face, time to look this stranger in the face. As we recognize that sin and evil really exist, and truly are *hateful*...at that point Jesus and the apostles hand us the meat cleaver. "Now use it," they say. "Deal with the hated thing. If you want to do what we say, you can't tolerate evil. You have to *hate* it."

At this point we come to a fork in the road. In which direction are we going to point hatred of evil—toward evil in the world, toward evil in others...or toward evil in ourselves? Contrary as it seems, this is not a *world-change* command. *Hate evil* is a mirror command. The evil we are supposed to hate more than any other is the evil that lurks in the shadows of our own souls. That's what the meat cleaver is for—not to wage war on the world's sin...but mine. At last the reality comes all the way home. Suddenly recognition dawns. The stranger we have bumped into is Jesus himself. Now he reminds us of his own words, "Be pure...be righteous...be perfect."

The terrible reality is that I *don't* hate what lurks in the shadows of my character. I have learned to justify it, because actually I don't mind it that much. "It's the way I am," I say to myself. "It's just a foible of personality. No big deal. How strenuous does God expect me to be? He loves me as I am. It is such a tiny anger, such an insignificant unforgiveness, such an invisible selfishness, such an unseen lust, such a well-disguised covetousness. No one will ever know. I'm sure God doesn't mind." So I put the meat cleaver back into storage, and lock it safely away. Perhaps I will get it out again at some future time when the saints of God will be called upon to wage end-time spiritual warfare against the hosts of Satan. As to the use for which it was forged on a hill called Calvary, for that purpose, I never let it see the light of day.

Our society far too easily deludes us into tolerance for the world's sin because deep inside we are far too tolerant of our own.

How much do I hate evil? Truth be told, not that much. I hate what I see in the world. But I'm pretty comfortable with my sin. This is the age of tolerance, after all.

"Foolish is the man, and there are many such men, who would rid himself or his fellows of discomfort by setting the world right, by waging war on the evils around him, while he neglects that integral part of the world where lies...his first business—namely, his own character and conduct...

"The wrong, the evil is in him; he must be set free from...the sins in his being which spoil his nature—the wrongness in him...the sin he is, which makes him do the sin he does." (George MacDonald, *The Hope of the Gospel*, "Salvation From Sin.")

Hate what is evil...Be guileless as to what is evil. (Romans 12:9; 16:19)
Shun immorality...Be babes in evil. (1 Corinthians 6:18; 14:20)
Let us cleanse ourselves from every defilement. (2 Corinthians 7:1)

---

34. Sin No More—Do Not Yield to Sin

The progression of commands in this section grows probing, stringent, convicting...even, perhaps we should say, impossible.

At last the rubber meets the road. With some piercing looks in the mirror we've explored the imperatives of repentance, non-conformity, and hatred of evil. Now it's decision time. A hundred times a day decision time. My very personal decision time.

The apostles now turn straight toward us, zero in eyeball to eyeball, and command with utter simplicity, with no possibility of misunderstanding: *Sin no More.*

Our daily choices suddenly confront us one after the other. For most these are not choices whether to get drunk, rob a bank, or host a wild orgy of promiscuity and debauchery. Paul warns against such clear sins of the flesh, of course. But for most of us, once we are walking with God, the daily sin-choices come more subtly, in smaller doses.

What are the daily sin-choices you confront? Mine creep out of the shadowy regions of attitude, response, thought...glances and expressions...kindnesses I could have shown but didn't, smiles I could have sent out but didn't, gracious words left unsaid, muttered frustrations rather than whispered thankfulnesses, conversations turned upon myself, needs of others ignored, flashes of envy or covetousness...and how many other tiny revelations of my ugly self. My sin may not be an orgy but a second look, not robbing a bank but wishing I had another $40 in my wallet. Yet aren't the roots identical?

The Bible's contrasts are full of insight. We have focused on Paul's distinction between flesh-walking and Spirit-walking. The practical mechanics of that either-or contrast is illuminated by the word *yield.* Like all the command-terms by which we practicalize the imperatives of the New Testament, yield is a *verb*—a verb of choosing, a verb of will-movement, a verb pinpointing laziness or strength, a verb of giving in or of spiritual muscle flexing. The contrast sits starkly before us. It is a contrast that defines the direction of our spiritual journey. We began this study with, *Yield to God.* Now we encounter the contrasting opposite, *Do not yield to sin.*

In which direction will our yieldings move us—toward Christlikeness, or toward conformity with the world? We *will* yield. What forces and impulses are we yielding to?

The following quote has recently made the internet rounds. It brings home the inescapable imperative of choice in the commands: "Everything you do is based on the choices you make. It's not your parents, your past relationships, your job, the economy, the weather, an argument, or your age that is to blame. You and only you are responsible for every decision and choice you make. Period." (Author unknown)

Consider yourselves dead to sin and alive to God in Christ Jesus. (Romans 6:11)

Do not yield your members to sin. (Romans 6:13)

Let us then cast off the works of darkness...Let us conduct ourselves becomingly...not in reveling and drunkenness, not in debauchery and licentiousness, not in quarreling and jealousy...Make no provision for the flesh, to gratify its desires. (Romans 13:12-14)

Do not desire evil...Do not indulge in immorality. (1 Corinthians 10:6, 8)

Come to your right mind and sin no more. (1 Corinthians 15:34)

Do not gratify the desires of the flesh...immorality, impurity, licentiousness, idolatry, sorcery, enmity, strife, envy, drunkenness, carousing, and the like. (Galatians 5:16, 19-21)

Put off your old nature. (Ephesians 4:22)

Put to death therefore what is earthly in you: immorality, impurity, passion, evil desire, and covetousness, which is idolatry...Put off the practices of the old nature. (Colossians 3:5, 9)

Abstain from every form of evil. (1 Thessalonians 5:22)

Put away all filthiness and wickedness. (James 1:21)

Resist the devil and he will flee from you. (James 1:21; 4:7)

As aliens and exiles, abstain from the passions of the flesh. (1 Peter 2:11)

Live...no longer by human passions. (1 Peter 4:2)

---

35. Do Not Participate in the Sin of Others

The practicality of the progression continues to tighten like a noose around our necks. Can it get any more *real* than this—Do not participate in the sin of others.

How subtly the "sin of others" intrudes. The merest word, smile, or glance is enough to send invisible tentacles of inducement into our brains...luring us toward the outlook, the frame of reference, the thought patterns of those around us...enticing us to condone, tolerate, look the other way, and thus become silent co-conspirators and participants.

Resisting the urge to "indulge in immorality," as Paul phrases it in 1 Corinthians 10:8 is so subtle, even so appealing a snare. Again, for 99% of us, we're not talking about wild drunkenness, orgies, promiscuity, robbing banks, or killing people. We're talking about sins *indulged* in. That may be the sin of the second look with the guys at work, the sin of the gossip indulged in with the ladies at coffee, the sin of eagerly sharing in a gripe session with friends lamenting our woes and blaming everyone but ourselves. Is it really a "sin" simply to *indulge* ourselves in such acceptable indiscretions?

How personal would the above command be if we rephrased it to read: *Do not indulge in the sins of others that you enjoy being part of?* Changing the active verb of the command from "participate" to *indulge* brings it too close for comfort. Truth be told, we *do* enjoy such indulgences.

Even when the words and behavior of those around us makes us a little uncomfortable, we put up with them. We tolerate the sins of others by our own silent participation, because...well, they're such *small* sins. We don't want people thinking we're getting judgmental on them.

How much, as we asked before, do we really "hate" evil? Or do we enjoy our indulgences? Going along with the crowd, participating in its perspective, condoning its behavior, is more serious than pampering ourselves with an indulgence for chocolate or cheesecake. Allowing ourselves to be drawn into the sin of others is a deadly game.

Bystanding leads to consequences. The law condemns equally the friend standing by along with the one who pulled the trigger. How many crimes might be prevented had bystanders and fringe participants had the courage to walk away. In the eyes of the law, participation equals guilt. Bystanding becomes participation even without conscious effort. Subtly we cross a line we didn't even see. Suddenly we are in over our heads.

Both legally and scripturally, participation *is* sin. If we're not careful, what seems an insignificant indulgence, over time, sweeps us further into sins of the mind and heart than we intended. We are well-familiar with C.S. Lewis's illumination of this principle:

"Every time you make a choice you are turning the central part of you...into something a little different from what it was before...Good and evil both increase at compound interest. That is why the little decisions you and I make every day are of such infinite importance. The smallest good act today is the capture of a strategic point from which, a few months later, you may be able to go on to victories you never dreamed of. An apparently trivial indulgence in lust or anger today is the loss of a ridge or railway line or bridgehead from which the enemy may launch an attack otherwise impossible." (C.S. Lewis, *Mere Christianity,* "Morality and Psychoanalysis, Charity.")

The principle is constantly at work in our souls. The eternal consequences in the inward parts of bystanding indulgent sin may be just as deadly to character as participation in murder.

Do not be overcome by evil. (Romans 12:21)
Do not be deceived, "Bad company ruins good morals." (1 Corinthians 15:33)
Give no opportunity to the devil. (Ephesians 4:27)
Do not associate with the sons of disobedience. (Ephesians 5:7)
Do not participate in another man's sins. (1 Timothy 5:22)
Shun all these evils and distractions. (1 Timothy 6:11)

---

36. Do not Associate With Immorality

The mirror probes deeper. *Indulgence* in sin may be passive. *Participation* raises the stakes a little higher. Now the command becomes active, forceful, imperative: Don't even *associate* with immorality. Turn your back and walk away. Renounce it altogether. It is an all-or-nothing command. You're in or you're out.

But what constitutes immorality? If we never associated with sinners, it would be a lonely life! I would have no friends, because I am a sinner. Obviously we enjoy relationship with sinners because that includes us all. Where do we draw the line, then, between "sin" and *immorality*? What do we tolerate as the sin of the human condition that stains every one of us, and the immorality that will draw us into disobedience? Paul goes so far as to say, "Shun immorality." What do we do with this command? Do we ignore this command because it is politically incorrect?

The principle at root in this series of commands is a simple one: Sin rubs off. Sin is a catchable virus. We catch it from being around it. That's why Paul warns us to stay away from people whose lives are not dedicated to fighting sin, to keep out of situations where sin is the ruling and pervading outlook. Of course you and I sin. We still have relationship. We're talking about avoiding *intentional* and *purposeful* sin. That's different than "original sin." The germs of the intentional sin-virus are in the air around us. We catch it as easily as a cold. Every seemingly insignificant off-color smile, back-biting comment, tiny untruth, thread of gossip, ethical line crossed, or ridicule of moral virtue are the coughs and sneezes and handshakes by which the virus is constantly assaulting us.

Obviously in this life we cannot quarantine ourselves entirely from sin. But we tempt fate by making a habit of foolishly exposing ourselves to it. Sin is contagious. Avoiding intentional sin is not judgmentalism but simple prudence. We must take precautions to avoid the virus. We can, so to speak, keep our hands clean. There's no reason not to fight against it with all the weapons—ie, the spiritual antibiotics and antiviral medicines and antidotes and health regimens—that God makes available in the Christian's medicine cabinet. The simplest weapon is what we remember every day to keep from catching colds. If you don't want to catch a cold, you've got to avoid other people's sneezes.

The notion of "avoiding" sin is probably more repugnant to the world than any other element of the Christian faith. It is not our beliefs themselves that so alienate the world. It is the idea that we take our beliefs seriously and that we have the arrogance to call our beliefs *true* by an absolute standard. Perhaps what the world finds most odious of all is our audacity to insist that such a thing as *sin* exists...and that some people are living in it and we choose not to associate with them. The world wouldn't mind our *beliefs* if we never took this stand. It is its uncompromising stance against sin that makes the world hate Christianity above all religions. Because the world cannot look into the mirror and perceive its own bigotry, judgmentalism, and intolerance, it hates Christians all the more. The world will always be most critical in Christians of its *own* most glaring blind spots.

Jesus went among sinners because he came as a Physician to cure their sin. We cannot cure sin. Therefore, we must keep from ingesting the germs from other people's sneezes. We love them. We can hand them a Kleenex. We can encourage them to go to Jesus for healing. But if we don't take precautions, we're going to catch their germs.

Do not gratify the desires of the flesh...immorality, impurity, licentiousness, idolatry, sorcery, enmity, strife, envy, drunkenness, carousing, and the like. (Galatians 5:16, 19-21)

Do not associate with the sons of disobedience. (Ephesians 5:7)

Avoid those who are puffed up with conceit. 1 Timothy 6:4)

Men will be lovers of self, lovers of money, proud, arrogant, abusive, disobedient to their parents, ungrateful, unholy...slanderers...haters of good, treacherous, reckless, swollen with conceit, lovers of pleasure rather than lovers of God, holding the form of religion but denying the power of it. Avoid such people...men of corrupt minds. (2 Timothy 3:2-5, 8)

37. Avoid Worldly-Minded Believers

This is clearly the most difficult of the three "avoidance commands" (participation, association, avoidance) to lay hold of. It is not hard to see that we mustn't participate in the immorality of the world. But avoiding intentionally sinning *Christians* is another matter. Many do not even realize that such a command exists in the New Testament at all.

It is a matter of motive and life-direction. We are in the fight together. We are trying to reject the world's priorities, and learn to walk by the Spirit. In that very personal war, you and I are comrades. I recognize that you are a sinner. You recognize that I am a sinner. We may catch a few of each other's germs now and then. I apologize in advance for any sneezes of mine that come near you. Yet we each recognize in the other an ally in the fight. We know we are purposed together in the life-objective of rejecting the world's priorities, of resisting the pull and lure of the walk of the flesh. As comrades in arms, we are dedicated to walking in the Spirit. In that mutual rejection and dedication we are brothers and sisters, allies and friends. In spite of my sin, perhaps in some way I can help you. In spite of your sin, perhaps in some way you can help me. We will not stamp out the sin virus. But together we can help each other live healthy growing spiritual lives.

There are others, however, my brother and sister Christians among them, whose life dedication and direction is not one I share. That does not make me judgmental, it is merely a statement of recognized spiritual fact. We are going different directions. We are driven by different life-goals. I recognize their life-goals as contrary to mine. Does it make me intolerant because I have chosen a different life-path? Am I judgmental because I choose to avoid the road they are walking on as unhelpful to the direction I want to go?

I happen to be careful about nutrition. I eat very little wheat, red meat, or processed foods. Much of my diet is comprised of fruits and vegetables, a good portion of it raw. When I am in a social setting, I choose foods that fit in with my life goals. Does it make me intolerant for choosing snacks from the vegetable tray rather than the dessert tray? Does it make me judgmental in a restaurant for ordering a vegetable stir-fry rather than a steak? We make choices according to our life's goals. I don't tell those I meet what they should or shouldn't eat. That's their business. They have their own health regimens.

Similarly, I read Paul's warning against mixing with the idle, arrogant, proud, unthankful, unsubmissive, rebellious, and contentious as very practical. Why should I expose myself to the habits and life-goals of those who are not my allies in the fight, who would probably, if given the chance, tell me I am wrong to set Christlikeness as my highest prayer, and might even try to undermine that prayer? Walking by the fruits of the Spirit is hard enough. Why make it immeasurably more difficult by intentionally mixing with Christians whose desire is to walk in the flesh? I don't judge them. But it is unhealthy to my spiritual diet to partake of what they choose to put on their plates.

That's all Paul was saying. There are those in the church who take discipleship seriously enough to pray the prayer of Christlikeness, and there are those who don't. Make spiritual allies of those who will help you walk in the Spirit.

Avoid those who create divisions. (Romans 16:17)

I wrote you not to associate with any one who bears the name of brother if he is guilty of immorality or greed, or is an idolater, reviler, drunkard or robber—do not even eat with such a one. (1 Corinthians 5:11)

Keep away from any brother who is living in idleness. (2 Thessalonians 3:6)

Avoid those who are puffed up with conceit. (1 Timothy 6:4)

Men will be lovers of self, lovers of money, proud, arrogant, abusive, disobedient to their parents, ungrateful, unholy...slanderers...haters of good, treacherous, reckless, swollen with conceit, lovers of pleasure rather than lovers of God, holding the form of religion but denying the power of it. Avoid such people...men of corrupt minds. (2 Timothy 3:2-5, 8)

---

38. Revere No Idols

This sounds like a command straight out of the Old Testament. What came to your mind when you read the words—a crucifix or icon on the wall, a statuette, a golden calf, a revered *object* such as people have been falsely worshipping for thousands of years? However, here we're talking about idols of another kind. We are trying to identify the invisible shrines we build to the *heart-idols* and *mind-idols* nearest and dearest to us.

Idols come in all sizes and shapes. We build our own very personal invisible shrines in the rooms of our mental homes. We revere people-idols, possession-idols, money-idols, goal-idols, idea-idols. Many make idols of their infirmities, others worship their looks, their athletic prowess, their skills and abilities, their intellect, their powers of persuasion. Parents make idols of their children. Christians make idols of their leaders and pastors and gurus. The church as well as the world has its "rock-stars"—musicians, actors, models, and personalities. Power and money are among the enduring idols of every age. The supreme gods of our time may be Independence and Narcissism. That they are such acceptable idols makes them more deadly to our souls. For they are the idols of anti-childship and therefore anti-Christlikeness. The fact that some of the most revered men and women in the world, especially in politics and entertainment, are filled to the satiation point with self-worship should place us daily on guard. How easy it is to follow in the well-trod ruts of their public example, seeking to emulate the very qualities of independence and narcissism that will subvert and eventually kill spiritual growth.

We even make idols of good things. It is easy for me to "idolize" books and favorite authors. I have been involved in discussions too numerous to count with Christians who have made idols of their doctrines and beliefs. Some of these ideas are *true*...yet they are still idols. Not all idols are false and evil. It is fearfully easy, as I say, to make idols of good things, good people, and good ideas. Whose pictures do you have on your wall?

Not long ago a brief mention during a television program of an imaginary "Last Supper Twelve" sent my mind spinning. The question was asked who were the twelve most revered men and women—other than family—one would choose to spend the last evening of life with. Some of the names thrown out were expected—Abraham Lincoln, Ghandi, the Pope, etc. When I heard the name John Lennon, however, I stared back at the screen in disbelief. No mention of Jesus, only a man who would be lower on my list than almost any famous personality I could imagine. What does such a selection say about someone's values? If we are not honoring humility, selflessness, and character in those we revere, what *are* we honoring? *Why* we honor may be as significant as *who* we honor.

I've been thinking about my own such list ever since. What would my Last Supper Twelve say about *me*—about my life priorities, about what I revere? If I shared my list with you, if you studied it carefully, even if you knew nothing about me, you would probably be able to construct a reasonably accurate character portrait of me, possibly even a thumbnail biography of my spiritual journey. George MacDonald and C.S. Lewis would be two names near the top of my list. I revere both men as pivotally influential in my life. My veneration for them reminds me to keep my honor of all whom I revere in perspective. So now I turn the question around: What would your list reveal about *you*?

Why we honor those we do reveals more about ourselves than them. It reveals what kind of person we desire to be ourselves. It's not as easy as making a list that includes Jesus, Winston Churchill, or Leonardo da Vinci. We may include them. But who are the unknown mentors, those men and women whose life-examples have made us more able to pray the prayer of Christlikeness in our own lives? Who are our *character* heroes?

Do not be idolaters...Shun the worship of idols. (1 Corinthians 10:7, 14)
Put to death therefore what is earthly in you: immorality, impurity, passion, evil desire, and covetousness, which is idolatry. (Colossians 3:5)
Keep yourself from idols. (1 John 5:21)

---

39. Confess Your Sins

We are familiar with the saying, "Confession is good for the soul." There is little doubt that confession is cleansing. Yet *why* does confession makes us feel better?

Great difference of opinion exists about the nature of confession, and to whom we ought to confess. The confessional represents a central feature of Catholicism. While the process and enforced habit of confession may be healthy, making confession to a priest is a difficult pattern to locate in the teaching of the New Testament.

Jesus speaks forcefully about confessing to those we have sinned against. Such is the root necessity in the restoration of relationship, and thus in forgiveness and healing between individuals. When James commands, "Confess your sins to one another," was he reiterating this command of the Lord's, or was he pointing more generally toward open sharing among Christians and being willing to "bare our souls" before one another?

At an even more fundamental level is the need to confess to God. It is him we have sinned against. Our entire lives of self-driven independence stand as a gigantic "sin" against our Father-Creator. To confess to him is to yield to his Fatherhood, to say, "I am your child...I want to walk as your child...I commit myself henceforth to lay down my self-will and yield myself to you."

These many forms of confession—from salvationary repentance, to a weekly visit with one's priest, to a tearful apology to one we have wronged, to the sharing of struggles and weaknesses with our brothers and sisters—are certainly, each in their own way, cleansing and "good for the soul."

There may, however, be a far deeper and more fundamental necessity involved. By its very nature sin *hides*. Sin *covers* itself. Sin seeks the *shadows*. Sin is of the night, not the day. Light exposes sin, rips it from its hiding place, shoves it into the spotlight for all to see. This contrast between light and darkness identifies the essence of hypocrisy. Hypocrisy is nothing more than the attempt to hide our true selves in the shadows, and present a face of sinless respectability to the world. We're not fooling God, of course. But we'll worry about that later. For now, we're content if we can fool most of the people most of the time. We also keep sin in the shadows to protect our own pride. We don't want to admit what's there. If we hide them deep enough in the basement where the lights are never turned on, eventually we may convince ourselves that some sins we used to worry about were really nothing but imaginary boogiemen.

We might legitimately ask why confess our sin at all. We may be hypocrites to one another—pretending to be what we're not. But we're not hypocrites to God. He sees all. There is no hiding from *him*. So why bother confessing? Because the cleansing comes from the acknowledgment, to God, that *we* see what *he* sees. It represents the end of the game. The sham is over. Hypocrisy is laid on the altar to be consumed with all the pretence and games we play. The confessional is the mirror. No priest is on the other side. The only one looking out of the mirror is me. I must act as my own priest. In acknowledging to myself, "I am a sinner," I have thrust wide the doors into my innermost being. There the cleansing light explodes in the darkness. I have unlocked the basement and sent in the searchlights. No more pretending. I am saying to myself, to others, and to the universe, "I have sinned. I am a sinner. I acknowledge the Light before a watching world. I am ready to slay the demons that have dwelt far too long in the darkness."

What additional confessions may follow, we each have to answer that question in our own way. As the mirror-confessional is personal, so too are its relational consequences. But we must make no mistake about where confession begins.

The person we most need to confess to is ourselves.

Confess your sins to one another. (James 5:16)

If we confess our sins, he is faithful and just, and will forgive our sins and cleanse us from all unrighteousness. (1 John 1:9)

40. Keep Your Conscience Clear

In now climaxing this series of 'Turn from sin" commands, we recognize that it would have been equally appropriate to have begun with the *conscience* as with the admonition to *repent*. The two commands are intrinsically linked as bookends unifying everything between. The conscience urges us toward right, toward repentance, toward yielding to God rather than sin. The mechanism we call the "conscience" is the very personal internal regulator between right and wrong. It gives power to all the commands.

Secularists, of course, dismiss the conscience. In the eyes of modernity no absolute *truth* or *right* or *wrong* exists. The notion of an unseen mechanism within the instinct of humanity pointing toward *right* is therefore an illusion. Secularism is quick to reject the power of the conscience because its existence proves beyond doubt the truth of Genesis 1:26. God invented the conscience as an internal searchlight to govern character and behavior. The conscience is the internal evidence of "the image of God" implanted into each of us by our Creator. It is nothing more nor less than the fingerprint of God.

Think of that the next time your conscience urges you toward "right," or warns you against a violation of truth. Suddenly God's finger across your mind and heart has pressed down hard. You felt his hand! If spiritual instruments existed to probe deeply enough, they would find God's fingerprint emblazoned across my soul. I can never erase it. All my life long, I will be urged toward right and warned against wrong by that finger pressing against my will. The Bible also calls this the "still small voice." How I respond to that inner Voice will determine the life-biography of my developing eternal character.

As George MacDonald illuminates, conscience is the starting point for obedience. A vigorously speaking conscience is the originating power in combating sin. A troubled conscience is one trying to keep sin in the shadows. Sin exposed, confessed, repented of, and turned from is a conscience cleansed.

The negative function of the conscience is the warning light on our human instrument panel. When that red light comes on, we know there is danger ahead. We've all felt those internal warnings. But we're not cars. We won't eventually break down from ignoring the warnings. We can keep right on going until the lights stop blinking. The more we *disregard* the conscience, the softer grows its voice. We have it in our power to deaden it altogether. Every time we *obey* the conscience, the louder it grows. Therefore, we also have it in our power to increase the clarity with which God speaks.

Do we want God speaking to us or not? The still small Voice is equipped with volume control. That volume knob is not in God's hands...it's in ours.

Many find the voice of conscience troublesome and uncomfortable. For the man or woman of God, however, the conscience is a daily guide indicting the right path to take, a constant and helpful warning when we diverge toward a direction we should avoid.

The voice of conscience precedes the decision of will. When the conscience speaks the will faces a moment of truth. Will it act in line with the way the conscience points? The more often the will obeys the voice of conscience, the more keen becomes that regulating Still Small Voice speaking into the human spirit. Obedience creates a finely tuned spiritual mechanism wonderfully in tune with the internal leading of God's Spirit.

"We must learn to obey him in everything, and so must begin somewhere: let it be at once, and in the very next thing that lies at the door of our conscience!" (George MacDonald, *Unspoken Sermons, Second Series,* "The Truth in Jesus")

"'What, then, is the way that lies before my own door?...It is just the old way—as old as the conscience—that of obedience to any and every law of personal duty.'" (George MacDonald, *The Marquis of Lossie,* ch. 53)

Keep your aim love that issues from a pure heart, a good conscience, and sincere faith. (1 Timothy 1:5)

Hold to faith and a good conscience. (1 Timothy 1:19)

"THE THESSALONICA COMMANDS"

Live God's Priorities at Home

CHRISTIAN MATURITY AND LEADERSHIP BEGIN IN THE FAMILY

THESSALONICA — MISPLACED FOCUS...PAUL RETURNS A CHURCH TO FOUNDATIONAL PRIORITIES

Paul's second missionary journey (50-52 A.D.) was full of memorable visits to cities whose names we know well. Corinth and Thessalonica are unique among them for several reasons. Problems arose in both churches that Paul found it necessary to address by letter. They are thus the first two city-churches to receive letters from Paul. Both cities also received *multiple* letters—yet another factor that sets them apart from the other churches to whom Paul wrote. The two Thessalonian letters are further unique in that they *may* (depending on the disputed dating of *Galatians*) actually be Paul's very first letters. What is beyond dispute is that they were written during Paul's first trip to Greece, possibly as early as the year 50, several years prior to the Corinthian correspondence.

In Thessalonica, a huge cosmopolitan seaport and the capital of the Roman province of Macedonia (Greece), Paul and his companions stirred up great controversy. After preaching in the Jewish synagogue of Thessalonica, some Jews and many Greeks converted to Christianity. This mass of conversions stirred up violent opposition. Before long, Thessalonica was in an uproar, with mobs threatening their lives. They fled the city.

Their flight took Paul and his companions to Athens where Paul's "Men of Athens, I see that you are very religious men..." speech took place on Mars Hill (Acts 17.) At some point Paul sent Timothy back to Thessalonica to see how the recent converts were making out after their hasty departure. Timothy rejoined Paul in Corinth. There, based on Timothy's favorable report, Paul wrote *1 Thessalonians*. Timothy and Silas then set out north from Corinth to deliver the letter to Thessalonica, while Paul remained at Corinth.

The two men must have remained in Thessalonica long enough after delivering Paul's letter to assess its impact. They returned with news that his teaching about the second coming was being seriously misinterpreted. The misunderstandings were so widespread that many in the Thessalonian church were quitting jobs and lazily slacking off on their responsibilities as they waited for the Lord's return. Paul quickly sent back a second letter to place his prophetic teaching into perspective. In it Paul reins in their enthusiasm with a return to fundamentals: Do your work with diligence, be at peace, live quiet orderly lives, and establish yourselves in good words and good works.

All the books of the Bible have some controversy surrounding dating and authorship. The major uncertainty regarding the Thessalonian epistles involves the order of the two letters. Some scholars believe that *2 Thessalonians* was actually written first. There are also doubts that Paul was the author of *2 Thessalonians*. No compelling evidence exists to validate either a different order or different authorship. Commentaries on the Thessalonian letters, however, are full of various theories, including the conjecture that Silas wrote *2 Thessalonians* under Paul's general oversight.

One of the chief arguments in favor of different authorship for the two books is the distinctive outlook presented in each on the *parousia*, or second coming of Christ. In the first letter it is more imminent, while the second seems to suggest a longer timetable, emphasizing everything that must take place prior to Christ's return. The second letter is also more formal than the warm and affectionate tone of the first. Some of these difficulties are removed by reversing the order of the writing.

The simplest explanation is simply that Paul wrote the second letter in a less exuberant mood, concerned by the report that the Thessalonians had gone over the top in their fanatic enthusiasm. In his second letter, Paul attempted to place future events into a longer-range perspective. This remains the majority view of most scholars.

The loving personal note, highlighting Paul's pastoral concern for the congregation, comes through loud and clear At the same time, his words about idleness are blunt and forceful. His overriding message to the Thessalonians is clear—Don't get swept up in second coming fever, or any other kind of doctrinal or experiential excitement. Keep your focus clear on the present not the future. Spirituality begins where you live.

SERIES FIVE

CHRISTIAN MATURITY AND LEADERSHIP BEGIN IN THE FAMILY

41. Christian leaders, live exemplary lives.

42. Honor marriage.

43. Husbands, love, honor, and serve your wives.

44. Wives, respect and submit to your husbands.

45. Children, obey and honor your parents.

46. Practice hospitality.

47. Manage your households well.

48. Raise your children in the wisdom of the Lord.

49. Train young men to be self-controlled, young women to be chaste and domestic.

50. Care for widows and orphans.

41. Christian Leaders, Live Exemplary Lives

Though we have taken the two letters to the Thessalonians as our starting point for the next series of commands, Paul does not directly address home and family issues to a great extent in those letters. Most of his family-specific commands come later, notably in *Ephesians* and *Colossians* as well as, interestingly, in the letters to the two single men, Timothy and Titus. It is in these latter three Pastoral Epistles, penned a dozen or more years after the Thessalonian correspondence, that Paul specifically addresses leadership in the church. There he spells out the qualifications and character attributes that men and women must demonstrate before being considered for leadership.

These instructions and guidelines from the Timothy and Titus letters can concisely be summarized in seven words: *Maturity and Christian leadership begin at home.*

Years ago I was stunned as I read an article in a local Christian paper by a church leader in our area. In it he discussed the occasional conflict between ministry and family. I have never forgotten his chilling conclusion—that family must take a back seat to the all important and more spiritually significant work of church ministry. Our own pastor shared a similar outlook. Early in our marriage, realizing we were struggling with a great adjustment, Judy and I withdrew from the whirlwind of church activity that had been consuming our time in order to focus on our relationship. We recognized that we simply needed to spend more time *together*. At that point, our friend and mentor, the pastor who had married us, turned hostile. We had sinned the unforgiveable sin. We had elevated our marriage above church. We began to receive pastoral calls of "concern." The word *backsliding* was raised. Concern turned to criticism, some of it angry.

These sadly misplaced priorities are not uncommon in today's "ministry" intoxicated church. Unfortunately this priority structure is exactly the reverse of what Paul taught. As I look back now forty years later, my heart breaks for these two men, both dear friends. I grieve because the results of getting God's intended order backwards is predictable. The wives of both men eventually left them. One remarried. Violating the qualifications outlined by Paul, both men continued in leadership. This disconnect between family life and church leadership continues. We are still getting the cart before the horse. Our churches are full to overflowing with so called "leaders" who would fail the test of Paul's leadership qualification with marks of 50% or less.

Our responsibility, however, is not to point fingers but to heed Paul's words *ourselves*. If we would aspire to leadership of any kind, in the church or outside it, being able to do so effectively begins with personal character and integrity, and with the relationships we have established in our families. That's where we learn to communicate, negotiate, lay down self, put others first, walk in humility, and exercise patience. If we do not demonstrate such traits of character at home, we will do so nowhere else.

No marriage is perfect. But do we have functional *working* relationships? *Exemplary* does not mean perfect, but capable of being exampled. Is my *example* one that others could follow? Then I may have a right to teach and speak about the things of God. If not, I need to set my own house in order before I try to instruct others about theirs.

A bishop must be above reproach, married only once, temperate, sensible, dignified, hospitable...gentle, not quarrelsome, and no lover of money. (1 Timothy 3:2-3)

Deacons likewise must be serious, not double-tongued...not greedy for gain...the women likewise must be serious, no slanderers, but temperate, faithful in all things. Let deacons be married only once. (1 Timothy 3:8-9, 11-12)

Appoint elders...who are blameless, married only once, whose children are believers...For a bishop, as God's steward, must be blameless; he must not be arrogant or quick-tempered or a drunkard or violent or greedy for gain, but hospitable, a lover of goodness, master of himself, upright, holy, and self-controlled; he must hold firm to the sure word...so that he may be able to give instruction in sound doctrine...Show yourself in all respects a model of good deeds...integrity, gravity, and sound speech. (Titus 1:5-9; 2:7-8)

42. Honor Marriage

It has almost become a cliché in our time to declare that "the institution of marriage is under attack." It is a cliché because it is true. An all out war is on to destroy marriage as Christians understand it. Even within the church, the entire perspective of marriage has changed. The books that most young Christian couples were being counseled to read about marriage forty years ago are nowhere to be found today. The church has happily adapted to the world's changing mores about marriage so completely that a "Christian" marriage today is simply a worldly marriage cloaked in an external set of doctrinal beliefs that can loosely be called "Christian." Unfortunately, these do not impact the marital relationship at the fundamental level of its origins.

It takes little insight to rail against the cultural shift that has produced this change. The outlook of progressivism is an easy target because it is obviously responsible and so clearly to blame. Condemning the cumulative impact over the last two generations of moral relativism, genderlessness, abortion, rampant divorce, promiscuity, teen pregnancy, non-traditional families, and the sins of our culture is an easy condemnation to deliver. The list of factors goes on and on. We could cite the impact of television, Hollywood, academia, the political agenda of liberalism to normalize practices that in most eras were nothing more nor less than sin. *Nothing* is sin anymore. Tolerance is the god of our age.

Condemnation of such factors is simple. It is what many Christians focus on, which is fine for those who consider that their calling. The important question is: What good does it do? Perhaps such outspoken condemnation in the cultural arena is useful. But our focus here is the commands. Will condemning the culture help you and me obey *this* command to honor marriage? In this book, we are not trying to change the world. We are trying to change ourselves by learning obedience to the apostolic commands. To do so, we continually return in the solitude of our prayer closets to the mirror.

Therefore, this is perhaps the time for us to look into those two eyes staring back at us and ask in what ways the culture has subtly and invisibly infected our *own* perspectives with the cancer of its lies about marriage. Have we, too, been anesthetized in ways we do not realize? Perhaps it is time to remind ourselves that marriage is an institution that belongs on a pedestal. It is worthy of our honor, respect, and veneration.

As we read the above words, *Honor marriage* is a command directed to you and me, not to Congress, the White House, Planned Parenthood, network executives, Hollywood producers, your local Board of Education, the Supreme Court, or the Board of Governors of our leading educational institutions. We have to take for granted that these institutions have long-since given themselves over to the lie of secular progressivism. How are you and I going to obey the command when *we* look in the mirror?

I cannot predict what you will see when you look into that mirror. That's none of my business. I can only say what this ancient command says to me. It tells me to rekindle my first love, to reaffirm scriptural priorities, to resist the cultural infiltration of worldly mores into *my* marriage. I am a man, so *Honor marriage* means nothing more nor less than to honor my wife, to honor the fact that marriage is sacred to her, that our marriage is her life, her covering, her protection, that she cherishes our marriage, that she has taken my name for hers, that she has given her whole self to me. I do not deserve such love and devotion. Yet she has given them because she honors marriage and all it stands for.

Therefore I honor *her*. And I dedicate myself to find ways to demonstrate that I honor *her*, and thus to honor the life we have together. I can honor marriage by honoring her desires, hopes, and dreams. I honor marriage by making *her* priorities my priorities, by dedicating myself to fulfilling *her* needs and hopes and dreams.

I will not change the culture this day. But I can honor my marriage this day.

Do not be mismated with unbelievers. (2 Corinthians 6:14)
Let marriage be held in honor...let the marriage bed be undefiled. (Hebrews 13:4)

43. Husbands, Love, Honor, and Serve Your Wives

Authority and submission, as they apply to masculine and feminine roles in marriage, were among the most discussed and argued about topics consuming the evangelical church during the 1970s. It was out of the milieu of this teaching concerning scriptural roles in marriage that Judy's and my own marriage emerged. We struggled to learn and apply, and indeed to *love,* the principles laid out by Paul for husbands and wives within a framework of mutual honor and respect. We have lived by these principles for what will soon be forty-five years together. During that time we have seen a dramatic shift not only in cultural perspectives about marriage, but in the outlook of the church and Christians in general toward the functions of husband and wife. Sadly, they are changes *away* from the scriptural standard, and *toward* a wholesale adaptation of the world's perspective.

No one is talking about authority and submission now, except to deride both as anachronistic reminders of a puritanical outlook that should have been tossed on the scrapheap long ago. The church is saying this along with the world. Marriage has become a business partnership, a negotiated contract between equals, each with clearly defined spheres of influence into which the other agrees not to intrude or interfere. "Everyone," in the words of the Old Testament, is free "to do what is right in his own eyes."

None would argue that much immaturity and unscriptural practice was perpetrated under the banners of *authority* and *submission.* Indeed, few New Testament commands have been so misapplied as Paul's instructions to husbands and wives. Yet that fact does not justify striking the reality of these powerful truths from the biblical lexicon. We still have a responsibility to uphold, properly understand, and seek to live by them.

The misunderstanding begins with the husband's half of the marriage assignment. Now while authority, properly understood, is essential to life and intrinsic to marriage, nowhere are husbands commanded to *take* authority. Authority does not enter into Paul's family instructions anywhere. The word simply isn't there. A husband is commanded to be a sacrificial and loving servant to his wife. How are we to do that? By *sacrificing* ourselves and *giving ourselves* to our wives, "as Christ loved the church."

That is a tall order! This changes everything about the so-called authority and submission debate! Authority is off the table. Men—we are commanded to love, honor, serve, and sacrifice. That's it. This is how we honor marriage—by serving our wives.

In Paul's words to husbands and wives we again find the commands demanding what most of us do not want to give—an uncommon level of sacrifice. For marriage to function as Paul outlines, mutual *servanthood* is the transformative foundation that validates love. The husband's love is the *love of sacrifice.* The woman's submission is the *submission of sacrifice.* Marriage is no 50%-50% proposition, no business arrangement between co-equals. It is a 100%-0% partnership of servanthood, in which both husband and wife take *100%* of that servanthood upon themselves, and expect nothing in return.

To gain an accurate and balanced perspective of Christian marriage requires reassessing both faulty images. We must forward the discussion beyond the "authority-submission" debate of the 1970s. And we must reject the "business-partnership" contract of the third millennium. We have to expand Paul's dual admonitions to emphasize mutuality in two directions—*respect and honor* and *servanthood and sacrifice.*

Let us each look to the mirror, and love one another as Christ loved the church and gave himself for her.

Husbands, sacrifice yourself for and be considerate to your wives in all ways.

Husbands, love your wives, as Christ loved the church and gave himself up for her. (Eph. 5:25)
Husbands should love their wives as their own bodies. (Ephesians 5:28)
Husbands, love your wives, and do not be harsh with them. (Colossians 3:19)
Husbands, live considerately with your wives, bestowing honor on the woman as the weaker sex. (1 Peter 3:7)

44. Wives, Respect and Submit to Your Husbands

If husbands have to recognize servanthood rather than authority as the foundation of their role, where does a wife's half of the servanthood equation begin? Modern women will hate the offensive words: "*Submit* to your husbands." Yet what do we do with this command? The misunderstanding of the authority-submission controversy cuts both ways. Women are equally to blame for *omitting* "submission" from their Bibles as men are for *adding* "take authority" to theirs. If men can't make excuses, neither can women.

It is especially dangerous for a *man* to speak about the *wife's* role in marriage, all the more so for a man to tell women that they are required to submit to their husbands. Submission is all the more bitter a pill to swallow when that command comes from a man like Paul, who, feminists contend, didn't like women anyway. This highlights the longstanding complaint from certain Christian woman about submission, domesticity, silence in the church, and the prohibition against teaching. All these impositions on women were not only delivered by a man, they came from an *unmarried* man. What right did Paul have to tell women what they should or shouldn't do?

It is not difficult, however, to detect the superficiality of this complaint. Women who use this argument to justify their own rebellion have not studied Paul's words as deeply as they may think. Paul has no ax to grind against women. When one examines the thing in depth, he is harder on men than women. He commands men to *sacrifice* themselves for their wives and to love as Christ loved the church. A man is commanded to give his whole life for his wife, to die for her if it comes to that. By any standard, that is a more sweeping and stringent command than merely to honor and submit. Children and slaves come in for their share of hard commands as well. In speaking of order, obedience, and love in the home and family, Paul addresses everyone equally and fairly with a consistent message—love, honor, respect, and serve one another. When it comes to Christlikeness of behavior, Paul is hard on *everyone*! Women are not singled out in the least.

We must therefore rid ourselves of the complaint that Paul's commands to women are unfair, chauvinistic, culturally biased, anachronistic, and outdated. An honest and humble reading of the family sections of *Ephesians* and *Colossians* reveal none of this. They reveal only fair, sound, wise, and balanced common sense: *Husbands, wives, and children—love, honor, and respect each other.*

The complaints that men and women raise about their half of the marriage equation reveal latent rebellion in both. Husbands justify their rebellion. Wives justify theirs. It is easy to be distracted by the shortcomings of the man or woman on the other side of the fence. However, Paul is only addressing one person: *Me.* Paul nowhere commands the husband to monitor his wife's submission, nor commands the wife to monitor her husband's sacrificial love. The regions dealing with the other's obedience are off-limits.

When a husband looks at his wife's submission, or worse, tells her she needs to submit, he has gone off the rails. That's none of his business. A husband's sole charge is to love, honor, and sacrificially serve his wife. He is not even allowed to *think* about his wife's submission. Likewise, when a wife notices, or worse, comments on her husband's lack of love, she has gone off the rails. That is none of her business. Her duty is to respect and submit to her husband. How he does his job has no bearing on *her* wifely charge.

Wives, show your husbands respect, deference, and submission.

Wives, be subject to your husbands, as to the Lord...As the church is subject to Christ, let wives also be subject in everything to their husbands. (Eph. 5:22, 24)

Let the wife see that she respects her husband. (Ephesians 5:33)

Wives, be subject to your husbands. (Colossians 3:18)

Bid the older women...to train the young women to love their husbands and children....to be submissive to their husbands. (Titus 2:4-5)

Wives, be submissive to your husbands. (1 Peter 3:1)

Thus are holy women adorned who are submissive to their husbands. (1 Peter 3:5)

---

45. Children, Obey and Honor Your Parents

If it is a cliché to say that the family is under attack, it is because it is so desperately true. These are perilous times for the values that hold marriage and the family together. The assault is not primarily one of ideas, as important as that is, it is an attack against relationships. We may rail against abortion, divorce, governmental anti-Christian bias, and the numerous sins normalized by our culture. But these are symptoms of a cancer eating away at the *relational* fabric of the family. Two relationships sit squarely between the crosshairs—that between husbands and wives, and that between parents and children. In both cases, a lie has infiltrated the outlook of the church as well as the world. This lie has birthed the destructive cancer that is eating away at both fundamental relationships.

God established *honor* as the strengthening relational virtue that holds the family together. We might go so far as to say that honor holds the universe together. Reading the Ten Commandments through the lens of honor explodes the ancient commands open with new insight. A slight rewording reveals the value God places on honor.

Honor me as your God—have no other gods before me.

Honor me as your *only* God—do not make idols to worship instead of me.

Honor my name—do not take the name of the Lord your God in vain.

Honor the Sabbath day and keep it holy.

Honor your father and mother.

Honor your fellow man—you shall not kill.

Honor your husbands and wives and marriages—you shall not commit adultery.

Honor the possessions of others—you shall not steal.

Honor truth—you shall not bear false witness against your neighbor.

Honor your neighbor—you shall not covet anything of your neighbor's.

Honor is established and built in the family—honor of husbands toward wives, honor of wives toward husbands, honor of children toward parents. Honor is the intermingling warp and woof upon which the whole fabric of marriage and the family is woven.

However, the enemy has planted the seed of a lie to destroy honor. The world now says: You are only required to honor what is honorable. In other words, we honor *because* something or someone is honorable. That all-important *because* breeds the lethal cancer. It implies that without a compelling reason, we are not required to give honor.

The devious subtlety whispers in the ear of Christians along with everyone else:

Honor your parents *because* they are honorable and only *if* they are honorable.

Honor your husbands *because* they are honorable but only *if* they are honorable.

Honor your wives *because* they are honorable and only *if* they are honorable.

About all three, and honor in general, the world turns the because-seed into the deliciously alluring lie: If they are *not* honorable you are not required to honor them.

This "because" is at root in Satan's lie. Children are to honor bad parents no less than good parents. Wives are to honor bad husbands no less than good ones. Husbands are to honor bad wives as well as good ones. There is no *because* in biblical honor.

Neither is there an *until*. The world feeds another lie to sons and daughters—You are only required to obey your parents *until* you feel capable of self-rule. But the Fifth Commandment is lifelong. Childness has no age limit. Neither do Paul's instructions in *Ephesians* and *Colossians* have an end point. Childness is the life Jesus brought to the world. The first steps in learning to live in eternal childness begin at home.

It may be the Christian young people of the next few generations that determine whether the family, as we know it, will endure. The strength of the biblical family begins with honor of parents—without the twin lies of *because* and *until* undermining them.

Children, obey your parents in the Lord, for this is right. (Ephesians 6:1)

"Honor your father and mother...that it may be well with you." (Ephesians 6:2-3)

Children, obey your parents in everything, for this pleases the Lord. (Colossians 3:20)

72

46. Practice Hospitality

Hospitality as commanded of Christians in the New Testament does not mean throwing cocktail and dinner parties. That is often what first comes to mind when we hear the word "hospitality"—having people over for dinner, Thanksgiving feasts, laughter, toasts, gaiety, etc. A moment's reflection, however, reveals the superficiality of this image. All we have to do is ask if Paul was a dinner party sort of guy. It is doubtful.

It is true that we can envision Peter enjoying a good time with his friends. However, I think we may safely conclude that something very different was going on in the first century church than cocktail parties which prompted both Peter and Paul to write, "Practice hospitality." There is a big difference between *entertainment* and *hospitality*.

Paul's second missionary journey may give us a more accurate picture. When Timothy and Silas delivered Paul's letter to the Thessalonians, they remained for an extended time. *Where* did they stay? Not in Motel 6. Obviously they stayed with fellow Christians. During the same time in Corinth, where did *Paul* stay? In this case we happen to know. He stayed at the home of Aquila and Priscilla. He probably spent over a year with them. Aquila and Priscilla later relocated to Ephesus where church meetings were held in their home (Paul calls it "the church in their house.") During his third missionary journey, Paul spent three years in Ephesus. In all likelihood, he was again a guest with them. Indeed, this well known first century couple is known throughout Christendom for their open-hearted *hospitality*. They never wrote a letter. We have no word recorded that either of them spoke. But they appear throughout Paul's letters as a recurring theme. The home of Aquila and Priscilla was an *open* home where people came and went regularly.

Here we begin to probe the essence of what Peter and Paul meant by the word—the open home, the unlocked door, the welcoming invitation, the spare bed, the kitchen and teapot and warm fire ready to embrace any visitor whether friend or stranger.

One of the lasting legacies left by my father and mother is the memory of an *open* home. After my sisters and I were on our way to adulthood, our parents began selectively taking in people in need. A young couple from our church lived with us for a time. Foster children came and went. One of the precious memories of my life is of the final years of an elderly lifelong friend of my grandmother's who, by the time she reached her 90s, had no living relatives left. "Aunt Luella" spent her last years in our home, cared for until her death by my mother. I keep her well-marked Bible from the early 1900s on my shelf, a treasured reminder of this godly woman, no relation, whom my mother loved.

The "open door" policy of my parents' home took some getting used to for Judy. The first time I spontaneously invited her home for dinner, long before we were married and without notifying my mom, she was stunned. "But...I can't just show up! Won't your mother mind?" she said. "Of course not," I replied. "She'll love it!"

I cannot recall a single "dinner party" in my parents' home. No entertainments, no festive toasts. Just the memory of Aunt Luella's peaceful final years and my mom's compassionate ministrations. My mother was a "Priscilla," and I honor her for that.

I hope some of her influence has rubbed off. Our house has been a temporary home for brothers, sisters, friends, students, nieces, parents, out of town bookstore customers, stranded travelers, fans, friends whose marriages broke apart, even—really!—itinerant street preachers, not to mention visiting adult sons. One of the highest compliments one of our grown sons paid us was his laughing comment when we mentioned someone staying with us: "I can never keep track of who you have living with you!"

I was warmed by his words. My mother's legacy lives on.

Practice hospitality...Welcome one another as Christ has welcomed you. (Romans 12:13; 15:7)
Widen your hearts. (2 Corinthians 6:13)
Appoint elders...who are...hospitable. (Titus 1:5, 6, 8)
Practice hospitality ungrudgingly to one another. (1 Peter 4:9)

47. Manage Your Households Well

How do we define "manage?" What does it mean to *manage* a household? The word is fraught with potential misunderstanding. Are we to imagine that Paul envisioned the husband and father as a C.E.O. whose duty it is to run the home with the authority and efficiency of a business—turning the family into the proverbial "well-oiled machine?"

What kind of model is that of the Godhead—the ultimate Ideal of which the earthly family is intended to be the human representation? Related questions come storming at the gates of our minds. Is the husband to "manage" the wife? Wives won't like that. Is the mother to "manage" the young people? They won't like that. Who manages the husband and father? How quickly we bristle at the idea of being managed only reveals how deeply the lie of Independence from the garden remains humanity's cancerous Achilles Heel. Or are we talking about financial management...or a house that is clean and tidy with food always on the table? Was Paul talking administratively, organizationally, or relationally?

This command is filled with land mines for modernity. Once we begin to pick at the edges, *nobody* is going to find it pleasant, except perhaps authoritarian men.

What makes these family commands most difficult is that we live, as mentioned earlier, in a culture ruled by the principle of doing what is right in our own eyes. We live in a *manage-less* environment, not a well-*managed* one. Wives resent being "managed." So they do what is right in their own eyes. Sons and daughters resent being "managed." Not wanting to engage in constant bickering and argumentation, parents give in and allow them to do what is right in their own eyes. And it is in men's nature to do what is right in their own eyes. And therefore, because "management" in families is as odious to modernity as "submission," *everyone* does what is right in his or her own eyes.

Christian families universally disregard this command up and down the spectrum of responsibility, from husbands and fathers, to wives and mothers, to sons and daughters. In the trenches of real life, there are no simple solutions to the selfishness, rebellion, and independence that are so endemic to family life in our day. Judy and I have struggled with these dichotomies and uncertainties in our family for forty years. More than at any time in my life, after more than four decades as a husband and father, I labor under the burden of having been a poor manager of my household. I have managed our finances adequately. Judy has kept an orderly, clean, hospitable home. We managed businesses and a home school. But did we "manage our household *well?*"

This raises a question on the flip side of the command—is it a father's or mother's fault that a son or daughter does not follow the values and spiritual training they have tried to instill? Surely in some cases the roots of rebellion *can* be traced to a lack of healthy parental models. Yet even in well "managed" homes where influences have been sound, wisdom taught, and example consistent, rebellion nevertheless erupts to fracture families. Are fathers and mothers to be condemned whenever honor, respect, and godliness of character are lacking? At what point does Command #45 move to center stage? When does accountability shift from manager to *managee?*

Such questions have become more probing and heart-wrenching in our own time when rejection of core biblical perspectives among Christian young people has never been higher. Who is responsible—church leaders, parents, or young people themselves? It may take the perspective of history, looking back on our time, to determine an answer.

Let us have no provoking of one another. (Galatians 5:26)

Fathers, do not provoke your children to anger. (Ephesians 6:4)

Fathers, do not provoke your children, lest they become discouraged. (Colossians 3:21)

A bishop must manage his own household well, keeping his children submissive and respectful in every way...Let deacons...manage their children and their households well. (1 Timothy 3:4, 12)

Appoint elders...who are blameless, married only once, whose children are believers...For a bishop, as God's steward, must be blameless...a lover of goodness, master of himself. (Titus 1:5-8)

48. Raise Your Children in the Wisdom of the Lord

How one reads and responds to this command will almost entirely depend on where on life's spectrum one finds oneself.

For the eager new parent, this command is filled with optimism and challenge. What could be more exciting than to mold a young life in the ways of God so that he or she develops into maturity as a growing and conscientious Christian?

For a child, however—whether of ten or twenty, it may grate like fingernails on a chalkboard. The world's lies assault young people from the moment they open their eyes and awaken to their own personhood. By ten or twelve, the world has ingrained into the deepest marrow of their beings a very different perspective than what Christian parents hope for: "I will decide for myself what constitutes wisdom," they boldly proclaim. "I will do and think and believe whatever I want. I'll have none of your parental instruction or discipline, thank you very much." The harder a parent tries sincerely to obey this command, the more their efforts are resented. In this single area of Christian practice, it seems that the *most* obedient parents are the *least* honored.

For the Christian parent who has been through the relational wars of parenting, and has the battle scars and fragmented relationships to prove it, reminders of the past are often tinged with melancholy. "I did my best to obey this command," they think wistfully. "Yet what good did it do? My children are bitter about much of what I did." I understand the heart-wrenching quandary. This is an easy command to idealize, but a difficult command to see to the end of.

Parents can but prayerfully and humbly try to obey as the Lord gives them insight, and hope for the best. We would like to add that we can leave the results in God's hands. But at the end of the day parents actually have to leave the results in the hands of their sons and daughters. *They* are the only ones who will decide whether their parents' training will ultimately shape their character.

Perhaps that is the point—parents are called to do their best to obey without being able to see to the end of it. Moses did not foresee what a troubled future lay ahead for his "family," the nation of Israel. He had not been a perfect father to that family. But he had been an obedient father. He had done his best to raise his family in the wisdom of the Lord. Yet they rebelled. Moses could not prevent it. He was given a difficult assignment and he carried it out faithfully. The Israelites rebelled anyway.

Moses' words remain the charge to us. Some of our children will heed our instruction and grow in wisdom. Others will stray. There will always be two kinds of people in the world. There were two kinds of Israelites. There are two kinds of sons and daughters.

Hear, O Israel: The Lord our God is one Lord; and you shall love the Lord your God with all your heart, and with all your soul, and with all your might. And these words which I command you this day shall be upon your heart; and you shall teach them diligently to your children, and shall talk of them when you sit in your house, and when you walk by the way, and when you lie down, and when you rise. (Deuteronomy 6:4-7)

Whether I did a good job in conveying the commands to my earthly sons may be a question I will never be able to answer. But it is in obedience to this passage, now that they are grown, that I have embarked on this series of books: *And you shall write them.*

In the end, it is only the living example of our lives, priorities, relationships, outlook, humility, consistency, sacrifice, attitudes, responses, kindness, and our *love* that that will instill the wisdom of God into our sons and daughters.

Yet even after all this, no matter how faithfully these principles may be lived by parents, sons and daughters will be urged by the world in a thousand ways to do what is right in their own eyes. The story of the Israelites remains poignantly contemporary.

Bring your children up in the discipline and instruction of the Lord. (Ephesians 6:4)
Appoint elders...whose children are believers. (Titus 1:5-6)

---

49. Train Young Men to be Self-Controlled, Young Women to be Chaste and Domestic

The commands slice into our flesh in many ways. They slice uniquely and personally into my flesh at precisely the point of *my* rebellion and *my* independence. They will slice into your flesh in different ways than they do mine.

So what do we do with those particularly irritating commands that cut most deeply? Do we humble ourselves and quietly whisper, "I don't like this, Lord. In fact, I hate it. But here it is in your Word in black and white. Therefore I will humbly pray with Mary, *Be it unto me according to your Word.* Help me to obey this very difficult command."

Or, when independence rises up, is that when we begin cherry-picking the commands, as if they are a smorgasbord from which we are free to choose those where perhaps obedience comes somewhat easily, and disregard those uncomfortably personal commands? Is that the point where we say, "Oh, well *that* was meant for first century Christians. But times have changed. That no longer applies to *me*. I can ignore it."

However subtly you mask it, many of you are probably reading this book as if passing along a spiritual buffet table, picking and choosing as you go. So am I. Even as I urge obedience, the buffet-mentality sneaks into my perspectives too. I have my favorite (easy) commands, and those other (hard) commands that I keep locked away in the basement so they do not escape into the convicting sunlight of my daily life.

None of us *like* the commands. None of us enjoy being commanded. If we're going to call ourselves Christians, however, that's the name of the game. We are under orders. We are a people under command. Christianity was not presented by its Founder as a lifestyle of *suggestions*. It was never a smorgasbord. "These things I *command* you..."

Not only do we personally dislike the most probing commands, the world feeds us continual lies that make it easy to disregard anything that modernity finds offensive. It's never been easier to play the game of pretense Christianity. Our culture makes it easy to call oneself a Christian while ignoring all but the most bland and societally-acceptable commands. *Cultural Christianity* is in...*Command Christianity* is on its way to extinction unless the few bold thinking Christians of our time plant enough seeds during their lifetimes to keep the commands alive for the remnant Christians of future generations.

This command before us may be the most culturally incorrect command of all. It shouts to the modernism of our culture, "You lie!" It shouts to the young people who will become the next pivotal generation of remnant seed-planting "command Christians." It shouts with clarity and without compromise: *Reject what the world tells you. Young men, young women...set an example for your times by being teachable, humble, obedient, self-controlled, pure, chaste, domestic, thoughtful, selfless, and kind.*

Nothing is more despised by our progressive culture than domesticity as a life's ambition for young women, and humble self-control in young men. We live in a youth-driven era when young men and young women are taught to go for everything they can get as soon as they can get it. The very notions of humility, self-control, chastity, and domesticity are laughably anachronistic in modernity's ears. So too is the notion that young people are under obligation to be taught by those older and wiser than themselves.

This command is positively hateful to modernity. Yet here it is in black and white—Older Christians are to teach younger Christians to be self-controlled, chaste, and domestic. Younger men and women are to heed and obey the teaching. This command hits us all: Older men, older women, younger men, younger women. Who in the church has the courage to obey it? Older men and women can obey this command by *teaching* God's precepts faithfully, but *obedience* to those teachings rests with the young. Young men and young women, the future of command-Christianity is on you.

Older women...teach what is good, and so train the younger women...to be chaste, domestic, kind, and submissive to their husband...Urge the younger men to control themselves. (Titus 2:4-6)

50. Care For Widows and Orphans

Without reading more meaning than probably exists into workmen being worthy of their hire, or elders being worthy of double honor, nowhere in the New Testament can we identify the precedent of huge church budgets for buildings, administrative staffs, music teams, or even paid clergy. In the first century, the church was a volunteer enterprise. Whether church buildings can be justified scripturally is another matter that has perhaps never been scrutinized closely enough. This, along with the general question whether the changes that have come to the "corporate church universal" are healthy, scriptural, and intended by God, obviously raises controversial matters best left for another discussion.

There is, however, New Testament precedent for the collection basket. The question is: What is the money to be used for? How did first century Christians put their collections to wise use? Those uses, as a careful study reveals, are much different that the expenditures listed on 99% of church budgets.

We can identify the scriptural precedent for financial collections to be four—money for *missions*, the *poor*, beleaguered *sister churches*, and *widows*. We find no provision for "church expenses." What money a church raises, according to the New Testament, is for helping those in need.

The last of these four is particularly fascinating. Paul's instructions to Timothy about widows (1 Timothy 4) are convoluted and more than a little confusing—especially when he launches into a diatribe against immaturity in young widows, and tries to clarify himself by differentiating between "*real* widows" and "*young* widows." Much in this passage may cause offense. It is not one of Paul's most triumphant or lucid moments.

Overlooking Paul's fumbling inconsistency, however, we note with interest that the church of the first century had an official "role" for widows for whom financial provision was made. This involved what we can only assume to be a "widow's fund." If the New Testament is our example, how many church budgets make provision for such a fund? We find no fund in any of Paul's instructions for pastoral staff, nothing for a building fund or church maintenance. Yet we see the early church collecting money to provide for the living expenses of its widows, and to help the famine-stricken church in Jerusalem.

Since churches through the years have in general invested their financial priorities in other directions, it falls to individual Christian men and women to seek the ways and means to obey this command. Obviously times are different. Widows today are better provided for than would have been the case in the first century. Though some are, of course, most widows today are not destitute. Nevertheless, the command is laid upon us to care for widows and orphans, not make excuses by saying they don't really need it. Whether they need financial assistance or not, they do need the companionship and care of friendship and love. This is the most personal "care" we can give. James does not speak to financial need at all. He is more practical than that. He simply says, "*Visit* widows and orphans." That is something anyone can do. It costs only time.

"Nothing has so distinguished Christianity throughout its history more than its compassionate ministry to the needy, starving, and suffering...to the widow and the orphan. Nor is this Command one to be obeyed only with bills in a collection plate, coins in a tin cup, or a check sent to missions...Into the life of every Christian intent upon obedience will be sent 'poor' who are suffering in many forms of poverty. We are not merely called to give money to the financially strapped, but to *give* to any and all of the poor that God sends uniquely into our lives...

"You and I, as *individuals*, are...called to address suffering existing close beside us." (*The Commands of Jesus*, p. 42)

Honor widows. (1 Timothy 5:3)
Let the church assist those who are real widows. (1 Timothy 5:16)
Visit widows and orphans in their affliction. (James 1:27)

SERIES SIX

"THE LAODICEA COMMANDS"

Show Respect in Relationships

HOW WE TREAT OTHERS REFLECTS OUR LOVE FOR CHRIST

LAODICEA—COMPASSION FOR A SLAVE REVEALS PAUL'S PRIORITIES IN PERSONAL RELATIONSHIPS

The only association many Christians have with the church in the mystery city of Laodicea comes from Revelation 3 where the term "lukewarm" originates in characterizing lazy faith. Jesus' words to the Laodicean church—"Because you are lukewarm, and neither cold nor hot, I will spew you out of my mouth...you are wretched, pitiable, poor, blind, and naked." (Rev. 3:16)—have unfortunately painted this church with an image that may not be entirely accurate.

Further examination of this passage reveals one of the Lord's most memorable and important challenges and promises, "I counsel you to buy from me gold refined by fire, that you may be rich, and white garments to clothe you...Behold, I stand at the door and knock: if any one hears my voice and opens the door, I will come in to him and eat with him, and he with me." The message to Laodicea in *Revelation*, therefore, may be more complex than the one-dimensionality often ascribed to it.

Our interest is heightened when we discover that Paul wrote a letter to Laodicea (Colossians 4:16) which was either lost or misnamed. Many scholars believe that the letter that has come down to us as *Ephesians* was actually originally written to Laodicea.

Of one thing we can be certain, the cities of Laodicea, Colossae, and Hierapolis were close enough together (within ten miles) to be almost one, as were the Christian fellowships of the three cities. They were located about a hundred miles east of the major seaport of Ephesus and are thus also linked to the Ephesian church.

An intriguing story exists between the lines tying these cities to the fortunes of an otherwise insignificant slave by the name of Onesimus. We would never have heard of him had not the early church fathers decided to include Paul's tiny letter of *Philemon* in the New Testament. The circumstances of the letter arose several years after Paul's first visit to the region. By then he was in prison in Rome. There he encountered the slave Onesimus who had become a Christian. This Onesimus was from the tri-city region east of Ephesus, probably from the tiny town of Colossae, slave to one of the church leaders there—either Philemon or a man by the name of Archippus. Becoming acquainted with Onesimus as a Christian brother, Paul wrote to Philemon in Colossae requesting him (or Archippus—the exact details are vague) to receive Onesimus back as a brother rather than punishing him for running away. As he wrote to the Galatians, "There is neither Jew nor Greek...neither slave nor free." Paul saw all men as equal.

Paul refers to these circumstances in his letter to Colossae, possibly written at the same time and delivered by the same messenger (Epaphras,) in which he mentions his enigmatic letter to the Laodiceans. This intricate scenario linking these cities highlights an underlying message—that Paul placed huge value on personal human relationships. One glance through the list of salutations with which he concludes most of his letters tells the tale. All taken together it is a huge list. Paul valued people!

Between the lines remains the mystery letter to Laodicea. We have titled this series "The Laodicean Commands," to underscore not only Paul's compassion for a slave and emphasis on relationships, but also to remind us of the fact that there remain many uncertainties about the unfolding biblical drama that we may never completely unravel.

The following summation of Paul's letter to Colossae, though not mentioning Philemon or Onesimus by name, draws many of these underlying themes together:

*Epaphras, who is one of yourselves...greets you, always remembering you earnestly in his prayers...For I bear him witness that he has worked hard for you and for those in Laodicea and in Hierapolis. Luke the beloved physician and Demas greet you. Give my greetings to the brethren at Laodicea, and to Nympha and the church in her house. And when this letter has been read among you, have it read also in the church of the Laodiceans; and see that you read also the letter from Laodicea. And say to Archippus, "See that you fulfil the ministry which you have received in the Lord." (*Col. 4:12-17)

SERIES SIX

HOW WE TREAT OTHERS REFLECTS OUR LOVE FOR CHRIST

51. Show honor and respect to all.

52. Seek the good of others.

53. Put others first.

54. Be merciful and full of sympathy.

55. Harbor no grievances or animosities.

56. Avoid the shallow and hypocritical who do not live their faith.

57. Control anger.

58. Don't judge.

59. Associate with the lowly.

60. Place no stumbling blocks in the way of another's faith.

51. Show Honor and Respect to All

From home and family relationships, the apostolic commands widen to embrace *all* relationships. As Christian ministry begins in the home and expands into the church, so too does the capacity and training to treat others in ways that reflect Christlikeness. What happens in the home does not stay in the home. Who we are in the home is the real us. It is only a hypocrite who treats wife, husband, children, or parents without humility, honor, respect, and servanthood, and who then goes out to work or school or church and puts on a mask of kindness and respectfulness with friends and colleagues and fellow church members. Of course it is better to treat people respectfully and kindly than otherwise. It may still be hypocrisy.

That's why we return again to the all-important virtue of honor. This is where deep, wholesome, integritous, loving relationship begins. As honor and respect were pivotal threads running through every aspect of the family commands, they are likewise the foundational virtues that strengthen and deepen *all* human relationship.

Honor and respect have two components—*external* (how I treat others) and *internal* (what I think about others.) We encounter many whom it is difficult to find reasons to respect. We meet people who are consumed by unforgiveness and hatred. How can we honor selfishness, greed, anger, bitterness? It is obviously possible to treat an individual with kindness and respect even though I may not actually respect him. I should treat him kindly (with external respect) even though I may not feel (internal) honor and respect toward him. To do so is not hypocrisy but is simple grace and kindness.

We find ourselves again sidetracked by the world's lie of "because." Once we remove *because* from the equation of honor and respect, the fog clears. We honor and respect all men and women, not for their virtuous character, but for their *humanity*. All men, all women, all children are created in God's image. Whether they know it or not, whether they are living in the reality of that truth or not, there yet remains the germ of God's imageness at the core of their personhood. That we can honor. God *loves* them, and thus we can *honor* them. All humanity lies at our doorstep to honor because it is God's humanity. Surely that is reason enough.

This wonderfully expanded perspective reveals a yet deeper truth. It reveals a truth about me. The internal half of honor speaks not merely about whether I feel honor toward someone. It reveals a deep truth about my character. Does honor dwell within me? Am I a man *of* honor? This is much different than whether I am honorable? My human flaws make me no more or less qualified for honor on the basis of "because" than anyone else. But am I an *honoring* man? Do I honor others because of who I *am*, not because they are honorable or because I am honorable? In other words, all relationships begin from a foundation that we are all flawed human beings together. We are all hypocrites to some degree. None of us *deserve* honor. That is given. But in my flawed humanity, am I an *honoring* man who has determined to honor others in spite of their flaws?

Suddenly I have plunged to the heart of honor. Respect and honor of others flows out of *my* character, out of my *honoring* heart. In a sense, it has nothing to do with anyone else. It has everything to do with me. That's why I can honor a stranger as well as my wife, though I know nothing about him. I may honor Judy because I know many honorable facets of her character. But I honor the stranger simply because I am an honoring man who honors all that God has made. Then I honor Judy also for that reason as well. She is therefore, as Paul says of elders, "worthy of double honor."

Outdo one another in showing honor....Pay all of them their due...respect to whom respect is due, honor to whom honor is due. (Romans 12:10, 13:7)

Highly esteem those over you in love. (1 Thessalonians 5:13)

Live a quiet and peaceable life...respectful in every way. (1 Timothy 2:2)

Honor all men. (1 Peter 2:17)

52. Seek the Good of Others

We speak a great deal about servanthood as the fundamental characteristic of Christian conduct. There are *internal virtues* (the fruits of the Spirit, the person I am inside, the transformative Christlikeness I am allowing the Holy Spirit to develop within me) and *external ethics* (my attitude and behavior toward others, the Christlikeness of behavior, deportment, manners, and responses by which I live my relationships.) The two are clearly intertwined. As Jesus said, the external always flows out of the internal. Ethics in behavior flow out of virtues that dwell in the heart. Servanthood brings both internal virtue and external ethic into the unity lived and exampled by Jesus. "The greatest among you shall be your *servant*...if any one would be first, let him be...*servant* of all." Any idea of Christianity apart from *obedience* to the Commands of Christ and *servanthood* toward others is dead religion not the living faith that Jesus died to bring to the world.

But servanthood is a double-sided coin. Contrary as it seems, it has a potential dark side that can reveal itself in two ways. It can become an entry-point for pride. (Look at *me*...my willing service and everything I do for others makes me incredibly virtuous.) It can also become a source of bitterness. (I may be serving on the outside, but inside I am hating every minute of it.) Obviously the servanthood Jesus spoke of is neither of these— neither prideful nor begrudging. *Christ-servanthood* marries the *internal virtue* (the fruits of the spirit...service with a humble, joyful, thankful, gracious, kind, peaceful heart) with the *external ethic* of duty and faithful service that reflects the model of Jesus himself.

Such a level of servanthood is more than passively acting as a domestic—cooking meals, washing dishes, sweeping floors, and cleaning toilets. Servanthood may take these and a thousand forms. But the servanthood of Christlikeness moves from the passive to the pro-active. As I meet needs, I also find myself working toward the deeper *good*, the ultimate *best*, of all with whom I share life on any level. This takes service to a higher level. I am no longer a mere caregiver, housekeeper, maid, valet, or cook. My goal is to work toward the best of those both under my charge and those whom I serve. Few of the people I meet in the course of a day are "under my charge." The good I can do for someone whose path I cross in the aisles of the grocery store is limited to a smile, kind word, or courteous gesture. Yet in both cases we see the distinction between *passive service* and *active good-seeking*. The service Jesus demonstrated was active not passive. He energetically dedicated his every minute to the eternal good of those he encountered.

What, then, is the ultimate "good" we can seek for others? It is God's intent for humanity to dwell together in unity and harmony. Peacemaking and fence building thus contribute to the good of those around us. While recognizing that not all temporal goals contribute to eternal good, embracing another's goals in life can also be a vital aspect of good-seeking. Probing the good of the whole man or whole woman, however, will extend much deeper. To meet human need means coming alongside those God sends us, affirming personhood in ways that reach far beyond helping someone get a job, work toward a degree, or write a book. It may be easing the pain of loneliness, grief, heartache, and sickness with simple compassion. There are no models or outlines for how exactly to do this in any individual situation or relationship. Every man or woman's "good" uniquely takes into account his entire life story. To work toward that good requires prayerful attentiveness to God's invisible hand in that story. It therefore behooves us to tread gently and humbly, co-workers with God's Spirit in human life. One thing I must never do is impose *my* will, *my* perceived best, on the life of another. What is good for me may not be the "good" God intends for him. "Love seeks not its own."

Let each of us please his neighbor for his good, to edify him. (Romans 15:2)
Let no one seek his own good, but the good of his neighbor. (1 Corinthians 10:24)
    Through love be servants of one another...As we have opportunity, let us do good to all men. (Galatians 5:14, 6:10) Always seek to do good to all. (1 Thessalonians 5:15)

53. Put Others First

Servanthood again rises as the informing virtue and ethic in our lifelong self-training exercise to put others first. This effort is equally multi-dimensional as yesterday's command to seek the good of our neighbor. We see an obvious *external* application (letting another go ahead of me in line, offering the plate of cookies to someone else before taking one myself, yielding to the car that arrived at the intersection the same time I did.) We also see the *internal* attitude and perspective that results in the external act (viewing myself as a servant and thus seeing others as deserving to go ahead of me.) Again we are also aware of the potential dark side. I may pretend to be nice by offering you the plate of cookies, but secretly I hope you will take the top one without noticing the big one underneath I've got my eye on. No matter what the command, pretense is always possible.

This is a more subtle and intricate command than first meets the eye. In how many subtle ways do we steer relationships and conversations upon ourselves? In a thousand ways, we make it "all about me." Putting others first may be as simple as listening instead of talking. What is 90% of our endless talk but barging our way to the front of the conversational line? Instead, move to the back of the line for a change. Let other people go first. What a simple way to discover obedience to this command!

Putting others first is doubly paradoxical when we consider Paul's enigmatic command in Philippians 2:3, "In humility count others better than yourselves." He goes on in verse 4, *Let each of you look not only to his own interests, but also to the interests of others.* This is Paul at his best. Surely this simple injunction must rank beside the Golden Rule in moment-by-moment importance in our lives. Let us all commit to memorizing these few words until we know them as well as we know, *Do unto others.*

But we are left scratching our heads at the first half of the verse. What a remarkable statement. Does Paul really mean what the words say? In this era of self-worshp, nobody-will-tell-me-what-to-do, my life is my own...a sentiment such as *Count others better than yourself* sounds positively absurd. How the world scoffs at meekness. Even many Christians would say that humility carried to such an extreme as to count others as better than your self is nothing short of an insane prescription for life. Yet this is exactly what is commanded of us. Will we adopt the world's view...or that of the New Testament?

Practically, what does counting others as better than myself mean? Do I open the door for another to let them go ahead of me, do I listen without trying to monopolize the conversation...because I think he or she is *better* than me? The rendition of the verse given by the King James Version sheds great insight: "In lowliness of mind let each esteem other better than themselves." They are not "better" as people, of more value in God's eyes. However, in obedience to this command, taking upon myself the lower part, I choose to esteem them *as if* they are better than me. I choose to esteem every individual I meet. I choose to treat them *as if* they are my superior. It is another form of honor.

This says nothing about intrinsic worth of personhood. It says everything about the value I place on the personhood of others. I simply recognize the truth of Matthew 25:40—the "least of these" whom we encounter throughout every day are images of Jesus himself. If Jesus is found in the faces of those who cross my path, it is the most natural thing in the world to count others as better than myself! If truth exists in the maxim, "Treat everyone you meet as the most important person in the world," how much greater is the truth: *Treat every person you meet as if it is Jesus himself.*

Be subject to one another out of reverence to Christ. (Ephesians 5:21)
Let each of you look not only to his own interests, but also to the interests of others. (Phil. 2:4)
Have this mind among yourselves, which was also in Christ Jesus, who...took the form of a servant. (Philippians 2:5-7)
Render service to the brethren. (2 John 5)

54. Be Merciful and Full of Sympathy

Sometimes the most wonderful scriptural insights are hidden in the most obscure words or phrases. We find one of these in the passage 2 Corinthians 6:11-13. In the ongoing dispute with the Corinthians, Paul uses a word that is full of illumination. The King James translates PEPLATYNTAI of 2 Cor. 6:11 (and PLATYNTHĒTE of 6:13) as "enlarge." The Revised Standard adds a slightly different nuance with *widen* ("has been widened.") Paul is pleading with the Corinthians for sympathetic hearts of understanding. "Widen your hearts," he writes. Either rendition of Paul's charge illuminates the essence of human compassion, mercy, and sympathy—*a large heart.*

Many labor sadly through life with constricted hearts. They are afraid to embrace the glorious depth and breadth of God's expansive human family. Many are also afraid to enlarge their hearts to the expansiveness and eternal forgiveness of God's infinite Fatherhood. They bring constricted hearts into their doctrines about God. They prefer to dwell in man's small-visioned theologies rather than embrace the infinite reach of God's eternal character, and purpose. Paul's charge, therefore, is a universal one with many applications: *Widen your hearts.*

What a lovely phrase. And so practical. You I will encounter a dozen or more opportunities this very day to throw wide the doors of our hearts to those around us. We will encounter people. We will encounter new ideas. Will we widen our hearts? Or will we creep quietly to the door and squint through the peephole first to see if the human brother or sister who has crossed our path, or the unfamiliar idea that has been posed, is worthy of our sympathy? Is he or she one to whom we will open the door? Or will we keep our heart's door closed? Is the new idea too unfamiliar to invite in for a mind-expanding discussion?

If we could imprint those three words on our hearts and brains, and take them out into the world this day to inform every response, every word, every expression, how different the world would look—*Widen your hearts!* How different do the people around me look when I am gazing into their faces—hurried, beleaguered, angry, frustrated, hurting, sad, lonely, prideful, self-centered, confused—with the silent prayer on my lips, "Lord, widen my heart toward these of your children."

George MacDonald focuses the practicality of the heart "widened" toward our neighbor: "Then my second neighbour appears, and who is he?...He with whom I have any transactions, any human dealings whatever...the man who makes my clothes; the man who prints my book; the man who drives me in his cab; the man who begs from me in the street...yea, even the man who condescends to me. With all and each there is a chance of doing the part of a neighbour, if in no other way yet by speaking truly, acting justly, and thinking kindly...A man must not choose his neighbour; he must take the neighbour that God sends him. In him, whoever he be, lies, hidden or revealed, a beautiful brother. The neighbour is just the man who is next to you at the moment, the man with whom any business has brought you in contact.

"Thus will love spread and spread in wider and stronger pulses till the whole human race will be...sacredly lovely. Drink-debased, vice-defeatured, pride-puffed, wealth-bollen, vanity-smeared, they will yet be brothers, yet be sisters, yet be God-born neighbours. Any rough-hewn semblance of humanity will at length be enough to move the man to reverence and affection... "Ah brother! thou hast a soul like mine...Thou art oppressed with thy sorrows, uplifted with thy joys. Perhaps thou knowest not so well as I, that a region of gladness surrounds all thy grief, of light all thy darkness, of peace all thy tumult. Oh, my brother! I will love thee." (George MacDonald, *Unspoken Sermons, First Series,* "Love Thy Neighbour.")

Show God's wisdom by being full of mercy. (James 3:17)
All of you, have unity of spirit, sympathy, love...a tender heart and a humble mind. (1 Peter 3:8)

55. Harbor No Grievances or Animosities

Forgiveness is one of the most difficult requirements of the Christian life. It is true that many (perhaps most) people don't want to forgive. If we have been wronged, we would prefer to get even. Forgiveness doesn't rank high on the list of what first comes to mind. We cherish our grudges against those who have hurt us. We nurse our resentments like private treasures kept in the memory bank of life's grievances.

It is a curious thing, humanity's love affair with unforgiveness. It eats us up inside, consuming our relational health and vigor like an invisible cancer. Yet we cling to unforgiveness with the passion reserved for a secret lover—knowing the affair is ruining us, yet addicted to the pleasure of the destructive evil.

For Christians, however, the case is different. Though we may struggle with the above tendencies, we yet *want* to forgive. It is not our intent or desire to nurse the cancer of unforgiveness. We want rid of it. At least on one level we want to forgive.

But the cure—forgiveness—is difficult to lay hold of. There are many dimensions to unforgiveness. It's not a matter of simple obedience. It's not even a matter of *trying* to forgive. We can say to God, to ourselves, even to one we feel has wronged us, "I forgive." But in the middle of the night the sense of grievance creeps back. We discover unforgiveness lurking with a more powerful hold on our thoughts than we had realized. Forgiveness is not a feeling we can summon to banish it as easily as we might like.

Perhaps our way through the difficulty begins by recognizing forgiveness for the elusive thing it is. We return to seek the essence of our responsibility in the region of *do* rather than *feel*. So what can we do? At such times, even absent *feelings* of forgiveness, we can refuse to *act* on those feelings of injury that may remain even after we have said, "I forgive." We can refuse to avenge ourselves, refuse any idea of getting even, refuse the idea of eye for eye and tooth for tooth. These responses are dead to us.

We will later consider Ephesians 4:26. It may give helpful insight here as well if we modify it slightly to read, *In your grievance, do not sin...do not let the sun go down on your unforgiveness.*

We determine to *act* in forgiveness. Even if we don't feel it, we determine that our "do" shall be the do of forgiveness. We will speak no word—neither by gesture, tone or implication—to convey the slightest hint of hurt, injustice, or injury. Kindness will be our only response. If the mind continues to battle with feelings of having been wronged, the face and hands and tongue will never betray it. No one shall know it. We will enter into forgiveness through the doorway of behavior and conduct, even if our minds, perhaps even our hearts, are slow to follow. When we continue occasionally to be plagued with contrary thoughts and feelings, we refuse to nurse and cherish them. Treating such thoughts as an enemy not a lover, we banish them from our presence.

The final phrase of Ephesians 4:26 puts this strategy into perspective: "Give no opportunity to the devil." By *acting* in forgiveness, and *forbidding* ourselves to nurse animosities, we allow the enemy no foothold. We will not let our mental gardens be planted with seeds of bitterness. He can plant no seeds without our permission, and that permission we disdain to give.

Thus, though we may still struggle, by conduct and behavior we refuse to give refuge or safe-harbor to ongoing feelings of offence or animosity. They may keep trying to enter, but we deny them residence.

> Repay no one evil for evil. (Romans 12:17
> Never avenge yourselves. (Romans 12:19)
> Turn to forgive and comfort. (2 Corinthians 2:7)
> As the Lord has forgiven you, so you also must forgive. (Colossians 3:13)
> See to it that no root of bitterness spring up. (Hebrews 12:15)

56. Avoid the Shallow and Hypocritical Who Do Not Live Their Faith

We previously examined the commands to avoid those living in obvious sin, both believers and non-believers. Paul's description of those we must keep clear of in 2 Timothy 3 are unambiguous—profligates, haters of good, treacherous, fierce, abusive, those swollen with conceit. Why would we want to be around such behavior? Not allowing the habits of such people to rub off on us is a no-brainer.

Paul's conclusion to the passage, however, contains a shocking addition. We are also to avoid those who "hold the form of religion but deny the power of it." Suddenly Paul has thrown us a curveball. He is not talking about *sin*, as such, but spiritual shallowness and hypocrisy. He is talking about those who play games with religion. It is what we have previously called "pretense Christianity."

Two kinds of hypocrisy infect Christianity. In the first sense, we are all hypocrites. We are engaged in a daily battle between flesh and spirit. Sometimes we don't do very well. Christlikeness may be the eternal objective, but while we remain in the flesh we are fallen human creatures who sin and who continue to sin. Picking ourselves up, with God's help we continue on. This is the Christian life. Our human weakness, flaws and all, is built into what Christianity is. So in the sense that we do not live our faith perfectly, that we are striving to be something we're not, we might be called *admitted* hypocrites. We're not pretending. I know what I am. I hold my hand to the charge and say, "You're absolutely right. I am not what I hope someday to be. God be merciful to me a sinner."

This is not what Jesus means when he uses the word "hypocrite." He is talking about *intentional* hypocrisy—hiding behind a shell of religiosity, *pretending* to be what we're not. He's talking about those whose goal is not righteousness but who only want to look like "good Christians." It is what Paul describes as "holding the *form* of religion."

Many of the world's "religions" are almost entirely made up of the outward forms and rituals of such sham religiosity. But what we have called "cultural Christianity" has also become a breeding ground for powerless pretentious pretended faith.

Motive is everything. We are not called to judge. We are simply called to quiet attentiveness to the motives swirling about us. Then we are instructed to associate with those with whom we share the goal of Christlikeness. When I sense the shallow "form of religion" with no motive but to dress up worldly priorities in spiritual clothes, it is time to quietly seek more command-helpful associations in my spiritual journey. I am not seeking perfection in relationships. I simply choose to ally myself with imperfect brothers and sisters (admitted hypocrites like myself) who are moving in the same direction.

The several "sin-avoidance" commands we have considered may be among the most difficult in this book to obey without fanfare or judgment. We are to avoid immorality and hypocrisy *within our hearts and minds*. We are not commanded to tell anyone where we think they are wrong, to make a display of our convictions, or condemn anyone else's life or Christian walk. Most such avoidance will be silent. We simply turn the other way. We choose our associations carefully. We try to be prudent about the circumstances we allow ourselves to be part of. These are not "world change" commands. We are not called to soapbox preaching about hypocrisy any more than about lifestyle sins, drunkenness, or atheism. We are only called to avoid those whose lifestyles are defined by *intentional* violations of scriptural virtue. Love remains.

In the last days...men will be lovers of self...lovers of pleasure rather than lovers of God, holding the form of religion but denying the power of it. Avoid such people. (2 Timothy 3:1-2, 4-5)
Renounce irreligion. (Titus 2:12)
Do not deceive your heart with vain religion. (James 1:26)
Do not pretend to have faith without works. (James 2:17)
If we say we have fellowship with him while we walk in darkness, we lie and do not walk according to the truth. (1 John 1:6)

---

57. Control Anger

Paul's words in Ephesians 4:26 are unlike anything we read elsewhere in the New Testament. The biblical writers are usually unequivocal—*Do this...don't do that.* They give no quarter to waffling, fence-sitting, or excuse-making. Most commands are blunt and forceful. The delineation between obedience and disobedience is clear and precise.

Yet in this intriguing command Paul seems to say that it is okay to get angry...just don't *stay* angry for too long: *Be angry, but do not sin; do not let the sun go down on your anger, and give no opportunity to the devil.* It sounds like Paul is endorsing anger.

In one sense, I positively love this verse. It recognizes the predicament in which we find ourselves—that our flesh *does* blow it, that it is not always a sin to react with human emotion. Then we have to regroup, ask forgiveness if necessary, make amends, give the enemy no chance to plant seeds of animosity, deal with what was perhaps an outburst, an ungracious word, and "not let the sun go down" without wiping the relational slate clean.

We have repeatedly noted the distinction between two kinds of commands. There are *commands of thought and emotion* that we cannot always control with the flip of a switch—envy, fear, anxiety, impatience, etc. Then there are *commands of behavior* which address conduct and habit patterns that we *can* control—sexual purity, drunkenness, associating with the immoral, obedience to parents, showing kindness, etc.

In the case of the former, we recognize that the "sin" does not come with the thought, but with what we do with it. Do we *yield* to thoughts and emotions that are contrary to Christlikeness? Do we allow them to influence our behavior and conduct? Or do we reject those contrary feelings, and keep the seat of action focused on obeying in spite of what we might think or feel? The question is: Which kind of sin is anger? Or is it a sin at all? Is anger an emotion we cannot always control (like anxiety)? Or is it a response which lies in the strict realm of obedience or disobedience? Can we *control* anger?

The moment we probe into such questions we come back to the words of Jesus. He paints a very different picture than Paul's. Not only is anger a sin, he says, it is a very serious sin: *I say to you that every one who is angry with his brother shall be liable to judgment...whoever says, "You fool" shall be liable to the hell of fire."* (Matthew 5:22)

So did Paul misspeak? If the words of Jesus are our guide, we have to admit that possibility. Yet we cannot say for *certain* that Paul was wrong. Because the second phrase of the verse is full of insight. His words give encouragement that there is hope in the midst of human weakness. This is an important truth. In my weakness, anger will rise up within me. But God provides a remedy—I have it in my power to make it right before the sun goes down. I cannot ignore Jesus' words. My anger *is* a sin. I must admit that fact. When I give in to anger, I have sinned. No pretending that Paul is endorsing anger here. Now, look to the sun. It is still high in the sky. Don't let too much time pass before allowing repentance and forgiveness to heal whatever breach my anger has caused.

That we must regard anger as a sin not a justifiable emotion is confirmed by what Paul says further along in this passage: *Let no evil talk come out of your mouths, but only such as is good for edifying...Let all bitterness and wrath and anger...be put away from you...and be kind to one another, tenderhearted, forgiving one another...*We find no loophole for "justified anger." If we would understand Paul's heart in the matter of anger, I think we do well to take this passage in its entirety, with his climax as the final word: *Let all...anger...be put away from you...and be kind...tenderhearted, forgiving.*

Do not let the sun go down on your anger, and give no opportunity to the devil. (Ephesians 4:26)
Let all bitterness and wrath and anger and clamor and slander be put away from you, with all malice, and be kind to one another, tenderhearted, forgiving one another. (Ephesians 4:32-32)
Put away also all these: anger, wrath, malice, slander, and foul talk. (Colossians 3:8)
A bishop must not be quick tempered (Titus 1:7) Let every man be slow to anger. (James 1:19)

58. Don't Judge

One of the most striking aspects of the command against judgment is that the entire Old Testament image of God was as a fierce and unyielding Judge. When Jesus said, "Judge not," he was not merely laying down a prescription for human conduct and relationships, at the same time he was wiping the slate clean of that Old Testament image. God is your *Father*, he proclaimed, not an unforgiving judge. This command, therefore, contains far-reaching theological implications that stretch into the unknowable domain of eternity. How will God ultimately deal with sin—as a Judge, or as a Father?

In reflecting on this command that is so central to Christianity, I find little additional insight coming to mind beyond what I wrote previously in considering Jesus' command not to judge. I therefore quote a portion of that selection here.

"Many of the Commands are implied, but this is a direct, clear, forceful, and unyielding command—*Judge not.* The Lord's words in Luke 6:37 are absolutely total and consuming—*Don't judge, don't condemn. Instead forgive.* Matthew adds the pithy image of trying to take a speck out of someone else's eye when there are blind spots in our own life the size of logs.

"But it is so *easy*, so natural, enjoyable, and satisfying to the flesh to notice those blind spots in everyone else...They jump out for all the world to see—those annoying mannerisms, those obvious examples of self-centeredness, those immaturities...that propensity always to talk about oneself, the hogging of the limelight...that habit of interrupting, of having to be right, of always getting the last word...

"All these traits are so *obvious*. How can they not see them?

"Imagine the eye-opening shock if we truly saw ourselves as others see us. All these little specks we see in others...they detect the same things in us—and more besides!...

"When Jesus says that we will be judged and forgiven by the same measure with which we judge and forgive others, he is not saying that God will *refuse* to forgive us if we judge others harshly. He is merely stating a fact of life—everyone by nature judges others more harshly than they do themselves. Turn that principle around, he says. Look to your *own* sins and weaknesses and selfishnesses first. Show leniency and understanding and forgiveness to others, and lo and behold...you will find that same spirit of generosity and kindness coming back to you.

"In truth, however, this principle represents a basic tenet of first-grade spirituality. When we move into graduate level Christlikeness, the weakness of others ceases to move the compass needle of our thoughts a hair's breadth. We choose to see those whose paths cross ours as God sees them—by looking *into* them. We choose to behold not what they may be now, but what God is making of them. We do not focus on the outer shell of weak humanity, but rather upon the radiant seed of eternal God-ness struggling to come to life within them...

"As for ourselves, we turn the searchlight of our prayers inward, toward no one but ourselves. We ask for the illumination of the Holy Spirit to give us sight to see our *own* blind spots, that we may walk humbly before God, and before our brothers and sisters, fully aware what small and fragile and weak and self-centered creatures we are. With David, the prayers of the 19th and 51st Psalms breathe silently from our lips: *Cleanse me from my hidden faults...Wash me thoroughly from my iniquity, and cleanse me from my sin...purge me...Create in me a clean heart, O God, and renew a right spirit within me.*" (*The Commands of Jesus*, p. 107)

Do not judge another man. (Romans 2:1)
Let us no more pass judgment on one another. (Romans 14:13)
Do not judge your neighbor. (James 4:12)

---

59. Associate With the Lowly

The Bible's commands are so wonderfully diverse...and often unexpected. From the lofty heights of *Yield to God* and *Grow in righteousness*, we crash to earth with such unbelievable practicality as, "Associate with the lowly." Truly, the biblical writers leave the self no place to hide. No facet of attitude, character, or conduct is left untouched by the demand of Christlikeness.

The opening line of introduction from *James*, likely the first surviving document of Christendom, is breathtaking and profound: "James, a servant of God and of the Lord Jesus Christ." When we observe how Paul began his letters ("Paul, an apostle"), James' humble and unassuming words are poignantly wonderful: *James, a servant...*

Nothing more. Just a servant. They focus James' desire to *serve* God by *obeying* the commands his brother had laid out in his teaching. James' entire letter exudes this tone of humility. His words about showing no partiality carry all the more weight realizing that he is a living example of the very principle he is speaking about.

While Paul's letters are full of theology, *James* is simple, straightforward, and so beautifully in harmony with the practicality of the Sermon on the Mount. It is as though the two brothers, Jesus and James, thought alike and saw things alike—practically.

Jesus says *Give to him that asks...lend money...agree with your adversary before he takes you to court...give to beggars...let him have your cloak as well.*

James echoes his brother with: *Bridle your tongue...visit orphans and widows...be slow to speak...do good works...don't speak evil against your brothers...ask for wisdom...don't swear...pray for one another.*

It is a wonderful expansion of the Lord's message for a new era. James brings obedience to the Lord's commands into daily life.

The Lord's brother, then, ever the practicalist, sets the stage for today's down-to-earth command that provides such an illuminating window into character. The command against partiality essentially reduces to: *Where do your eyes turn?* To whom do you look first—to the powerful and wealthy and honored, or to the weak and poor and dishonored?

Let's get more practical yet. Who would you rather spend time with or engage in conversation—the cool, hip, "in", good-looking, intelligent, articulate, winsome, likable life of the party whom everyone admires and wants to be around...or the annoying, shabby, smelly, rude, self-centered, obnoxious, loudmouth that everyone tries to avoid?

James sets up this contrast in the second chapter of his letter with an image that is as contemporary and relevant as your next Bible study or worship service. When you walk into a room, where are your attentions drawn? Again, *where do your eyes turn?* Or, as James has it, when two men walk into a gathering—which he contrasts as a rich man and a poor man—who is shown the most attention? Again, let's get personal—whom do you walk over to and invite to sit next to you—the personable man or woman everyone loves...or the annoying bore no one wants to be caught dead with?

"Show no partiality" reduces to this: Don't allow yourself to be partial to and drawn to the external lures of appearance, wealth, and status. Give all men and women equally of your attention, your honor, your kindness, and your love.

The subtlety of this command probes deeper and deeper the more layers of the onion we peel off. Who is *the least of these* whom Jesus would seek out? *Show no partiality* is another way of articulating a familiar truth, that in the ways of the world "God is no respecter of persons."

Do nothing from partiality. (1 Timothy 5:21)
Show no partiality...if you show partiality, you commit sin. (James 2:1, 9)

60. Place No Stumbling Blocks In the Way of Another's Faith

The term "stumbling block" is familiar to most Christians. We use it in a variety of ways to indicate anything we do or say that in some way hinders or blocks or impedes or "stumbles" the spiritual growth of another. Paul's use of the term was very specific. He used it exclusively about mature Christians not stumbling the less mature with "liberties" of faith—specifically in reference to laws and customs pertaining to food and eating. If a mature Christian considered himself no longer bound by Jewish laws about eating meat or food offered to idols, for example, Paul would tell him not to flaunt that liberty in front of those younger and weaker Christians who might still be struggling to incorporate aspects of the old law into their new faith. Today Paul might say, "Don't make a big deal of your liberty. Don't push your freedoms onto others. Don't speak of them. Give the weak time to grow into mature faith." Theologians may analyze it along different lines, but that seems the general gist of Paul's thoughts in Romans 14 and 1 Corinthians 8.

This is fine as far as it goes. We are deeply indebted to Paul for the principle of the stumbling block. Yet his analysis contains hints of condescension and self-righteousness. It implies that he, Paul, and those who think like him, are automatically strong and mature alongside "weaker" brethren who happen to view food regulations differently. This is exactly how Paul viewed Peter and Barnabas at Antioch—he, though a younger Christian, thought himself strong and mature and justified in publicly exposing their "weakness." This is a flimsy foundation upon which to base the important principle of stumbling blocks because it so easily admits the prideful assumption of *my* maturity alongside the weaknesses of others. This is a dangerous basis for any doctrine. It is dangerous for us. It was dangerous for Paul. His flagrant failure to practice what he preached at Antioch, as recounted in *Galatians,* placed the stumbling block of the "public rebuke" into the lexicon of church practice, where it has remained for 2,000 years.

Though the principle of the stumbling block began with food regulations, we recognize its expansion to include anything that hinders another's growth. When humility, not a vaunted sense of my maturity, is the foundation, then this command illuminates a deep truth of human relationship. That is simply that we are all on unique and personal pilgrimages toward Christlikeness. We cannot assume that God's methods and timetable and specific revelations in our lives will apply to everyone.

As we have said about many principles of faith, stumbling blocks come in all sizes and shapes. The tiniest word or act, seemingly insignificant, may be seen or heard and stumble another in ways we cannot predict. Doctrine remains a huge potential stumbling block today. It should not come between Christians. But it does. Paul is right in saying that doctrine is a stumbling block because of weakness and immaturity of faith. But it may be weakness and immaturity on *both* sides. It is not so black and white as Paul makes it. As we have seen, Paul had his blind spots too. It is our natural tendency to assume that we are the strong. This was Paul's assumption too. What if in fact I have it backwards? What if in a certain instance *I* am the weak who does not perceive full truth?

This is one of the reasons I do not speak overmuch about certain perspectives I hold that may differ with the doctrinal views of some friends and brother and sister Christians. It is not because I consider myself more mature alongside my weaker brethren. Heavens no! I keep my own counsel because I realize that I am still growing and do not see full truth. My brothers will see truth that I do not see. Like Paul, I have blind spots too. I am not so concerned about my maturity being a stumbling block...I want to make certain that I stumble no one by my *weakness.*

Decide never to put a stumbling-block or hindrance in the way of a brother. (Romans 14:13)
If a brother is being injured by what you eat, you are no longer walking in love. (Romans 14:15)
It is right not to...do anything that makes your brother stumble. (Romans 14:21)
Take care lest that this liberty... somehow become a stumbling-block to the weak. (1 Cor. 8:9)

"THE ATHENS COMMANDS"

Develop Wise and Gracious Habits

DAILY HABITS THAT REVEAL INNER CHARACTER

The image of "St. Paul Preaching at Athens," immortalized in the classic tapestries of Raphael, shows Paul arguing and debating religion with the philosophers of Greece in the Areopagus. That is the image that comes to mind when we think of Paul introducing the gospel of Jesus Christ to the ancient Greek civilization. Paul's sojourn in Athens is recounted in the latter half of Acts 17. It came during Paul's second missionary journey between his time in Thessalonica and Corinth.

Little is known about Paul's time in Athens beyond the famous speech recorded in Acts which begins, "Men of Athens, I perceive that in every way you are very religious." Yet as always, we discover between the lines an intriguing fact that may reveal interesting details about Paul's priorities.

Paul and his companions had essentially been run out of Thessalonica on a rail. They eventually came to Athens where, concerned for the brethren they had so hastily left behind, Paul wrote the first letter to a single church to flow from his pen. That is the letter we know as *1 Thessalonians.* Obviously many more such letters would follow. Then Paul placed the letter in the hands of Timothy and Silas to be delivered to Thessalonica. Paul, meanwhile, waited in Athens. Why he stayed behind and sent them back with the letter alone is a mystery, unless it was simply to avoid creating another uproar in the city. Eventually the two men returned to Paul with news from the Thessalonian church, which then prompted *2 Thessalonians.*

While Paul's stay in Athens is remembered to history for its apologetic to the intellectual world of Greek culture, the letter Paul wrote while there, in a sense, tells a different story. *1 Thessalonians,* too, is remembered to history primarily for its second coming passage in Chapters 4 and 5 as we have already discussed. Neither an intellectual Christian apologetic nor the *parousia*, however, represent what Paul chiefly attempted to communicate in this all-important early letter to flow from his pen.

He was most concerned simply about how Christians live their faith in daily life through habits of behavior and relationship. "We were willing to be left behind at Athens alone, and we sent Timothy..." Paul writes in 1 Thessalonians 3:1. He then goes on to exhort the Thessalonians largely with practicalities not theology.

Abound in love to one another and to all men. (3:12)

We beseech and exhort you in the Lord...how you ought to live. (4:1)

Abstain from immorality. (4:3)

You have been taught by God to love one another. (4:9)

Aspire to live quietly. (4:11)

Mind your own affairs. (4:11)

Work with your hands. (4:11)

Respect those who labor among you and...esteem them very highly. (5:12-13)

Be at peace among yourselves. (5:13)

Encourage the fainthearted. (5:14)

Help the weak. (5:14)

Be patient with them all. (5:14)

Always seek to do good to one another and to all. (5:15)

Rejoice always, pray constantly, give thanks in all circumstances. (5:16-18)

Hold fast what is good. (5:21)

Abstain from every form of evil. (5:22)

Here we find nearly all the fruits of the spirits, the entire "practical gospel" of Paul, laid out to the Thessalonians during Paul's solitary sojourn in Athens while he waited for the return of Timothy and Silas.

DAILY HABITS THAT REVEAL INNER CHARACTER

61. Conduct yourself becomingly.

62. Be courteous and full of grace toward all.

63. Do not insist on your own way.

64. Don't yield to or allow suspicions to fester.

65. Live without guile.

66. Do not be irritable or resentful.

67. Do not be foolish.

68. Mind your own business.

69. Give generously.

70. Owe no one anything.

61. Conduct Yourself Becomingly

The translation of Romans 13:13 is full of interest. It contains relational significance literally every time we encounter another person, whether friend, family member or stranger, whether the meeting is a chance encounter or a lifelong relationship. Paul's words, however, are enigmatic and difficult to pinpoint with precision. The RSV renders it, "Let us conduct ourselves *becomingly*." The King James translates the pivotal word *honestly*, the NIV *decently*. Though it is a somewhat old-fashioned term, "becomingly" seems best to capture the wide scope of the nuances implied.

The Greek EUSCHEMONOS carries several shades of meaning—graceful, seemly, comely, honorable. Perhaps "grace" comes as close as any other definition. We usually invest grace in our minds with its theological associations. Even more important may be the "gracefulness" of our carriage, demeanor, speech, conduct, and habits in the world of men. Observers and those with whom we relate as we go about our daily activities may know nothing about what we *believe* concerning grace from the book of *Galatians*. But they will be *very* aware of our deportment, carriage, and behavior. In most circumstances, everyone notices a man or woman of grace, dignity, and courtesy in their midst. In a time when virtues of character are disappearing from our culture, the *grace of seemliness* stands out as a refreshing reminder that goodness, kindness, humility, and selflessness still exist in the world. The world may not always know whence springs the root of such grace. We know, however, that it is the *grace of Christ* shining through—not the grace of theology, but the grace of comeliness.

It is easy to assume that grace and dignity of carriage are inborn, having more to do with looks and personality than chosen behavior. This is what we might call the Grace Kelly and Cary Grant syndrome. Because an individual is handsome or beautiful, stands tall, and carries himself or herself with a gentle and reserved demeanor, we assume these to be the reasons we sense an elusive quality of grace. But it is not the externals at all. That same grace of "becomingness" is available to all. More than that, it is commanded of us even if we do not have the stature of Cary Grant or the looks of Grace Kelly. Seemliness is born in behavior not beauty.

Finding apt defining definitions points us in many helpful directions that all originate not in inborn personality but in chosen habits and behavior. We might begin with *reserved humility*—not thinking too highly of myself nor pushing myself to the forefront. Seemliness is willing to stand back, out of the spotlight, content, humble, soft-spoken, and at peace. We might also identify the habit of finding ways to *gently put others at their ease*. This I can do anytime, anywhere—the upbuilding word of reassurance, the kindly gesture, the cheerful smile, the gentle touch, the affirmation of personhood, the soothing of anxiety. Then, too, seemliness is ever conscious of opportunities to *bestow on others the dignity of honor and respect*. Few gifts are as powerful as to convey to another individual—man, woman, child...young or old...happy or hurting...brimming with confidence or floundering in self-doubt—I believe in you, you are special to God and to me, I honor you for the person you are. We will make anyone's day to whom we convey the unmistakable message, "There is no one in the world I would rather spend this minute or this hour with than you. I respect you. I value your thoughts, your feelings, your aspirations, your heartaches."

All these, along with simple polite, smiling, gentle, gracious, soft-spoken courtesy, combine to exude a grace and comeliness in our manner that people will *feel*, even if but through a chance encounter.

Let us conduct ourselves becomingly. (Romans 13:13)

[Love]...doth not behave itself unseemly. (1 Cor 13:5, KJV)

Whatever is true...honorable...pure...lovely...gracious...think about these things. (Philippians 4:8)

Bid the older women to be reverent in behavior. (Titus 2:3)

62. Be Courteous and Full of Grace Toward All.

What we call common courtesy represents one of the greatest yet overlooked fruits of spiritual maturity. It is not that courtesy alone implies spiritual maturity. Clearly more is involved in maturity than a single virtue. But the reverse is always true: Spiritual maturity *will* imply courtesy.

Henry Drummond relates courtesy to the outflowing of love. Love, he says, simply cannot behave in an uncourteous manner. We have quoted his words before, but they are so important they bear repeating. "*Courtesy.* This is Love in society, Love in relation to etiquette," Drummond writes. "'Love doth not behave itself unseemly.' Politeness has been defined as love in trifles. Courtesy is said to be love in little things...Love *cannot* behave itself unseemly...The gentle man cannot in the nature of things do an ungentle, an ungentlemanly thing." (Henry Drummond, *The Greatest Thing in the World.*)

In fact, the expression "common courtesy" we often hear is not really accurate. There is nothing *common* about courtesy whatever. It is a high and exalted virtue that displays one's respect and honor and love for others. In truth, it is not common enough.

We're not talking about mere manners of etiquette—which fork to use, whether to set the napkin to the right or left of the plate, how to hold a coffee cup, or how to delicately consume soup without slurping. The courtesy of Christlike grace strikes much deeper than such surface indicators. Manners may be part of it. Yet these are largely defined by society. In many times and cultures, eating with one's fingers was the norm and a burp was the accepted sign of respect for one's hostess. Yet imagine such practices in a high-society dining room today. The courteous individual will be attentive to the manners appropriate to his particular time and place and circumstances. Though we recognize the changeable nature of the specifics, respect for others implies fitting in with *their* culturally accepted code of manners.

Manners themselves, however, only represent the first step toward courteous and graceful demeanor. Looking beyond what we might call societal etiquette, we discover an intrinsic connection between honor and courtesy. Commands 51 and 62 flow out of the same source. Courtesy is the outward manifestation of honor. When we honor, we will behave with courtesy. Respect requires courtesy or it is no respect at all.

To honor another means honoring *their* standards of manners and etiquette, *their* priorities, *their* values, what makes *them* comfortable. What in my behavior will put *another* at ease. That I will courteously try to do.

Courtesy makes it all about others, not about me. I fit in and flow with what is considerate to those around me. My speech is soft, my matter deferential, my conduct respectful, my gestures and expressions and mannerisms gracious. I deflect notice, not draw it. Nothing in my deportment calls attention to *me* or draws eyes in *my* direction, except it be my kindness. Customs and fashions may change. Selflessness and humility are virtues of eternity. Courtesy is simply putting others first in society. All these habits by which I comport myself and which define the carriage of my personality and relationships might be summed up by the word graciousness.

Hear what associations Webster's 1828 Dictionary likens to *grace* and its associated adjective *gracious*: "Favor; good will; kindness; disposition to oblige...a liberal disposition...meekness, humility, patience...that in manner, deportment, or language which renders it appropriate and agreeable; suitableness, elegance with appropriate dignity...Favorable, kind, friendly...benevolent, merciful...expressing kindness and favor."

Remind them...to be gentle, and to show perfect courtesy toward all men. (Titus 3:1-2)

63. Do Not Insist On Your Own Way

We all *want* our own way. We would hardly be human if we didn't. Wanting our own way is in the nature of things. If we would live in the region of love, however, which Paul lays out for us in 1 Corinthians 13, we choose not to *insist* on it. The word "insist" in this command is the sticking point, the stumbling-block to the flesh.

In a sense, the practical reality of this command embedded in the heart of the "love chapter" to the Corinthians simply states in a different way what is at the heart of all the commands—self-denial, relinquishment of my priorities, putting God and others ahead of myself. This emphasis is laid upon us in dozens of ways by all the commands. Yet Paul's singular word use here pokes and prods, digging to loosen the scab hiding my reluctance to lay my self entirely on the altar. By the many subtleties you bring into your relationships, your conversations, your mannerisms, even your doctrinal beliefs, says Paul, do not *insist* on your own way. When you insist on insisting on your own way, you are not walking in love.

This strikes home in a thousand ways—from discussions on matters of scriptural interpretation and belief to which direction to hang the toilet paper. In how many ways through the course of a day do we insist on our own way without realizing it? Not only do we ignore this command all too easily and invisibly, we do so purposefully. We justify doing so because what we have insisted on is the "right" way. It is not difficult to obey this command in little things. When two people arrive at a door at the same time, it is an easy matter to yield and defer with a smile. It costs us nothing not to insist on our own way. Indeed, we are rewarded for letting the other go first with the smile and good feeling we receive in return.

That's easy. But abdicating the need to be right when discussing ideas is not so appealing. The next time you are involved in a contentious debate over politics, abortion, a presidential election, or a matter of difficult doctrinal ambiguity in Scripture such as hell, the atonement, or predestination...how easy is it then not to insist on your own way? Convinced that I am *right* and that opposing viewpoints are *wrong*, does not truth demand that I "insist on my own way." We tell ourselves that it is *right* to insist that our viewpoint is the correct one. Truth is at stake. We must stand up for truth.

I think Paul would reply, "Let me show you a more excellent way. Love does not insist on its own way. Love is willing to lay down the desire to prove itself right. Whether you actually *are* right is beside the point. Don't insist on it. Lay it down. Let the discussion go on without you. In a verbal battle, let the other fellow win. The call upon your life is not to get the last word in an argument, but to love. And love does not insist on its own way."

Insistence in itself is a contentious verbal habit, a relationship killer, an indication of self-centeredness at the core of discussion not a love of truth at all. No one wants to be around an argumentative, importune, remonstrative windbag who has an opinion on every subject, who believes he is right about every topic, and who can out-talk everyone else in the room by persistent insistence that his or her points of view are the final word.

The antidote to insistence is the simplest one in the world. Silence. Just stop talking. This may be the easiest command of all to obey. With my mouth closed, it is impossible to insist on my own way.

Love does not insist on its own way. (1 Corinthians 13:5)

Let every may be quick to hear, slow to speak, slow to anger. (James 1:19)

If any man thinks he is religious, and does not bridle his tongue but deceives his heart, this man's religion is vain. (James 1:26)

The wisdom from above is...open to reason. (James 3:17)

64. Don't Be Suspicious

This is one of those commands listed in Appendix 2 as an "implied" command which we infer from the actual words. What Paul says in 1 Timothy 6:4 is, "If anyone teaches otherwise...he knows nothing; he has a morbid craving for...base suspicions." The passage is lengthy and lists other attributes of those whom Paul says "know nothing." Such mini-tirades against those whom Paul judges to be false teachers are common in his writings. Sometimes we have to take these with a grain of salt. In other instances, however, we pull important truths out of such passages. This is one of those. The attributes Paul enumerates here to be avoided are notable because we find so many of them prevalent in the church: craving for controversy, dissension, envy, wrangling, disputes about words. It sounds like our last home Bible study!

Among these cancerous tendencies is the curious poisoner of relationship *suspicion*. It is a poison as lethal as gossip, and intrinsically related. Paul states it in slightly different terms in 1 Corinthians 13:6, "Love does not rejoice at wrong." This exactly describes the root of suspicion—relishing in someone else's wrongdoing. When was the last time you were privy to gossip about someone in your church or circle of friends concerning something honorable? We don't gossip about the good. We gossip about the low and unseemly. That's why Paul calls them "base" suspicions—because suspicions are always low. No one spreads rumors and suspicions about acts of Christlikeness.

Those suspicions that feed the cancer most vigorously are those we nurture and enjoy. Nothing is more delightful than sharing them with another set of itchy ears. Yet suspicion ruins relationship. Even if completely untrue, when we allow suspicion to take root, it sows seeds of mistrust, secrecy, dishonor. Our relational gardens fill with weeds rather than flowers. Suspicion eats away at the fabric of relationships. Many friendships are destroyed by the tiniest of suspicions that one of the individuals allows to take hold.

About a year ago a friend of many years told me a "secret" about another friend of even longer duration, a man, recently passed away, whom I had admired above nearly all men, and whom I knew on a far more intimate basis than my gossip-peddling friend. It was a terrible secret with far-reaching implications. I was stunned, but also offended that she had spoken with seeming knowledge about an incident from forty years before about which she had no first hand information. What she passed on to me was little more than hearsay. I then had a choice. I could embrace, harbor, and "receive" the revelation—and thus allow it to be planted in my mind as a base suspicion. Had I done so, it would have poisoned one of the important relationships of my spiritual life. I chose instead to reject it. I chose to disbelieve the gossip as a lie of the enemy. Having been closely involved with the principle players in the incident related, I had compelling reasons for believing it exactly that—a lie. And that's where it stands. I harbor no suspicion about my late friend. He stands as highly in my memory as ever, a man of God whom I honor.

But what, it may be argued, if it *is* true? Some suspicions are indeed true. Of course. Yet I am wary of inserting myself into areas that are none of my business. This is none of my business, nor the business of the one who relayed the information. In my opinion, she sinned against the man involved and against me. Her sin was not for being wrong, but for engaging in gossip that was none of her business. She let a loose tongue spread a base rumor. The truth or falsehood of the thing is in God's hands to deal appropriately with as need be. I am commanded to honor all men, and to reject gossip and suspicion.

Don't yield to suspicious thoughts, or allow suspicions to fester.

If anyone teaches otherwise...he knows nothing; he has a morbid craving for...base suspicions. (1 Timothy 6:4)

Love does not rejoice at wrong, but rejoices in the right. (1 Corinthians 13:6)

Finally, brethren, whatever is true, whatever is honorable, whatever is just, whatever is pure, whatever is lovely, whatever is gracious, if there is any excellence, if there is anything worthy of praise, think about these things. (Philippians 4:8)

65. Live Without Guile

Guilelessness is one of the most intriguing of all the New Testament virtues, possibly because guile is not a word we use in everyday conversation. We know generally what it means. But its subtleties and nuances mostly escape us.

Again we look to the original Webster of 1828 to provide insight: "Guile...craft; cunning; artifice; duplicity; deceit...to disguise craftily...intended to deceive." And: "Guileless...artless; frank; sincere; honest...simplicity."

Guile at its root is duplicity—having mixed motives which we cunningly keep hidden from view. It is not merely pretending to be what we're not, it's the intentional hiding of motives we don't want seen for the purpose of deception. Guile is not reserved for criminals or those trying to hide moral and ethical sins. More subtle forms of guile creep into our behavior and thought-patterns without us even knowing it. Guile is first cousin to hypocrisy, putting on a demeanor of pleasant respectability and spiritual maturity to hide those aspects of our true character we don't want seen.

The memorable encounter between Jesus and Nathaniel in the first chapter of John gives us our New Testament introduction to this somewhat cryptic word that reveals such an all-important spiritual virtue. There Jesus said, "Behold, an Israelite indeed, in whom is no guile!" What a wonderful quality for the Lord to observe in a man! It is the very opposite of what he saw when he encountered the Pharisees. Their entire nature was guile personified. When he looked into Nathaniel's face, he saw reflected out into the world exactly what was in his heart.

At its most basic, guile is secrecy. Its opposite is transparency. Guile dwells in the shadows. Guilelessness lives in the light. Is our innermost soul transparent to God, to others, and to ourselves? When others are with us, do they meet the *real* us, or do we present a different face to the world than what we are inside? And who are we really trying to hide from with guile but ourselves? Transparency begins in the mirror.

Being without guile does not imply constantly *talking* about ourselves, *sharing* every tidbit and personality quirk, *confessing* every tiny sin, being transparent by being completely self-absorbed. It doesn't require "opening up" and "spilling our guts" every five minutes. It simply means having nothing to hide. When Nathaniel and Jesus walked toward one another and met face to face, Nathaniel didn't *say* anything. Jesus read guilelessness in the transparency of his countenance. The circumspect, quiet, humble, selfless individual in your group may be a man or woman of less guile than the one constantly talking about himself. Guile has little to do with constant talk, it has everything to do with transparency of character.

Run through the list of virtues Paul commands of us in Philippians 4:8. Every one represents the opposite of the two most recent commands, guile and suspicion—truth, honor, justice, purity, loveliness, grace, excellence.

These are virtues of light! Guile and suspicion dwell in darkness. Neither can dwell in the heart of one living guilelessly within the reality of Philippians 4:8.

Be honest, sincere, and transparent, and never superficially religious.

I would have you wise as to what is good and guileless as to what is evil. (Romans 16:19)

We commend ourselves...by...genuine love, truthful speech. (2 Corinthians 6:7)

Whatever is true...honorable...just...pure...lovely...gracious, if there is any excellence, if there is anything worthy of praise, think about these things. (Philippians 4:8)

The wisdom from above is first pure...gentle...without uncertainty or insincerity. (James 3:17)

Put away...all guile and insincerity. (1 Peter 2:1)

He that would love life and see good days, let him keep his tongue from evil and his lips from speaking guile. (1 Peter 3:10)

He who says he is in the light and hates his brother is in the darkness still. (1 John 2:9)

66. Do Not Be Irritable or Resentful

The familiar words of 1 Corinthians 13:5 provide an intriguing example where different translations render a passage of Scripture with distinct shades of meaning. The particular phrase of interest to us here reads, *Love... "is not irritable or resentful,"* in the RSV. The NIV has it, *Love... "is not easily angered."* Finally, the KJV presents the same passage as, *Love... "is not easily provoked."* It is clear that all three shed enormous light on this often overlooked attribute of love.

As we discussed earlier, Paul elsewhere seems to condone anger with his "do not let the sun go down on your anger." Here, however, he makes clear that anger is *not* an expression of love. Even the word *"easily* provoked" offers no wiggle room for those who would excuse their anger. However, the "easily" does not appear in the Greek. The phrase simply reads, "is not provoked/angered."

The RSV's word choice gets under our skin and digs at our flesh like a festering splinter. *Irritable...*what an incredibly self-exposing word! *So* many things irritate me. If I let myself, I could find a hundred annoyances to irritate me from morning till night. Yet what does this say about me? If Paul is right, it says that every single one of those irritations, if I allow myself to brood on it, will banish love from my heart. When an irritation rises, love has flown. Love cannot co-exist with irritation, resentment, or anger. If irritation, resentment, or anger are stewing within me, love is gone. It's that simple. The point is so important it bears re-emphasis—brooding on our angers and irritations, allowing people or circumstances to provoke silent annoyances and resentments, will expel love from our heart. If I would be a man characterized by love, then I must instead banish anger, irritability, and resentment. I must not allow myself to be provoked.

"The next ingredient is a very remarkable one: Good Temper. 'Love is not easily provoked.' Nothing could be more striking than to find this here. We are inclined to look upon bad temper as a very harmless weakness. We speak of it as a mere infirmity of nature, a family failing, a matter of temperament, not a thing to take into very serious account in estimating a man's character. And yet here, right in the heart of this analysis of love, it finds a place; and the Bible again returns to condemn it as one of the most destructive elements in human nature.

"The peculiarity of ill temper is that it is the vice of the virtuous. It is often the one blot on an otherwise noble character. You know men who are all but perfect, and women who would be entirely perfect, but for an easily ruffled, quick-tempered, or 'touchy' disposition...The truth is there are two great classes of sins—sins of the Body, and sins of the Disposition. The Prodigal Son may be taken as a type of the first, the Elder Brother of the second. Now society has no doubt whatever as to which of these is the worse. Its brand falls, without a challenge, upon the Prodigal.

"But are we right...Analyse, as a study in temper, the thunder-cloud itself as it gathers upon the Elder Brother's brow. What is it made of? Jealousy, anger, pride, uncharity, cruelty, self-righteousness, touchiness, doggedness, sullenness—these are the ingredients of this dark and loveless soul...

"You will see...why Temper is significant. It is not in what it is alone, but in what it reveals...It is a test for love, a symptom, a revelation of an unloving nature at bottom. It is the intermittent fever which bespeaks unintermittent disease within; the occasional bubble escaping to the surface which betrays some rottenness underneath...For a want of patience, a want of kindness, a want of generosity, a want of courtesy, a want of unselfishness, are all instantaneously symbolized in one flash of Temper." (Henry Drummond, *The Greatest Thing in the World.)*

Love...is not irritable or resentful. (1 Corinthians 13:5)
If you have bitter jealousy and selfish ambition in your hearts, do not boast and be false to the truth. (James 3:14)

67. Do Not Be Foolish

Foolishness and wisdom are mirror opposite traits about which it is easy to make several wrong assumptions. The most serious of these is the assumption that both are somehow inborn. We might not necessarily say about a wise individual, "It's a gift, he was born that way," though such thoughts subconsciously color our perceptions. But we *do* often respond to the foolish man or woman with, "Oh, that's just the way he (or she) is. He's always been that way."

The biblical writers, however, do not urge impossible commands on their readers. Foolishness and wisdom are commanded of us—Avoid the one...Get the other. The entire book of Proverbs was written as an exhortation to *Get wisdom* and to *Avoid foolishness,* both in others and oneself.

The fear of the Lord is the beginning of knowledge; fools despise wisdom and instruction. (Proverbs 1:7)

My son, if you receive my words and treasure up my commandments...making your ear attentive to wisdom...then you will understand the fear of the Lord and find the knowledge of God. For the Lord gives wisdom; from his mouth come knowledge and understanding. (Proverbs 2:1, 5-6)

Hear, O sons, a father's instruction...When I was a son with my father...he taught me..."Let your heart hold fast my words: keep my commandments ...Get wisdom; get insight...The beginning of wisdom is this: Get wisdom...get insight..." (Prov. 4:1, 3-5, 7)

Does not wisdom call...O foolish men, pay attention. (Proverbs 8:1, 5)

A wise son makes a glad father, but a foolish son is a sorrow to his mother. (Proverbs 10:1)

It is easy to see that wisdom is deepened within us by maturity and obedience—that we train ourselves in the ways of wisdom over the course of a lifetime by the priorities and responses we cultivate. What is more difficult to recognize, if we are not paying attention, is that we may potentially be training ourselves in foolishness too. Foolishness lurks at the door of our minds every second, looking for opportunities to develop itself into our characters. But whereas wisdom training is hard, usually means going against the world's current, requires making difficult decisions, and necessitates an eternal outlook and selfless responses, foolishness, on the other hand, is *easy.* Foolishness is deepened within us every time we take the comfortable path or make a spineless choice, whenever we opt for temporal rather than eternal gain, when we put ourselves first, when we respond with haste rather than forethought, and especially when we heed bad advice and surround ourselves with the worldly-minded rather than the heavenly minded.

In other words, foolishness, like wisdom, is an *acquired* character trait. The foolish man or woman was not born that way. He or she has usually spent a lifetime training himself or herself in foolish habits. What we observe as foolishness is the cumulative effect of a lifetime of poor choices. Neither wisdom nor foolishness are inborn. We decide along which life's road we want to travel, and what is the ultimate objective at the end of that road—a life characterized by *Wisdom*...or a life characterized by *Foolishness.*

Who am I listening to? What mentors am I trying to emulate? How do I make decisions? Who are my friends? What are my lifetime goals and objectives? What am I seeking in life—fun, gain, wealth, and a happy time of it, or the deepening of Christlikeness in my character? Am I planting weeds or flowers in my internal garden?

All these determine whether we wake up one day at the end of life to discover Wisdom or Foolishness waiting as the reward of character we have spent our lives developing.

That day will come to us all. I will see that I built my eternal character by the building blocks of either Foolishness or Wisdom every day of my earthly life.

Do not be foolish, but understand what the will of the Lord is. (Ephesians 5:17)

68. Mind Your Own Business

Judy and I try to live by a maxim which is simply stated: *If you are not part of the problem, and not potentially part of the solution, stay out of it.*

We use this as a guide to our responses in countless ways. It is astonishing how much information comes to us on the gossip and rumor pipeline, spread by people who are completely disconnected from the circumstances and relationships involved. Yet they thrive on being part of the delicious informational conduit, passing along into every new set of ears that comes along that which is none of their business.

This is a far more cancerous character flaw than most people have any idea. We've got to recognize it for exactly what it is. It is *sin*. We are commanded not to gossip, not to relish in secrets and suspicions about others, and to mind our own business. The moment we make ourselves an active participant in the informational circuit, we have committed four or five command-sins in one fell swoop.

We cannot stop information coming to us. We are surrounded by gossips, busybodies, and rumor-mongers. They will go on sinning. They will continue to yield to their addiction. But it is the easiest thing in the world to stop the informational flow at my own doorstep. I simply don't pass it on. The flow stops with me. Silence is my chosen response to conversations I have no business jumping into the middle of.

We also need to reflect on our conduct in discussions about situations that do, in fact, require solutions. Gossip may not be involved at all. How often I find myself listening to a friend's heartfelt "sharing" of a problem, *assuming* he is asking for my input. Yet in fact he doesn't want my advice at all. If I am not involved, and my counsel has not been specifically sought, I have no business weighing in. If I cannot be part of a solution, my opinions are a distraction. The discussion may grow vigorous around me, but the first half of 1 Thessalonians 4:11 is my guide—*quietness*. If I am neither part of the problem nor a solution, it is time to obey this command, remain quiet…and mind my own business.

I have had to heed this command in my professional as well as my personal life. Many years ago, long before I dreamed of becoming a novelist, when I was filled with visions of changing the world through Christian social commentary, the Lord pointed me to the example of George MacDonald. In the midst of great cultural upheaval in the 19th century, MacDonald kept his eye on the bull's eye—the nature and character of God's Fatherhood and his purposes in the hearts of men and women. MacDonald seldom diverged into tangents. His message remained focused on who God is, and what does he want for my life. I felt God laying that same charge upon me. *Write about me. Others may speak to the culture, but that is not what I want from you. Tell your readers what kind of God I am. Mind this business, nothing else.*

It has not always been an easy directive to obey. I have opinions like everyone else. I have insights that I consider true. Time and again, however, as I feel the temptation rising within me to "speak out" on some cultural issue facing the church, always comes the still small Voice...*Not now, not you...if you are neither part of the problem nor the solution, mind your own business—the business I have given you.*

So I take a deep breath, occasionally with a pang, and again turn my gaze from without to within, from the television screen to the mirror. My mirror is my confessional, my prayer closet, and also the fountainhead for my writing. If I am to be faithful to the charge to speak to first causes, to spirituality not culture, to foundations not results, to roots not symptoms, to eternal outlooks not temporal responses…that charge begins with *me*. My response to the world begins with my own childship as I enter my prayer closet and climb into God's lap and say, "Be it unto me as you desire. My will is your will."

The world will not be changed except as individual men and women are changed. And I can change no one but myself. *This* is the business God has given me to be about.

Aspire to live quietly, to mind your own affairs. (1 Thessalonians 4:11)

69. Give Generously

Giving comes in many forms. The least important may be financial giving. That is not to say that financial generosity is *un*important, only that it may be far down the list of virtues emphasized in the New Testament. It is fearfully easy to give to a church or charity more to placate the conscience than because of a generous heart. Sending in a check or tossing a few coins or bills into a collection plate conveniently keeps us from involving ourselves in the more personal discipline of meeting people's needs where they actually live. The most important regions where generosity is required are time, energy, friendship, and compassion. We give most deeply and generously when we give *ourselves.*

The ten percent tithe, which for many Christians remains the foundation stone of financial giving to the church, is purely an Old Testament tradition originating in the Law of Moses. It is never enjoined on Christians. It has been incorporated into church practice along with many legalisms more for the purpose of sustaining the bloated bureaucracy of the church and its priesthood than for its basis in Scripture. Neither Paul, Peter, John, nor James so much as mention the tithe. Jesus mentions it on a handful of occasions, but always in connection with pharisaic legalism, not as a command on his disciples. Of further interest is the fact that the giving urged throughout Paul's letters is almost entirely devoted to raising contributions for the famine-stricken church in Jerusalem. Paul never asks for money to support his own "ministry" or its so-called "staff" of travel companions, assistants, and secretaries. Is there a lesson here for the church? It may be that raising contributions for special needs is in reality the only truly New Testament basis for passing the collection plate, box, or bag.

This is not to imply that one should not give to the church, nor that Christians are immune from financial obligation. We must simply be clear that the tithe, and financial giving to support the staff and ministry of a specific church, are not principles taught in the New Testament. Giving generously is commanded...the tithe is not. Meeting the needs of one's fellow Christians, and all men in need, is taught...supporting the administrative requirements of a church and its ministry is not.

With these facts before us, the command *Give generously* takes on wider import. In whatever manner one feels called upon to give—of money, time, talents, resources, gifts, skills, insights, energy, possessions—ten percent has nothing to do with the equation. One might give 5% another 45%. But we must erase the tithe from our considerations.

Paul speaks of giving "according to their means" and "beyond their means." For some 10% may be a crippling and unattainable burden of legalism. For others 10% may be a cheap and easy way to satisfy the conscience that one is doing all that is "required," but not a penny more. Jesus' poignant comparison in Luke 21 between the widow's mites and the lavish "giving" of the rich is all the example we need to emphasize that dollar amounts and percentages fade into insignificance as we consider this command.

The true New Testament standard is not the tithe, but *according to and beyond one's means.* That is the only rule Paul lays upon believers. Even this is not phrased as a command, but as an example to follow.

The writer of *Hebrews* insightfully adds what may be the most useful injunction of all: "Share what you have."

That may not necessarily be money. It may involve money. But it will not *only* be money.

Contribute to the needs of the saints. (Romans 12:13)

They gave according to their means...and beyond their means...see that you excel in this gracious work also. (2 Corinthians 8:3, 7)

Do not neglect to share what you have. (Hebrews 13:16)

70. Owe No One Anything

Some of the commands are more difficult to write about, and personally for me to feel that I have laid hold of in a helpful way, than others. This is one of those. Many use this command as a basis for living debt free. I applaud that objective. With a sense of wistful longing, I find myself at times wishing that such had been more feasible in my marriage and in our home and business life.

Unfortunately, it has not been practically realistic or attainable. When one operates businesses and buys homes and is dynamically engaged in a network of family and friends where financial need and provision is not one-dimensional, unless one has inherited wealth, debt-free living is extremely difficult. There are those who would object to that statement and say that with self-discipline anyone can live debt free. But the fact is, no matter how diligent one is with finances, debt free living in our time is a luxury mostly reserved for the few who happen to have the financial wherewithal to do so. For the rest, home mortgages and credit buying for business are facts of life. In addition to requiring independent means available to very few, much of what passes in our society for "debt free" living also requires some level of escapism both from society and from the command to meet the needs of others. Many things would be possible if I were living as an island unto myself. They become practically unrealistic the more deeply I involve myself with others, especially when I make my resources available to help those who are struggling, and to do my utmost to enable those close to me to live a good life.

So what do we do with this command? Honestly, I don't know. What I have said above sounds fearfully like excuse making. I fear lest it seem that I am justifying disobedience to this command.

I return to what I have said before, that the Bible does not present us with impossible commands. Yet we always find ourselves face to face with Jesus' clearly "impossible" command: *Be perfect as your heavenly Father is perfect.* I am thus aware, even as I say, "There are no impossible commands," that there are apparently impossible commands.

We are left having to figure out where to discover obedience even in what seem on the surface to be extremely difficult, if not impossible, commands. In the matter of perfection, I have urged us to look in the directions of motive and life's goals to discover the region of our obedience. Are we committed to perfection? In our growth as Christians are we dedicated to the level of (imperfect) obedience that will keep us moving toward the eternal objective? I find consistency within this apparent contradiction by remembering the father's wonderful proclamation in Mark 9: *I believe, help my unbelief.* We are not perfect, but we are commanded to be perfect. We are people of unfaith, yet we are commanded to have faith.

Perhaps we discover that same principle at work here, and in all the commands that seem unattainable. Are we moving *toward* the high goal? Are we committed to owing no man anything? Are we working diligently toward that end? Are we living within our means? Are we being wise in our financial stewardship...all with the goal (though we have not yet attained it) of owing no one anything.

Looking beyond finances, we may also discover here the command to discharge all *spiritual* debts—to be free of the debts required by love, forgiveness, and the will of God.

"You will be compelled to pay...all you owe...A love unpaid you...will not absolve you of the debt of a love unpaid, a justice not done, a praise withheld, a false judgment passed: these uttermost farthings...you must pay...The main debts whose payment God demands are those which lie at the root of all right, those we owe in mind, and soul, and being. Whatever in us can be or make an adversary, whatever could prevent us from doing the will of God, or from agreeing with our fellow—all must be yielded." (George MacDonald, *Unspoken Sermons, Second Series,* "The Uttermost Farthing.")

Owe no one anything, except to love one another. (Romans 13:8)

105

Speak With Grace

THE GRACE OF CHRIST BEGINS WITH THE TONGUE,
MIRROR OF THE SOUL.

CAESSAREA — PAUL AND JAMES PRESENT DIVERGENT PERSPECTIVES ABOUT CHRISTIAN SPEECH

As we discussed in Volume 1 of *The Eyewitness Bible,* the Lord's brother James and Paul presented distinct views about the basis of Christian faith. They articulated their convictions in two New Testament documents that began to circulate in the early church during the late 40s.

"*James* and *Galatians* were the first New Testament books written...These two letters may have appeared within a year or two of one another. A between-the-lines rivalry had been shaping up between Paul and James over certain matters of doctrine. When they wrote these letters, the two church leaders presented two *very* different perspectives—James emphasizing the importance of *works* and *good deeds*, Paul emphasizing *faith* over works. It seems that James and Paul were each responding to what they considered the imbalance of the other. Place the two letters beside one another and the impact is explosive!

"Paul writes: *'A man is not justified by...works...but through faith....We may be justified by faith...and not by works...'*

"James comes back with: *'What use is it...if a man says he has faith but he has no works...faith, if it has no works, is dead...I will show you my faith by my works...faith without works is useless.'...*

"It is positively fascinating...This same debate is still a matter of controversy within Christendom. Which is the true basis of true Christianity—*faith* or *works*?" (*The Eyewitness Bible, New Testament, Volume 1,* "Introduction")

James and Paul also present divergent perspectives on the tongue and the power of speech. Paul is often called the preeminent Christian "spokesman" of the first century, Christianity's "mouthpiece" to the Roman world. Paul was a communicator. He spoke, wrote, preached, exhorted, debated, railed, argued. It would not be far off the mark to characterize Paul, as we say, as a man who "loved the sound of his own voice."

When he returned to Palestine at the conclusion of his third missionary journey sometime about the year 57-58, Paul landed at Caesarea and then went on to Jerusalem. There he was arrested. He spent the next several years in detention, both in Jerusalem and in Caesarea. During these years, many opportunities were given Paul to "speak out" for his faith and defend himself. He used these opportunities before Roman and Jewish tribunes, priests, governors, and kings, to give testimony to his faith. This Paul does *at length*! He goes on for three entire chapters (22, 24, 26) in the book of *Acts*. While incarcerated at Caesarea, Paul takes full advantage of the opportunity to *speak* for the faith. How different is this approach to that of Jesus, who, when he was similarly questioned by a parallel tribunal of Romans and Jews, remained mostly silent. Jesus' words after his arrest we can count on our fingers. Paul's monologues go on for pages and pages in our Bibles.

Now we turn to *James*. James had learned from his brother well. Whenever we meet him in *Acts*, we find the Lord's brother circumspect and slow to offer his opinion. During the Jerusalem Conference to discuss the matter of Gentile converts which is related in Acts 15, it is Paul and Barnabas who take center stage. Luke writes, "And all the assembly kept silence; and they listened to Barnabas and Paul..." Only when everyone else was through does James, as the leader of the church, take the floor. We read, "After they finished speaking, James replied..."

James is a living example of the very principle he emphasized in his letter, *Let every man be quick to hear, slow to speak...bridle your tongue...the tongue is a fire.*

Paul was eager to speak. James was slow to speak. Christians thus have two very different perspectives with which to evaluate the commands in this section on the tongue, mirror of the soul.

SERIES EIGHT

THE GRACE OF CHRIST BEGINS WITH THE TONGUE, MIRROR OF THE SOUL

71. Speak graciously.

72. Control your tongue.

73. Be quick to listen, slow to speak.

74. Say what you mean.

75. Do not grumble, complain, or speak against others.

76. Do not gossip, slander, or lie.

77. Do not swear.

78. Do not quarrel.

79. Speak to edify, encourage, and bless one another.

80. Speak not to flatter, impress, or please men.

71. Speak Graciously

It may seem to some readers as if we have been talking about gracious speech all along. Now we come to a series of ten commands *all* focused on Christian speech. What more is there to be said? Is the manner in which we talk and use our tongue really of such importance?

Yes.

Few attributes of personality and character are more indicative of what lives in the depths of one's heart. The tongue is not only the mirror of the soul, it is one of the primary indications either of spiritual maturity or immaturity. How we conduct ourselves verbally, our habits of speech, our spoken patterns of interaction with others, truly reflect spiritual character. A loose, uncontrolled, reckless tongue exposes the immaturity of first grade Christianity. A mature, gracious, controlled tongue reveals the character of one who has moved into the high regions of graduate level spirituality.

The way I talk, my mannerisms, how I talk about others and myself, how I conduct myself in groups, the way I voice my opinions and how I respond to the ideas of others, how I express gratitude and complaint, how I express joy and suffering, my tone of voice, my responses to sudden crises or disappointments, what I say and do when angry, my exclamations when the hammer slams down on my hand, my verbal responses to one who has insulted or criticized me...every word to come out of my mouth, and the *way* it comes out of my mouth, is an indicator of maturity or immaturity. There may be no more readily visible image of either Christlikeness or *un*Christlikeness that I present to the world than this.

Where do our eyes flit when we look into someone's face? To his or her mouth. When the mouth is in constant motion, our eyes remain fixed on those moving lips. Only when the voice stills, and calmness of countenance reigns, do we have leisure to probe more deeply. Slowly our gaze drifts to the eyes. There, in the silence, we begin to detect the marks of inner character.

The question the mirror poses is simple and convicting: *When I speak, do my words and tone sound like Jesus?* Would he speak as I am speaking? Would his expression sound like mine? Would he say what I just heard myself say? Would he turn a conversation upon himself like I just did? Would he lose no opportunity to get in a subtle dig of annoyance or complaint as I am so fond of doing? Would he respond to criticism as I do? What were his exclamations of pain when he hurt himself in the carpenter's shop—would he have used the kinds of words I use?

How much does my speech resemble that of Jesus?

The command is to speak *graciously*...for our words and speech and tone and manner and expression to be seasoned with *grace*. We are not measuring only the contrast between being soft-spoken, reserved, and quiet on the one hand, and being a talkative extrovert on the other. That contrast will come in the two commands that follow. Here we are talking about the *seasoning* of our speech.

However much we talk, in whatever circumstances we find ourselves, we have the opportunity to speak graciously. This implies gentleness and courtesy, kindness and sympathy in our speech. A loud, forceful, pushy, insistent, opinionated, domineering style of conversation is unknown among those who are gracious of speech. Their words, rather, are soft, soothing, healing. Theirs is the speech of refreshing streams through quiet meadows, not the breaking of stormy waves upon a rocky shore. Their tone does not shout with kettle drums, but vibrates gently into the spirit with harp strings of grace.

Love is not rude. (1 Corinthians 13:5)
Let your speech always be gracious, seasoned with salt. (Colossians 4:6)
Show perfect courtesy toward all men. (Titus 3:2)

72. Control Your Tongue

Speaking and listening are intrinsically linked. Not only are the tongue and the ears physically located in close proximity—the back of the tongue and the two inner ears all function within a couple inches of each other—their seemingly opposite function is not opposite at all. They represent the two sides of the *same* coin.

The tongue *speaks* words that are *heard* by the ear. Speaking and listening work like the two blades of a pair of scissors—in tandem, in harmony. They function *together*.

What, then, can we learn about wise speech from what we know about wise listening? The commands of Jesus point the way. Often overlooked in the Gospels is the frequency with which Jesus exhorts his disciples and listeners (more than mere "exhortation," indeed, *commanding* it of them) with some form of: *Listen, listen carefully, be clear-minded, apply yourself to think, learn, and understand.* Jesus did more than exhort his disciples to listen. He knew they had to listen *carefully.* He knew that his disciples had to cultivate the habit and skill of listening with clarity and wisdom. His oft-used "Behold" indicates far more than seeing with the eyes but always implies "inner vision"—look earnestly, contemplate, regard, perceive, observe, understand, apprehend. In other words—Listen *carefully*, hear what I am saying *truly*, apprehend my meaning in the *depths* of your meaning.

We can take these same exhortations as applying equally to the opposite side of the speech-hearing coin. *Speak* carefully, *speak* truly, *speak* to the depths. Jesus' *Behold* applies with equal precision to the care with which we speak—*Behold how you express yourself, speak carefully, be clear-minded and apply yourself to speak with understanding, clarity, and wisdom. Be earnest and perceiving of speech. Speak truly.*

Jesus pinpoints this command yet further in Luke 8:18: *Take heed then how you hear.* Carefully contemplate that pivotal word "how." Everyone has two ears and a tongue. We are all *capable* of talking and hearing. Indeed, we do both almost non-stop from morning till night. But *how* do we hear and speak? With wisdom or with foolishness? With care, foresight, clear-mindedness, and truth? Or with superficial responses and from-the-hip opinions and comments?

Jesus' injunction might also read: *Take care, then, how you speak.*

James gives us three perfect images in which to encapsulate this truth—a wild horse, a ship's rudder, and a forest fire. Little more needs be said because we are well familiar with his metaphors. The tiny rudder controls the whole ship. The bridle controls the direction of the horse. A tiny spark can set a forest ablaze.

The tongue is not evil, but it can do evil. It is one of our most powerful gifts, and one of our most lethal enemies. Therefore, the command, *Bridle your tongue* does not merely focus an important spiritual principle...it is good practical advice. The unbridled tongue, the spark that sets a fire ablaze, may not only do mischief and harm in the lives of others, it may boomerang back on you. Suddenly you may find that the wild horse is stampeding toward *you* and it is your *own* house that has been set on fire.

There are *seed-sins* and *boomerang-sins*. The careless talk of an uncontrolled tongue is both.

Walk by the Spirit...the fruit of the Spirit is...self-control...if we live by the Spirit, let us also walk by the Spirit. (Galatians 5:16, 22-23, 25)

Let every man be...slow to speak. (James 1:19)

If any one thinks he is religious, and does not bridle his tongue...this man's religion is vain. (James 1:26)

---

73. Be Quick to Listen, Slow to Speak

The two brothers, Jesus and James, left the church with many of the same messages, exhortations, and commands. One signature tune they share is this: *Listen.*

The letter of *James* is memorable for a number of its themes. Its discussion of the power and potential destructiveness of the tongue tops that list. It might be said that his pithy command encapsulates one of the great contrasts of human relationships: *Be quick to listen, slow to speak.* The power of those simple words is profound and breathtaking.

Less acknowledged, however, is that James got this message straight from Jesus. Most Christians tend to focus on Jesus' *final* earthly exhortation rather than one of his most frequent *early* commands. They amplify this imbalance by mistakenly reading *Preach the gospel* into Matthew's Great Commission (Matthew 28:18-19), something Jesus did not say, thus justifying a *talking* rather than a *listening* witness to the world.

In actual fact, one of Jesus' most frequently given commands came in the form of a single word: *Behold.* Occasionally translated "listen," this command implies everything James meant, and more. The word contains multifold meanings, and speaks of mental and *spiritual receptiveness,* of a *hearing heart* more than just listening with the ears. It carries the implication of *mental perception,* of *earnest contemplation,* of *attentiveness* and *understanding.* When Jesus said, "Behold," he was really saying: *Listen, perceive, pay attention, and apply your minds to understand.* This cannot happen when we are talking. It only takes place when we are *listening.*

James gleans his own priority straight from his brother. Jesus used *Behold* over sixty times. He told his disciples to "preach" less than ten. The contrast is patently obvious, though the church has been slow to apprehend its significance to evangelism. We have instead taken the lesser of the Jesus commands and exalted it into the greater.

With *Behold,* Jesus is saying, "Close your mouth and hear what I have to say."...

Listening is so imperative to a growing Christian life because the natural human tendency is to blab first and ask questions later. Whenever we're confronted with a new idea, a new experience, a new insight, we immediately start talking about it. However, this is probably the time we should *not* be talking about it, but rather quietly trying to absorb what this new truth has to teach us. Reflection, not talk, is the mark of a heart learning and growing in wisdom. How much foolishness has been spread by the proclamations of the spiritually immature? The first thing a new Christian wants to do is announce everything that comes into his head.

But it's backwards. The *first* thing is to listen. The wise man and woman know that wisdom comes, not from spouting off their opinions at the drop of a hat, but from a quiet and listening spirit.

"This is the imperative message of Proverbs. Paul, too, is clear that *Faith comes from hearing, and hearing from the Word of God.* (Rom. 10:17) He does not say that faith comes from talking, but faith comes from *hearing.*

"The wisdom of Christlikeness is grown in us by attentively absorbing the Lord's teachings and putting them into practice. We must *absorb* and *receive* truth before attempting to proclaim it." (From *The Commands of Jesus,* p. 27)

"The word *obedient* comes from the Latin word *audire,* which means "listening"...a life in which there is some free inner space where we can listen to our God and follow his guidance. Jesus' life was a life of obedience. He was always listening to the Father, always attentive to his voice, always alert for his directions. Jesus was 'all ear.' That is true prayer; being all ear for God. The core of all prayer is indeed listening, obediently standing in the presence of God." (Henri J. M. Nouwen, *Making All Things New,* From *Devotional Classics,* Richard Foster, ed., p. 95)

> Be quick to listen, slow to speak. If any one thinks he is religious, but does not bridle his tongue...this man's religion is vain. (James 1:19, 26)

74. Say What You Mean

We all have our favorite passages of Scripture. These two are among mine. Matthew 5:37: *Let your "Yes" be "Yes," and your "No," "No."* (NIV) Later James quotes his brother almost word for word. James 5:12: *Let your yes be yes and your no be no.* (RSV)

Our favorite passages are usually ones that confirm our most cherished ideas and doctrines. We don't include among our favorites those that are most convicting and that expose our flesh, immaturity, and hypocrisy. Among the commands, we probably like the *most* are those that require the *least* from us.

I include this among my favorites list for a different reason. I include it because I see the extreme importance of this command. I do not exaggerate when I say that I rank this command among the top ten commands in importance for Christians in all the Bible. In many ways, our entire witness hangs on attentiveness to this command. The world will not pay attention to people whose word, even in the tiny things, is not to be relied on.

We live in a culture where people speak with forked tongues from morning till night. *Not* saying what we mean is a cancer. It used to be said of a man of integrity, *His word is his bond.* But nobody's word is his bond anymore. Christians along with the rest of the world play games with words all day long. We make statements that do *not* represent what we mean, and which we are *not* prepared to back up. How often do we rearrange our schedule after being told, "I'll call you tomorrow morning...I'll let you know Wednesday afternoon," yet the call never comes. Not doing what you say you will do not only represents disobedience to the Bible, it is rudeness of the highest order. Therefore, I choose my words with care. I take even tiny commitments to be somewhere or do something with the seriousness of having signed a written contract of truth. I do not make commitments I cannot follow through on. If I say I will do it, I will do it.

"James is making a simple but profound point: *Say what you mean*...Not only do not speak *carelessly*, speak *accurately*...Nor is it merely a question of speaking...truthfully. It is larger than that. James is speaking of dependability, commitment, follow-through, predictability, accountability. Not just *say* what you mean, *do* what you mean...

"If you say you will be somewhere...*be* there. If you promise to do something...*do* it. The Lord's people are meant to be men and women you can trust implicitly. Their words can be depended on...Their entire character can be depended on...[This] magnificent challenge...touches every aspect of life—*Let your yes be yes, and your no be no.*

"Sadly, there are Christians [who]...don't stop to consider what flighty, inconsistent, unreliable, erratic unpredictability says to a watching world. Their yes means if they get around to it...their no means maybe...Staying power, constancy, steadfastness, a long obedience in the same direction—these do not enter into the calculus of their spiritual focus. But they are not worried—grace covers all.

"Being an individual whose yes means yes and whose no means no contains important implications about how one conducts himself or herself in conversation. Ideas, opinions, and plans are measured out judiciously. Another of James' injunctions—being slow to speak—is always on the mind of one whose yes means yes and whose no means no, lest, speaking too hastily and without forethought, a word might later have to be withdrawn and it will turn out that yes wasn't *exactly* yes, and no wasn't *quite* no...Better to keep one's own counsel and remain silent until certain that the *yes* or *no* can be spoken with confidence, and with the staying power to back it up. (From *The Commands of Jesus*, p. 123)

Let your yes be yes and your no be no. (James 5:12)

Speaking the truth in love, we are to grow up in every way...into Christ...Let every one speak the truth with his neighbor...Let there be no...silly talk. (Ephesians 4:15, 25; 5:4)

The wisdom from above is first pure...without uncertainty or insincerity. (James 3:17)

Put away...guile and insincerity. (1 Peter 2:1)

---

75. Do Not Grumble, Complain, or Speak Against Others

. Consider the fascinating word *grumble*. At first glance it seems like such a minor violation of gracious speech. What's the big deal? Why does Paul command us not to grumble? Because it is a *seed-sin*. It acts like a mustard seed. From it, bigger things grow. Grumbling yields fruit. Its fruits lead to more serious sins.

The King James translates the same word GONGUZO as "murmur." It is used of the Pharisees complaining and speaking against Jesus. This sense of the word implies a muttered, half-whispered, low-toned complaint. The Pharisees "murmured" (*grumbled*) about Jesus...Paul tells the Corinthians and Philippians not to "murmur" (*grumble*.) Grumbling poisons the outlook by planting seeds of dissatisfaction, resentment, irritation, and complaint. Every one of these has roots like a dandelion. They go deeper and deeper until you can't get rid of them.

We all know whiners. If they indulge in the habit long enough, they will become those in old age of whom it will be said, "He's an old grouch." What a sad punctuation mark to define one's character at the end of life—a sour, complaining disposition that loses no opportunity to express dissatisfaction.

Murmuring is such a personal sin, easy to hide at first. We murmur quietly, under the breath. We murmur with thoughts as much as with words, allowing annoyance and irritation to plant their seeds. But the seeds sprout and grow. Before we know it, we are grumbling aloud, seeking ears into which we can spread asperity, protest, discord, blame, and accusation. We have progressed to a more serious sin. We are in danger of leading others into the sin of unthankfulness. We have become a purveyor of complaint, a grumbling evangelist, anxious to pass on our sour outlook.

All these manifestations are poison to a healthy life perspective, poison to relationships, and poison to our growth as Christians.

That is why Paul, James, the book of *Proverbs*, and indeed the entire Bible, emphasize the *extreme* importance of the power of speech. In hundreds of ways they tell us over and over, as the song goes, to accentuate the positive. It sounds like such a simple principle. Yet in some ways all other character traits flow out of this.

So how do we break the habit of murmuring, grumbling, and complaint? By training ourselves to do exactly the opposite, to do what Paul tells us to—speak of the good, the nice, the pleasant...to speak about what has gone right not what has gone wrong...to speak of what we like about others not what annoys us...in short, to find ways to express *satisfaction* not *dis*satisfaction. The antidote is a simple matter of speaking goodness, speaking gratitude, speaking *light*. Continually we are reminded of Paul's triumphant climax when writing to the Philippians. By changing a single word, his exhortation becomes a crystalline guide to Godliness in our speech habits.

"Finally, brethren, whatever is true, whatever is honorable, whatever is just, whatever is pure, whatever is lovely, whatever is gracious, if there is any excellence, if there is anything worthy of praise, *speak about* these things." (Philippians 4:8)

Do not murmur, grumble, complain, or speak against others. Instead speak of what is true, honorable, just, pure, lovely, gracious, and excellent. Spread words of light with your tongue. Plant seeds that will grow roots of healing, kindness, sympathy, encouragement, generosity, grace, and Christlikeness in all those who come within sound of your voice.

We must not...grumble. (1 Corinthians 10:10)
Let no evil talk come out of your mouths, but only such as is good for edifying, as fits the occasion. (Ephesians 4:29)
Do all things without grumbling. (Philippians 2:14)
Do not speak evil against one another. (James 4:11)

76. Do Not Gossip, Slander, or Lie

Most of us reading this command will not automatically think of ourselves in connection with such clear violations of integrity as these words indicate.

If you were to ask, "Do you lie?" I would quickly reply, "Of course not."

"Are you in the habit of slandering people?" you might ask next. "*Me*...absolutely not!" would again be my answer.

"Are you a gossip, then?" *No!* I would answer emphatically.

It is always possible to read the commands on two levels: The *hands off method*, keeping them safely at arm's length, and the *mirror method*, in which we invite every command into the deepest corners of being to accomplish its self-convicting work. The above responses represent the "hands off method" for dealing with difficult commands.

Let's try again, this time using the "mirror method."

"Do you ever pass along tidbits of information, something that you know will be of interest to one of your friends? Whose information it is, and thus who has the proprietary right to decide whether the information is spread, does not cross your mind. It is just an innocent little tidbit of gossip. What could be the harm of passing it along?"

"Well...when you put it like *that*," I answer, "sure...I suppose *occasionally* I do."

Then you have the right to conclude that I am a *gossip*.

"Do you ever speak accusations, perhaps about some minor violation of right and wrong as you see it, without absolute proof or first hand knowledge of the circumstances involved? Perhaps your statement is based on what you heard from someone else?"

"Well...I suppose I *might* have."

Then again I must face a sobering fact—You have the right to call me a *slanderer*.

"Do you ever fudge the truth so as to allow another to believe something that isn't 100% true? Do you sometimes tell half a story, coloring motives and responses in such a way as to influence the conclusions your hearers draw that might be less than fully accurate? Do you occasionally allow little white fibs to smooth your way and help you avoid uncomfortable consequences which the full truth might raise? Have you ever stretched the truth just a smidgeon, enhanced the facts, shaded your representation of circumstances in such a way as to put yourself in the best possible light?"

None of those may make me a liar. But they certainly make me a dabbler and trifler with truth, not a man *of* truth.

The words, *Let no evil talk come out of your mouth,* are easily misunderstood by the same hands-off reasoning. I might think that I would never speak *evil*. But let the mirror method translate "evil" as negative, suspicious, secretive, rude, mean-spirited, unkind, harsh, unforgiving, accusative. Suddenly Paul's words slam forcefully into my face. Let *no* unkind talk come out of your mouth...Let *no* rude, harsh, or unforgiving talk come out of your mouth...Let *no* secretive, accusing, or mean-spirited talk come out of your mouth.

The hands-off response always says, *Not me.* The mirror response acknowledges, "In my fallen humanity I am susceptible to *all* the sins that beset humankind."

Paul's contrast illuminates what should come out of our mouths—*edifying, fitting speech that imparts grace.* What a wonderful image—speaking to impart grace.

Let no evil talk come out of your mouths, but only such as is good for edifying...that it may impart grace to those who hear...Let all...slander be put away from you. (Ephesians 4:29, 31)

Put away...malice, slander, and foul talk...Do not lie to one another. (Colossians 4:8-9)

The women likewise must be...no slanderers. (1 Timothy 3:11)

Avoid such godless chatter, for it will lead people into more and more ungodliness, and their talk will eat its way like gangrene. (2 Timothy 2:16)

Speak evil of no one...be gentle, and...show perfect courtesy toward all men. (Titus 3:2)

If any one thinks he is religious, but does not bridle his tongue...this man's religion is vain...Do not speak evil against one another. (James 1:26; 4:11)

Let him keep his tongue from evil and his lips from speaking guile. (1 Peter 3:10)

---

77. Do Not Swear

We might try the same little test with this command as we did with the last.

"Do you swear?"

"Certainly not. Profanity...not from *my* mouth."

The hands-off method quickly discovers as many justifications as needed to weasel out of this command. It's one of the easiest in the book to sidestep. "Oh, well that's not *really* a swear word...it's just, well...you know—everybody says *that*."

The mirror-method looks deeper into the nature of speech itself. The mirror does not examine for loopholes, but for purity. The mirror seeks no excuses, but Christlikeness. The only question the mirror asks about our speech habits is: "If you glanced around and saw Jesus standing at your side, would you be pleased or embarrassed that he heard what just popped out of your mouth? Would you be pleased or embarrassed that he heard the words you just whispered under your breath that no one else ever heard?"

It is true that in speaking of oaths, Jesus was not speaking primarily of profanity, but the sealing of a word or agreement by an oath. When he speaks of *swearing* by heaven, Jerusalem, the temple, the altar, or even by one's head, he was condemning the use of holy things to enforce a binding pledge. But the apostles are even more rigid in their condemnation of loose and careless talk. They are unequivocal: Do not swear. Do not speak guile. Let no evil, foul, loose, degrading, evil talk come from your lips. Bridle your tongue.

"As we have stressed many times, we have to seek the heart of Jesus' intent. Here we can see that he was laying down no legalistic code about oaths. He was speaking rather about the entire nature of how we express ourselves—in particular about employing holy things to punctuate and enforce our speech...

"All loose, crude, unthinking, irreverent talk, all oaths and exclamations whether holy or vulgar, used to add 'color' to speech, or shouted in outbursts of anger, are an abomination to God's ears...Our minds have been polluted by such expletives from constant exposure. In the world we are barraged from morning to night with filthy, degrading, coarse, lewd, and suggestive expressions. But God *hates* such talk. May we never cease to be shocked and appalled by it.

"Worst of all, however, must be the ease with which the world has accustomed itself to using God's name in vain. The use of the holy name *God* to punctuate careless speech has become an epidemic in our time. How shocked would be the unthinking young person to count the number of times *God* is sprinkled through speech as if it is no more important a word than *the* or *and*. Yet Jesus says that we will be held accountable for *every* careless word...

"Indeed, as James says, the tongue is a fire. Loose speech may seem like one of the most insignificant of sins. But in truth, the tongue is an open window into the soul. The words it speaks are one of the most accurate measures of what lies deep inside. Careless talk reveals careless character." (From *The Commands of Jesus*, p. 113)

Let no evil talk come out of your mouths, but only such as is good for edifying, as fits the occasion. (Ephesians 4:29)

Let there be no filthiness. (Ephesians 5:4)

Put away...foul talk from your mouth. (Colossians 4:8)

If any one thinks he is religious, but does not bridle his tongue...this man's religion is vain. (James 1:26)

From the same mouth come blessing and cursing. My brethren, this ought not to be so. (James 3:10)

Do not swear. (James 5:12)

Let him keep his tongue from evil and his lips from speaking guile. (1 Peter 3:10)

78. Do Not Quarrel

The injunction against quarreling is fascinating to find among the commands, not because it comes as a surprise, but because of how completely accepted it is in the body of Christ. Is there any more commonplace relational dynamic in the church than this?

Has *love* been the most visible historical hallmark of the church through the centuries?

Have graciousness, kindness, unity, humility, wisdom, and Christlikeness been universally visible manifestations of the sons and daughters of God in their relationships with one another and their dealings with the world?

Or has a disputatious, argumentative, squabbling, contentious party spirit characterized Christ's church to a watching world?

This is remarkable indeed. We find ourselves compelled to admit that one of the most recognized and universal traits of the body of Christ is something the Lord's followers are specifically and repeatedly told *not* to do.

Is quarreling perhaps the church's ensnaring "besetting sin?"

How is the scourge of intra-family squabbling to be purged when it is so endemic to the pastime many Christians seem to love more than anything else?

The reality is that we *won't* purge the church of the compulsion to bicker over words, ideas, doctrines, traditions, practices, and interpretations of Scripture. Christians will quarrel until the end of time. What Paul calls "wrangling over words" will continue until the Lord himself separates the wheat from the chaff.

You and I, however, can purge *ourselves* of the compunction and entertaining desire to quarrel by recognizing argumentativeness as a direct slap in Jesus' face. We can simply stop quarreling. When disputes come, we go silent. It's as simple as that.

I often find myself in discussions that seem to be flowing along fine—with open-minded give and take of ideas, respect of diverse opinions, intellectual honesty—when all at once comes a change. One individual seizes on something just said and counters with a recognizable edge of tone. The next words to fall from his lips are imbued with new weight. His opinion is *right* and *true*. Opposing opinions are *wrong*. This may not be succinctly stated, but tone and gesture and intensity of delivery unmistakably imply it. The discussion has entered a new phase. The atmosphere has changed. A challenge has been laid down. What has been spoken is the *true* perspective and, implied yet further, the *only* true perspective. Another individual takes the bait and bats the tennis ball of opinion back with a divergent point of view. The *quarrel* has begun.

That's when I withdraw into myself and go dark. I sit in silence and watch the ball fly back and forth over the net. But I refuse to weigh in. Right and wrong on the issue under scrutiny matters nothing to me. What matters is that I do not slap Jesus in the face by entering the argumentative fray and begin wrangling over words with everyone else.

I may not be able to change the body of Christ. But I can change the little corner of it occupied by the chair I am sitting in.

Let us conduct ourselves becomingly…not in quarreling. (Romans 13:13)

Agree with one another. (2 Corinthians 13:11)

The works of the flesh are…enmity, strife…anger…dissension, party spirit. (Galatians 5:19-20)

Let us have no…provoking of one another. (Galatians 5:26)

A bishop must be…not quarrelsome. (1 Timothy 3:3)

Avoid disputing about words. (2 Timothy 2:14)

The Lord's servant must not be quarrelsome. (2 Timothy 2:24)

Avoid quarreling…be gentle, and…show perfect courtesy toward all men. (Titus 3:2)

Avoid stupid controversies…dissensions, and quarrels over the law…As for a man who is factious, after admonishing him…have nothing more to do with him. (Titus 3:9-10)

If any one thinks he is religious, but does not bridle his tongue…this man's religion is vain. (James 1:26)

79. Speak to Edify, Encourage, and Bless One Another

The final two commands of this section are intrinsically related, yet they point in opposite directions. Speech will always build up or tear down *someone*. These last two commands identify the two objects of that building or tearing—others or ourselves.

We cannot build others up with flattering superficialities. Sincerity of speech is required in all ten of these speech-commands. However, nowhere is it more imperative than when attempting to build up one in need. The greater that need, the more mere words won't help. People know when we're faking it. Cheery, overly optimistic, unrealistic, and occasionally patronizing pep talks telling someone how he or she ought to feel and how fantastic life is if they only looked on the bright side isn't always what's called for. We've all been on the receiving end of those sanguine but unhelpful sermonettes. When we are low, discouraged, heartsick, or suffering physically, we don't want to be told that everything is rosy, that we are great, and that life is one enormous bowl of peaches and cream. Yet there are those who go through life spreading a light-hearted, Pollyanna outlook without pausing long enough to look into the hearts of those they pass. In their own way, they resemble the priest and Levite who pass by on the other side of the road. Meeting needs requires more than strewing verbal petals as we pass—pretty and fragrant, it may be, but not touching people where they live. It takes time to cross over and involve ourselves in the lives of those God brings us.

Most of us won't encounter those who have been beaten by robbers and left for dead beside the path. Every day, however, we encounter men and women with *inner* hurts and anxieties perhaps no less traumatic. To these we are sent as Samaritans. Spiritually and emotionally they may indeed be lying half dead alongside the road. How can we help?

First, we have to identify their suffering. We don't have to know details. We're trying to listen to hearts. We don't probe and question as if standing beside a psychologist's couch. We simply *listen*. Now is the time to bring together all the commands we have considered. I must cultivate the gift, the art, the skill, the practiced habit of listening with my heart to the hearts of those around me. Gradually we cultivate an orientation of live-listening. We are *always* listening...with the eyes, with all the senses, listening to the inner stories those around us are keeping hidden but cannot help telling. The perceptive Samaritan *feels* these stories without words. Then he or she moves gently to become a character in the story himself. He or she enters the stories of those about them all day long, with a smile, a touch, an embrace, or a gently administered blessing of encouragement. Our listening hearts, and the words of our mouths, are the Samaritan-gifts we have been given with which to minister kindness.

It is not only the suffering whom we are commanded to encourage, edify, and bless, but *all* men, in *every* encounter, in all circumstances and relationships. How? By affirming personhood. By conveying that one whose path we have crossed at some given moment is important, that his or her life and concerns and joys and sorrows *matter*. We edify by saying—in word, deed, expression, by all we are—*You matter!*

When I know I *matter* to another human being, that single fact is a powerful ray of sunlight exploding through the clouds of my discouragement. The fact that my personhood matters sends shock waves of new life straight into my heart. If I matter to you, I must matter to God too!

What a revelation...my personhood is significant. *I matter.*

Edify, bless, and encourage those around you this day. Affirm personhood with kind words of grace. *Make people matter.*

Love is not rude. (1 Corinthians 13:5)

Let no evil talk come out of your mouths, but only such as is good for edifying, as fits the occasion. (Ephesians 4:29)

Bless, for to this you have been called. (1 Peter 3:9)

80. Speak Not to Flatter, Impress, or Please Men

Let us pose a probing question. The more personal layers of the onion we peel off in formulating an answer may reveal startling, even shocking, truths about ourselves.

How much of our speech is subtly laced with the hidden desire to impress?

Unvarnished flattery is usually easy to detect. Even the term "man pleaser" is not difficult to observe at work. This does not mean we do not succumb to flattery and speaking to please on occasion. But if we know ourselves at all, we recognize—after the fact, perhaps—when we have slipped into cajolery and praise that might be a little overdone.

Yet how subtly does the desire to impress sneak into our speech in the most invisible ways. We do it all the time without ever noticing what we're doing. The simplest turn of phrase, the most infinitesimal enhancement to a story, the tiniest amplification of my role in events, the most seemingly innocent stretching of fact...and voila, I have aggrandized myself at the expense of truth. It's what Paul so insightfully calls "puffing oneself up."

It is *so* easy, so natural. Our choices of words, phrases, and expressions are adapted from a lifetime of practice to shine the light upon ourselves. With cunning skill we turn to show our best side to the camera that will hide our warts and flaws.

So many of these integrity-practices require retraining ourselves in ways no one else may see. But God sees. Aware of this universal tendency toward resume enhancement, some time ago I began retraining myself in one of the tiniest ways imaginable. I determined to make it a matter of obedience to this command. Whenever I return from a bicycle ride, Judy usually asks, "How far did you go?" If my odometer reads 24.9 miles, it's the most natural thing in the world to answer, "Twenty-five miles." Therefore, I intentionally began rounding down not up. Even if the odometer reads 34.95, I now say, "Thirty-four." I said nothing to her, of course. To voice my commitment would only deepen the subtly of the temptation to *impress* her by my truthfulness. These subtleties will attack us from every side! And now that I have let the cat out of the bag, she will know my secret along with everyone else. Hopefully doing so may accomplish a greater good for one of you.

This command is extraordinarily difficult to live by in today's world. On every side we are told to blow our own horns. You would be astonished to know how often agents and editors and publishers tell authors that selling books is all about self-promotion. Could any quality of character be more anathematic to Christlikeness than that? The idea is positively hateful to me. Yet for over thirty years it has been pounded into me that my writing career depends on it. Now more than ever, "platform" defines success in every endeavor—writing, ministry, evangelism. Even a pastor who wants the ministry of his church to have an impact must engage in this hideous practice of *self*-promotion in order to build a reputation and platform. Look around at nearly every well-known Christian leader, teacher, author, musician, or speaker. Chances are about 89% that they either got where they are, or, having got there, are managing to stay in the public spotlight, by assiduously marketed and shrewdly targeted self-promotion.

Let us categorically reject the desire to *build ourselves up* and *impress* and *self-promote*. Let us reject these in all their ugly forms for they are an insult to Jesus Christ!

Self-promotion is anti-Christlikeness. I would paraphrase this command simply to read: *When speaking of yourself, round down not up.*

We speak, not to please men, but to please God. (1 Thessalonians 2:4)

We never used either words of flattery...or a cloak for greed...nor did we seek glory from men. (1 Thessalonians 2:5-6)

"THE PHILIPPI COMMANDS"

Reflect Christlikeness of Character

THE ULTIMATE LIFE GOAL FOR CHRISTIANS

PHILIPPI—THE CHURCH PAUL LOVED

The result of Paul's arrest in Palestine in the late 50s and his various trials, imprisonments, and public defenses was inconclusive. The Roman authorities didn't know what to do with the outspoken Jewish Christian. He had broken no laws. But the tribune and governor were so adamant upon pleasing the powerful Jewish leaders who were clamoring for Paul's head, that they could not bring themselves simply to let him go. Because of Paul's Roman citizenship, and his famous demand, "I appeal to Caesar," he was eventually sent from Caesarea to Rome for Caesar to decide his case.

Paul had long planned to visit Rome. He had written his *magnum opus* letter of *Romans* in 55-56 from Corinth at the conclusion of his third missionary trip. He planned to make a quick visit to Palestine, then to set out again, this time for Rome. His plans were preempted by his arrest and imprisonment. Yet in the end, after a delay of several years as recounted in Acts 21-26, Paul's wish came to fulfillment, though in a different way than he had anticipated. At last he was on his way to the center of the Empire.

Paul arrived in Rome, under guard, in the early 60s. While waiting for his case to be heard by Caesar, Paul was kept under what was a reasonably comfortable "house arrest." He was allowed to have guests, and apparently even hosted small groups of Christians. Paul's fellow workers came and went. It seems that Paul was able to direct a vigorous campaign of Christian activity in Rome during approximately the years 61-63. As the community of believers in Rome increased, Paul's influence extended through the Roman Guard, even into the household of Caesar himself. It was during these years that the incident related earlier with Philemon and Onesimus took place.

This period of Paul's Roman imprisonment is memorable to history largely because of three hugely significant letters he wrote during this time to churches he had previously visited during his missionary trips of the early and mid-50s. Neither of the three is particularly long. Yet they represent the apex of Paul's thought, the crowning summation of his written corpus. They are the letters of *Philippians, Ephesians,* and *Colossians.* Taken together, the three present an image of Christ and his work far more sophisticated than anything Paul had set forth before. The doctrine of the trinity was later developed on the basis of these three letters. And in *Ephesians* Paul presents a vision of the church— both individual and corporate—that is breathtaking and wonderful.

Paul's visit to Philippi in the early 50s during his travels around Macedonia had been pleasant and memorable. It contained none of the strife and controversy of, say, his relationship with the Corinthian church, or the doctrinal imbalance Paul had to address with the Thessalonians. It was simply a happy time. Therefore, when years later Paul wrote to the Philippians, his spirit is one of joy. *Philippians* is a bright letter of rejoicing.

Paul opens with insight into his imprisonment: "I hold you all in my heart as partakers with me of grace, both in my imprisonment and in the defense and confirmation of the gospel...I want you to know, brethren, that what has happened to me has really served to advance the gospel, so that it has become known throughout the whole praetorian guard and to all the rest that my imprisonment is for Christ; and most of the brethren have been made confident in the Lord because of my imprisonment, and are much more bold to speak the word of God without fear." (Phil. 1:7, 12-14)

The life Paul sets before the Philippians is nothing short of a life in which Christians are being trained, molded, nurtured, and transformed into the Christlikeness of Jesus himself. This vision Paul articulates succinctly in a statement made about the same time to the Ephesians: "...until we all attain to the unity of the faith...to mature manhood, to the measure of the stature of the fullness of Christ." (Ephesians 4:13)

Paul's conclusion stands as one of the towering illuminations of Christian character and outlook that surely surpasses all Paul's theology in eternal import: "Finally, brethren, whatever is true, whatever is honorable, whatever is just, whatever is pure, whatever is lovely, whatever is gracious, if there is any excellence, if there is anything worthy of praise, think about these things." (Phil. 4:8)

THE ULTIMATE LIFE GOAL FOR CHRISTIANS

81. Put on the character of Christ.

82. Seek God's will and live by it.

83. Pray for wisdom and walk in wisdom.

84. Be pure.

85. See through God's eyes by developing the mind of Christ.

86. Do not be covetous, greedy, or a lover of money.

87. Clothe yourself with humility.

88. Eagerly rejoice in right and goodness.

89. Endure suffering with faith, fortitude, grace, and courage.

90. Wage victorious spiritual warfare.

81. Put On the Character of Christ

"There are many secondary aspects of God's will that are good, right, and scriptural elements of spirituality with which we should be concerned. We do well to understand these, and to pray for God to develop them within us...

"But what is God's *primary* will for his people...What is it that God wants to do in your life, and in mine, above *all* other things?

"What is the *summum bonum,* the greatest thing, the 'supreme good' of life—the most perfect, ultimate purpose that is in God's mind and heart when he thinks of *you* and *me?* It can be simply stated: That we become sons and daughters of God who are conformed to the image of Christ.

"Jesus was *the* Son of God, the 'only begotten' Son. God's design is that we too become sons and daughters, his younger brothers and sisters, who are *like* him—who love like him, think like him, respond like him, resist the enemy like him, trust the Father like him, and who pray like him.

"We will never be like him in his perfection, but we *are* to become like him in attitude, thought, and motive. Only *one* Son brought salvation to the world. But *all* God's sons and daughters are to partake of that salvation by growing into the Christlikeness that it makes possible.

"Obviously this is a process—a *long* process, a lifelong process. We *don't* love or think or respond or trust God like Jesus did.

"But make no mistake, to turn us into the kind of people who *can* do so—with infinitesimally tiny baby steps to begin with, then growing steadily more capable of it as our lives progress—is the whole point of Christianity. There is simply nothing else that the Christian life is about than this. We will never do so perfectly in this life. But it is toward this end that God is leading us, and toward this divine 'center' that the prayer of Christlikeness aims us.

"It will be obvious that such a transformation into men and women that reflect the nature of Jesus Christ is not something that can be accomplished externally. Christians these days are fond of external proclamations. But we're talking here about something of an entirely different nature than a bumper sticker or worship service or thirty day program can achieve.

"The kind of sonship and daughterhood that is in God's heart to accomplish will not come about by outward manifestation. It can only happen inwardly, as we become people of a certain nature and character.

"God wants more than mere believers. He wants more than mere worshippers. He wants more than people who can parrot back doctrinally correct spiritual phrases. He wants more than men and women forever seeking new experiences and highs and blessings.

"He is involved in the enterprise of fashioning sons and daughters.

"In the same way that he stooped down and created Adam and Eve out of the dust of the ground, he similarly takes each one of us when we give our lives to him, takes us in the midst of our sinful and selfish natures, and to the extent we yield to that remaking process, as with our ancient ancestors in Eden, begins to fashion children who will one day bear the image and reflect the nature of his firstborn Son, Jesus Christ himself." (Michael Phillips, *Make Me Like Jesus,* "Introduction.")

So shall we all at last attain to...mature manhood, measured by nothing less than the full stature of Christ. (Ephesians 4:13, NEB)

Be imitators of God, as beloved children. And walk in love, as Christ loved us. (Eph. 5:1-2)

As therefore you received Christ Jesus the Lord, so live in him. (Colossians 2:6)

We always pray...that the name of our Lord Jesus may be glorified in you, and you in him. (2 Thessalonians 1:11-12)

82. Seek God's Will and Live by It

The question we are about to pose may at first glance seem simplistic, almost a cliché, like something from an old-fashioned salvation tract. Let us try, however, to listen to the words with fresh insight, and bring the question all the way inside. Let us see what it might have to tell us about ourselves.

What are you living for?

Perhaps we should begin our probe into the hidden veins of motive and life orientation by rephrasing our inquiry with more specific focus: *What are your life's goals? What are you trying to accomplish in life? What are your dreams? Where do you hope to be and what do you hope to be doing in ten years…in twenty years? At the end of your life, what do you hope to be able to look back on with the greatest satisfaction and sense of completion and fulfillment?*

And then what is perhaps the most important question of all: *How did you arrive at those goals, dreams, and objectives?*

There are two general ways to answer this last question. Probably most arrive where they are by circumstance of family, background, upbringing, and where they were and with whom and what factors were influencing them at certain critical crossroads moments. They moved along through life as situations and opportunities presented themselves. They ended up where they are more by *accident* than design. Others, however, will have *planned* out a course of life to specifically follow their dreams. They are where they are because they knew what they wanted, then they pursued those goals.

How many, even among Christians, would answer, "I got where I am, and I am on the life course I am following, because I asked God what *he* would have me do with my life, what *he* wanted my life's objectives to be, and then I did my best to yield to *his* guiding and nurturing hand to allow *his* will to be fulfilled in my life."

All the above questions really reduce to this: Whose will are we living by, God's or our own? We're not talking about vocation. The jobs we hold are mere sidelights to life's deeper and more eternal objectives. We're talking about the people we are in the process of becoming, and *how* we are becoming those people. Vocation is part of that, of course, but is not central to it. We're talking about inner goals of growth and character.

What direction are we moving in? How and by whom were our goals of growth and character established?

The person we want to become is the foundation for everything else. Vocation, marriage, family, friendships, church life, where we live, how we spend our money, leisure, relationships…everything flows out of the person we want to be. Garbage collector or lawyer, teacher or rocket scientist, investment banker or secretary, retail clerk or business manager, policeman or librarian, custodian or taxi driver, factory worker or congressman. God values none of these over any other. His will is not primarily concerned with life accomplishments but with the development of personhood.

What will we be thinking about on our deathbed? What will we wish we had spent *more* energy on? What will we wish we had spent *less* energy on? These are the things God is thinking about *now*. It is these eternal priorities that make up what we call "God's will." The deathbed is no time to start thinking about eternity, or to decide that it's high time to live by God's will and become the kind of person he wants me to be. The time to think about who God wants me to be, and what is his will for my life, is today.

> Do not be foolish, but understand what the will of the Lord is. (Ephesians 5:17)
> We…pray for you, asking that you may be filled with the knowledge of his will in all spiritual wisdom and understanding. (Colossians 1:9)
> Give thanks in all circumstances; for this is the will of God in Christ Jesus for you. (1 Thessalonians 5:17)
> May…God…equip you with everything good that you may do his will. (Hebrews 13:20-21)

83. Pray For Wisdom and Walk in Wisdom

Of the many commands we have considered, which are those at the top of the list? Which are those that incorporate all the others into them? We immediately recognize *Christlikeness* as a recurring signature tune of the commands. Obviously *obedience* is the doorway into the Christlikeness God desires to develop within us. And when we attempt to isolate scriptural first causes, we are also plunged into the book of *Proverbs* which extols wisdom as the highest virtue in the world. Its overriding message is...*get wisdom!* From the life of Solomon, however, we know that wisdom *alone* can lead to emptiness, vanity, and a failed life. Wise as he was, Solomon failed to discover life's highest good.

So how do we balance these three "highest" things—Christlikeness, obedience, and wisdom? Let us coin a phrase to identify this threefold scriptural priority toward which life is intended to lead us: *Obedient wisdom unto Christlikeness.* Wisdom and obedience mutually are intended each to produce the other. Obedience leads to wisdom. Wisdom is intended to produce obedience. When both function in harmony with God's purpose, over a lifetime Christlikeness is developed within the character of God's sons and daughters.

What is the secret, then to Solomon's command of Proverbs 4:5-7: *Get wisdom.*

It is a two-phase process which we glean from the example of Solomon's life. James writes, "If any of you lacks wisdom, let him ask God...and it will be given him." (James 1:5) This is an astonishing promise. The cause-and-effect simplicity is breathtaking—*Ask God, he will give wisdom.* Wow! This Solomon did in 2 Chronicles 1:10. God promised to give him what he asked for. Solomon asked for wisdom and knowledge. God granted his request because it was a wise request. Solomon became the wisest man in the world.

When it came to the obedience of step two, however, Solomon failed mightily. He did not obey the precepts of the very wisdom God had given him. Obedience did not characterize his life. His heart did not, like that of his father David's, yearn for Godliness. So while David was not as wise as his son, and indeed his biography was marred by several glaringly foolish blunders, the yearning of his heart was higher than his son's.

Pray for wisdom...obey the commands. The two high things go hand in hand.

Early in my spiritual pilgrimage, struck with the power of the *Proverbs* and the glorious magnitude of "the prize of the high calling" of wisdom, I asked my former pastor and spiritual mentor how one acquired wisdom. He did not hesitate a second, "Pray for it," was his instant reply. I was stunned by the simplicity of his answer. Then he pointed me to James 1:5. He was telling me exactly the same thing that James said.

I began following James' exhortation that very day. As Solomon had done, I prayed and asked God for wisdom. Soon after that, my then current pastor issued a challenge that led me straight into the commands of the New Testament. In many ways, that challenge has represented the focus of my life ever since. This book is one result. Praying for wisdom was the easy part. The forty-five years since have been an often difficult school of learning obedience to the commands that represent the second, and perhaps most important part of the wisdom-obedience partnership. How grateful I am to these two men of God, my two pastors, each in their own way, who pointed me early in my life to the dual high calling: *Obedient wisdom unto Christlikeness.*

Be wise as to what is good. (Romans 16:19)

If any one among you thinks that he is wise in this age, let him become a fool that he might become wise. (1 Cor. 3:18)

Look carefully then how you walk, not as unwise men, but as wise. (Ephesians 5:15)

We...pray...that you may be filled with...all spiritual wisdom and understanding, to lead a life worthy of the Lord...and increasing in the knowledge of God. (Colossians 1:9-10)

If any of you lacks wisdom, let him ask God who gives to all men generously. (James 1:5)

Who is wise among you...By his good life let him show his works in the meekness of wisdom...The wisdom from above is first pure, then peaceable, gentle, open to reason, full of mercy and good fruits. (James 3:13, 17)

---

84. Be Pure

It would make an interesting experiment to attempt to identify the single principle of spirituality that the world vilifies, mocks, and rejects more than any other. Many options leap to mind: righteousness, authority, obedience, humility.

Another possibility may surprise us—purity. *Why* does the world hate purity? It is a mystery. Why are not goodness, humility, respect, and purity admired?

We are pounded all day long by subtle voices (from entertainment and the media most of all) telling us that *impurity* is normal, and that purity is abnormal, if not downright weird. No one would think of buying gold, silver, aspirin, or Vitamin C if they were not guaranteed to be "99.999% pure." *Purity* in precious metals, chemical compounds, drugs, medicines, supplements, and scientific experiments is absolutely essential. Purity of character in the human soul and heart, however, is ridiculed. The illogical self-contradictory schizophrenia of modernity is truly astonishing.

So how does the command *Be pure* impact the decisions you and I will face today? For most Christians, the answer will come in tiny, unseen ways. That's where we are called to walk differently than the world in regions of life no one sees. Blatant sins of the flesh are self-condemning—sexual impurity, adultery, lying, stealing, promiscuity. These need no commentary other than the reminder of Jesus' stark and unyielding command, *Go and sin no more.*

For most, however, the command *Be pure* assaults us in smaller doses.

"Purity in all aspects of life…—in attitude *and* behavior—has monstrous consequences for the Christian. The hidden sin, sketchy business deal, flirtatious glance, or off-color comment…the semi-truth, the fudging of an application, the stretching of accuracy, the exaggeration to put oneself in a favorable light…a lust indulged, a suggestive laugh, an ethical boundary pushed to the limit, a whispered curse, an immodest neckline…the grudge nursed, the lurking unforgiveness, the outburst of temper, the inattention to influences of unedifying music and film, the justified untruth—mostly unseen by any other human eye…these all build up like scales over spiritual eyesight, dulling true vision, preventing the development of God-eyes.

"Yet how easily even Christians justify such violations of purity, thinking their impact negligible on character. How much more lethal to vision capable of seeing God are the gross sins against purity…We live in an era that is quick to excuse even these sins of the flesh. But for the Christian who wants to see like God…there is no justification. *All* impurity dulls and blurs the vision—from the dirty joke to the clandestine affair.

"Nor must we forget that Jesus condemns impurity of mind, motive, and heart no less than the impurity that leads to visible sin. Impure motives produce what…James…calls 'a double-minded man'—one who isn't yet quite sure whether he *wants* to obey the Commands of Jesus in all things. *Impurity of motive*—a sort of halfway house of discipleship, where one is able to keep all options on the table in the event selfishness or loose ethics or moral slippage become expedient—will never produce Christlikeness nor reveal the Father of Jesus to the world…Scarce wonder that Jesus says that we must become as children to enter the kingdom. Purity is the heart orientation and spiritual outlook of the childlike." (From *Commands of Jesus,* p. 22)

Be…guileless as to what is evil. (Romans 16:19)
We commend ourselves…by purity. (2 Corinthians 6:4, 6)
It is my prayer that your love may abound…and may be pure. (Philippians 1:9-10)
Whatever is pure…think about these things. (Philippians 4:8)
The aim of our charge is love that issues from a pure heart. (1 Timothy 1:5)
Keep yourself pure. (1 Timothy 5:22)
Train the young women…to be…chaste. (Titus 2:4-5)
Cleanse your hands…and purify your hearts. (James 4:8)

---

85. See Through God's Eyes By Developing the Mind of Christ

To see through anyone else's eyes requires looking in the same direction they are. When someone says, "Look!" then stretches out his arm and finger, we have to align ourselves with them as if looking along a rifle barrel to see exactly what he is looking at. When Jesus said, "Behold," however, he wasn't pointing with his hand. He was talking about another kind of vision—*inner* vision. He was talking about seeing with God's eyes.

The principle is the same. To see with God's eyes requires seeing what God sees, looking in the same direction he is looking. We have to pay attention where God's hand is pointing. We have likened it to wearing "God glasses." But the prescription only works when we are peering *straight* through the lenses, not off to the side, looking in the same direction God is. That's when "God eyes" come into focus.

Frank Laubauch wrote, "I choose to look at people through God, using God as my glasses, colored with His love for them." (*Letters By A Modern Mystic,* Sept 28, 1931)

We are well familiar with the sixth Beautitude in Matthew 5:8: "Blessed are the pure in heart, for they shall see God." Might we here also discover a doorway from the previous command into the reality of today's command? Let us take the liberty of temporarily adding a single word to the text. Doing so, I believe, sends us deep into the heart of Jesus' meaning: "Blessed are the pure in heart, for they shall see *like* God?"

Only purity produces God-like vision. Only the pure in heart are capable of perceiving life and the world and the people around them as God perceives them. Purity produces God-eyes. Only God-eyes, vision pure as God's vision is pure, makes it possible to see God as he truly is. Seeing *like* God enables us to see God *himself.*

Yet all around us are sights, sounds, voices, priorities, advertisements, music, and influences that blare at us literally every second, telling us to wear the world's glasses, to see things with the eyes of modernism, independence, me-first, and self-fulfillment. We can't wear two pair of glasses at once. We're going to be looking at everything about us—situations, people, circumstances, relationships, culture, politics, and ourselves—wearing either the world's glasses or God-glasses. It's a choice we make every morning when we climb out of bed and face the day. Which pair of glasses will we put on?

God-glasses enable us to see people (including ourselves!) stripped of the silly fleeting superficialities that the world's glasses focus on—looks, prestige, personality, money, self-confidence, power, influence. The moment we take off the world's glasses, all these suddenly vanish into thin air. When we put on God's 3-D glasses, the flat and superficial perspective of the world fades away. Suddenly an entirely new set of perceptions comes into focus. The world's ridiculous priorities evaporate. We see *into* people. We see who they are and what they are becoming. We sense their hurts and anxieties, dreams and disappointments. We see precious children of God's creation whom their heavenly Father loves. This new outlook illuminates Paul's exhortation to look at people with the mind of Christ. It is how Jesus looked at people.

Accustoming oneself to seeing with the mind of Christ takes getting used to. We may stumble about a bit at first. The vision is so acute and clear that we are amazed we got by for so long looking at life with the one-dimensional, stale, black-and-white, uninteresting perspective of the world. The mind of Christ changes everything.

Put on God's glasses and suddenly that overweight, unattractive, boorish, infirm man or woman, overlooked and rendered completely invisible in the world's eyes, jumps into focus as a lovely, careworn, child whom the Father loves. The beautiful charismatic man or woman on stage or on the television screen suddenly loses interest to us. What is worldly acclaim in our eyes? The Father has given us his sons and daughters to love!

We regard no one from a human point of view. (2 Corinthians 5:16)
Have this mind among yourselves, which you have in Christ Jesus. (Philippians 2:5)
We have the mind of Christ. (1 Corinthians 2:16)

128

86. Do Not Be Covetous, Greedy, Or a Lover of Money

If we are brutally honest with ourselves, our responses to the commands reveal the state of our spiritual condition. A probing test is a dead giveaway when stagnation has settled in like an invisible fog. It is the *Oh-but-that-doesn't-apply-to-me* test. Check how often that reaction is the first thing that pops into your head when you turn the page and read a new command. If you are anything like me, taking your pulse with this test will yield some occasionally unpleasant revelations.

There are two kinds of commands that prompt almost instant excuse making: The *do* and *be* commands of character...and the do *not* commands. The first we excuse by saying that the standard is unrealistic, that no one could possibly measure up. *Be pure, be righteous, be humble, be perfect.* Who can possibly be *that* virtuous? So we excuse ourselves because the demand is too high. The second, the *do not* commands, we excuse for just the opposite reason, because they point to such low failings of character and behavior they could not possibly apply to *me*.

But when I am seeing with the mind of Christ and looking at *myself* with God-glasses, I perceive that *all* the commands apply to me.

Excuses and justifications expose stagnation like a spiritual thermometer. C.S. Lewis nails this universal tendency toward excuse making as it applies to his exposition of the Law of Human Nature: "There may be all sorts of excuses for us...I am just the same. That is to say, I do not succeed in keeping the Law of Nature very well, and the moment anyone tells me I am not keeping it, there starts up in my mind a string of excuses as long as your arm." (C.S. Lewis, *Mere Christianity,* "The Law of Human Nature.")

So here we face a truly unpleasant and ugly command. What...*me*...are you telling me that I am greedy, a mammon worshipper, a lover of money? Surely *this*, of all the commands...surely this one can't *possibly* apply to me...you don't really mean...*me*?

That is the one thing we must not say. The commands of the Lord, and the commands of the Apostles—including this one—are meant for *me* and no one else. Obedience is commanded of me and *only* me. In the light of that reality, all excuses and justifications evaporate.

Every command presents us with life's moment of truth. Every one is stark, uncompromising, definite, unyielding. There is no place to hide. We have been undressed. We stand naked before the Commands.

Suddenly there is no everybody else. Only me. And the Word spoken...the Word exampled...the Word commanded.

Therefore, let us admit—each in our own way, that this command is meant for us. We *are* greedy. We want *more* than we have. If I were presented two piles of bills on a table and told that I may have either, no strings attached, as a gift from an anonymous benefactor—one a stack of a hundred $1 bills, and the other an equal stack of a thousand dollar bills—remember, not a single string attached...which stack would I take?

Would I have the courage, peace of mind, and complete contentment with what I have to walk away and take neither? What would my choice indicate about my level of financial contentment?

Where does my choice leave me alongside this command?

Naked in front of the mirror.

A bishop must be above reproach...no lover of money....Deacons likewise must be serious...not greedy for gain. (1 Timothy 3:2-3, 8)

Those who desire to be rich fall into temptation...For the love of money is the root of all evils...As for the rich in this world, charge them not to...set their hopes on uncertain riches. (1 Timothy 6:9-10, 12)

Keep your life free from love of money, and be content with what you have. (Hebrews 13:5)

87. Clothe Yourself With Humility

It is easy to look upon the Bible's *Be* commands as more passive than they really are. We do this simply because "be" is a passive verb. It points to intrinsic character of being more than the *do* of action and decision. Therefore, whenever we encounter a command such as *Be Pure,* we have to translate the "be" of character into the "do" of obedience.

Now *Be* is a good verb. We might even say that it is the most significant word in the English language. It was this verb that God chose to identify himself to Moses. *I am* is God's name. In marking intrinsic quality of character, "be" is the most important concept in the world because it is a reflection of God's own character, his "Being." The commands of *be*-ing identify the men and women we *are* in our hearts and souls.

The wording of this command, taken from Peter's charge in 1 Peter 5:5, shows us practically how to "translate" the commands of character into practical commands of *do.* Peter does not admonish his listeners merely to "*Be* humble." That would have been a perfectly appropriate and powerful command. Yet Peter goes farther. He tells us *how* to walk in humility. He likens humility to clothes we "put on." We might not claim to *be* humble. If we are honest with ourselves, we know we are *not* humble. None of us are. That's part of the human condition. But humility is nevertheless a quality of character and an attribute of Jesus' being that we can wear. We can put on humility. Thus Peter's beautifully phrased command: *Clothe yourselves in humility.*

It is the same admonition given by Paul. In Romans 13:14, he says, *Put on the Lord Jesus Christ.* In Colossians 3:12, Paul tells us to *put on* kindness, humility, and patience.

C.S. Lewis speaks of the same principle of obedience, calling it "dressing up" as Christ. "To put it bluntly, you are *dressing up as Christ.* If you like, you are pretending. Because, of course...you realize that you are not a son of God...you are a bundle of self-centered fears, hopes, greeds, jealousies, and self-conceit...

"But...the pretence leads up to the real thing. When you are not feeling particularly friendly but know you ought to be, the best thing you can do, very often, is to put on a friendly manner...And in a few minutes, as we have all noticed, you will be really feeling friendlier than you were. Very often the only way to get a quality in reality is to start behaving as if you had it already." (C.S. Lewis, *Mere Christianity,* "Let's Pretend")

Does this make us hypocrites, pretending to be what we're not? Perhaps, if we're only going through the motions of religiosity to deceive people, to put on a sham shell of niceness when inside we're sneering and mocking all the fools around us. But if we are genuinely attempting to model our lives in obedience after the Lord's, it is not hypocrisy at all...it is obedience. We simply recognize what we are, what we are not, and what we are trying to become. We are growing into Christlikeness by obediently trying to wear the clothes of Christlikeness. We are behaving like the Lord's followers by trying to model our lives after his. We are trying to do what Jesus said.

So beside that rack in the hall by the door is another one, invisible but even more important than where we hang our coats, hats, and jackets. On its pegs hang the virtues of Christlikeness: kindness, humility, patience, and all the rest. These are the clothes we are commanded to wear every day. "And above all these," Paul adds in Colossians 3:14, "*put on love,* which binds everything together in perfect harmony."

I bid every one among you not to think more highly of himself than he ought to think, but to think with sober judgment. (Romans 12:3)

Lead a life worthy of the calling to which you have been called, with all lowliness and meekness. (Ephesians 4:1-2)

In humility count others better than yourselves. (Philippians 2:3)

Put on...compassion, kindness, lowliness, meekness. (Colossians 3:12)

Humble yourselves before the Lord. (James 4:10)

Have...a tender heart and a humble mind...Clothe yourselves...with humility. (1 Peter 3:8; 5:5)

---

88. Eagerly Rejoice in Right and Goodness

We are familiar with Paul's timeless words in 1 Corinthians 13, "Love...does not rejoice at wrong, but rejoices in the right." The NIV has it, "does not *delight* in evil." That simple word change may reveal a great deal about ourselves.

We encounter here another example where the familiarity of the words of Scripture, and the somewhat unusual turn of phrase, can obscure the enormity and practical impact of Paul's meaning. Who would admit to "rejoicing" in evil? Yet in so many subtle ways we take perverse, even perhaps a secret and unspoken *delight*, in all the ugly gossip we can get hold of. We have raised the question before: Who spreads gossip about the *good* in others? By its very nature, gossip thrives on the low, the sordid, the wrong, the sin, the weaknesses, the failings of those we love talking about. We take pleasure in knocking people down a notch. "I happen to know that so-and-so isn't the saint everyone thinks he is...would you like to hear about it!" How many times have you been on the receiving end of a juicy story that begins with such a tantalizing lead-in.

Sadly, however, the opposite kind of "good" news isn't usually discussed with the same enthusiasm,. "Hey, did you hear about Maggie and Joe—they just celebrated their 30th anniversary, and have been completely faithful to each other! It's fantastic!" It isn't these stories that are spread about hungrily from one set of itching ears to the next. Rather, it's usually just the opposite. "Did you hear about poor Maggie? Yeah, Joe is cheating on her." We profess sadness as we pass the story along the grapevine. In reality, we are enjoying every minute of it. The human craving for evil takes many perverse forms. Delighting in the failings of others is one of the worst.

All this is wrong, says Paul. It reflects the very opposite of love. As God's people, charged with sending love into the world at every opportunity, we are commanded to rejoice and take delight in the *truth*, in what is *right*, in *goodness*, in *virtue*, in *character*, in *righteousness*.

We've all lamented the fact that the only news reported is bad news. It's because that's what people "delight" in. In heaven, however, we're going to tune in to an altogether different kind of programming: "We have an exciting new documentary beginning tonight. It will chronicle the ten million acts of kindness, generosity, and love displayed during the earthly life of one of our newly arrived saints. The series will run for the next few hundred years. Don't miss a single episode."

Whether the ugly, sordid, gruesome, corrupt, and selfish will be topics of interest in the "other place," I have no idea. But in heaven, stories of goodness, truth, and righteousness will be the only ones we will be interested in.

I determine to get in practice by training myself to eagerly delight in right and goodness now. So let me take the opportunity to rejoice in *you*. I rejoice that you are reading and taking the commands of the apostles seriously in your life. I delight in your attempt to obey the commands. That is a good thing that will influence the world around you in the ways and truths of God. I honor you for your obedience. I will pray for you in your pilgrimage with God to walk by the commands. I covet your prayers for me in my attempt to walk the same road. It is a difficult quest. Obedience to the commands is not easy. I am weak and human as I know you are. Sometimes it seems as if it is five steps forward and four-and-a-half steps back in the lifetime journey toward Christlikeness. But I delight with you in those half-steps we are taking together! That is where we will focus our rejoicings—in the truth, the good, the virtuous, and the right. Thus, I honor you, I delight in you, I rejoice in you.

Take no pleasure in wrong, untruth, failings, impurity, disobedience, or evil.

Love...does not rejoice at wrong, but rejoices in the right. (1 Corinthians 13:5-6)

Whatever is true...honorable...just...pure...lovely...gracious, if there is any excellence, if there is anything worthy of praise, think about these things. (Philippians 4:8)

---

89. Endure Suffering With Faith, Fortitude, Grace, and Courage

If one were to formulate a perspective of *What Christianity is* from the preaching and teaching of modern evangelicalism, many might conclude it a religion whose foundation is a Genie in a bottle ready and able to do man's bidding if we just rub in the right place, while repeating the correct doctrinal incantations. Blessings, happiness, contentment, fulfillment, wonderful relationships, financial prosperity, success in the world...all these and more are just waiting for today's Christian. Live by these principles, pray these words, believe these doctrines...and all the Genie's blessings will be yours. Indeed, it is upon precisely this house of cards that many of today's most well known Christian ministries, churches, and teachings are based. Of course the God-in-a-bottle motif is shrewdly disguised. But dig deep enough and you will find this underlying perspective at the foundation—Become a Christian, join our church, follow our teaching...and good things will flood into your life. The Genie is waiting to bless you! It is no wonder these mega-ministries and appealing teachings garner such huge followings. They tell people what they want to hear. They are feeding them spiritual junk food.

How different was the teaching of the first century. The underlying message of the Christianity of those days was different: *Christianity may cost you your life.* The "blessings" Paul spoke of as coming to Christians in Ephesians 1:3 were blessings "in heavenly places," not earthly blessings. This contrast may be seen from a startling fact. The words *blessing* and *blessings* appear fourteen times in the New Testament. *Trials, suffering* and *sufferings*, and *tribulations* occur over seventy.

Of course, Jesus emphasized that his followers would be "blessed." But the word did not imply earthly gifts from the Genie's bottle, but eternal happiness. In describing it, most often Jesus said that such blessedness would result from trials, tribulations, suffering, and from being mocked and persecuted and reviled.

We are commanded both to *rejoice* in our sufferings, and also to *endure* them with patience, faith, fortitude, courage, and grace. Rejoicing in suffering may be a tall order. But being faithful to endure it with courage is an obedience that lies open to us all.

Such "enduring rejoicing" begins with the simple recognition that good will come to us in the end by meeting life's trials, disappointments, heartaches, and griefs with faith, fortitude, and grace. In this the modern blessings peddlers are right—*good will come.* But not in the way they preach, nor the kind of blessings-good they promise. It is the good of eternal character worked deep into the hearts of those who make themselves faithful, enduring, courageous, grace-ful partakers of the sufferings of Jesus. This is the reason Jesus tells us to rejoice—suffering produces spiritual character in a way mere blessing never can. So what do we want to pray for—temporal blessing or eternal character?

"We rejoice in our sufferings, knowing that suffering produces endurance, and endurance produces character, and character produces hope, and hope does not disappoint us, because God's love has been poured into our hearts." (Romans 5:3-5)

Value suffering for the spiritual tool it is in the chiseling of eternal character.

We rejoice in our sufferings, knowing that suffering produces endurance, and endurance produces character. (Romans 5:3-4)

Love bears all things...endures all things. (1 Corinthians 13:7)

We commend ourselves...by forbearance. (2 Corinthians 6: 4, 6)

Take your share of suffering as a good soldier of Christ Jesus. (2 Timothy 2:3)

Endure suffering. (2 Timothy 4:5)

Let us run with perseverance the race that is set before us. (Hebrews 12:1)

Count it all joy...when you meet various trials, for you know that the testing of your faith produces steadfastness. (James 1:2-3)

Blessed is the man who endures trial. (James 1:12)

Rejoice in so far as you share Christ's sufferings. (1 Peter 4:13)

Do not wonder...that the world hates you. (1 John 3:13)

90. Wage Vigorous Spiritual Warfare

Few commands give such wide berth to a diversity of interpretations as this. How do we define "spiritual warfare?" The question is complex and raises a multitude of scripturally entangling conundrums that are not simple to resolve.

Is the warfare demanded of Christians a full-scale onslaught against the societal godlessness that characterizes the world we live in? Are we to wage war against loss of individual freedoms, progressivism, sexual immorality, relativism, abortion, and other so-called "sins of the world," by activism in the world's events and affairs?

Or are we to read this command in the context of demonology? Most of modernism considers Satan a myth and demons an imaginary anachronism perpetuated by cultural superstition. Even modern-thinking Christians tend to pass over the demon-possession passages of the New Testament with a wink and a nod. For others, however, battling against Satan in the name and power of Jesus, breaking strongholds, standing against principalities in the heavenlies, and casting out demons within others and themselves, is as real in their daily walk of faith as breathing.

Others read spiritual warfare as vigorous prayer, and term those active in this fight "prayer warriors." Paul also speaks of the warfare of apologetics, of battling untruth in the arena of ideas, contending and arguing for the faith against the falsehoods of the world. Still others view the necessary warfare as entirely personal, battling against sin within myself in the inner and very individual war that Paul describes in Romans 7.

So we will all seek to obey this command in different ways. But however we read Paul's marching orders, it is clear he is talking about a *real* war being waged invisibly about us. It is a war that requires specialized weapons. These Paul specifies as the "armor of God." He identifies its components: The breastplate of righteousness, the shoes of the gospel of peace, the shield of faith, the helmet of salvation, and the sword of the Spirit.

One look at these weapons tells us clearly that it is not a worldly war. It cannot be waged in the political or cultural arena. These weapons exist in another realm altogether. We will never succeed in legislating the gospel of Jesus Christ. Trying to use the world's methods and systems to transform the world's values will *always* fail. Our warfare lies elsewhere than in spiritualizing the world into a "better place." This Paul makes abundantly clear. "For though we live in the world *we are not carrying on a worldly war,*" he writes to the Corinthians. "For the weapons of our warfare are not worldly but have divine power to destroy strongholds." (2 Corinthians 10:3-4) To the Ephesians he adds, "For we are not contending against flesh and blood, but against principalities, against...the spiritual hosts of wickedness in the heavenly places." (Ephesians 6:12)

It behooves us, therefore, to read the spiritual warfare commands of the New Testament very personally. Acknowledging oneself a Christian requires the recognition that we have enlisted as soldiers in a war. How you and I define our own calling within that battle may vary widely. But we cannot harbor the illusion that we can coast along in the current of modernism and worldliness and still really be a *Christian* in the full sense of what the word means. Paul does not leave that option open to us. We are at war against *everything* the world stands for. We are either in the world's army...or Christ's.

Cast off the works of darkness and put on the armor of light. (Romans 13:12)

I do not want you to be partners with demons. (1 Corinthians 10:20)

Give no opportunity to the devil. (Ephesians 4:27)

Be strong in the Lord and in the strength of his might. Put on the whole armor of God, that you may be able to stand against the wiles of the devil. For we are not contending against flesh and blood, but against principalities, against...the spiritual hosts of wickedness in the heavenly places. Therefore take the whole armor of God, that you may be able...to stand. Stand therefore. (Ephesians 6:10-14)

Wage the good warfare...Fight the good fight of faith. (1 Timothy 1:18; 6:12)

Resist the devil and he will flee from you. (James 4:7)...Your adversary the devil prowls around like a roaring lion, seeking someone to devour. Resist him, firm in your faith. (1 Peter 5:8-9)

"THE COLOSSAE COMMANDS"

Build Mature Beliefs

DEVELOPING RIGOROUS INTELLECTUAL FOUNDATIONS FOR FAITH

COLOSSAE—PAUL BUILDS A THEOLOGICAL FOUNDATION FOR THE TRINITY AND ALL CHRISTIAN DOCTRINE

While in prison in Rome in the early 60s, Paul wrote three wonderful and significant letters to Philippi, Ephesus, and Colossae. The letter of Colossians is noteworthy for several reasons. The gospel probably came to the tri-city region of Colossae, Laodicea, and Hierapolis through Epaphras who had been converted to Christianity during Paul's three year stay at nearby Ephesus. Though Paul had never visited Colossae personally, *Colossians* stands as one of his most theologically significant works, like *Romans*, written to a city Paul had not even visited. Additionally, Colossae was a minor and insignificant town in the region. *Colossians*, therefore, further reminds us of the principle Paul speaks of in *1 Corinthians* of the inferior member being accorded the greater honor.

When Epaphras came to visit Paul in prison in Rome, besides involving Paul in the intriguing case of Onesimus and Philemon, he brought with him reports of false teachers and heretical ideas circulating in the area. This concern, which many commentators identify as a germinal form of Gnosticism, may have prompted Paul to set pen to parchment. One of Christendom's most profound theological treatises resulted.

In *Colossians*, Paul sets forth the doctrinal foundations for the eternal nature of Christ as the full embodiment of God himself. The theological progression as Paul's spirit takes flight is breathtaking: "He is the image of the invisible God, the first-born of all creation; for in him all things were created, in heaven and on earth, visible and invisible...all things were created through him and for him. He is before all things, and in him all things hold together...For in him all the fullness of God was pleased to dwell, and through him to reconcile to himself all things, whether on earth or in heaven, making peace by the blood of his cross. (Colossians 1:15-17, 19-20) From this, and the rest of the letter, it is obvious how the doctrine of the Trinity was developed. Paul himself did not set forth the Trinity, but he laid the foundation for others to build upon in later centuries. Intriguingly, in the same way that *Colossians* establishes a basis for Trinitarianism (which became "orthodox" belief in most of the church), it also lays a scriptural base for universal salvation ("through him to reconcile to himself *all* things"...which became "unorthodox" doctrine.) Both belief systems can be derived from this *same* passage! It is yet one more case where we read into Scripture what we want to read into it.

The depth and profundity of *Colossians* shouts "Build mature beliefs" in every verse. But a more subtle message exists between the lines. That is the example of Paul's own life. It shows how we *grow* and *mature* in belief, how we must "leave the elementary doctrines of Christ and go on to maturity." (Hebrews 6:1) Maturity is a *growth* process. Discerning deeper truth, leaving shallowness, superficiality, and legalisms, and growing into *mature* faith, largely rests on our own heads. We have to *leave* superficiality. This may mean walking a different path than some of our brethren who are bound by legalities of doctrine (of which there are just as many in Christianity as there were in Judaism.)

Paul's example points the way. A dozen years earlier, he was contentious, possessive of his apostleship, defensive, embroiled in disputes with Peter, Barnabas, and Mark. Now, however, the words that flow from Paul's pen ring with a more mature tone. These relationships have been healed. Mark is now one of his most trusted lieutenants. Though we still see hints of the "old Paul," we yet observe that they are tempered by a gentler spirit, and a mind and heart responsive to lofty themes of enormous eternal import.

In observing this growth into maturity of a living, breathing man, we appreciate all the more the glory of the man Paul truly was...the man he allowed himself to become. Paul examples what it means to "build mature faith." C.S. Lewis puts it beautifully: "In St. Paul...The crabbedness, the...sophistry, the turbulent mixture of petty detail, personal complaint, practical advice, and lyrical rapture, finally let through what matters more than ideas—a whole Christian life in operation—better say, Christ Himself operating in a man's life." (C.S. Lewis, *The Reflections on the Psalms,* Ch. 11.)

DEVELOPING RIGOROUS INTELLECTUAL FOUNDATIONS FOR FAITH

91. Be mature in your thinking and wise in doctrine.

92. Increase your knowledge of God.

93. Build on a foundation of Jesus Christ.

94. Love truth.

95. Do not be ruled by legalisms.

96. Do not be shallow of belief.

97. Do not be deceived.

98. Do not dispute over doctrine.

99. Walk with discernment.

100. Equip yourselves for fitness to teach spiritual completeness.

91. Be Mature in Your Thinking and Wise in Doctrine

Speaking personally from the depth of my heart, I consider this among the most imperative of all the commands for our time. After an active life with God of over fifty years, I am more concerned than ever with the jargonistic superficiality, doctrinal formulism, and parroted cliché that rules so much of Christendom. This rote externalism is a more grievous threat to our witness than all the secularism and godlessness of the age put together. The church's most dangerous enemy is within.

Counterintuitive as it seems, however, this cosmetic Christianity is actually fed by what masquerades as depth and erudition. Among Christendom's many interconnected obsessions are two of special malignancy. One, a passion for theology, analysis, debate, knowledge, and persuasion concerning the *tenets* of Christianity. And two, a hunger to sustain the signs, wonders, blessings, and assorted feel-good perks and *feelings* of Christianity. We might term these *doctrinal intellectualism* and *personal experientialism.*

Yet high theology and impressionistic fervor may be skin deep facades to hide something other than the daily discipleship of humble obedient Christlikeness as the *raison d'être* for calling oneself a follower of Jesus Christ. As impressive as theological intellectualism and visible experientialism appear, they may actually sit at the heart of Christendom as fertile soil for propagating a superficiality all their own.

To discover what is meant by Christian maturity, we must ask how mature belief is built. We take as our starting point how we grow into responsible adulthood. As children, we are taught a range of truths and trained according to certain principles. Growing into mature men and women, we gradually make that teaching and training our own. The purpose is that we develop the "character" of maturity intended by and embodied in our early training. Along the way, we assess the tenets of what we were taught for ourselves. Hopefully we do so with wisdom and sound judgment. We are anxious not to cast off what we were taught nor blame our parents for their failings, but to deepen life's principles into our own character. We develop a personal understanding of life, God, and ourselves. Some former ideas we may leave behind. This does not necessarily mean they were wrong, but that we come to understand them in deeper and more personal ways. Training and teaching becomes a doorway into individual maturity as men and women.

Spiritual maturity is developed in the same way. Wise in doctrine means summoning wisdom, as Paul says, to "rightly divide" truth from falsehood…wisdom to discern what makes sense from what doesn't. Maturity weaves together intellectual rigor, experiential reality, and obedient discipleship. This process is energized and wisdom deepened as one yields to Scripture's commands. *Obedience* transforms the ideas and experiences of faith into the maturity of Christlikeness. Obedience thus becomes the door to wisdom.

George MacDonald's emphasis is clear-visioned and unequivocal: "Obedience alone holds wide the door for the entrance of the spirit of wisdom." "Obedience is the soul of knowledge…Upon obedience must our energy be spent; understanding will follow." "Obedience is the opener of eyes." (*Sir Gibbie,* ch. 38; *The Hope of the Gospel,* "Salvation from Sin"; *Unspoken Sermons, Second Series,* "The Way")

Do not be children in your thinking…in thinking be mature. ("In understanding be men," KJV…1 Corinthians 14:20)

And his gifts were…for building up the body of Christ, until we all attain…to mature manhood…so that we may no longer be children, tossed to and fro and carried about with every wind of doctrine. (Ephesians 4:11-14)

We are to grow up in every way into him who is the head, into Christ. (Ephesians 4:15)

Work out your own salvation with fear and trembling. (Philippians 2:12)

Present yourself to God as one approved…rightly handling the word of truth. (2 Timothy 2:15)

Let us leave the elementary doctrines of Christ and go on to maturity. (Hebrews 6:1)

Gird up your minds…Grow up to salvation. (1 Peter 1:13; 2:2)

92. Increase Your Knowledge of God

What *is* knowledge of God? Many potential counterfeits spring to mind: A salvation experience, so-called doctrinal orthodoxy, an accumulated storehouse of spiritual learning, a great prayer life, a vast familiarity with Scripture, spiritual revelations and experiences, faithful church involvement or leadership. For all we know, however, Judas might have been able to point to many of these in his life. He certainly had spiritual experiences we would consider astounding. He saw miracles worked and people healed by his own hand. But where did he arrive in the end? Did Judas "know" God truly?

One of the modern classics of our time is ambitiously titled *Knowing God.* The entire volume, however, represents but an extensive doctrinal treatise. The author's underlying message is: Believe the correct *doctrine* about God, and you will "know" God. Yet can such a sweeping promise really deliver? Does doctrine *about* God produce knowledge of God? Clearly the answer is no. The entire premise is a house of cards. Doctrine will never reveal character.

What, then, is *true* knowledge of God? What characterized Jesus' "knowledge" of God? The answer to both questions begins with knowing who God really is as a Father, then submitting oneself in intimate relationship to his Fatherhood-being and Fathering-nature. Growing out of this foundation evolves an understanding of his eternal plan and purposes. What is it that God desires, *as Father,* to accomplish in the lives of the men and women of his creation?

It is clear that "doctrinal correctness" has little to do with any of this. Our ideas about God certainly have to be correct ones. But if those ideas *about* God exist in a vacuum separated from his intrinsic Fatherhood, or if they are at cross purposes from his eternal purposes, then those ideas and doctrines do not produce true knowing. We may possess an entire catalog of doctrines in the storehouse of the brain, yet God *himself* may remain a closed book to the true knowing of the heart. Doctrine offers no door into intimacy.

Many define God by his almighty sovereignty and holiness. He is for them the great Judge who must punish all unforgiven sin unto eternity. But those who seek an approach to God through his "attributes" will never know God as Jesus knew his Father. The chapters of the book mentioned earlier read like a laundry list of God's attributes—grace, unchangeability, majesty, judgment, wrath, severity, jealousy—rather than a description of divine Fatherhood. Where in such attributes is the invitation to daily intimacy?

There is one door into the knowledge of God: *Fatherhood.* It is the *only* door.

To know God, we have to approach him as Jesus came to him—as a good, loving, faithful, creating, sovereign, holy, forgiving *Father.* We begin to know God when we come to him as sons and daughters, entering the arms of his embrace to be made good, clean, and obedient children. This is his eternal purpose—not to punish his wayward children for their sin, but to bring them into the home of his heart. Only there can he grow them into the same Christlikeness that Jesus came to earth to example through his own obedient Sonship. True "knowledge of God" thus begins by entering into the eternal purpose of God's Fatherhood through our obedient return to his Fathering embrace.

We commend ourselves...by...knowledge. (2 Corinthians 6:4, 6)

And his gifts were...for building up the body of Christ, until we all attain to...the knowledge of the Son of God. (Ephesians 4:11-13)

It is my prayer that your love may abound more and more, with knowledge and all discernment. (Philippians 1:9)

We have not ceased to pray for you,. Asking that you may be filled with the knowledge of his will in all spiritual wisdom and understanding...increasing in the knowledge of God. (Col. 1:9-10)

For I want you...to have all the riches of assured understanding and the knowledge of God's mystery, of Christ, in whom are hid all the treasures of wisdom and knowledge. (Colossians 2:1, 2-3)

Supplement your faith with virtue, and virtue with knowledge. (2 Peter 1:5)

Grow in the grace and knowledge of our Lord and Savior Jesus Christ. (2 Peter 3:18)

93. Build On a Foundation of Jesus Christ

Theological interpretations, doctrinal precepts, and individual spiritualizations abound to explain what it means to "build on a foundation" of Jesus Christ.

Most will read the above words through a doctrinal lens. The "foundation," as they view it, is comprised of a series of ideas, truths, and doctrines which, taken together, comprise foundationally correct "belief" in Jesus. Believe certain precepts—the Trinity, for example, or that the Bible is the Word of God, that Jesus is the son of God who died for our sins, that he rose from the dead and I have accepted him into my heart...add your own specifics to the list—and your "foundation" is solidly laid. Every Christian emphasizes a unique set of beliefs, experiences, and church practices that he or she views as essential. They are as varied as the multitude of denominations in Christendom.

Yet the question must be asked whether the foundation of true spirituality is comprised of a paradigm of precepts, creeds, prayers, experiences, or church traditions at all. Is this what Jesus meant by, "Believe in God, believe also in me." (John 14:1)

To find the answer, we need look no further than the foundation Jesus himself built into the lives of his disciples. What foundation did *he* lay in *their* lives? Surely we want that same foundation in ours. How did he establish them on a firm footing? What did he say that would grow their roots deep? What truths did he leave them to carry on after he was gone?

The answer to these questions is found in the upper room. It was there that Jesus set out with perfect clarity the life-foundation he expected his disciples to build on. Remarkably, however, we find nothing there about doctrine, theology, or correct belief. He made no mention of salvation prayers or baptism or the Trinity. He spoke not a word about forgiveness or that he was dying for anyone's sins. It will no doubt surprise many readers to learn that the words *forgive* and *forgiveness* do not appear once in the gospel of John. In the entire upper room discourse of five full chapters (John 13-17) the word *sin* only appears in two brief passages about the sin of the world. Jesus did not leave his disciples with a theological treatise that spelled out what they were to believe about his work, the cross, salvation, the Trinity, or about sin and forgiveness. He told them simply to *love* him, to *love* one another, and to *abide* in him. This was the belief he urged upon them—exampled, fulfilled, and lived in one way and *only* one way: Obedience.

Jesus left his disciples with a single resounding message—*Do what I have commanded.* (John 14:15, 21; 15:10, 17)

The foundation Jesus laid is found in his commands. He said it over and over—*Abide in me by keeping my commandments...do what I command you...love one another.*

There is no other foundation than this: The Commands. All the so-called "correct belief" in the universe will produce not an atom of spiritual maturity without practical daily obedience to the Commands as a foundation underlying that belief.

Let each man take care how he builds...For no other foundation can any one lay than that which is laid, which is Jesus Christ. (1 Corinthians 3:10-11)

And his gifts were...for building up the body of Christ, until we all attain to the unity of the faith and of the knowledge of the Son of God, to mature manhood, to the measure of the stature of the fullness of Christ. (Ephesians 4:11-13)

Work out your own salvation with fear and trembling. (Philippians 2:12)

For I want you...to have all the riches of assured understanding and the knowledge of God's mystery, of Christ, in whom are hid all the treasures of wisdom and knowledge. (Colossians 2:1, 2-3)

As therefore you received Christ Jesus the Lord, so live in him, rooted and built up in him and established in the faith. (Colossians 2:6-7)

We must pay the closer attention to what we have heard, lest we drift away from it. (Heb. 2:1)

Like living stones be yourselves built into a spiritual house, to be a holy priesthood, to offer spiritual sacrifices acceptable to God through Jesus Christ. (1 Peter 2:5)

Grow in the grace and knowledge of our Lord and Savior Jesus Christ. (2 Peter 3:18)

94. Love Truth

There is an enormous difference between loving *truth,* loving *doctrine,* and loving *opinion.* It is fearfully easy, however, to confuse the three. We *all* love our opinions. That is one of life's givens. Few things are so precious to us. Likewise, we all love the spiritual ideas that make up our belief systems. That, too, is a given.

Truth, however, exists on a higher plane than either opinion or doctrine.

The true lover of truth recognizes at the outset that his own opinions are flawed. They are the very human attempt of his mind to sift and sort his perceptions and conclusions, using the training and teaching he has received, to make sense of life and the world. But he recognizes that his range of opinions is not perfect. They cannot thus be said to represent Truth. Some of his opinions will be true, but he will find that some of them are also wrong. And as C.S. Lewis says, even among his wrong ideas, some are nearer truth than others. The lover of truth will recognize the same thing about his beliefs. No belief system, no catalog of spiritual precepts, can be 100% accurate. So even as he endorses ideas that he believes to be true, he does so knowing that the possibility exists for error. He recognizes his opinions and beliefs as incomplete signposts on life's progressive journey toward ultimate Truth.

For such a one, then, what he calls Truth, represents the eternal prize, the high calling, as Paul calls it, toward which he is growing but which he realizes he will never completely reach in this life. Opinions and beliefs are fluid. They remain subject to change as we move along life's road. As experience, fresh ideas, a wider range of relationships, and the deeper appropriation of previous beliefs all mature and expand, our perceptions and beliefs expand with them. The Christian man or woman sees the Holy Spirit as guiding this progression of growth, development, and deepening wisdom according to the promise Jesus gave his disciples to send them the "Spirit of truth."

Loving *Truth,* then, requires the recognition that our opinions and beliefs do not represent *full* Truth. They are revelations *toward* Truth. The self-righteous insistence that "I am right" and "You are wrong" has been an Achilles heel to Christendom's witness through the ages. Contrary as it seems, this insistence is not founded on love of truth at all, but love of doctrinal opinion. Humility concerning our opinions and doctrines, therefore, is one of the first and most important ingredients in love of truth.

Having laid this foundation, I am free to seek and *love* Truth hungrily and eagerly, stretching my heart and brain into realms "beyond" opinion and doctrine, and especially beyond my own partial grasp of what I call truth. The quest for Truth becomes no mere accumulation of that driest of empty husks called "spiritual knowledge." It is rather an ever-enlarging, ever-expanding awareness of the great *More* of eternity which God is anxious to reveal and is beginning to reveal to obedient hearts. Not content with the status quo of doctrine or opinion, with David we cry to God to *enlarge* our understanding.

Psalm 119 resounds with the heart's cry of growth: "I will delight in thy statutes... Open my eyes that I may behold wondrous things...I am a sojourner on earth...I will run in the way of thy commandments when thou enlargest my understanding...give me understanding...Thy statutes have been my songs in the house of my pilgrimage...I hasten and do not delay to keep thy commandments...Oh, how I love thy law!"

Love...rejoices with the truth. (1 Corinthians 13:5-6, NIV)

We commend ourselves...by...truthful speech. (2 Corinthians 6:4, 7)

Speaking the truth in love, we are to grow up in every way...Putting away falsehood, let every one speak the truth with his neighbor...Let no evil talk come out of your mouths, but only such as is good for edifying...that it may impart grace to those who hear. (Ephesians 4:15, 25, 29)

Whatever is true...think about these things. (Philippians 4:8)

Guard the truth. (2 Timothy 1:14)

Whoever knows what is right to do and fails to do it, for him it is sin. (James 4:17)

95. Do Not Be Ruled By Legalisms

It is customary to think of religious "legalisms" as superficial rites, rituals, and observances such as those Jesus identified in Mark 7. ("For the Pharisees, and all the Jews, do not eat unless they wash their hands, observing the tradition of the elders; and when they come from the market place, they do not eat unless they purify themselves; and there are many other traditions which they observe, the washing of cups and pots and vessels of bronze."—Mark 7:3-4) We identify Judaism and Islam in particular with such legalistic observances, those of Judaism deriving from the Old Testament Levitical Law.

Though in general Christian teaching in the New Testament emphasizes "freedom from law," rituals nevertheless worm their way in. If we are not careful, these external legalisms can turn vibrancy of faith into mere ceremony, custom, and habit. Crossing oneself is probably the most common legalism practiced untold millions of times a day. But how often does it prompt prayerful thought for what the sacrificial death of Jesus on the cross really means in daily life. Likewise, the celebration of communion or the Eucharist, the confessional, wearing Christian jewelry, a St. Christopher on the dashboard, a memorized prayer at every meal, baptism, even the strict attendance of a worship service every week all point to potential legalistic habits we adhere to without corresponding depth of meaning. Catholics, Protestants, Orthodox, Evangelicals...we all drift into legalism if we're not on our spiritual toes. Even those aspects of faith that are deeply personal—any or all of the above—can become a legalism if, when the meaning begins to drift away, we continue to worship the practice of its outer shell.

The above examples in themselves do not constitute legalisms. Paul tells us that nothing is unclean in itself. It is what we make of our observances that turns them into legalisms. The highest of truths can become a legalism. Likewise, the most mundane of observances can stimulate deeply prayerful exchanges with God. It is not the thing itself, it is whether we use our observances as opportunities for prayerful yielding-exchanges with our heavenly Father. Thus, prayer at meals, the communion celebration, baptism, confession, weekly church attendance...these can all be healthy components of a vibrant walk with God, *or* dead legalisms.

Another subtle form of legalism is equally invasive to vibrancy of faith. It is deadening because it is so entirely accepted as normal. That is doctrinal legalism. Christians consider themselves free from Old Testament "Law." But what of less obvious idea-legalisms that infiltrate our belief systems which we come to worship more than the God those doctrines are intended to reveal? Whatever depth of meaning may originally have existed in them gradually fades. Only the outer shell remains. It finds its place on a pedestal along with the other doctrine-idols of one's particular belief system.

Christianity's teachings are constantly enfeebled into such legalisms. Catholics recite their formula with the rosary. The Westminster Confession of 17th century Protestantism set out its legalistic recipe in 196 succinct points which good Scottish Calvinists were taught to memorize. The Four Spiritual Laws of the last century reduced the points of the salvationary formula to four. But the flaw of all these legalisms is identical.

You hear few pastors, priests, and Christian teachers saying: I'm not going to dish out spiritual recipes and clichés that are too easily turned into doctrinal legalisms. Instead, we are going to discover essential principles of faith by which we can *live*.

How can you turn back again to the weak and beggarly elemental spirits. (Galatians 4:9)
Let no one deceive you with empty words. (Ephesians 5:6)
Let no one pass judgment...with regard to a festival or a new moon or a Sabbath. These are only a shadow of what is to come...Why do you submit to regulations, "Do not handle, Do not taste, Do not touch"...according to human precepts and doctrines? These have indeed an appearance of wisdom in promoting rigor or devotion...but they are of no value in checking the indulgence of the flesh. (Colossians 2:16-17, 21-23)

96. Do Not Be Shallow of Belief

Three kinds of shallow beliefs are constant internal battles for the serious Christian. If we are not alert, they will infiltrate at every opportunity, and turn rigorous, practical, dynamic, growing faith into shallow, dogmatic, formularistic religion.

First, we find shallowness in those beliefs I have not made my own. The atonement is a great truth, but if I have not personalized and appropriated the combined miracle and example of what Jesus' death means in an ongoing moment-by-moment way in my daily life, then for *me* the atonement lacks depth. I have not appropriated its eternal and practical mystery. The truth is profound, but *my* belief is shallow.

We also discover shallowness in those ideas of my belief system I have been taught and have accepted as formularistic precepts without thinking them through. I have been told they are correct and orthodox, so I have neither analyzed their depth of meaning nor potential implications. We had a friend who said to Judy and me one day: "We believe in the five points of Calvinism. I don't know what they are, but we believe them." Sadly, this is exactly the sandy foundation upon which the beliefs of many Christians are built.

A third form of shallowness remains surprisingly prevalent in Christendom, that is the dogmatic adherence to *untrue* beliefs. There is obviously much overlap with the first two. One's rigid insistence on believing ideas that logical, reasoned, intellectually honest, and open-minded scrutiny would expose as false may result from the fact that one hasn't investigated or appropriated the principles involved. We'll take one example from Catholicism and one from evangelicalism so that everyone is offended together. Many Catholics are taught to believe that Mary was a virgin all her life. This doctrine goes against common sense, and against what the New Testament teaches (unless one employs interpretive sleight of hand and maintains that Jesus' brothers and sisters weren't *really* his brothers and sisters.) On any level of common sense, humanity, and the way God works, Mary and Joseph had a normal marriage. Yet many Catholics simply close their eyes and hold to the doctrine. On the conservative side, many evangelicals hold to an equally suspect view of salvation, believing that those who have prayed a certain prayer containing the correct salvationary ingredients will gain instant entry into heaven. Those who have not prayed such a prayer will go straight to hell. That's it—black and white, sheep and goats. No middle ground. Salvation, in this view, has nothing to do with how one lives his or her life. Again, this is contrary to what both Jesus and Paul taught, contrary to common sense, and contrary to the entire spirit of the New Testament.

These may be stark examples. It is easy to point fingers. But the mirror stands ready to expose our own areas of shallow belief. It may not be any of the above. Yet what aspects of *my* belief system have I failed to personally appropriate into my daily relationships and attitudes? How much of what I say I "believe" would more truthfully be described by saying, "This is what I have been taught." Where has untruth if not outright falsehood infiltrated my beliefs and spiritual perspectives without my being aware of it?

This is a command that points nowhere but inside. It exposes my own shallowness, no one else's.

Do not be moved and swayed by every wind of doctrine. Keep from being lured and led away by superficial, tantalizing, and unusual teachings that pamper pride and vanity.

Widen your hearts. (2 Corinthians 6:13)

Continue in the faith, stable and steadfast, not shifting from the hope of the gospel...For I want you...to have all the riches of assured understanding and the knowledge of God's mystery, of Christ, in whom are hid all the treasures of wisdom and knowledge. (Colossians 1:23; 2:1, 2-3)

We beg you, brethren, not to be quickly shaken in mind or excited. (2 Thessalonians 2:1-2)

Do not be led away by strange and diverse teachings. (Hebrews 13:9)

Gird up your minds...Grow up to salvation. (1 Peter 1:13; 2:2)

97. Walk With Discernment

It has been customary in recent years to equate what we call "discernment" with the spiritual gift mentioned in 1 Corinthians 12:10. Sandwiched between the gifts of prophecy and speaking in tongues in Paul's list, the easy assumption is that discernment is a miraculous manifestation given only to a few individuals. Certainly this is one aspect of scriptural discernment, what some translations amplify as, "the ability to distinguish between spirits."

But discernment exists in a much broader and more life-encompassing context than what might be evidenced in a worship setting as a singular "gift." We are all meant to exercise discernment in our lives and relationships. Discernment is to be a daily and continual aspect of our character and walk with God. If it were reserved for a few select individuals, it would not be commanded of us.

While discernment may be more than a gift given to some, neither is it automatic. It is a quality of maturity and wisdom that accompanies love of truth. These must be nurtured, developed, cultivated, and practiced. Discernment, like wisdom, is a lifetime virtue. The book of *Proverbs* illuminates the principles by which discernment is nurtured and grown in our lives. It is developed by seeking wisdom in one's own life, by learning to detect wisdom in others, training oneself to distinguish wisdom from foolishness, and above all by making wise choices.

James' words about speaking and listening give us what may be the most important clue how to develop discernment: "Let every man be quick to hear, slow to speak." (James 1:19) Translated for our purpose, we might read, "Let every man first listen, observe, watch, and reflect before arriving at any conclusions. Sift the evidence carefully. Do not respond hastily. Feel the spirit of those around you. Allow time to discern truth from falsehood, to judge between sincerity and insincerity, to weigh motives and assess possibilities."

In other words, discernment is in no rush. Discernment listens, observes, weighs. It keeps its powder dry. Discernment takes its time. Discernment is not afraid of waiting, patient silences. Discernment waits for wisdom to be revealed.

These are *learned* qualities. We nurture them by ceaseless *practice*. We develop them by living and obeying the proverbs.

An enthusiastic young Christian came to me years ago full of boundless eagerness to work for me and hitch himself to my vision of God's work in our community. "God told me I was to work for you!" he exclaimed passionately and with a great smile on his face. I think he expected to start that very day.

"That's great," I said, nodding slowly. "Come back in six months. If God is still telling you that you are to work for me, then we'll talk. We'll see if by then he is getting through to me with the same message."

Like the rich young ruler, he went away sorrowful and, I think, shocked at my response. I never heard from him again.

I have not always been the discerning judge of character I would like to have been. I have been taken in by empty words that were not backed up by character. My family has on more than one occasion paid a heavy price for my lack of discernment. This command is therefore a poignant one for me to reflect on, and one I read with the utmost sobriety.

Let no one deceive you with empty words. (Ephesians 5:6)

It is my prayer that your love may abound more and more, with knowledge and all discernment, so that you may approve what is excellent. (Philippians 1:9-10)

Test everything. (1 Thessalonians 5:21)

The Lord will grant you understanding in everything. (2 Timothy 2:7)

Do not believe every spirit, but test the spirits to see whether they are of God...every spirit which does not confess Jesus is not of God. This is the spirit of antichrist...by this we know the spirit of truth and the spirit of error. (1 John 4:1, 3, 6)

98. Do Not Dispute Over Doctrine

What is one of the favorite intellectual pastime of Christians?

We all know the answer because we've engaged in it ourselves probably more times than we can count—arguing over doctrine.

It has been the favorite activity of Christians since 50 A.D. when Paul and Barnabas toured Galatia. Not long after their return, Paul launched a series of vehement and passionate diatribes against those Christian teachers who believed Christians were still in some measure subject to Jewish law. He disagreed with that perspective of what Christianity ought to be. It was a doctrinal dispute within the fledgling church, with men of stature, integrity, and knowledge of Scripture on both sides. Paul framed his occasionally angry arguments both verbally and in writing. He left us a record of both in his letter of *Galatians*. The controversy resulted in a break between Paul and Barnabas and Paul's public rebuke of Peter at Antioch. The doctrinal debate was so intense it dominated the church for twenty years.

Remarkably lenient, tolerant, and open-minded in many areas, Paul was a dog with a bone about this Judaizing and circumcision debate. He lost no opportunity to harp on it. Nearly every one of his letters mentions it. More than twenty years after *Galatians* and his public criticism of Peter and Barnabas, Paul was still beating the same drum. His letter of *Philippians*, written from Rome in the early 60s, contains a caustic harangue against those he calls the "dogs" and "evil-workers" on the other side of this doctrinal divide. Was this perhaps his thorn in the flesh, an argumentative spirit that refused to stop harping on his pet doctrines? Paul simply refused to let the controversy die.

Yet it was this same Paul who repeatedly exhorted in his letters *not* to dispute over doctrine. We are thus faced with one of Scripture's many conundrums—the dichotomy between Paul's words and his example. Over and over he tells us not to quarrel, to avoid dissension and controversy...yet his own example reveals a contentious, argumentative, and arrogant spirit toward any and all who disagreed with him. This is the great black spot on Paul's remarkable career as a Christian communicator. It set dreadful trends in motion in the church which remain with us to this day.

We will probably never rid Christendom of its love of disputation, argumentation, and doctrinal controversy. But we can at least rid *ourselves* of it, and stop spreading the cancer in our own little corners of the Christian world. Doing so, however, may require a hard look at Paul's example, and the recognition of the damage done because he did not practice what he preached. Paul often told his listeners, "Imitate me." This is one case where we have to do just the opposite and reject Paul's example.

My own practice, whenever I sense the doctrinal tennis ball starting to be hit back and forth in discussion is simply to shut up. Let others pick up their rackets of opinion as they run onto the court to have their own whack at the ball. I lay mine down and say nothing. I have doctrinal opinions like everyone else. But I choose not to debate them.

I appeal to you, brethren...that all of you agree and that there be no dissensions among you, but that you be united in the same mind. (1 Corinthians 1:10)

The works of the flesh are plain...enmity, strife, dissension, party spirit. (Galatians 5:19-20)

A bishop must be above reproach...not quarrelsome. (1 Timothy 3:2-3)

If any one teaches otherwise...he has a morbid craving for controversy and for disputes about words, which produce...dissension...and wrangling among men. (1 Timothy 6:3-5)

Avoid the godless chatter and contradictions of what is falsely called knowledge. (1 Timothy 6:20)

Charge them before the Lord to avoid disputing about words, which does no good...Have nothing to do with stupid, senseless controversies...that breed quarrels. (2 Timothy 2:14, 23)

Avoid stupid controversies...dissensions, and quarrels over the law, for they are unprofitable and futile. (Titus 3:9)

---

99. Do Not Be Deceived

The two "D's" we considered earlier are intrinsically linked—*Discernment* and *Deception*. Obviously they are opposites. It is discernment that guards against deception. In that sense, *Walk in discernment* and *Do not be deceived* read as a single command. Yet the apostles repeatedly urge both exhortations on us, each with its particular nuances of importance.

Paul and John, as we see in the list of passages below, warn us against three kinds of deception. Discernment is our protection against all three. They are: *Self deception,* the deception of *untrue people*, and the deception of *untrue ideas*.

We recognized patience as one of the key elements in a discerning outlook—taking time to think and evaluate and reflect...listening...observing...waiting...allowing time to reveal truth. We discover that same necessity in avoiding deception. We see it clearly, say, in the business opportunity or investment or sales pitch that is too good to be true, that we have to take advantage of *today*.

The imperative of haste is invariably a signal as obvious as a red flag that something is amiss, that it is time for waiting discernment to step forward and take over.

The best things in life happen slowly, over time. Haste is one of nature's warning signs. Whenever I find myself pressed to make a quick decision, I back off and take a deep breath. If the "fantastic opportunity" passes me by, it was not meant to be.

Likewise, we find ourselves constantly confronting *ideas* and *people* intent to deceive. All these deceptions work together. Untrue people deceive with beguiling ideas that appeal to the fleshly nature. When a temptation seems unrealistically optimistic, wait...observe...listen...keep your powder dry, and be wise.

These principles come calling in Christendom all the time with deceptions that are gullibly swallowed because they are so appealing. Christianity is full of blessings deceptions, victimhood deceptions, self-righteousness deceptions, legalism deceptions, God-wants-you-rich deceptions, political deceptions, racist (white, brown, and black) deceptions, and all manner of doctrinal deceptions. These deceptions and the hucksters who promote them are so successful because they tell people what they *want* to believe. They have been active in the church since the first century. Yet Paul's repeated warnings against "empty words" and "beguiling speech" and "empty deceit" and "itching ears" are as contemporary as ever.

Paul's words sound eerily prophetic for our own time. "People will not endure sound teaching...they will accumulate for themselves teachers to suit their own liking." (2 Timothy 4:3) Sound familiar? That's why all deceptions, at root, are *self*-deceptions. We *allow* ourselves to be deceived because we "accumulate for ourselves teachers to suit our own liking." That's why Paul says over and over: "Do not deceive *yourselves*."

Jesus did not tailor his message to suit the likings of his hearers. He said, *Obey my commands. Obey the ones you don't like as well as the ones you do. Deny yourself, take up your cross, and follow me.* He did not appeal to people's fleshly natures by offering beguiling deceptions of blessings and spiritual pots of gold. He offered the cross. Therefore, let no one deceive himself about what discipleship is.

Let no one deceive himself...Do not be deceived. (1 Corinthians 3:18;15:33)

If any one thinks he is something, when he is nothing, he deceives himself...Do not be deceived; God is not mocked, for whatever a man sows, that he will also reap. (Galatians 6:3,7)

Let no one deceive you with empty words. (Ephesians 5:6)

I say this...that no one may delude you with beguiling speech...See to it that no one makes a prey of you by philosophy and empty deceit, according to human tradition. (Colossians 2:4, 8)

Let no one deceive you in any way. (2 Thessalonians 2:3)

The time is coming when people will not endure sound teaching, but having itching ears they will accumulate for themselves teachers to suit their own likings. (2 Timothy 4:3)

Let no one deceive you. He who does right is righteous, as he is righteous. (1 John 3:7)

---

100. Equip Yourselves For Fitness to Teach Spiritual Completeness

We climax this series of commands to build mature beliefs (Hebrews 6:1: *Let us...go on to maturity*) with an exhortation that expands maturity out of the merely personal.

Spiritual maturity clearly begins with oneself. All spiritual foundations are laid within the holy sanctuary of our hearts and minds where communion with and obedience to God begins. But with those underpinnings of maturity laid, higher obligations present themselves—responsibilities toward family, friends, and the wider body of Christ. Personal growth does not exist in a vacuum. We live as part of an interconnected family network of believers. Paul's relationship with Timothy reveals a wonderful model. Paul taught and trained and exhorted Timothy into personal maturity. All the while, however, he was also training him to train and teach others after him. Paul was always mindful of what he calls "the equipment of the saints, for the work of ministry, for building up the body of Christ." (Ephesians 4:12) His heart's desire was to prepare the whole church, each part individually as well as the whole together, for completeness. This exhortation, therefore, leads naturally into the series of commands that follows. As we continue, we will discover the church as a unity "knit together" into maturity as a living, breathing, functioning body that, in Paul's words, "upbuilds itself in love." (Ephesians 4:16)

This implies no anxiety to speak and teach and become Christian "leaders." Such often evidences the very opposite of true maturity. Maturity is passed on not primarily by words, certainly not by seizing every opportunity to share everything we know, nor by stepping into the limelight to "teach." It is passed on by character. Spiritual maturity, as it were, draws others into its wake. The obligation upon us is to recognize that our lives influence those around us for the building up and equipping of Christ's body into completeness. As we mature, younger Timothys will come to be part of our lives. We do not *seek* others to lead into deep spiritual waters. They will simply come. Wisdom draws.

Paul uses the heavily laden word "fitness" to describe the mature completeness that will equip us to teach, train, pass on, and fulfill our function within Christ's body. This tiny overlooked word is found in the Greek original of Colossians 1:12. Paul's words read: "...giving thanks to the Father, who has made you *fit* to share in the part of the lot of the saints..." Most Bibles, however, blot out the DO of obedience. No hint of spiritual fitness remains. Instead, you will read that the Father has *qualified* us "to share in the *inheritance* of the saints." All trace of the training regimen Paul laid out is gone.

The difference the translators have slipped in is enormous. Being *made fit* implies training, it implies a progression of growth. Paul is articulating a muscular vigorous faith that grows us to endure. Let us therefore commit ourselves to diligent *fitness* training not with passive doctrines that excuse spiritual laziness, but with obedience to the commands. Such fitness will draw and equip others likewise into maturity and completeness.

And his gifts were...for the equipment of the saints, for the work of ministry, for building up the body of Christ...we are to grow up in every way...into Christ, from whom the whole body...upbuilds itself in love. (Ephesians 4:11-12, 15-16)

A bishop must be...an apt teacher...Command and teach these things...Set the believers an example in speech and conduct, in love, in faith, in purity. (1 Timothy 3:2; 4:11-12)

What you have heard from me...entrust to faithful men who will be able to teach others also...Continue in what you have learned and have firmly believed...All scripture is inspired by God and profitable for teaching, for reproof, for correction, and for training in righteousness, that the man of God may be complete, equipped for every good work. (2 Timothy 2:2; 3:14, 16-7)

A bishop...must be able to give instruction in sound doctrine. (Titus 1:7, 9)

May the God of peace...equip you with everything good that you may do his will. (Heb. 13:21)

Let steadfastness have its full effect, that you may be perfect and complete, lacking in nothing. (James 1:4)

Exemplify Unity and Servanthood in Church Life

SERVING AND BECOMING ONE WITH THE BRETHREN

EPHESUS—A CHURCH KNIT TOGETHER
IN THE UNITY INHERENT IN FAITH

Ephesus is one of the New Testament's pivotal cities for several reasons. Paul obviously liked it there. He spent three years in Ephesus during his third missionary journey from approximately 53 to 55. It was obviously a fertile environment to serve as a base of operations in the region around the Aegean Sea. Paul's later "prison letter" to Ephesus (from Rome, along with *Philippians* and *Colossians* c. 60-62) is intriguing as well, believed by many actually to be the mysterious missing letter to Laodicea.

In *Ephesians* we are presented with a comprehensive treatise of Christian living that grows organically out of, and builds upon, the foundation of Paul's earlier letter to Rome. *Romans* explains the theological foundation of Christianity. *Ephesians* describes the life that results. Intrinsic to that life is the corporate dynamic of the Christian family. *Ephesians* illuminates Paul's vision for the "Church," the new universal community of God's people that has replaced the old legalistically defined Hebrew community. The purpose of that corporate body is to produce growth toward Christlikeness ("the fullness of Christ") in each of its members. One phrase from *Ephesians* leaps out as a white-hot light of truth into our hearts. We can be eternally grateful to the translators of the New English Bible (1970) for their inspired rendition of Ephesians 4:13. In this verse, a single word captures with exquisite precision the wondrous message of this profound and far-reaching book—unity, growth, maturity, and Christlikeness.

So shall we all at last attain to the unity inherent in our faith and our knowledge of the Son of God—to mature manhood, measured by nothing less than the full stature of Christ.(Ephesians 4:13, NEB)

It may be that no statement in the New Testament so succinctly captures the essence of God's purpose and plan for his sons and daughters. Unity is and will eternally remain the *inherent* hallmark of the Church's discipleship to Jesus Christ.

Ephesians also clarifies the truth that the doctrinal, structural, organization that came to be called the "church" is something very different from the spotless, blemishless bride that fills Paul's heart with such soaring vision. The historic "church" of schism and division is not the *Church* of unity, maturity, and Christlikeness Paul is speaking of.

Paul is here articulating a vision of the upper-case Church, the *true* Church. *Ephesians* illuminates the character of the *universal* Church, not its local and individualized shadow. This Church of unity will indeed be the living, breathing body of Christ, a Church of energetic, loving, selfless disciples—men and women individually and corporately growing into the mature sonship and daughterhood that reflects to the world the very stature of Christ.

Paul's description in *Ephesians* of what God is making of his people carries us away in wonder and glory. Our hearts are caught up, as Paul might say, to the third heaven in the mere contemplation of the unity that is to come. In that day the spiritual building of Ephesians 2:21—of which *we* are the living stones!—will truly be bonded together and grow into a holy temple and spiritual dwelling for God!

Legend has it that the disciple John spent his last years at the end of the first century in Ephesus. Over a lifetime, John was given extraordinary insight into the very love of God about which he wrote so eloquently. In John we observe the miraculous result of "abiding" in the vine-life of Christ over a lifetime. That result is love.

Whether it is legend or fact, Jerome tells a touching story of John's dying charge. It is in perfect keeping with the message for which John is primarily known. It is said that his disciples asked John if he had any parting words to leave with them.

"Little children," he replied, "love one another."

He repeated the words several times. Finally they asked if this was all he had to say.

"It is enough," John answered, "for it is the Lord's command."

SERVING AND BECOMING ONE WITH THE BRETHREN

101. Do not be anxious to teach or
place the immature in leadership.

102. Older men and women, teach younger men and women.

103. Pursue and emphasize what builds up the body of Christ.

104. Encourage one another.

105. Be sensitive to the weak in faith.

106. Use your gifts wisely.

107. Do all things decently and in order.

108. Deal with body conflicts in the church.

109. Don't neglect fellowship with your brothers and sisters.

110. Maintain unity.

101. Do Not Be Anxious to Teach or Place the Immature in Leadership

The "young prodigy" and "famous star" syndromes represent constant temptations for modern Christendom, especially in an era of worldwide entertainment and media exposure. A flashy youngster or well-known celebrity brings notoriety and attention to the Christian message. The automatic assumption is that this is a "good witness" to the world. New Christian celebrities are regularly trotted out and placed in the spotlight while they are yet babes in faith. The result is often tragic. Many of these quickly fall away while still toddling about in spiritual diapers. Examples are too numerous to site of child-star evangelists being put on stage to delight a crowd, only for their lives to fall apart when they reach their teens or twenties.

This tendency has always existed. When youthful aristocrat William Penn converted to Quakerism in the seventeenth century, it caused a stir through all England. He quickly became Quakerism's most visible spokesman, a "star" who gave the fringe movement stature. His conversion is probably one of the reasons Quakerism continued to grow as it did, and eventually became such a dominant influence in America. But there was a difference between his experience and that of today's media celebrities who are treated like Christian rock stars. William Penn was thrown in prison for his trouble. How many of today's "media Christians" would be so eager to sign autographs and stand before fawning fans if they knew they were going to be arrested the next day for doing so?

The celebrity mentality so infecting contemporary Christendom is potentially more dangerous than at any time in Christianity's history. If we knew that placing a new Christian celebrity on the podium, rushing him into a book contract, or sending him out on a speaking tour would ultimately result in his rejecting his faith two years later, would we be so anxious to disobey the command against placing the immature in leadership?

Even more widespread is the related passion—this one more personal...within *ourselves*—to lead and teach. No one is satisfied to sit in the background and listen, receive, absorb, ponder, and pray. Everyone has to find their leadership and ministry niche. It's not enough to quietly learn and grow. We have to start a blog, lead a Bible study, join the worship team. If all else fails, we'll just rent a storefront and start our own church. Instant leadership on the *No-scriptural-qualifications-required* plan.

All this directly contradicts the clear instructions laid out by Paul for leadership in the church. We are *not* eagerly to seek leadership. We are commanded *not* to rush to lay the hands of imprimatur and approbation on an immature Christian no matter how great his or her star power. Paul goes so far as to counsel against wanting to teach at all.

Yet the cancer infects us all. Who wouldn't want the acclaim of thousands hanging on our every word? The cancer infects the pastorate, Christian publishing, and is perhaps nowhere more lethal than in the Christian music industry. Christians the world over endorse and deepen the cancer by their passion for stardom rather than character.

The solution to this cancerous tendency begins at home. It begins with *me*. Let *me* sit in the back row and say nothing. Let *my* activities be ones of service not leadership. Let *me* offer to clean bathrooms and leave the leading of Bible studies to the spiritually ambitious. Let God raise me up in quietness and meekness. Let me not crowd to the front of the line in my own strength. Let me take the low road, not clamor toward the podium. Let silence, self-control, and humility be the traits by which I seek to emulate the leadership style of Jesus Christ, rather than that of the charismatic, flashy, articulate television personality, healing evangelist, or motivational speaker.

A bishop must...not be a recent convert. (1 Timothy 3:2, 6)

Do not be hasty in the laying on of hands. (1 Timothy 5:22)

Deacons likewise must be...tested first; then if they prove themselves...let them serve as deacons. (1 Timothy 3:8, 10)

Let not many of you become teachers. (James 3:1)

Christian teaching is built on maturity not celebrity. Gray hair not star power is the guide for leadership in the church. But intoxication with "star power" is not the only obstacle that sabotages the church's obedience to the leadership commands. Obedience is compromised by simple ego. We want to bask in the spotlight rather than sit in the audience. We are more anxious to preach and share than to listen and absorb.

Every subtlety implied by "the old teaching the young" goes against the grain of modernity. Everyone is in a headlong rush to be heard, to promote one's cause, to speak, to entertain. Everyone wants to teach, but few want to be taught. The podium, the spotlight, the pulpit, the speaker's chair lure and pull the immature from the moment they leave their knees as newborn Christians. How many in their twenties, thirties, or forties go to those Christians in their fifties, sixties, and seventies with the words, "I want to learn from you. Will you teach me what your years have taught you about walking with God? I want to sit at your feet." More likely they are announcing in the church newsletter, "Hey everyone, I am starting a group...a study...a ministry. Come and be led by *me*. Come listen to all the wisdom my few years with the Lord have taught *me*."

I keep a photo at my desk of five men. I am standing in front, a youthful forty-six. Behind me stand my dad, two pastors, and my youth leader from early college days. Three of the four are mostly bald and gray. It is a visual image I treasure. I gaze upon it every day to remind me of my roots. How fortunate I was to have such men in my life, and to have been able to gather them all in one place on that memorable occasion when I had dedicated a book to them. My father and spiritual mentors are all gone now. But their legacy lives on in the influence of their character in my life. I, too, was caught up in the rush to change the world by the time I was thirty, anxious to write, to share, to teach. How thankful I am, however, in the midst of my immaturity, that I had the good sense to learn and glean and be mentored by those four men.

On the shelf above that photo stands a handful of books, the names on whose spines remind me of my literary mentors of faith—men whose ideas and writings, more importantly whose characters—have guided and molded and influenced my growth. Joining the four men of the photograph through their books are George MacDonald, C.S. Lewis, Thomas Kelly, Frank Laubach, Henry Drummond, William Barclay, and the writings of a few others—Thomas Kempis, Francis Schaeffer, Brother Lawrence, Glenn Clark, and John Woolman. On another bookshelf I also keep a treasured set of Bibles passed down as a precious legacy from my grandfather, my father-in-law, and my mother, all links in a mentoring older-to-younger legacy that I value and treasure.

All these serve as practical daily reminders of the great truth that the old and wise are to teach and influence the young. These men and women are still working the strength of their example and character into the soil of my spiritual being. I look in the mirror and now see that my own head is covered with gray. I am as old as the men were when Judy stood behind the camera to take the picture of me with my four mentors. The years race on. I am as old as MacDonald was in most of the familiar photographs taken of him. I have already outlived C.S. Lewis by five years.

In spite of my own advancing years, however, these will forever be *my* elders in the faith. I will continue to honor them and learn from them—along with what new elder-teachers it may please the Lord to send me. If one should ever come to me and say, "I want to learn from the wisdom of your years," I would merely point to these and say, "First learn from these men."

Bid the older women...to teach what is good, and so train the younger women. (Titus 2:3-4)
Elders...tend the flock of God that is your charge...being examples to your flock. (1 Peter 5:1-3)
You that are younger be subject to the elders. Clothe yourselves, all of you, with humility toward one another. (1 Peter 5:5)

103. Pursue and Emphasize What Builds up the Body of Christ

The analogy of building is used throughout Scripture as symbolic of spiritual growth and development. It is an especially apt image with respect to the church. Peter and Paul both speak of our being built *into* a spiritual house or temple. This is a forceful and significant image. Paul's letter to the Ephesians is full of this dynamic perspective of a growing expanding church being fashioned into a dwelling place for God.

With this model before us, then, what is it that "builds up" the body of Christ? It is customary in some circles to assume that such things as leading a Bible study, giving a word of prophecy, sharing a word or a song with the congregation, being on the worship team, etc. are all activities that "build up" the church. While there may be some occasional lasting value to these, as often as not they mostly build up the vanity of one who wants to be at the center of attention. True Christlike compassion prompts far less of what passes for Christian "ministry" than good old fashioned spiritual pride.

What are the components of the spiritual house that is being built? We know the answer from Peter's words. That house is forged and sculpted one brick at a time with *living* stones. You and I are those stones. As yet, however, we are imperfectly shaped stones. We need to be chiseled and shaped. Rough and uneven bits have to be chipped away. We must be made to fit perfectly together with all the other stones in the building.

And here is a great truth. As we are living stones, we are fluid, pliable, unshaped, malleable stones. We are not chunks of granite—we are capable of changing our shape. To fit compatibly and comfortably next to you in God's building, I find that your rough edges and jagged bits of personality and mannerisms poke uncomfortably at me. You don't fit very well next to my nicely shaped stone. If only you would take care of those rough spots. Then the Master Builder reminds me of a simple principle of spiritual masonry. Perhaps I might pliably and graciously adapt my stone to accommodate all the jagged bits about me. Maybe all the stones surrounding me don't have to be perfectly shaped. They all must simply fit together. I can do my part to allow that to happen.

Lo and behold, then another great truth strikes home—my stone has just as many jagged bits as yours! You are having just as difficult a time accommodating to me as I am to you. Building up the body of Christ may require not my ministry but my adaptability to your foibles and weaknesses, just as you are adapting to mine.

The Lord's words about beams and specks in the eye give us all the insight we need about the process by which he is raising his building. Anything you and I can do to help one another achieve a little more of the ultimate shape God intends will truly contribute toward "building up" our little corner of that eternal dwelling place. My job is to help you into your final shape, adjusting myself in the process. Yours is to help me into mine. In this mutual upbuilding, you do not need my critique, nor I yours. What we need from one another is the encouraging adaptation of brotherhood, the strengthening kind word, the helping hand, the shoulder to lean on as we work together to grow into fitly shaped and molded stones. We are growth encouragers together, smoothing the rough edges of our mutual jaggedness in the gentle tumbler of relationship. Thus we grow into shape to be set, wedged, and mortared together into God's house.

Let us then pursue what makes for peace and mutual upbuilding. (Romans 14:19)

Lead a life worthy of the calling to which you have been called…eager to maintain the unity of the Spirit in the bond of peace. (Ephesians 4:1, 3)

And his gifts were…for the equipment of the saints, for the work of ministry, for building up the body of Christ…Speaking the truth in love, we are to grow up in every way into him who is the head, into Christ, from whom the whole body, joined and knit together by every joint with which it is supplied, when each part is working properly, makes bodily growth and upbuilds itself in love. (Ephesians 4:11-12, 15-16)

Let no evil talk come out of your mouths, but only such as is good for edifying…that it may impart grace to those who hear. (Ephesians 4:29)

104. Encourage One Another

Encouragement is personal. This command clearly comes as a corollary to building up the body of Christ. It is not limited, however, to our relationships with Christians or to a church environment. We are exhorted to encourage *all* men, *all* women, *all* children, in *all* circumstances. This is a 24/7 command.

Encouragement is such a familiar term. We rarely pause to consider the breadth of subtleties the word contains. Nor do we explore the wealth of means at our disposal for transmitting the blessed thing into the heart of one who crosses our path. Obviously a gracious or affirming word, a smile, a listening ear, a gentle touch are the most obvious ways to communicate, "I believe in you. You are significant. Your concerns matter. God is with you and in you and cares about you." These are imperative and powerful truths which every human being needs to be reminded of again and again. Yet they represent the mere surface means to communicate a deeper and more eternal truth—*You are loved!*

This is the heart of encouragement. *Love!*

Every person we meet is hungry for love. Reflect on an astounding truth—no one has *enough* love. Every person on this planet needs *more*. And there is no shortage. Love to fill every human need, every human hurt, every sorrow and loneliness, exists aplenty and to spare. You and I possess love in limitless supply to impart into those love-hungry faces whom we pass every day. Love is a commodity that *increases* the more it is *given away*.

What, then, is this familiar yet potentially life-changing thing we call *encouragement* which God places into our hands to transmit to those around us? A few words of definition and clarification may help us practicalize exactly how to encourage one another. We see that encouragement means: Affirm, hearten, cheer up, give hope, boost, invigorate, help, reassure, motivate, sympathize with. Pondering these words, we discover all the practical guidance we need.

Are these definitions too lofty to be lived, to be *done*? I would reply that they are so down-to-earth and real that we are presented dozens of opportunities a day to do them. For many, however, encouragement does not come naturally. We become so consumed by our own troubles we do not see those around us with God-eyes. We are like the man Jesus healed who said he saw men walking around, but they looked like trees. It takes a second touch on our eyes to see them "like men." As is true with all virtues, therefore, encouragement is a developed and practiced habit, a learned art and skill of human interaction. Self must vanish. The person before us emerges from the faceless haze of obscurity and becomes Jesus in the flesh—the least of these, God among us—to whom we have the eternal privilege of sharing a cup of cold water in a love-starved world.

Therefore, friends...spread encouragement as you go! Without analysis, contrivance, or expectation of return. Without timidity, without delay. Lavish it among the aging, the hopeless, the suffering, the neglected, the poor, and the unlovely where it is so thankfully received. The simplest kindness revives the downcast human spirit like a thirsty flower drinking in heavenly rain. Spread it with abundance even among the pompous, the self-absorbed, the rude, and the self-righteous where perhaps it may be needed the most.

Exhort, hearten, comfort, nurture, and bear one another's burdens...and *encourage!*

Rejoice with those who rejoice, weep with those who weep. (Romans 12:15)
Let all things be done for edification. (1 Corinthians 14:26)
Bear one another's burdens, and so fulfill the law of Christ. (Galatians 6:2)
For I want you to...be encouraged as they are knit together in love. (Colossians 2:1-2)
Comfort one another with these words. (1 Thessalonians 4:18)
Encourage one another and build one another up. (1 Thessalonians 5:11)
Encourage the fainthearted, help the weak. (1 Thessalonians 5:14)
Exhort one another every day. (Hebrews 3:13)
Let us consider how to stir up one another to love and good works (Hebrews 10:24)

---

105. Be Sensitive to the Weak in Faith

It is occasionally easy to read Paul's words about the "weak in faith" from the self-aggrandizing perspective of *my* maturity. We must admit that this is exactly what Paul himself often conveys.

To get to the practical heart of this command, therefore, we have to penetrate deeper. We are given no license here to nourish that disease flourishing so mightily in the evangelical church of the third millennium—self-righteousness. Instead, we are presented with yet one more opportunity to obey the two previous commands—*Build up the body of Christ,* and *Encourage one another.*

Now we are called upon to nurture and support and sensitively give a helping hand to those of our brothers and sisters struggling to make the commands their own. It is our responsibility to find ways to help them grow into maturity. How can I sensitively encourage *others* to take a few steps forward in faith? How can I strengthen *their* spiritual legs?

If I am in tune with the spirit of this command, my life and walk and thoughts and ideas and doctrines all fade into the background. I simply move with sympathy and sensitivity to love and encourage and build up one who needs the strengthening and sustaining hand of love. I have no interest in *speaking* to them from my storehouse of wisdom. My desire, rather, is to *listen* to their need. The tongue is the least important tool for this impartation of loving encouragement. Say nothing. Move in sympathy to the point of need. Words not required.

Paul's admonition in Romans 14:1 sheds fascinating light. "Weakness" of faith is often interpreted as holding incorrect doctrinal beliefs. Many view it as the responsibility of those older and wiser in faith to instruct and teach the young, immature, and "weak" in correct doctrinal orthodoxy. This is not at all what is implied by this command. Paul states clearly that our welcoming, helping, encouraging, burden-sharing sensitivity toward the weak is *not* for the purpose of resolving disputes over opinion and doctrine. The New English Bible gives an interesting turn of phrase to this verse, adding the wonderfully instructive phrase, "without attempting to settle doubtful points."

Helping and encouraging the weak implies not only leniency, acceptance, broadmindedness, and non-judgment on points of theology and doctrine, but also a forgiving spirit in the face of personal failing, weakness, and sin. We find a balance here with the numerous exhortations we considered earlier to root out intentional sin from the church.

How, then, do we balance intolerance toward sin (Commands 35-37) with what Paul says in Romans 15:1, "Bear with the failings of the weak." We find ourselves hindered again by Paul's, "We who are strong." Since we cannot know Paul personally in the flesh, he is a difficult man to assess. He comes across as pompous and full of himself, so convinced of his own maturity and wisdom alongside the weak, that we have to wonder if we are losing something in the translation. Was the *real* Paul perhaps more humble than his words imply?

As always, the commands are complex and multi-dimensional. They point in what appear diverse directions, yet with a harmony and unity of balance that brings rejoicing to the discerning eye of wisdom. Here we find that diversity and balance in merging *Root out sin* and *Be patient with the weak of faith.*

As for the man who is weak in faith, welcome him, but not for disputes over opinions. (Romans 14:1)

Bear with the failings of the weak. (Romans 15:1)

If a man is overtaken in any trespass, you who are spiritual should restore him in a spirit of gentleness. (Galatians 6:1)

Bear one another's burdens, and so fulfill the law of Christ. (Galatians 6:2)

Encourage the fainthearted, help the weak. (1 Thessalonians 5:14)

Elders...tend the flock of God that is your charge...being examples to your flock. (1 Peter 5:1-3)

106. Use Your Gifts Wisely

At first read, this command seems so obvious as to be unnecessary. Who would chose to use a gift *un*wisely? No one intentionally breaks a Christmas gift, or intentionally uses a hammer to hit his thumb instead of the nail.

But when it comes to the *spiritual* gifts—tools intended for the strengthening and mutual building up of the body of Christ—these precious commodities are all too often the source of excess, lack of wisdom, and self-glorification. Humility, which is the regulating energy of all the gifts, is grievously lacking in the church's practice of many spiritual gifts. How often have we squirmed uncomfortably listening to an outpouring of tongues or prophecy which accomplished little more than puffing up the prophetic tongue-speaker in his or her own eyes? How many "music ministry" teams so drip with rock star wannabe ego as to infect their worship services with a spirit of Self not Christ? Thrusting oneself into the spotlight can never accurately be called "ministry."

All the commands, and especially this one, hit the modern self-glorifying church squarely in the solar plexus. *Why* are so many eager to sing and perform in the front of a congregation? What stirs in the heart that would make one desire all eyes on him? To what extent are humility, Christlikeness, and self-abasement the motivating factors? Do Christian authors humbly treat their opportunities and good fortune as from God's hand to build up the body of Christ, or do ego and pride worm their way in to hear one's efforts praised and lauded? We each have to write our own mirror responses to this command. You have to write yours. I have just written one of mine.

It might be appropriate to read this command as: Humbly and wisely use your gifts in anonymity.

This idea has prompted my reflection on a very soul searching question. How many musicians would be eager to join the music team if the music was piped in from a hideaway in the basement and no one *saw* them, if no one knew who was on the music team...ever? No one *ever* knew. All participation on the music team was forever and completely anonymous. How many would clamor to "minister" unseen and unknown?

How many inspired words of prophecy would be spoken if they were delivered from a hidden room with voices disguised such that no one *ever* knew who had delivered the message?

How might my motivation as a writer be different if my name never appeared on a single book, and no one ever knew that I was a writer? *Ever*.

How much do we flatter our pride with the misuse of the holy word *ministry*? We ought to be ashamed of our easy and hypocritical use of the word. How would today's Christian enterprise change if *all* so-called ministry were anonymous? If all Christian music, all writing, all preaching, all teaching, all service, all evangelism, all worship were completely void of personality...if every book, every song, every sermon was anonymous...if the music and message had to stand on their own without names or faces and personalities attached.

It is an extremely sobering question to stand in front of the mirror, look ourselves in the eyeball, and ask: *Do you, Michael Phillips, always use your gifts sensitively, wisely, sympathetically, gently, anonymously, and humbly?*

Having gifts that differ...let us use them. (Romans 12:6)

And his gifts were...for the equipment of the saints, for the work of ministry, for building up the body of Christ. (Ephesians 4:11-12)

Do not neglect the gift you have. (1 Timothy 4:14)

Fulfill your ministry. (2 Timothy 4:5)

As each has received a gift, employ it for one another, as good stewards of God's varied grace. (1 Peter 4:10)

157

107. Do All Things Decently and In Order

Paul wrote these words to sum up the 14th chapter of 1 Corinthians in which he had been setting forth guidelines for the use and operation of the spiritual gifts (speaking in tongues, prophecy, interpretation, etc.) For those who regularly participate in charismatic and Pentecostal worship services, the command requires little explanation. In such settings where spontaneity, fervor, and demonstrative outpourings at times create unpredictability in worship, it is not unusual for chaos to replace calm and orderliness. Paul's instructions may be paraphrased simply: *Don't let it get out of hand. Be sensitive to one another. Be orderly in worship.*

It may be, however, that his words are not limited to worship. This injunction brings with it a broad perspective that encompasses all aspects of behavior. It starts in the church. But as we read these words personally, many areas leap to mind where we are perhaps not as "orderly" in our lives and routines and practices as we ought to be. Frequently as we progress through the commands we are reminded that our witness to the world comes more through behavior, demeanor, and personal habits than from our words of belief. Nothing so quickly and visibly undermines that witness as a disheveled, random, scattered, frantic, chaotic, flustered, ship-shod, undisciplined personal life.

We've all known those who are perpetually late, who forget appointments, and whose days are ruled by pandemonium. It's easy to laugh it off. But personal disorganization is a bad witness. There is nothing else to call it. Do *all* things decently and in order. The Greek implies not so much "decently," which is a peculiar translation to have been perpetuated through the years. The actual word is "becomingly." Making this change plunges us into the heart of Paul's intent. It is not "becoming" in anyone's eyes, especially the world's, to observe a life in disarray.

This is clearly not a command reserved for Sunday mornings. It is a challenge to bring discipline, harmony, and *order* into our days, into the stateliness and sobriety with which we conduct our relationships, into the thoughtful wisdom we bring to our decisions. Paul does not only say to worship in an orderly manner, but to do ALL things becomingly and in order.

As we read the gospels, we often sense a flurry of turbulence, uncertainty, question, anger, and a hundred other emotions and reactions flying around the outer circles of the storm that hit Palestine in the late 20s A.D. At the eye of the hurricane, however, all was calm, sedate, peaceful, orderly. That's where Jesus lived—at the heart, in the calm of the Center. In this command Paul is reminding us where we live. At the eye, not in the storm.

My thoughts inevitably return to my mentor of the Center, Quaker Thomas Kelly.

"Over the margins of life comes a whisper, a faint call, a premonition of richer living which we know we are passing by. Strained by the very mad pace of our daily outer burdens, we are further strained by an inward uneasiness, because we have hints that there is a way of life vastly richer and deeper...a life of unhurried serenity and peace...If only we could slip over into that Center! If only we could find the Silence which is the source of sound! We have seen and known some people who seem to have found this deep Center of living, where the fretful calls of life are integrated....Surrounding the trifles of their daily life is an aura of infinite peace and power and joy...

"Life is meant to be lived from a Center, a divine Center. Each one of us can live such a life of...peace and serenity, of integration and confidence and simplified multiplicity...*if we really want to.* There is a divine Abyss within us all, a holy Infinite Center, a Heart, a Life who speaks to us and through us to the world. We have all heard this holy Whisper at times. At times we have followed the Whisper, and amazing equilibrium of life...set in. But too many of us...I fear, have not surrendered all else, in order to attend to the Holy Within." (Thomas Kelly, *A Testament of Devotion,* p. 114-17)

Let all things be done decently and in order. (1 Corinthians 14:40, KJV)

108. Deal With Body Conflicts in the Church

This command contains two elements. One, when problems and conflicts arise in the church—deal with them. Two, when problems have to be resolved, don't involve outsiders. As much as possible keep them in the church.

Essentially the first can be paraphrased as: Don't procrastinate, excuse, justify, ignore, or sweep problems under the carpet. Be gentle, understanding, compassionate, and above all wise, loving, and mature in handling them. But find solutions promptly and judiciously. Don't let them become festering sores in the church body.

When word reached Paul that the church in Corinth was allowing sexual immorality in its midst by one of its members, he was stunned that church leaders had allowed such a situation to persist. He shot off a letter telling them to get with the program. Confront the sinning man and urge repentance, he said forcefully. If there is none, remove him from the church. In other words...*Deal with it!*

The second half of this command is more easily misunderstood, especially by the world. To the undiscerning eye it smacks of hypocrisy, as if he is saying: Hide your sin from public view. Though everyone knows otherwise, pretend that the church is full of squeaky clean people.

Something far more pragmatic, however, is on Paul's mind. The reason we are to deal with conflicts in the church as much as possible without involving outsiders stems directly from Jesus' own words. Brothers and sisters are to go to *one another* to resolve conflict. If they are unable to do so, they must go to the church and its leaders. Jesus says to agree with one's adversary in private, before the world's judges, courts, magistrates, and prisons are forced to intervene. It is not a command encouraging hypocrisy—hiding the church's dirty laundry from the world's eyes. We're not pretending to be other than we are. We simply recognize the practical fact that the world is incapable of judging situations, relationships, problems, and truth accurately.

Personal issues are to be dealt with inside the church as well. A Christian going to a non-Christian psychologist steeped in the psycho-babble of worldly progressivism is seeking help from the enemy camp. What can possibly result but confusion?

Dealing with internal struggles, marital and family issues, addictions, besetting sins, guilt, anger, unforgiveness, adultery, self-esteem...all these require the wisdom and insight of those equipped to turn the searchlight of the gospels onto the problem in order to bring about resolution, restoration, healing, forgiveness, and wholeness. The world will forever fumble about with politically correct responses that accomplish nothing but deepen independence, unaccountability, and blame of others for our problems. The only solutions capable of leading to the healing of the whole man, the only true resolution to conflict (internal and relational) will originate in a proper, humble, and repentant response to Jesus and his commands. The world cannot point in this direction. If we desire help from others, we have to seek it from men and women who have grown wise in the use of the command-mirror. Eternal wholeness of personhood is found nowhere else.

We might reword this command: Deal with conflict, sin, and personal issues in the gospels.

It is actually reported that there is immorality among you...Let him, who has done this be removed from among you. (1 Corinthians 5:1-2)

Cleanse out the old leaven. (1 Corinthians 5:7)

What have I to do with judging outsiders? Is it not those inside the church whom you are to judge? (1 Corinthians 5:12)

When one of you has a grievance against a brother, does he dare go to law before the unrighteous instead of the saints? (1 Corinthians 6:1)

Admonish the idle. (1 Thessalonians 5:14)

As for those who persist in sin, rebuke them in the presence of all. (1 Timothy 5:20)

As for a man who is factious, after admonishing him once or twice, have nothing more to do with him. (Titus 3:10)

109. Don't Neglect Fellowship With Your Brothers and Sisters

We find ourselves here facing a sometimes confusing, often misapplied, and complex command. The injunction in Hebrews 10:25, "...not forsaking the assembling of ourselves together," as the King James wording has it, is frequently used as a scriptural basis for the attendance legalism, *Be in church every Sunday without fail and without excuse,* and to condemn those who aren't. How many pastoral visits of concern are not motivated by a shepherding heart of concern, but rather begin with the words, "I haven't seen you in church recently." The legalism of "church attendance" as an indicator of spiritual health is one of many fallacies infecting the body of Christ. Unfortunately, mere regularity of church attendance accomplishes little to strengthen the church unto Christlikeness. It merely undergirds a new Christian legalism no less crippling to the flourishing of the Spirit as was its Old Testament Mosaic counterpart.

Therefore, we must look for deeper themes and purposes that God intends to accomplish through our fellowship with the brethren.

The King James "assembly" conveys an erroneous picture, implying regular structured church meetings. The RSV's "to meet together" brings the command down to a more personal level. The actual Greek meaning is even more individually rendered "to come together." There is no sense in the original of "gatherings." This verse has nothing to do with weekly worship services. We will more accurately read the passage as, *Do not neglect one another.* It is not "meetings" we are warned to be attentive of, but *each other.*

Let us, therefore, read the writer's intent in its positive sense: "Build up the body of Christ by being attentive to your brothers and sisters. Fellowship with them and come together with them. Do not isolate yourself and think only of your own spiritual health. You need the brethren and the brethren need you. Share your gifts, your hospitality, your encouragement. Knit yourselves together in love."

The great 17th and 18th century devotionalist William Law offered the following insight into the attendance legalism that plagued the church in his time as well.

"It is very observable that there is not one command in all the gospel for public worship. One could say that it is the duty that is least insisted upon in Scripture. Frequent church attendance is never so much as mentioned in all of the New Testament. But the command to have a faith which governs the ordinary actions of our lives is to be found in almost every verse of Scripture. Our blessed Savior and his Apostles were very intent on giving us teaching that relates to daily life. They teach us: to renounce the world and be different in our attitudes and ways of life; to renounce all its goods, to fear none of its evils, to reject its joys, and have no value for its happiness; to be as newborn babes who are born into a new state of things; to live as pilgrims in spiritual watching, in holy fear, and heavenly aspiring after another life; to take up our cross daily, to deny ourselves, to profess the blessedness of mourning, to seek the blessedness of poverty of spirit; to forsake the pride and vanity of riches, to take no thought for the morrow, to live in the profoundest state of humility, to rejoice in worldly sufferings; to reject the lust of the flesh, the lust of the eyes, and the pride of life; to bear injuries, to forgive and bless our enemies, and to love all people as God loves them; to give up our whole hearts and affections to God, and to strive to enter through the straight gate into a life of eternal glory.

"Isn't it strange that people place so much emphasis upon going to church when there is not one command from Jesus to do so, and yet neglect the basic duties of our ordinary life which are commanded in every page of the Gospels? (William Law, *A Serious Call to a Devout and Holy Life,* 1728, from pp. 192-92 of *Devotional Classics,* R. Foster, ed.)

> Let us consider how to stir up one another to love and good works, not neglecting to meet together...but encouraging one another. (Hebrews 10:24-25)
> Love the brotherhood. (1 Peter 2:17)

110. Maintain Unity

Unity is the great neglected virtue of the New Testament. It may, in fact, be the *most* important of all the virtues the church is to display to the world. Yet this command is also one of the *least* obeyed of all the commands. We do not exaggerate to say that *disunity*—such a grievous hallmark of the church throughout its history—is nothing less than a direct slap in Jesus' face. We ought to be ashamed of ourselves.

Jesus' prayer of John 17, in a sense, represents the highlight of the gospel story. In its own way it stands of equal significance alongside the Lord's garden prayer, his crucifixion, and then his resurrection. It may indeed offer a more reliable climax to New Testament prophecy than the entire book of *Revelation*. The reason is simple: In John 17 we have Jesus' final spoken words prior to his death concerning the future. That those words come in a prayer to his Father give them all the more weight. These are therefore words of prophetic intent which we can *know* of a certainty *will* be fulfilled. Only in John 17 is God's prophetic intent unmistakably clear. This prophetic utterance points the way to the destiny of his church.

The tense of the Greek of John 17:23 points both toward the present and the future. It is impossible to render exactly into English. It literally reads: *"...that they may be having been perfected in one..."* He is speaking both of present spiritual reality and future fact.

By only one means will the world know of God's love, and know the truth that Jesus is God's Son and that he came from the Father—by the UNITY of God's people, as they become not partially one but *perfectly* one. Without "oneness" visibly flowing among Christ's followers, the world cannot fully know Jesus and his Father.

The world still does not know that Jesus came from God for the simple reason that God's people are not one. All Christendom's alternate witnessing programs evaporate in the stunning present/future reality of John 17. Unity is the only meaningful witness. Without unity, we are wasting our time telling the world to believe.

This is the condition that must exist prior to the Lord's return. *Unity* within the body of Christ is the prophetic reality that will usher in the future. *Unity* rules the prophetic timetable. *Unity* is the prophetic vision. *Unity* in Christ's body is the gateway to eternity.

A simple principle unlocks the secret of unity and makes it attainable right now to you and me. It is just what we discussed earlier: *Widen your hearts...*widening our perception of the brotherhood. This requires an *inclusive* outlook of what comprises Christian belief. It requires laying down prized doctrinal legalisms—not because we believe them in error, but relinquishing the insistence that all Christians conform to the same dogmas of belief we do. Cherishing unity above doctrinal agreement, we seek to *include* not exclude, widening the arms of faith to embrace those of different practice and theologic persuasion. We recognize discipleship in the midst of difference. Abandoning doctrinal narrowness, the brotherhood flourishes into unity. Amish and Adventist, Baptist and Brethren, Catholic and Congregationalist, Methodist and Mennonite, Presbyterian and Pentecostal, Orthodox and Reformed and Quaker and Nazarene and Lutheran and Anglican all embrace in the unity of their shared faith.

Do not allow factions or a party spirit to exist among you. Pursue, value, and work toward unity. Knit yourselves together and be at peace with one another.

Let us then pursue what makes for peace and mutual upbuilding. (Romans 14:19)

I appeal to you, brethren...that all of you agree and that there be no dissensions among you, but that you be united in the same mind. (1 Corinthians 1:10)

Agree with one another, live in peace. (2 Corinthians 13:11)

Lead a life worthy of the calling to which you have been called...eager to maintain the unity of the Spirit in the bond of peace. (Ephesians 4:1, 3)

Complete my joy by being of the same mind, having the same love, being in full accord and of one mind. (Philippians 2:2)

"THE ROME COMMANDS"

Evidence Discipleship in the World

THE WORLD WILL KNOW THE TRUTH
BY OUR *BE* AND *DO*, NOT OUR *SAY*

ROME—LIFE WELL LIVED IN A HOSTILE WORLD

At last we arrive where it is said all roads lead…to Rome.

How fitting that this city at the center of the greatest empire the world had ever known, which Paul had aspired to reach for so many years, became his final destination and resting place. At the same time it became the launching point, in a sense, for the second phase of the expansion of the Christian gospel. The first phase took 35-40 years. During those decades the gospel expanded from Jerusalem to mighty Rome itself, largely through the efforts of Paul and the other apostles who carried that message personally abroad. Up to that point it was primarily a word-of-mouth expansion.

From Rome, however, that message would go viral. In Rome, the protégé of both Peter and Paul, John Mark himself, now a mature man and leader in the Christian movement, set quill to parchment and penned a new form of literary biography. He called his work a "gospel"—*good news*. As Jesus' life and teaching was now committed to writing, and with three more gospels to follow, the message of Christianity could literally be spread in every direction around the globe. With the example of *Mark* pointing to the imperative of *written* documentation to take Christian truth into the future, copies were also being made of the writings of Paul. Toward the end of the first century these began to be gathered together. To them were slowly added the writings of the other apostles. Throughout the following century, in many groupings and compilations, the early forms of what became the New Testament gradually came into being.

Rome was the final destination for Peter and Paul, who both died there, and at the same time the beginning of an explosive new era of Christian growth. So vividly do the Lord's prophetic words come to life, not only in his own example, but from the lives of the first generation of faithful followers and transmitters of his message: "Unless a grain of wheat falls into the earth and dies, it remains alone; but if it dies, it bears much fruit." (John 12:24) How magnificently was that truth fulfilled through the deaths of those very apostles whose commands we are attempting to incorporate into our lives—most notably Paul, Peter, James, and John. In large measure, Rome was the garden into which those dying seeds were planted and from which they indeed produced "much fruit." We do not know where James died. John presumably died in Ephesus, if not Patmos. But Peter and Paul were both martyred in Rome. Even as their lives were coming to an end, Mark was writing the gospel which would grow the dying seeds of their lives into a worldwide eternal harvest of spiritually living grain.

From Rome outward, Christianity threw off the limitation of being regarded as a minor Jewish sect. Now it became a religion for all men, all women, and all people everywhere.

To penetrate cultures and societies on a worldwide scale required more than a theology that would mean little to those unfamiliar with Judaism. How Christian men, women, and children *lived* and *behaved* and *thought* and *treated one another* would henceforth give validity and authenticity to Matthew, Mark, Luke, and John's riveting biographies of God's Son, as well as to the writings and commands of the apostles.

Theology would not be enough. How did Christians *live*?

This final series of apostolic commands, therefore, contains little theology, except perhaps for the final charge of Peter to the Church. In these commands we discover practicality in the attitudes and behaviors the world sees—our response to government, our diligence at work, how we conduct ourselves in relationships, whether we're hard workers or slackers, what we reflect in countenance and demeanor, even how we dress. All these are being observed every day, in circumstances large and small, as Christians go forth into the world with the message of the risen Christ.

And as it watches us, the world will know the Truth by our *be* and *do*, not our *say*.

THE WORLD WILL KNOW THE TRUTH BY OUR *BE* AND *DO*, NOT OUR *SAY*

111. Live quiet peaceable lives.

112. Live in harmony with all.

113. Honor and submit to authority.

114. Honor, respect, and give your best to your masters and employers.

115. Be modest in dress, manners, and demeanor.

116. Aim at what is honorable in men's eyes as well as God's.

117. Work diligently to earn your own living.

118. Live your faith with zeal, good cheer, and steadfastness.

119. Consider your witness.

120. Recognize yourselves as a people set apart.

111. Live Quiet Peaceable Lives

One of the first scriptures my mother taught my sisters and me was Romans 12:18. To this day the words are emblazoned on my memory where they were Scotch-taped to our refrigerator: *If possible, so far as it depends upon you, live peaceably with all.*

What a mighty legacy to leave a son! I am so thankful for that reminder. My mother lived her Christian faith in practical ways—helping people more than trying to ascertain whether or not they were going to heaven. How grateful I am for the memory of this verse (along with Deuteronomy 6:18: "Do what is right and good in the sight of the Lord,") stuck to that old white Westinghouse. My parents were not people whose emphasis was getting people saved. Neither of them ever led a Bible study in our church. I don't remember them even participating in one, individually or together. I never once saw my father reading the Bible. Yet the reputation that followed him during more than thirty years in business in the small northern California town where I grew up was as a "good" man who would do anything for anyone. My mother and father spent their lives trying to do "what was right and good." I learned early in life from this man and woman that faith is validated by how we interact with those around us.

Paul's injunction in my mother's refrigerator verse of Romans 12:18 contains a subtle twist. He does not promise that we *will* always, in every situation and with every person, be able to live in peace. He only says to make sure that *you* give no cause for dispute. "*If possible...so far as it depends on you...*live peaceably with all." He recognizes the fact that occasional difficulties with people are inevitable. Maybe it won't always be possible to avoid them. But don't *you* be the cause of them. Others may dispute and bicker, but *you*—maintain unity, and live in peace with all. The whole thing turns on that most fascinating "if" clause.

I think we would admit that we've got our hands full living in peace with all men. Christians through the years haven't generally done a very good job of it. But Paul doesn't stop there. Whenever he speaks of living "peaceably," he adds an unexpected virtue to that lifestyle. *Quietness* nearly always accompanies the command.

Quietness, he emphasizes, is no mere trait of personality, it is a virtue of spirituality!

This is totally unexpected. But there is no mistaking Paul's intent: Spiritual maturity exudes quietness. A spiritually mature life is a *quiet and peaceable* life. Over and over he repeats the two character qualities together. Live quiet and peaceable lives...work in quietness...aspire to live quietly.

What is this quiet life upon which Paul places such a high premium? Exactly what the word says. "Quiet" means *quiet*. Stop talking. Live and do your work without constant prattle. Absorb. Listen. Glean from others. Peaceability begins with quietness.

Most men and women simply talk too much. Christians try to set everyone straight too much. Preachers talk too much. Evangelists talk too much. Bible study leaders talk too much. Friends visiting with one another talk too much.

There is no mystery here. A Godly life is one lived in peace, quiet, respectfulness, sensitivity, harmony, minding one's own business. The next time you are in a group, try saying nothing. Add no words to the banter and discussion. You may thereby enter into one of the deep secrets of living in obedience to the commands of the Apostles.

If possible, so far as it depends upon you, live peaceably with all. (Romans 12:18)

Agree with one another, live in peace. (2 Corinthians 13:11)

Aspire to live quietly, to mind your own affairs, and to work with your hands...so that you may command the respect of outsiders, and be dependent on nobody. (1 Thessalonians 4:11-12)

We command and exhort in the Lord Jesus Christ to...work in quietness and to earn their own living. (2 Thessalonians 3:12)

I urge that...we may lead a quiet and peaceable life, godly and respectful in every way. (1 Timothy 2:1-2)

112. Live in Harmony With All

We have spoken about unity within Christ's body as the fulfillment of Jesus' intimate prayer to his Father of John 17. But the harmony of humanity we are to exhibit as God's ambassadors in the world, and as avowed disciples of his Son, goes much further. Unity is not limited to our relationships with Christians. We are commanded to live in accord, friendship, goodwill, and brotherhood with *all*. Obviously the unity Jesus prayed for will have distinctively *spiritual* characteristics not possible with non-Christians. Though giving special heed to unity within Christ's body, our charge is to live in harmony with those in the world also. Paul says, "Do good to all men...*especially* to those of the household of faith." (Gal. 6:10) However different may be the features of the two, there will yet be an observable harmony within all the relationships we are part of.

Some Christians question whether all men and women are truly God's children. They squirm whenever I speak of the "universal brotherhood." It is true that we are commanded to walk a tightrope between rejecting what the world stands for, while yet living in harmony, peace, brotherhood, and love with those who are immersed in the world. The balance is not always easy to find. Yet the command to live in peace is universal from the apostolic writers—from Paul, James, Peter, and the writer of *Hebrews*. Their message is unequivocal. They make few distinctions between Christians and non-Christians—Live in harmony with *all*...with the universal brotherhood of man.

In illuminating what "peacemaker" means, George MacDonald offers the following fascinating description of how the world's peacemakers sow unity, harmony, and peace in relationships, in the church, and in the world.

"The Lord calls those his children who, on their way home, are peace-makers in the travelling company...The true idea of the universe is the whole family in heaven and earth...God, then, would make of the world a true, divine family...The peace-makers quiet the winds of the world ever ready to be up and blowing; they tend and cherish the interlacing roots of the ministering grass; they spin and twist many uniting cords, and they weave many supporting bands; they are the servants, for the truth's sake, of the individual, of the family, of the world, of the great universal family of heaven and earth. They are the true children of that family, the allies and ministers of every clasping and consolidating force in it; fellow-workers they are with God in the creation of the family... They are the children of God, for like him they would be one with his creatures...

"This way and that, guided in dance inexplicable of prophetic harmony, move the children of God, the lights of the world, the lovers of men, the fellow-workers with God, the peace-makers—ever weaving, after a pattern devised by, and known only to him who orders their ways, the web of the world's history...Blessed are the peace-makers, for they shall be called the children of God—the children because they set the Father on the throne of the Family." (George MacDonald, *The Hope of the Gospel*, "God's Family")

Live in harmony with one another. (Romans 12:16)

Let us then pursue what makes for peace and mutual upbuilding. (Romans 14:19)

Agree with one another, live in peace. (2 Corinthians 13:11)

The works of the flesh are plain...enmity, strife, dissension, party spirit. (Galatians 5:19-20)

Lead a life worthy of the calling to which you have been called...eager to maintain the unity of the Spirit in the bond of peace. (Ephesians 4:1, 3)

Complete my joy by being of the same mind, having the same love, being in full accord and of one mind. (Philippians 2:2)

Be at peace among yourselves. (1 Thessalonians 5:13)

Strive for peace with all men. (Hebrews 12:14)

The wisdom from above is...peaceable, gentle, open to reason. (James 3:17)

The harvest of righteousness is sown in peace by those who make peace. (James 3:18)

Honor all men. (1 Peter 2:17)

Seek peace and pursue it. (1 Peter 3:11)

---

113. Honor and Submit To Authority

Christians in all times have found this a particularly odious command. Many today manufacture a variety of justifications why in this or that case Christians are not obligated to heed the strict letter of its requirement. It's not a simple matter of justifying jaywalking or exceeding the speed limit. Our entire perspective of government, authority, and respect for civil leaders has been contaminated by deep cynicism and silent anger. To be sure, how can we not disdain the judgment of leaders who are so blind to right and wrong as to legalize, normalize, and even encourage the practice of many disgusting and degrading practices now considered acceptable by a culture quickly sliding into moral ruin. Perhaps the worst of it is that the world's governments are not only legalizing such perversions, they are mandating that children be taught that they are normal "lifestyle choices." Any Christian whose blood does not run hot is not paying attention to the death of scriptural virtue taking place before their very eyes as the world sinks into the cesspool of liberal relativism.

Yes, this is an extremely difficult command to come to terms with. *How* do we honor those blind guides who are in authority in our governments, courts, schools, universities, and businesses? Yet Paul's words are indisputable and stringent: Honor and submit to authority. Is this a command to which we can simply turn a blind eye as if it is not there?

Let us pause a moment to consider the situation when Paul said that Christians were "to be submissive to rulers and authorities" (Titus 3:1) and, "Let every person be subject to the governing authorities." (Romans 13:1) The emperor of Rome at the time was none other than Nero himself, the most brutal persecutor of Christians in the first several generations of Christianity. And we think we have it bad! This is the tyrannical Roman government that Paul tells the Christians of his time to submit to with honor and respect.

We don't really have it so hard today. Yet the issues facing us are certainly compelling. They tax to its limit the integrity of our love for truth. It is simply not possible for a thinking, truth-loving individual to honor one who calls wrong right, and then who forces that wrong to be accepted as "normal" by an entire culture. Yet in this quagmire of hypocrisy and relativism, we are commanded not to fight cultural sin through political change. This is perhaps the most difficult aspect of the command. Everything in us wants to engage our energies in crusading against the outrages around us. But neither Jesus nor the Apostles sanction making such causes our focus. Rather they persistently bring us back to first causes—to conduct ourselves with quietness, respect, honor, and love.

This may be one of the most difficult of all the commands to obey. The specifics of this obedience are elusive. This is far more difficult than loving the sinner but not the sin. Love is easy alongside the command to give *honor* where honor is due.

It may be that the answer lies, not in honoring the corrupt policies being promulgated, but rather in honoring the position, the station, the office, so to speak. And then, as prayerful citizens who must live under their charge, loving the sinners holding those offices, praying for them, and upholding them in spite of their sin.

I offer this perspective, however, only as a struggling wayfarer whose practical grasp of this command is shadowy at best and admittedly incomplete.

Let every person be subject to the governing authorities...pay all of them their due, taxes to whom taxes are due, revenue to whom revenue is due, respect to whom respect is due, honor to whom honor is due. (Romans 13:1, 7)

I urge that supplications, prayers, intercessions, and thanksgivings be made for all men, for kings and all who are in high positions. (1 Timothy 2:1-2)

Remind them to be submissive to rulers and authorities. (Titus 3:1)

Be subject for the Lord's sake to every human institution. (1 Peter 2:13)

Honor the emperor. (1 Peter 2:17)

We take the world's habits and attitudes far too easily and thoughtlessly for granted. We scarcely pause to consider the hundreds of ways in which our habits, attitudes, and behavior patterns flow along with the world's current exactly like those of the staunchest unbeliever. How shocking many would find it to know that grousing about work, complaining about one's boss, and shutting down one's efforts at one minute before quitting time are actually examples of being *disobedient* to Scripture.

How often have you been frustrated when the window at the post office, bank, doctor's office, or governmental agency closes at two minutes *before* five, or, when you are waiting for a store to open and the clerk finally unlocks the door a minute or two *after* 9:30?

These are tiny examples in which people the world over train themselves in the habit of *not* giving their best to their employers. It is in the air of our culture to give the *least* we can, and to expect *more* for our efforts than we are really worth. If we were paid by how much we actually accomplish and how hard we work for our bosses, most of us would only get half of what we are currently receiving. Or less. We *don't* give of our best, and we feel perfectly justified in not doing so.

As Christians, you and I are supposed to be different. We are to be visible, living, breathing examples of Jesus to those around us. Anyone can conform to the world. Conformity to the world's ways requires only laziness. Who has the courage to live by a *different* example? Who cares enough about diligence to be well on the job and breaking a sweat by 8:02, and who doesn't relax his or her efforts on his boss's behalf until five or ten minutes *after* 5:00...or 5:30...or 6:00, expecting no overtime, intent only on giving the boss a full return on his day's investment? Who has the courage to give a *full* day's work for a day's pay? Who has the integrity to make up for all the squandered and wasted minutes that accumulate through the day when we are accomplishing nothing meaningful? Who makes up for all the minutes spent visiting with one's colleagues and fellow workers by staying on at day's end to repay those stolen minutes? Who brings such a level of integrity into their jobs?

How different would our work habits be if we were paid by what we accomplished rather than by the time we put in. We would no doubt think differently about coffee breaks, lunch hours, about chatting with co-workers, and about all the wasted minutes and hours in a week that add up to nothing lasting produced, nothing actually *done*.

If they were the living, breathing examples of Christ in the small things of life, Christians in the workplace would stand out like a sore thumb. From their lips would never fall a word of complaint about pay or criticism of their boss. They would be the first to arrive, the last to leave. The traditional, and in some eyes old-fashioned, virtues of duty, loyalty, and steadfastness, of doing one's best and going above and beyond the call of duty, would regulate their entire work ethic. All around them, employers and fellow-workers would say, "If you want it done right, if you want a full return on your investment, if you want a cheerful, productive, diligent worker and a job well done...hire a Christian."

Be obedient to those who are your earthly masters...in singleness of heart, as to Christ; not in the way of eyeservice, as men-pleasers, but as servants of Christ, doing the will of God from the heart, rendering service with a good will as to the Lord and not to men. (Ephesians 6:5-7; Colossians 3:22)

Whatever your task, work heartily, as serving the Lord and not men. (Colossians 3:23)

Obey your leaders and submit to them. (Hebrews 13:17)

Honor all men. (1 Peter 2:17)

Servants, be submissive to your masters with all respect, not only to the kind and gentle but also to the overbearing. (1 Peter 2:18)

115. Be Modest in Dress, Manners, and Demeanor

It is probably true that on the whole Paul's commands are more difficult for women to swallow than men. Paul irks modern sensibilities. Who wants to be told to submit, to keep quiet, to cover their head, and not to speak in church? These commands quickly raise the hackles. Paul may thus be viewed as the original male chauvinist, with the added observation that his words were culturally motivated and certainly not intended for today.

Today's church, therefore, subtly edits the text and essentially glosses over Paul's questionable instructions. *Husbands, love your wives* can stay. No one has a problem with that. But *Wives, submit to your husbands* has to go. It is stricken from the account. No one reads the Sermon on the Mount in this manner. The gospels remain in our New Testaments as they have come down to us through the ages. However, Paul's epistles are read with a redactive wink and grin to remove all trace of so-called anti-woman bias.

The Christian woman of today who desires to read the New Testament accurately and humbly, and who desires to obey its precepts whether they are comfortable to modernism or not, has a difficult time of it. She is swimming upstream against an entire culture of feminist narcissism telling her that she can ignore all those unpleasant passages. Even her Christian friends will tell her it is foolish to try to live by such chauvinistic ideas.

Perhaps these observations about Paul's teachings (even if they are excuses to avoid strict obedience) have merit. The viability of such commands, and how they are to be applied in our time, is certainly worthy of discussion and leniency of interpretation. We do live in a different culture. We *do* have to adapt and change with the times, as long as in so doing we seek *greater* obedience in our lives, not seek to justify a *lesser* obedience.

How grateful I am for my wife's determinative, vocal, and decision-making role in our marriage, which I have always viewed as a divinely appointed partnership. I praise God for it no less now after almost forty-five years than I did on the day we were married. I would be lost (or forever going off the rails!) without the balancing wisdom she brings to all facets of my life. Having said all that, we both also know that we must attentively heed Paul's difficult commands, and strike out *none* of them. That commitment is on my head too. Paul's commands to men are equally stringent.

And so we come to the command toward modesty of dress and demeanor. It is easy to overlook just how important modesty may actually be in reflecting Christlikeness to the world. Though Peter and Paul specifically address the charge of modesty to women, it is a universal command. Men and women alike are commanded to adorn themselves inwardly with a gentle and quiet spirit, not to make a show nor turn eyes upon themselves. Humility and grace identify the man or woman who is a disciple of Jesus, not surface appearance or an alluring demeanor.

The shocking practicality of this command strikes home as we reflect on how automatically and thoughtlessly Christians accept the world's standards of fashion without batting an eye. An obsession with clothes, styles, appearance, and adornment indicates a desire to conform to the world's fads and be acceptable in the world's eyes. Paul would be outraged to see the high skirts, low necklines, scanty swimsuits, and flirtatious mannerisms considered "normal" by today's Christian teens. To what extent is modesty taught as a virtue in today's youth groups? To what extent are Christian young people warned against a flirtatious spirit as sin?

Peter's and Paul's words speak for themselves.

I desire then that in every place...women should adorn themselves modestly and sensibly in seemly apparel, not with braided hair or gold or pearls or costly attire but by good deeds...in faith and love and holiness, with modesty. (1 Timothy 2:8-9,15)

Wives...let not yours be the outward adorning with braiding of hair, decoration of gold, and wearing of robes, but let it be the hidden person of the heart with the imperishable jewel of a gentle and quiet spirit, which in God's sight is very precious. (1 Peter 3:1, 3-4)

Having seen that scriptural modesty is undermined by an obsessive attempt to fit in with every fashion, we now find ourselves facing the question: How then are we to look in the world's eyes? Are we to comport ourselves wearing dowdy clothes and with such a dramatically *old*-fashioned lifestyle as to seem prudish, out of step, and irrelevant?

Obviously not. A distinctive life will be noticed, of course. But noticed *how*? With snickering and ridicule, or with the statement made about Christians in the second century? Roman emperor Hadrian had sent his man Aristides to investigate the Christian movement. Aristides' report came back: "Behold! How they love..."

We discover the secret of today's command in the simple yet profound word *honor*. A huge difference exists between trying to *turn eyes* versus arresting the world's esteem because we are noble, loving men and women of integrity. When Paul speaks of commanding respect and being well thought-of by the world, he is illuminating the natural result of honorable living...the consequence that flows out of obedience to the commands.

When we obey, the world will notice. When we don't obey, the world will notice.

Paul's multi-dimensional command in 1 Thessalonians 4:11-12 demands attention. Not a word about witnessing, attending a Bible study, or inviting non-Christians to church. Compel the respect of outsiders by *living quietly, minding your own business*, and *working with your hands*. To the Colossians and Titus Paul adds *wisdom, sobriety, uprightness,* and *godliness* to the virtues that will arrest the attention of the world.

What an inverted prescription this is for witnessing! To these we might add from yesterday, modesty. A modest quiet spirit carried with dignity, kindness, and grace, will compel the world's respect and honor far more than superficial appearances. This is the foundation of Paul's command: Honorability. It takes character to compel honor. Appearance, of course, reflects character too. Presenting oneself to the world clean, tidy, well-groomed—looking nice but without intentionally trying to attract attention—is another form of politeness, courtesy, decorum, and grace. Our appearance reflects not only on our witness but also on our boss. We owe him or her professionalism of appearance and demeanor. Modesty and professionalism go hand in hand.

For women, personal appearance and adornment may be the region where honorable modesty is first noticed. For men, perhaps the most significant arena where this command finds opportunity for obedience is in the workplace. Honorability will be noticed in not striving to get ahead at the expense of others. The noble and honorable man is one whose ambitions are self-contained, who would take not a single step toward advancement at the expense of a colleague, a man whose financial integrity is inviolate, who would sooner quit his job than convey a hint of untruth. He is a man of character and dignity whose dictum of life is defined in Micah 6:8: *He has showed you, O man, what is good; and what does the Lord require of you but to do justice, and to love kindness, and to walk humbly with your God?* Such men are honored within the world as well as within God's kingdom. Modesty and integrity compel honor.

Take thought for what is noble in the sight of all. (Romans 12:17)

Aim at what is honorable not only in the Lord's sight but also in the sight of men. (2 Corinthians 8:21)

Let all men know your forbearance. (Philippians 4:5)

Conduct yourselves wisely toward outsiders, making the most of the time. (Colossians 4:5)

Aspire to live quietly, to mind your own affairs, and to work with your hands...so that you may command the respect of outsiders. (1 Thessalonians 4:11-12)

A bishop must be...well thought-of by outsiders. (1 Timothy 3:2, 7)

Live sober, upright, godly lives in this world. (Titus 2:12)

Maintain good conduct among the Gentiles, so that...they may see your good deeds and glorify God. (1 Peter 2:12)

117. Work Diligently and Do Not Be Slothful or Idle

Paul was no fan of the welfare state. His disdain for laziness was so strong that he gave the Thessalonians the memorable command, *If a man will not work, let him not eat.* (2 Thessalonians 3:10) He went so far as to tell them to keep away from Christians living in idleness. (3:6) This is a strong and almost shocking statement. It is the same treatment he commands toward Christians living in immorality and sin. Paul had no tolerance for those slothfully idling away the time unproductively.

We note the enormous distinction between "having a job" and "work." The two may not be the same. Not everyone is always fortunate enough to have a job. That does not prevent work. Paul is not talking about a paycheck. He is talking about being industrious, busy, active, involved, engaged, and diligent. It is *work* that Paul commands. He wants us up and doing. He wants us *about* something. If we don't happen to have a job, we have friends and neighbors and churches to whom we can offer our services. Being unemployed is no invitation to the couch or TV. Rather it is an opportunity to find other "work," whether paid or not. There is always something to do, even if it means going to a friend or neighbor and saying, "What can I do for you today?"

Keeping industrious may mean developing a hobby—scrapbooking, gardening, woodworking, painting, crafts, quilting, writing. It might also take the form of learning a new skill, taking music lessons, enrolling in a computer class, reading, or study. If you think you have nothing to occupy your time and attention, write letters of encouragement to your friends and acquaintances, teach yourself to play the piano, research some subject of interest, volunteer at a church or charity or mission or farm that uses volunteer labor, write your memoirs, set a goal to read fifty books this year, reconfigure your garden, write a novel, join a book club or Bible study, visit those in need, volunteer at a hospital.

Slothfulness comes in all sizes and shapes. Going to work every day does not excuse the imperative of this command. It only transfers the environment of laziness to the workplace. Nowhere, in fact, is laziness *more* evident than among those who hold jobs and think too much is expected of them. The desire to do as little as possible and be paid maximum dollar for half-hearted efforts is epidemic. It is nothing but well-paid slothfulness. What do your co-workers think of you—that you work harder than anyone else, or that you take it as easy as you can?

Most today have such an exalted sense of their own worth that if they lift a finger they expect to be paid for it. In my boyhood I watched my father and his circle of church friends helping one another every weekend, often with enormous projects. Land was cleared, trees felled, houses remodeled, roofs put on, firewood cut, plumbing repairs made, and an entire new church building constructed...and no one thought of being paid. They functioned as a community of men *working* to help each other.

Diligence is the resounding message of the book of *Proverbs*. It is a foundational and instantly-noticed component of a "good witness" for Christ.

Be steadfast, immovable, always abounding in the work of the Lord, knowing that in the Lord your labor is not in vain. (1 Corinthians 15:58)

Each man will have to bear his own load. (Galatians 6:5)

Whatever your task, work heartily, as serving the Lord and not men. (Colossians 3:23)

Aspire to...work with your hands...and be dependent on nobody. (1 Thessalonians 4:11-12)

Keep away from any brother who is living in idleness. (2 Thessalonians 3:6)

If any one will not work, let him not eat. (2 Thessalonians 3:10)

We command and exhort in the Lord Jesus Christ to...work in quietness and to earn their own living. (2 Thessalonians 3:12)

Show yourself in all respects a model of good deeds. (Titus 2:7)

Remind them...to be ready for any honest work. (Titus 3:1)

We desire each one of you to show the same earnestness...so that you may not be sluggish, but imitators of those who through faith and patience inherit the promises. (Hebrews 6:11-12)

---

118. Live Your Faith With Zeal, Good Cheer, and Steadfastness

One of the hallmarks of youth is zealous energy and passionate vision.

How well I understand! After a nurturing grounding in the church, God took hold of my life in a more complete way one summer long ago on a farm in Germany. I was immediately filled with such spiritual energy I wanted to tell everyone of my deepening encounter with God. And urge them to follow in my footsteps (the preoccupation of youth with its *own* revelations!) This compulsion extended toward my German family, who, I am certain, hadn't a glimmer what I was talking about in my fumbling German.

Shortsighted and naïve as was my early-twenties perspective, I yet cherish those memories. The vision of a life lived in the Center, obedient to the commands of the New Testament, has never left me. Many life-themes sprouted and sent down roots in that rich German soil, priorities that remain with me to this day. My writing was one of those.

Yet with maturity comes a quieting and deepening. A long obedience in the same direction—that wonderful phrase coined by Eugene Peterson—is not a life that can be forever stoked by the fires of youthful zealotry. At the other end of life's spectrum, age chips away at zeal and vision. Weariness sets in. It is not easy to maintain the same level of passion for one's faith when one has been walking with God for forty or fifty years. Not all prayers are answered. God sometimes seems to go silent for years at a time. Blessings are eroded by disappointments and heartaches.

This I also understand. As I look back on those eventful months of 1969, I realize that part of me is tired. The years take a toll. I must admit that I have grown weary. Over forty-five years have passed since I prayerfully walked those German woods and fields with visions of changing the world for God. I am increasingly conscious these days of the wisdom of two proverbs: *The Lord is not doing so much through us, as he is in us,* and, *The greatest reward for a man's toil is not what he gets for it, but rather what he becomes by it.*

The apostolic writers wonderfully bring together these two emotional bookends of life, exhorting faithful steadfastness of good cheer, even zeal, as the years roll on. The excitement of youth will surely fade. But with patience and diligence, God's men and women labor on conscientiously with upbeat hearts—perhaps not every moment with the joyful vigor of youth, yet with quiet smiles and contented hearts

The scriptures below all speak of what I call the "faithfulness of years" rather than the excitement of the moment. What a wonderful vision of living life for the long haul.

I have this week been reading James Michener's autobiography, written at eighty-five. He tells of thirty more books he wants to write, and speaks of the eleven books he has just completed between eighty and eighty-five. His output at the end of life was staggering. He has given my flagging zeal a great boost of vision!

I determine to press on with Paul and James Michener toward the goal and high calling of life in God with good cheer, energy, and optimism.

Never flag in zeal, be aglow with the Spirit. (Romans 12:11)

Be steadfast, immovable, always abounding in the work of the Lord, knowing that in the Lord your labor is not in vain. (1 Corinthians 15:58)

Let us not grow weary in well-doing. (Galatians 6:9)

Look carefully then how you walk...making the most of the time, because the days are evil. (Ephesians 5:15-16)

Forgetting what lies behind and straining forward to what lies ahead, I press on toward the goal for the prize of the upward call of God in Christ Jesus. (Philippians 3:13-14)

Do not be weary in well-doing. (2 Thessalonians 3:13)

We desire each one of you to show the same earnestness...so that you may not be sluggish, but imitators of those who through faith and patience inherit the promises. (Hebrews 6:11-12)

Who is there to harm you if you are zealous for what is right? (1 Peter 3:13)

Be the more zealous to confirm your call. (2 Peter 1:10)

What is the first thing that comes to mind when a car speeds past five or ten miles above the speed limit, then recedes in the distance with a Christian bumper sticker flashing its tiny Christian "witness" as it leaves everyone else in the dust?

And what do we think when we read church message boards proclaiming, "We preach Christ crucified," or "We preach the gospel," or "We preach the *full* gospel," and the all-time favorite, "We preach the Word of God."

How many times have you read, *We preach the commands?*

A church message board two blocks from our house is changed every week, always with some clever saying or life-prescription. Never once have I seen the commands of the Bible mentioned. This is an astonishing fact. The *single* message Jesus left his disciples before he died through which he said his life would be transmitted to the world, was to do what he said—to obey his commands. Yet we never find churches promoting that priority on their message boards.

It might be said that there are two kinds of Christians in the world—*bumper sticker Christians* and *character Christians.* Or we might characterize the contrast as between *message board Christians* and *command Christians.*

These are, of course, generalizations. All generalizations are simplistic. There are as many kinds of Christians as there are Christians. We all live and share our faith uniquely. You and I will convey Christ to a watching world by a myriad of complexities known only to God.

But the contrast may be useful to focus our attention one final time, as has been our emphasis throughout, on the distinction—at once so patently obvious, yet so glaringly misconceived through the centuries by a clueless church—between the church's witness of *proclamation*, and its witness of personal and corporate *Christlikeness.* What fuels our daily *raison d'être* for calling ourselves "Christians"—cliché or command?

Today's exhortation emphasizes the principle underlying this entire final series of commands: "The world will know the truth by our *be* and *do,* not our *say.*" Little things matter. People are watching and observing. The world is judging Jesus by what they see in you and me, by what they hear when we open our mouths, by our behavior in the midst of frustration, suffering, setbacks, and disappointments.

The only Christians who truly change the corners of the world where they live are character and command Christians. "Character" cannot be applied to one's back or forehead like a bumper sticker. It is infused into us as we steep ourselves over a lifetime in the commands of the New Testament. Jesus calls this infusion "abiding." It is how our life-rudders set their direction, by infusion in the waters of the gospel.

Get rid of your bumper stickers. If you want to stick something to the back of your car, put a picture of yourself. It may not advertise a sound bite message about Christianity. But it will serve as a constant reminder to *you* of what your real witness is.

Aim at what is honorable, not only in the Lord's sight but also in the sight of men. (2 Cor. 8:21)

Let us not grow weary in well-doing. (Galatians 6:9; 2 Thess. 3:13))

Let all men know your forbearance. (Philippians 4:5)

Aspire to live quietly…so that you may command the respect of outsiders. (1 Thess. 4:11-12)

I urge…that we may lead a quiet and peaceable life, godly and respectful in every way. (1 Timothy 2:1-2)

A bishop must be…well thought of by outsiders. (1 Timothy 3:2, 7)

Show yourself in all respects a model of good deeds, and…integrity. (Titus 2:7)

For the grace of God has appeared for the salvation of all men, training us to…live sober, upright, and godly lives in this world. (Titus 2:11-12)

Live such good lives among the pagans that…they may see your good deeds and glorify God. (1 Peter 2:12, NIV)

120. Recognize Yourselves as a People Set Apart

Separation from the world is not high on the list of objectives for third millennium Christians. Just the opposite. If we were to poll one hundred Christians from a broad cross-section of church affiliations, it is doubtful the phrase "separation from the world" would register coherent meaning to more than five or ten. The goal of modern Christendom, rather, seems to be to preserve as much worldliness as possible in outlook, methodology, and behavior, while clinging to just enough abstract "belief" to retain the technical label of "Christian."

For the Hebrews of the Old Testament it was a different story. Separation from the surrounding peoples was a matter of national survival. Even so, the temptation to adopt the practices of those nations was a constant threat to Israel's spiritual and moral fabric. Thus the message was persistently voiced from Moses to Ezekiel and all the prophets between: *Come out from among them and be separate.* Loosely quoting these prophets in 2 Corinthians 6:17, Paul illuminates why God calls his people out of the world—so that he can be a Father to us, and so that we can be his sons and daughters.

This is no worldly Fatherhood or childship. It is *separation childship* ruled by a Fatherhood so high and wonderfully beyond anything the world can conceive that the word itself adds to the confusion. Childship in this universal family of Fatherhood cannot be nurtured in a milieu pervaded by the perspectives of the world. The world is consumed with and wholly committed to the *destruction* of Fatherhood and childship. It will destroy them in us if we do not reject everything it tells us about the origins of fulfilled and integrated personhood. The sole environment where childship can be birthed, rooted, and grounded into Christlikeness is an environment of separation. The holy relationship between heavenly Father and his sons and daughters can *only* flourish divorced from and utterly disconnected from the world's frame of reference.

Building on Paul's picture in *Ephesians* of God's temple being built of living human stones, Peter gives us a wonderful vision of God's family. He calls the body of Christ a "chosen race," a "royal priesthood," a holy family set apart—taken out of the world to be a light sent back into the world. This apartness originates in no selection of God's "elect." It is a chosen separation from the world's perspectives, attitudes, methods, and entire worldview. Christians *choose* whether or not to be of the elect by their responses to the world. God places no special imprimatur on certain individuals to destine them for eternal life. Election is our own daily choice. Obedient separation is the door into election.

Peter phrases his vision of Christ's body as a command. *Be built,* he says, *into a spiritual house, to be a holy priesthood.* The command is on us.

How fitting that we end with Peter himself. Peter issued the first apostolic commands in the book of *Acts.* We now draw our prayerful journey to a close with Peter's high vision of God's eternally growing, maturing, expanding separation-family.

What, then, is our calling according to the apostles? Casting our gaze back over the road through the commands we have taken together, we see that we are commanded to pursue godliness, nurture personal spirituality, grow the fruits of the Spirit, turn from sin, live God's priorities at home, show respect in relationships, develop wise and gracious habits, speak with grace, develop Christlikeness of character, build mature beliefs, exemplify unity and servanthood in church life, and evidence discipleship in the world.

For we are the temple of the living God; as God said, "I will live in them...and I will be their God, and they shall be my people. Therefore come out from them and be separate from them, says the Lord...and I will be a father to you, and you shall be my sons and daughters." (2 Corinthians 6:16-18)

Like living stones be yourselves built into a spiritual house, to be a holy priesthood...You are a chosen race, a royal priesthood, a holy nation, God's own people, that you may declare the wonderful deeds of him who called you out of darkness into his marvelous light. Once you were no people but now you are God's people. (1 Peter 2:5, 9-10)

Appendix 1

The Priorities in the Categorization and Organization of the Commands:

As those of you will know who have previously read *The Commands of Jesus,* the categorization and organization of the Commands of the Bible is a personal and highly subjective undertaking. As I made clear in Appendix 1 to that earlier volume, my objective was not to create a perfect list that every student of the Bible would agree with, but rather to discover ways to bolster my own prayer life and obedience to the commands of Scripture. I wrote: "This is my own personal devotional list. I have arranged and grouped the Commands in ways that have helped *me* remember them, think of them, and fill my mind with them throughout the day. I share it on that basis alone."

That same personal priority undergirds *The Commands of the Apostles.* Most of the means and methods I explained that guided me in compiling *The Commands of Jesus,* and the discussion of "implied" and "incident/person specific" commands, also apply to my treatment of the commands from the Apostles. If you want to know what I have done in more detail and why, I refer you to *The Commands of Jesus.* The underlying priority for both sets of commands is exactly the same: To get to the heart of God's intent, to discover what he wants us to DO—how he wants you and me to *live* as obedient Christians. That is the *only* objective of this book. There is no doctrinal nor theological agenda hidden between the lines. The Commands are given us to obey, not doctrinalize. The Commands are the great treasure of our faith. *Living* them, *obeying* them, is the entire and only purpose, foundation, and validation of Christianity's eternal truth.

As ambiguous and hyperbolic as are some of Jesus' statements, and as difficult as it can occasionally be to isolate exactly what he intended in some of his obscure teachings that are not phrased in the *form* of command, we nevertheless find most of the Lord's words to be remarkably succinct, pithy, concise, and above all eminently *practical.* When we move on to the commands of the Apostles, however, the complexities are multiplied tenfold. Laying hold of the imperative commands that are intended to rule my behavior, conduct, attitudes, and character, can be extremely difficult. Some of the commands of the Apostles are succinctly straightforward, others are impenetrable almost beyond belief. Some are as relevant as the day they were written. Others are hopelessly dated to a cultural milieu so different from ours as to be like night and day. The task before us in attempting to arrive at a universal list of commands from the words of the Apostles that applies to all Christians in all times is much more difficult and complicated than was the case with *The Commands of Jesus.*

I will briefly summarize a few of these difficulties. I will then explain the priorities I have used in sifting through the vast and complex list of scriptures in Appendix 2 to arrive at the 120 commands of the Apostles which I consider of universal application.

First and foremost, as alluded to in the Introduction, is the confusion that can result from the two broad and very different types of commands found throughout the New Testament—*individual* commands, and commands intended for the *church.* Even the word "command" is occasionally misleading when Paul is addressing himself to the churches. Everything he writes is not presented exactly in the *form* of command. We might call much that Paul writes to the churches "instructions" rather than commands. Sometimes they come across as mere "suggestions." It is therefore difficult to determine where universality is present that is intended to govern our own obedience as well as those in the first century to whom the letters were written. This is but one of many challenges we face in trying to discover universal practicality for our lives in the commands and instructions (and suggestions) of the Apostles.

The Commands of Jesus are, almost without exception, *individual* Commands. Jesus referred but twice to the "church." In neither case does he hint at the structure and organization which was built up in the three decades following his death. By the time that most of the New Testament epistles were written, however, that structure and organization had grown to significant size in nearly every corner of the Roman empire. Whether Jesus intended such a structured "church" to become what it became is a matter for discussion between theologians and historians. The fact is, it *did* become structured and organized, and much in the epistles is written with that in mind. Christianity was an explosively expanding movement. There were no handbooks on how things were to function. Much of it happened by the seat of the pants of Paul and other leaders who were doing their best to keep ahead of the wave. Theology developed jerkily, even randomly. Church order developed the same way. Thus the epistles sent about the Mediterranean, to be read in the homes where Christians met, provided leadership, order, direction, and guidance in the midst of this growth.

Thus, we find ourselves with two very distinct kinds of commands in the epistles—the *individual* and the *corporate*. There is certainly much overlap. Obviously commands to the church must be obeyed by individuals. But the complexion and dynamic of the "church" commands concerning, say, the operation of spiritual gifts in public worship, is much different from the "individual" commands to love, be watchful, live in peace, and remain pure.

The Commands of Jesus are universal. They are *all* meant for *all* Christians. We may not understand the full complexities involved in some cases, but none are to be neglected or ignored. The commands and instructions of the Apostles are different. They are probably *not* all universal. That is an intricate question of personal interpretation. But the fact is, Jesus alone is our Lord, Savior, and Master. To call oneself a Christian implies obedience to *his* Commands above all else. Peter, Paul, James, John, and the other New Testament writers were men...*fallible* men. When they set quill to papyrus or parchment, the last thing on their minds was that they were producing what later generations would consider "Scripture." They were writing letters to individuals, to home churches, mostly addressing specific issues and needs. Their words contain wisdom, and, we believe, carry the inspiration of the Holy Spirit. However, we also recognize that their human fallibility, and the specific issues of their time, must be kept in perspective. Their words cannot be placed on a level with those of the Lord. The Commands of Jesus represent the ultimate truth out of which the teachings of the Apostles must flow. If there appears to be a conflict, we must turn to the Commands of *Jesus* first, and, if necessary, lay aside the conflicting Apostolic teaching as potentially in error.

In order to clarify somewhat the individual situations and church issues addressed in the epistles, I have included an additional category in the listing of commands in Appendix 2: *Issue Specific Commands*. Every so-called "church" command will not fall into this category, and many important "individual" commands *will* be found in that column. Each will have to read and assess the commands of the Apostles prayerfully to determine their practical relevance in his or her life. There are no one-dimensional answers. But hopefully this added category will help us clarify the many different types of commands we find here.

Some of these "issues" will be extremely relevant. Others will have almost zero relevance for us today. Paul's commands about food offered to idols, for example, clearly does not cause too much confusion in our time. It is not a dilemma we face very often. Nor are his commands about slavery of great daily concern. On the other hand, some of Paul's specific commands are *very* troublesome—that women must not speak in church, that the unmarried should stay single because Paul is single, that a man should not touch a woman, that a woman who will not veil herself should cut off her hair. There are many such commands in the writings of Paul that are potential hornets' nests of controversy. Opinion varies widely. Are we, or are we not, bound to obey them? Even a command such as, "Wives, submit to your husbands," while hardly controversial a generation or two ago, has come to be widely rebuffed by modern women. (Though most remain entirely happy to preserve the other half of the Pauline marital equation, "Husbands, love your wives." Interpretation is indeed usually the child of individual bias as much as it is hunger for truth.)

In all these cases, it is hoped that the "Issue Specific" column in Appendix 2 will help readers weigh the complexities of the questions, "How does this command, or this group of commands, apply to me? To what extent is obedience demanded of me in this case? Is this an outdated command, perhaps one based merely on the author's opinion, or is it still of universal application to all Christians and all churches?"

Also heading the list of difficulties found here that we did not encounter in *The Commands of Jesus* would be Paul's convoluted writing style. C.S. Lewis humorously commented in his *Reflections on the Psalms*: "...we find a somewhat similar difficulty with St. Paul. I cannot be the only reader who has wondered why God, having given him so many gifts, withheld from him (what would to us seem so necessary for the first Christian theologian) that of lucidity and orderly exposition..."

This difficulty is not uniform through the Pauline epistles. When Paul focuses on concrete and specific commands, his staccato-like clarity has no equal: *Rejoice always. Pray constantly. Give thanks in all circumstances.* The precision and practicality of this threefold command is beautiful! His letters are full of such powerful two, three, and four word lightning bolts of practical Christianity. It is these that have formed the bedrock and foundational power of the 120 commands of the Apostles we have considered.

But Paul is a theologian. Like many preachers, he loves the sound of his own voice. The young man who toppled out the window because Paul was droning on so long was probably not the only man or woman to fall asleep during one of Paul's sermons. He tends toward wordiness and overmuch explanation. Some of his theological dissertations are so circuitous and convoluted as to confuse anyone at first read. Even his more straightforward commands and instructions could be much more clearly delivered.

For example, in Galatians 4:12, Paul writes, *Become as I am, for I have become as you are.* Who can possibly tell exactly what he means? In 1 Corinthians 7:30-31, he ambiguously commands: *Let those who rejoice live as though they were not rejoicing. Let those who buy live as though they had no goods. Let those who deal with the world live as though they had no dealings with the world.* His meaning is so unclear that these verses will probably be read differently by everyone. And in Philippians 2:1-2, Paul writes: *If there is any encouragement in Christ, any incentive of love, any participation in the Spirit, any affection and sympathy, be of the same mind, having the same love, being in full accord and of one mind.* It is a beautiful passage. Yet its sheer wordiness and cumbersome construction makes the command at the heart of it more difficult to lay hold of than would be the case if he had merely written, *Be of the same mind.* Nor can we be sure that this is all Paul meant. For he seems to be speaking of being in full accord and of one mind under certain conditions that he wanted to emphasize. We need not belabor the analysis so much that we miss the power of the passage. The point is only to illustrate that Paul's wordy style occasionally blurs the focus of what he intends to say.

Paul also mingles theology in some of the statements that come to us in the form of commands. In such cases it becomes difficult to untangle exactly what God expects of us. It's not as simple as the Lord's *Go and do likewise*, or Paul's *Rejoice always.* We find an example of this in Romans 11:25-26, where I take Paul's *I want you to understand this* as the phraseology of command. He writes: "I want you to understand this mystery: a hardening has come upon part of Israel, until the full number of Gentiles come in, and so that all Israel will be saved." It is an obvious "theological command," clearly not as down-to-earth as his "lightning bolts" of practical conduct.

The anonymous writer of *Hebrews*, too, suffers from the same tendency toward wordy theological ambiguity. *Fear lest you be judged to have failed to reach God's rest* (Hebrew 4:1) is a command whose meaning could be interpreted any number of ways. The same is true of, *Show earnestness in realizing the full assurance of hope until the end.* (Hebrews 7:11) The same writer also, like Paul, mingles theology in his commands.

This makes them difficult to put into easily *do-able* terms. Hebrews 6:1-2 presents a tangle of theological complexity included within the command to "go on to maturity." And it is difficult to know exactly how to "obey" in the daily up and downs of life a theological command such as, *See how great Melchizedek is.* (Hebrews 7:4) None of these can compare in practicality with Paul's pithy, common-sense, down-to-earth "lightning bolts."

Another related difficulty is the self-contradictory nature of certain Apostolic commands. In 1 Cor. 7:8, Paul says that the unmarried and widows should remain single. In 1 Timothy 5:12, he says that younger widows should remarry. Did Paul mistake? Did he change his mind? Do these contradictions cancel one another out?

Similarly, in his two letters to Timothy, he gives what appear to be directly opposing instructions: *Have nothing to do with controversies that breed quarrels* (2 Tim. 2:23); and, *A bishop must be able to give instruction in sound doctrine and be able to confute those who contradict it.* (1 Tim 1:9) Which is it? Are we to *avoid* doctrinal quarrels? Or are we to argue to contradict and confute those who disagree with us on points of doctrine? Which command did Paul intend Timothy to follow?

There are many such examples. Among the most glaring is Paul's personal behavior in light of certain of his commands. To put it bluntly, he doesn't always practice what he preaches. He repeatedly forbids "quarreling over the law" even as he does exactly that with respect to the question of circumcision. Indeed, heated arguments against the legitimacy of circumcision arise in most of his letters, even as he exhorts his readers *not* to argue about matters of the law.

This dichotomy is especially evident in *Titus*, written at the end of Paul's life and thus not excusable as a lapse of youthful immaturity. Within a few verses we find what can hardly be considered anything but a series of flagrant contradictions.

"Speak evil of no one," (3:2) comes on the heels of, "They are detestable, disobedient, unfit for any good deed." (1:16) And, "Avoid quarrels over the law" (3:9) follows soon after, "Silence the circumcisers...rebuke them sharply." (1:11, 13) It is difficult to see what to consider Paul's vehement condemnation of the circumcision party other than a "quarrel over the law."

Likewise, he exhorts his readers to humility and meekness, telling them *not* to set themselves over one another, and to count others as better than themselves. But then he charges Titus: "Let no one disregard you." (2:15) How does this fit with meekness? How does *asserting* one's leadership harmonize with Jesus' words about being last of all and NOT seeking to be over others? How does Paul's command to Titus fit with the Lord's *condemnation* of ambition and rank? These are difficult dichotomies to rationalize. Still more troublesome, Paul does not merely tell Timothy and Titus to assert *their* leadership, his letters are full of argumentative defensiveness about his *own* apostleship, in almost direct contradiction to the principle of counting others as better than oneself. He claims to boast only in his weakness. But a thorough reading of his epistles makes clear that Paul boasts in far more than that. He boasts about almost *everything* in his walk. These examples do not invalidate his commands, but they certainly detract from the weight of his words.

Still another potential interpretive difficulty concerns the liberties Paul takes. He leaves little room for alternate points of view or interpretations. On the basis of his Apostolic commission, he feels justified in essentially considering himself right...about *everything*. Those who disagree not only are wrong...they must be silenced, including even some of the very Apostles who lived and walked with Jesus. Paul's insistence that he alone is right is not necessarily always the surest path toward truth.

He goes so far as to take liberties with Jesus' words themselves. In 1 Corinthians 9:14, he universalizes the Lord's instructions when sending out the Twelve far beyond what can be surmised from Jesus' actual charge to the disciples. Paul writes, "The Lord commanded that those who proclaim the gospel should get their living by the gospel." Even a cursory reading of the gospel account shows that Jesus made no such universal

179

command. Paul has taken a liberty here, leading to the doctrine of a paid Christian clergy, which may *not* be what Jesus meant at all. We don't really know what Jesus intended. But we *do* know that Paul was in error by amplifying Jesus' words into a universal command.

But our job, as I have tried to do here, is to sift the wheat from the chaff. We have to read the commands of the Apostles with care, with prayerful common sense, and with one eye always focused on The Commands of Jesus for validation and confirmation. Whether Paul took liberties and was argumentative and defensive is beside the point. None of us live up to the commands. Why should Paul be any different? He is one of us. He is a brother—a brilliant, wise, insightful, but fallible brother. Therefore, *Do not quarrel over theological or doctrinal controversies* has been included among the commands of the Apostles as incumbent upon us all, as I believe Paul intended it to be. Paul did not live very well by his own command. But then neither do I. The command still applies to us both.

Perhaps the greatest difficulty facing us, mentioned in the Introduction, is simply the fact that many of the commands and instructions are not things that one can DO in a moment-by-moment life of obedience. Nearly all the Commands of Jesus pinpoint qualities of outlook, attitude, behavior, and character. They are Commands that you and I can DO...today, moment-by-moment, by obedience, and by the reorientation of our perspective to see the world and ourselves through the eyes of Jesus. But a great many, perhaps even a majority, of the commands and instructions of the rest of the New Testament are not so practical. They are theological or what we might term "spiritual." Jesus didn't like spiritualizations. When the rich young ruler came to him with spiritualizations, Jesus cut through it all with a down-to-earth command: *Go, sell all that you have and give the money to the poor, and come, follow me.*

Jesus is not interested in spiritual jargon, but practical obedience. Our difficulty is that the Apostles did not follow the simplicity of the Lord's example. Their spiritualized lingo is so long-winded and impractical at times as to be utterly incomprehensible. Out of this forest of jargon and theology, we have to weigh between those commands that reflect the practicality of the Commands of Jesus, and those that are too heavily spiritualized to be of much help in learning to walk in Christlikeness. ALL the commands and instructions have been listed so that you will be able to make such determinations for yourselves. You may find some of those I have not emphasized to be highly practical in *your* life of obedience. That is an inevitable consequence of the highly interpretive nature of these commands.

A few of what I have labeled "issue specific" commands will be completely meaningless to some readers. Those commands specific to the operation of the gifts of prophecy and speaking in tongues in public worship will have no relevance to those in congregations where the spiritual gifts do not play a prominent role. Those in congregations where the spiritual gifts *are* emphasized will find Paul's guidelines enormously practical and helpful. Some will find Paul's instructions about marriage, and male and female roles in the church, to be outmoded and irrelevant. Others *will* seek to model their lives according to Paul's commands in these areas.

These are highly personal and interpretative decisions. These commands, in a sense even more than the Commands of Jesus, require prayer, wisdom, insight, and humility to discover their applications to our daily lives. We cannot, however, simply assume that any command we don't like is outdated and can therefore be ignored. The serious Christian man and woman must engage with these Commands personally and prayerfully to discover God's intent.

For example, what if it *is* God's will that women do not teach in church? What does this Apostolic command have to contribute to the discussion of the modern trend of women in the pulpit? Are the Commands of the Bible to be simply thrown out because they don't mesh with progressive thought? I don't know the answers to these questions. But we mustn't dismiss *any* of the commands out of hand simply because they are inconvenient or run cross-grain to our personal preferences? Any woman who stands in a pulpit to preach or teach must recognize that in doing so she stands in unambiguous *disobedience* to a direct Apostolic command. I am a fairly progressive man. I recognize that the revelation of God is ongoing, that times change and that the truths of God must be reinterpreted anew in every successive generation. At the same time, I read the Commands of the Bible with the greatest solemnity. They are given us for a reason. That reason is not to be peremptorily laid aside for the sake of human ambition. I honestly don't know what God thinks of women in the pulpit in light of Paul's command. Such a development may well be part of God's expanding revelation according to another truth that comes to us from Paul's pen: *There is neither Jew nor Greek, slave nor free, male nor female.* (Galatians 3:28) I bring up this controversial matter to underscore that it is a solemn and serious matter to arrive at the conclusion, "I do not believe that this biblical injunction is one that is incumbent upon me to obey." We cannot draw that conclusion just because we don't like the command.

The fact is, however, we *will* all arrive at that conclusion in certain instances. The commands of the Apostles are so complex, occasionally contradictory, and often specific to issues and situations that are distinct from those we face in our own lives and our own era that it is impossible to live by *every* one of the commands of the New Testament. I have to be just as careful about those commands that I do not make a matter of obedience in *my* life as any woman considering entering the ministry. Let us simply be certain that when we lay aside a command as inapplicable to our personal obedience, we do so with prayerful humility. It can truthfully be said that all the commands are inconvenient to our laziness, our selfishness, our biases, and our comfort zones. Serious Christians have to take a deep breath, look in the mirror, and say, "God, what is your will for my life...today? Give me courage and humility to live by your commands."

For *The Commands of the Apostles*, I began by compiling a complete list of the post-gospel commands of the New Testament. This list is represented in Appendix 2. It is clearly of my own making. Others may compile different lists and groupings. Those who do will no doubt use different priorities. I decided to list *every* command, even those that are obviously not of universal application ("Greet Priscilla and Aquila," etc.), as well as those such as are found in the book of *Acts* that are not of Apostolic origin. This may seem like an exercise in futility. However, I felt that if a list of "the commands of the New Testament" was to be compiled, it ought to be as 100% complete as I could make it. I decided to leave the determination of what is applicable and what is not to the reader. Perhaps it is something like James Strong listing every use of "the" and "and" in the entire Bible. He set out to compile an "exhaustive" concordance, and that is what he did. Accounting for errors and oversights, then, my list of the post-gospel commands of the New Testament, in their various categories, follows in Appendix 2. This list has been the foundation for *The Commands of the Apostles*.

The category of "Implied Commands" is even more complex than for *The Commands of Jesus*. In that case, it was not usually difficult to see what charge Jesus intended to lay upon his disciples and listeners. It is more difficult here. Wordiness and mode of expression make that determination very difficult. Was the writer merely making an observation, or did he intend to lay the charge of obedience upon his readers? It is not always easy to tell. Perhaps more than at any other point, my own interpretation has had to guide me. I have prayerfully asked God to reveal both the writer's intent, and the Holy Spirit's, for *my* life. Where is obedience required of *me*? Others may not agree with a method that interprets words that are not literal "commands" as "implied commands." But I have done so here when I believe the author's intent was to speak instruction concerning personal character and conduct.

Two good examples of this ambiguity exist in 1 Corinthians 13:4-7 and Galatians 5:22—the familiar passages detailing the attributes of love and the fruits of the Spirit. Neither group is phrased *as* commands. Paul is defining and illuminating the characteristics of love, and the fruits of the Spirit-controlled life. As I read these two lists, however, I draw no other conclusion but that God does not merely want me to intellectually analyze love by its constituent elements, he wants me to *love*. I take 1 Corinthians 13:4-7 as a series of commands upon me to love with the love of Christ. Similarly, if the fruit of the Spirit is love, joy, peace, patience, kindness, goodness, etc., I take that as implying that I am *supposed* to live by those qualities of character. I take them as commands that are incumbent upon me.

Or 1 Corinthians 3:11: "For no other foundation can one lay than that which is laid, which is Jesus Christ." I have rendered this as an "implied" command: *Do not lay any other foundation other than that of Jesus Christ.*

An even more ambiguous group of implied commands arises when Paul speaks about himself, his own experiences, his personal walk with God. In some instances (though not all) I have felt that he is sharing personally for the express purpose that his readers take his example upon themselves. He often makes the bold command, "Imitate me." I take this to mean that he intends some of his statements about himself to be read as commands. Therefore, when he writes in 2 Corinthians 11:30, "If I must boast, I will boast in the things that show my weakness," I have rendered as an implied command: *If you boast, boast in the things that show your weakness.*

Two examples of yet greater stretches of interpretation of "implied command" are found in Ephesians. Though they are not technically phrased as commands, I have rendered them as follows because I believe this was the meaning Paul intended:

Allow Christ to dwell in your heart through faith; be rooted and grounded in love, so that you may have power to comprehend what is the breadth and length and height and depth of the love of Christ which surpasses knowledge, and so that you will be filled with all the fullness of God. (Eph. 3:17-19)

Use your calling (apostles, prophets, evangelists, pastors, teachers) for the equipment of the saints, for the work of ministry, for building up the body of Christ, so that we will all attain to the unity of the faith and the knowledge of the Son of God, to mature manhood, to the measure of the stature of the fullness of Christ. (Eph. 4:11-13)

I do not ask you to endorse my interpretive conclusions in every case. Others will arrive at different conclusions for specific passages. But it is important that you know what I have done and why.

It might be said that almost any passage of Scripture can be turned in this way into an implied command. Perhaps that is true. All I can say is that I have prayerfully tried to get at the heart of the writer's intent, and at a deeper level of God's intent for my own moment-by-moment walk with him.

The priority I have used in compiling the list of Implied Commands is based on a series of simple questions I asked myself in each instance:

Is this something I am supposed to DO?

Is this a quality of character I am meant to LIVE by?

Did the Apostolic writer mean this to be a matter of OBEDIENCE?

Does GOD intend for the principle of this passage to be a matter of obedience?

If I read a passage and answer yes to the above questions, then I have worded it accordingly and included it in the "Implied" column.

Phraseology is all important in attempting to ferret out the Commands of the Bible. I read Jesus' words *If any man...*or *Anyone who...*to mean that he intends his words as commands. I read certain phrases and expressions in the epistles in the same way. Included would be, *I bid you...Let us...Let each one...* and so on. Such statements are included in "Direct Commands." Even in these cases, however, ambiguity is possible. Paul writes to Titus: *Bid the older women to teach the younger women to be submissive to their husbands* (Titus 2:3-5) Is this command directed to *Titus*, to *older women*, or to *younger women*? Obviously all three. Younger women cannot ignore it on the technicality that Paul was actually addressing Titus. Yet it is a good example of what we are up against in untangling how and to whom the commands are to apply.

The Apostolic writers are fond of lists of instructions, character qualities, attributes of Christlikeness, and personal instruction. Some of these represent the most succinct and practical passages in the New Testament. We have already mentioned 1 Corinthians 13:4-7 and Galatians 5:22. We could also note: Romans 12:9-21, Colossians 3:12, 1 Thessalonians 5:11-18, 1 Timothy 6:11, and Titus 3:1-2. These are a few examples of the "lightning bolts" of practicality that are sprinkled throughout the epistles. In some cases where it seemed appropriate, the lists are kept intact in Appendix 2. But though they are familiar to us grouped together, I have usually listed each character attribute or command separately.

This broad, complex, multi-dimensional, sometimes confusing and contradictory, dated, and often ambiguous milieu of direct commands, indirect commands, person specific commands, and issue specific commands, has provided the raw material. Out of them I have isolated those commands that most succinctly and practically pinpoint the life God intends to be visibly demonstrated by his people, both individually and corporately. I have tried to identify those with the most widespread application for Christians of all backgrounds and in all denominational and church affiliations. I have not emphasized those "theological" or "spiritual" commands that have little bearing on personal character. God is certainly well able to use any and *all* the commands, no matter how specific, complex, or theological, to speak into our individual lives. However, commands such as *See how great Melchizedek is* have not been included in those commands which I take to be of universal application to Christians today.

Without question, the Commands of Jesus represent the bedrock of the Christian faith. The commands of the Apostles flow from them and harmonize with them. It is no surprise, as Jesus commanded us to love, pray, be kind, do good, and be watchful and patient, that the Apostles likewise command us to love, pray, be kind, do good, and be watchful and patient. Except in rare instances when I felt there to be a compelling reason to do so, those commands that have already been discussed in *The Commands of Jesus* have not been isolated for a repeat of the same detailed discussion here.

Obviously I have had to make certain value judgments about the relative importance of certain commands to the widest possible cross-section of Christians. Some will question my omissions. Speaking in tongues in public worship, for example, is not reflected here with the same weight of significance that Paul gives it. Similarly, because of their controversial nature, neither have I attempted to entirely untangle Paul's sometimes random, contradictory, and clearly opinionated instructions about head coverings, women's role in church, or the relationships between men and women, marriage, sex, divorce, and remarriage. For an unmarried man, Paul had stronger views on these matters than he perhaps had a right to, with the result that his instructions sometimes make no sense and are self-conflicting. I have not ignored the spiritual gifts nor the commands about marriage. However, I have tried to keep them in balance in light of the bigger picture of Christlikeness within the body of Christ.

These commands of the Apostles provide the practical foundation for vibrant and influential church life. There will be constant interplay between individual and corporate obedience. Clearly, every command must first of all be lived out in the day-to-day by the individual men, women, and children who call themselves Christians. Yet for the Church of Jesus Christ to effectively communicate the truths of the Gospel, these commands must also regulate their interactive life together before a watching world. These are our marching orders.

May God grant us the wisdom to seek the Spirit not worship the letter, and then summon the courage to live according to the commands and instructions set forth by the Lord's Apostles for Christ's body, his Church.

Appendix 2

A Listing of the Post-Gospel Commands of the New Testament

A Listing of the commands and instructions of the apostolic writings of the New Testament with numbers where included in *The Commands of the Apostles*. Some rewording liberties have been taken to incorporate command wording. Not all verses are quoted verbatim or in full. But they are mostly compatible with RSV language.

ACTS

Direct
    Implied
        Issue Specific
            Incident/Person/Doctrine Specific
                Of non-Apostolic or divine authority (spoken in *form* of
                      "command" only by miscellaneous persons)

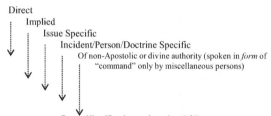

         Peter—His office, let another take. (1:20)

         Peter—Men of Israel, hear these words. (2:22)

Peter—Let all the house of Israel know that God has made Jesus both Lord and Christ. (2:36)

         Peter—Repent and be baptized in the name of Jesus. (2:38)31

         Peter—Look at us. (3:4)

         Peter—In the name of Jesus Christ of Nazareth, walk. (3:6)

         Peter—Repent and turn again. (3:19) 31

         Peter—Be it known to you that by the name of Jesus Christ of Nazareth this man is standing before you well. (4:10)

         Peter—Tell me whether you sold the land for so much. (5:8)

         Angel—Go and stand in the temple and speak to the people the words of Life. (5:20)

      Peter—Obey God rather than men. (5:29 11

             Gamaliel—Take care what you do with these men. (5:35)

             Gamaliel—Keep away from these men and let them alone; for if this undertaking is of men it will fail; but if it is of God, you will not be able to overcome them. You might even be found opposing God. (5:38-39)

         The twelve—Pick out from among you seven men of good repute, full of the Holy Spirit and of wisdom. (6:3)

         Steven—Brethren and fathers, hear me. (7:2)

             Simon the magician—Give me also this power, that anyone on whom I lay my hands may receive the Holy Spirit. (8:19)

         Peter—Repent therefore of this wickedness of yours, and pray to the Lord that the intent of your heart may be forgiven you. (8:22) 31

         Angel—Rise and go toward the south to the road that goes down from Jerusalem to Gaza. (8:26)

         The Spirit—Go up and join this chariot. (8:29)

         Jesus—Saul...Saul...I am Jesus whom you are persecuting; but rise and enter the city, and you will be told what you are to do. (9:4-6)

         Jesus—Ananias...rise and go to the street called Straight and inquire in the house of Judas for a man of Tarsus named Saul. (9:10-11)

         Jesus—Go, for he is a chosen instrument of mine to carry my name before the Gentiles.
    (9:15)

         Peter—Aeneas, Jesus Christ heals you; rise and make your bed. (9:34)

         Peter—Tabitha, rise. (9:40)

         Angel—Cornelius...send men to Joppa and bring one Simon called Peter. (10:3, 5)

Angel—Rise, Peter, kill and eat. (10:13)

The Spirit—Behold, three men are looking for you. Rise and go down, and accompany them without hesitation.. (10:19-20)

Peter—Stand up; I too am a man. (10:26)

Peter—Be baptized in the name of Jesus Christ. (10:48)

Barnabas—Remain faithful to the Lord with steadfast purpose. (11:23) 28

Angel—Get up quickly...dress yourself and put on your sandals...wrap your mantle around you and follow me. (12:7-10)

Peter—Tell this to James and the brethren. (12:17)

The Holy Spirit—Set apart for me Barnabas and Saul for the work to which I have called them. (13:2)

Paul—Men of Israel, and you that fear God, listen. (13:16)

Paul—Beware, therefore, lest there come upon you what is said in the prophets: Behold, you scoffers, and wonder, and perish. (13:40-41) 14, 17

Paul—Stand upright on your feet. (14:10)

James—Brethren, listen to me. (15:13)

James—We should not trouble those of the Gentiles who turn to God, but should write to them to abstain from the pollution of idols and from unchastity and from what is strangled and from blood. (15:19-20) 38, 94

Paul—Come, let us return and visit the brethren in every city where we proclaimed the word of the Lord. (15:36)

Angel in form of a Man of Macedonia—Come over to Macedonia and help us. (16:9)

Paul—I charge you in the name of Jesus Christ to come out of her. (16:18)

Paul—Do not harm yourself, for we are all here. (16:28)

Paul—Believe in the Lord Jesus Christ, and you will be saved, you and your household. (16:31)

Magistrate—Let these men go. (16:35)

Jailor—Come out and go in peace. (16:36)

Paul—Let them come themselves and take us out. (16:37)

God—All men everywhere, repent. (17:30)

Jesus—Do not be afraid, but speak and do not be silent. (18:9)

Jewish exorcists—I adjure you by the Jesus whom Paul preaches. (19:13)

Paul—Do not be alarmed, for his life is in him. (20:10) 16

Paul—Take heed to yourselves, and to all the flock, in which the Holy Spirit has made you guardians. (20:28) 14

Paul—Therefore, be alert. (20:31) 17

Paul—The will of the Lord be done. (21:14) 82

The elders—Do therefore what we tell you...take these men and purify yourself along with them. (21:23-23)

Paul—And the Lord said to me, Rise and go into Damascus, and there you will be told all that is appointed for you to do. (22:10)

Paul—I was praying in the temple, and saw him saying to me, Make haste and get quickly out of Jerusalem...depart. (22:18, 21)

Crowd—Away with such a fellow from the earth. (22:22)

Jesus—Take courage. (23:11)

Paul—Bring this young man to the tribune. (23:17)

Tribune—Tell no one that you have informed me of this. (23:22)

Tribune—At the third hour of the night get ready two hundred soldiers with seventy horsemen and two hundred spearmen to go as far as Caesarea. Also provide mounts for Paul to ride, and bring him safely to Felix the governor. (23:23-24)

Felix—Go away for the present; when I have an opportunity I will summon you. (24:25)

Festus—Let the men of authority among you go down with me, and if there is anything wrong about the man, let them accuse him. (25:5)

Paul—I heard a voice saying to me...Saul, Saul...I am Jesus whom you are persecuting, but rise and stand on your feet. (26:14-16)

Paul—I bid you to take heart. (27:22) 16

Angel—Do not be afraid, Paul, for you must stand before Caesar. (27:24)

Paul—Take heart, men, for I have faith in God. (27:25) 16

Paul—Let it be known to you that this salvation of God has been sent to the Gentiles. (28:30)

ROMANS

Direct
  Implied
    Issue Specific
      Incident/Person/Doctrine Specific

Do not judge another man. (2:1) 58

Rejoice in your sufferings, knowing that suffering produces endurance, and endurance produces character, and character produces hope, and hope does not disappoint. (5:3-4) 19, 23, 25, 84, 89

Consider yourselves dead to sin and alive to God in Christ Jesus. (6:11) 34

Do not yield your members to sin as instruments of wickedness. (6:13) 34

Yield yourselves to God. (6:13) 1

Do not become proud, but stand in awe. (11:20) 87

Note the kindness and severity of God: severity toward those who have fallen, but God's kindness to you, provided you continue in his kindness; otherwise you too will be cut off. (11:22) 92

      I want you to understand this mystery: a hardening has come upon part of Israel, until the full number of Gentiles come in, and so that all Israel will be saved. (11:25-26)

Present your bodies as a living sacrifice, holy and acceptable to God, which is your spiritual worship. (12:1)2

Do not be conformed to this world. (12:2) 32

Be transformed by the renewal of your mind, that you may prove what is the will of God, what is good and acceptable and perfect. (12:2) 1

I bid every one among you not to think of himself more highly than he ought. (12:3) 87

Think of yourself with sober judgment. (12:3) 87

Use your differing gifts according to the grace given you: if prophecy, in proportion to your faith; if service, in your serving; he who teaches, in your teaching; he who exhorts, in your exhortation; he who contributes, in liberality; he who gives aid, with zeal; he who does acts of mercy, with cheerfulness. (12:6-8) 106

Let love be genuine. (12:9) 22

Hate what is evil. (12:9) 33

Hold fast to what is good. (12:9) 27

Love one another with brotherly affection. (12:10) 22

Outdo one another in showing honor. (12:10) 51

Never flag in zeal. (12:11) 118

Be aglow with the Spirit. (12:11) 118

Serve the Lord. (12:11) 9

Rejoice in your hope. (12:12) 23

Be patient in tribulation. (12:12) 25

Be constant in prayer. (12:12) 5

Contribute to the needs of the saints. (12:13) 69

Practice hospitality. (12:13) 46

Bless those who persecute you; bless and do not curse them. (12:14) 27

Rejoice with those who rejoice, weep with those who weep. (12:15) 23, 104

Live in harmony with one another. (12:16) 110, 112

Do not be haughty. (12:16) 87

Associate with the lowly. (12:16) 59

Never be conceited. (12:16) 87

Repay no one evil for evil. (12:17) 27, 55

Take thought of what is noble in the sight of all. (12:17) 8,. (116/7)

If possible, so far as it depends upon you, live peaceably with all. (12:18) 103, 108, 112, 119

Never avenge yourselves, but leave it to the wrath of God. (12:19) 55

If your enemy is hungry, feed him; if he is thirsty, give him drink; for by so doing you will heap burning coals upon his head. (12:20) 27

Do not be overcome by evil, but overcome evil with good. (12:21) 27, 35

Be subject to the governing authorities. (13:1) 113

      Do not resist the authorities or you will be resisting what God appointed. (13:2) 113

Do what is good. (13:3) 27

If you do wrong, be afraid. (13:4)

Pay taxes to whom taxes are due. (13:7) 113
Pay revenue to whom revenue is due. (13:7) 113
Give respect to whom respect is due. (13:7) 51
Give honor to whom honor is due. (13:7) 51
Owe no one anything, except to love one another. (13:8) 70
Love your neighbor as yourself. (13:9) 22
    Wake from sleep. (13:11) 117, 118
Cast off the works of darkness and put on the armor of light. (13:12) 34, 90
Conduct yourself becomingly. (13:13) 61
Do not conduct yourself in reveling. (13:13) 34
Do not conduct yourself in drunkenness. (13:13) 34
Do not conduct yourself in debauchery. (13:13) 34
Do not conduct yourself in licentiousness. (13:13) 34
Do not conduct yourself by quarreling. (13:13) 78
Do not conduct yourself with jealousy. (13:13) 15
Put on the Lord Jesus Christ. (13:14) 81
Make no provision for the flesh, to gratify its desires. (13:14) 34
Welcome the man who is weak in faith, but not for disputes over opinions. (14:1) 19, 105
       COMMANDS SPECIFIC TO FOOD AND EATING:
       Despise no one or pass judgment for what he eats. (14:3) 58
       Let every one be fully convinced [on controversial points] in his own mind. (14:5) 91, 92
    Do not pass judgment on or despise your brother. (14:10) 58
       Do not pass judgment on one another. (14:13) 58
       Never put a stumbling block or hindrance in the way of a brother. (14:13) 60
       Do not let what you eat cause another to stumble. (14:15) 60
       Do not let what is good to you be spoken of as evil. (14:16)
Pursue what makes for peace and mutual upbuilding. (14:19) 103, 110, 112
    Do not for the sake of food destroy the work of God. (14:20) 60
  It is not right to do anything that makes your brother stumble. (14:21) 60
  Keep the faith that you have between yourself and God. (14:22) 28
If you are strong, bear with the failings of the weak, but not to please yourself. (15:1) 105
Please your neighbor for his good, to edify him. (15:2) 27, 52
Welcome one another as Christ has welcomed you, for the glory of God. (15:7) 46
       Greet Priscilla and Aquila, my fellow workers in Christ Jesus...greet also the church in their house. (16:3, 5)
       Greet my beloved Epaenetus, who was the first convert in Asia for Christ. (16:5)
       Greet Mary, who has worked hard among you. (16:6)
       Greet Andronicus and Junias, my kinsmen and my fellow prisoners. (16:7)
       Greet Ampliatus, my beloved in the Lord. (16:8)
       Greet Urbanus, our fellow worker in Christ, and my beloved Stachys. (16:9)
       Greet Apelles, who is approved in Christ. (16:10)
       Greet those who belong to the family of Aristobulus. (16:10)
       Greet my kinsman Herodion. (16:11)
       Greet those in the Lord who belong to the family of Narcissus. (16:11)
       Greet those workers in the Lord, Tryphaena and Tryphosa. (16:12)
       Greet the beloved Persis, who has worked hard in the Lord. (16:12)
       Greet Rufus, eminent in the Lord, also his mother and mine. (16:13)
       Greet Asyncritus, Phlegon, Hermes, Patrobas, Hermas, and the brethren who are with them. (16:14)
       Greet Philologus, Julia, Nereus and his sister, and Olympas, and all the saints who are with them. (15:15)
       Greet one another with a holy kiss. (16:16)
Avoid those who create dissensions and difficulties, in opposition to the doctrine which you have been taught. (16:17) 37
Be wise as to what is good. (16:19) 27, 83
Be guileless as to what is evil. (16:19) 33, 40, 65, 84

1 CORINTHIANS

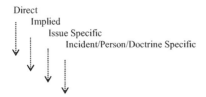

Direct

   Implied

      Issue Specific

         Incident/Person/Doctrine Specific

I appeal to you that all of you agree and that there be no dissensions among you, but that you remain united in the same mind and the same judgment. (1:10) 98, 110

Consider your call. (1:26)

Let him who boasts, boast of the Lord. (1:31) 87

Let each man take care how he builds on the foundation. (3:10) 92, 93

    Do not lay any other foundation other that that of Jesus Christ. (3:11) 93

Let no one deceive himself. (3:18) 99

If any one among you thinks he is wise in this age, let him become a fool that he might become wise. (3:18) 83, 87

Let no one boast of men. (3:21) 87

        COMMANDS SPECIFIC TO IMMORALITY IN THE CORINTHIAN CHURCH

        Do not pronounce judgment before the time, before the Lord comes. (4:5) 58

        Remove the immoral man from among you. (5:2) 108

        Deliver the immoral man to Satan for the destruction of the flesh, so that his spirit may be saved. (5:5) 108

Do not boast. (5:6) 87

    Cleanse out the old leaven that you may be a new lump. (5:7) 108

Let us celebrate the festival, not with the old leaven, the leaven of malice and evil, but with the unleavened bread of sincerity and truth. (5:8) 34

Do not associate with immoral men. (5:9) 36

    Do not associate with any one who bears the name of brother if he is guilty of immorality. (5:11) 36, 37

    Do not associate with any one who bears the name of brother if he is guilty of greed. (5:11) 37

    Do not associate with any one who bears the name of brother if he is an idolater. (5:11) 36, 37, 38

    Do not associate with any one who bears the name of brother if he is a reviler. (5:11) 36, 37

    Do not associate with any one who bears the name of brother if he is a drunkard. (5:11) 36, 37

    Do not associate with any one who bears the name of brother if he is a robber. (5:11) 36, 37

    Do not even eat with such individuals. (5:11) 36, 37

        Do not judge outsiders but judge those inside the church. (5:12) 108

            Drive out the wicked person from among you. (5:13) 108

    Handle grievances between brothers within the church. (6:1) 108

    Do not have lawsuits between brothers. (6:7) 108

Do not be deceived; neither the immoral, nor idolators, nor adulterers, nor homosexuals, nor thieves, nor the greedy, nor drunkards, nor revilers, nor robbers will inherit the kingdom of God. (6:9-10) 99

Shun immorality. (6:18) 33,34

Glorify God in your body. (6:20) 2, 9

        COMMANDS SPECIFIC TO SEXUALITY, MARRIAGE, AND CIRCUMCISION

        It is well for a man not to touch a woman. (7:1)

        Because of the temptation to immorality, each man should have his own wife. (7:2)

        The husband should give to his wife her conjugal rights, and likewise the wife to her husband. (7:3)

        Do not refuse one another except perhaps by agreement for a season. (7:5)

        To the unmarried and the widows, it is well for them to remain single as I do. (7:8)

        To the married I give charge that the wife should not separate from her husband. (but if she does, let her remain single or else be reconciled to her husband)—and that the husband should not divorce his wife. (7:10-11)

        If any brother has a wife who is an unbeliever, and she consents to live with him, he should not divorce her. (7:12)

        If any woman has a husband who is an unbeliever, and he consents to live with her, she should not divorce him. (7:13)

        If an unbelieving partner desires to separate, let it be so; in such a case the brother or sister is not bound. (7:15)

        Lead the life which the Lord has assigned to you and in which God has called you. (7:17)

        If you were circumcised at the time of your call, do not try to remove the marks of circumcision. (7:18)

If you were uncircumcised at the time of your call, do not seek circumcision. (7:18)

Everyone should remain in the state in which you were called. (7:20, 24)

If you were a slave when you were called, never mind. But if you can gain your freedom, avail yourself of the opportunity. (7:21)

If you are bound to a wife, do not seek to be free. (7:27)

Are you free from a wife, do not seek marriage. (7:27)

Let those who have wives live as though they had none. (7:29)

Let those who mourn live as though they were not mourners. (7:30)

Let those who rejoice live as though they were not rejoicing. (7:30)

Let those who buy live as though they had no goods. (7:30)

Let those who deal with the world live as though they had no dealings with the world. (7:31)

Be free from anxieties. (7:32) 20

If one thinks he is behaving improperly toward his betrothed with strong passions, it is no sin if they marry. (7:36)

Take care that your spiritual liberties do not become stumbling blocks to the weak. (8:9) 60, 105

Run the race that you may obtain the prize. (8:24)

The Lord commanded that those who proclaim the gospel should get their living by the gospel. (9:14)

Do not desire evil. (10:6) 33

Do not be idolaters. (10:7) 38

Do not indulge in immorality. (10:8) 34, 35, 36

Do not put the Lord to the test. (10:9) 33

Do not grumble. (10:10) 75

If you think you stand, take heed lest you fall. (10:12) 14, 87

Shun the worship of idols. (10:14) 38

Judge for yourselves what I say. (10:15) 97

COMMANDS SPECIFIC TO FOOD AND EATING

Consider the practice of Israel: are not those who eat the sacrifices partners in the altar. (10:18)

Do not be partners with demons. (10:20) 90

Let no one seek his own good, but the good of his neighbor. (10:24) 27, 52

Eat whatever is sold in the meat market without raising any question on the ground of conscience. (10:25)

If an unbeliever invites you to dinner, eat whatever is set before you without raising any question on the ground of conscience. (10:27)

If someone says to you, "This has been offered in sacrifice," then out of consideration for the man who informed you, do not eat it.. (10:28-29)

Whether you eat or drink or whatever you do, do all to the glory of God. (10:31) 9

Give no offense to Jews or to Greeks or to the church of God. (10:32) 60

Be imitators of me, as I am of Christ. (11:1)

COMMANDS SPECIFIC TO HEAD COVERINGS

Any man who prays or prophesies with his head covered dishonors his head. (11:4)

Any woman who prays or prophesies with her head unveiled dishonors her head. (11:5)

If a woman will not veil herself, then she should cut off her hair. (11:6)

A man ought not to cover his head. (11:7)

A woman ought to have a veil on her head, because of the angels. (11:10)

Judge for yourselves; is it proper for a woman to pray to God with her head uncovered. (11:13)

COMMANDS SPECIFIC TO THE CELEBRATION OF THE LORD'S SUPPER

I received from the Lord what I also delivered to you, that the Lord Jesus on the night when he was betrayed took bread...also the cup after supper, saying..."Do this in remembrance of me.". (11:22-25)

Let a man examine himself, and so eat of the bread and drink of the cup. (11:26)

When you come together to eat, wait for one another—if any one is hungry, let him eat at home—lest you come together to be condemned. (11:33-34)

Earnestly desire the higher gifts. (12:31)

IMPLIED COMMANDS OF LOVE

Love is patient. (13:4) 22, 25

Love is kind. (13:4) 22, 26

Love is not jealous. (13:4) 15, 22

Love is not boastful. (13:4) 22, 87

Love is not arrogant. (13:5) 22, 87

Love is not rude. (13:5) 22, 61, 71, 79

Love does not insist on its own way. (13:5) 22, 63

Love is not irritable. (13:5) 22, 66

189

Love is not resentful. (13:5) 22, 66
Love does not rejoice in wrong. (13:6) 22, 94
Love rejoices in the right. (13:6) 8, 22, 23, 88
Love bears all things. (13:7) 22, 89
Love hopes all things. (13:7) 22, 84
Love believes all things. (13:7) 22, 25, 91
Love endures all things. (13:7) 22, 25, 89
Love never ends. (13:8) 22

Make love your aim. (14:1) 22

COMMANDS SPECIFIC TO SPIRITUAL GIFTS AND SPEAKING IN CHURCH

Earnestly desire the spiritual gifts, especially that you may prophesy. (14:1)
I want you to speak in tongues, but even more to prophesy. (14:5)
Strive to excel in building up the church. (14:12)
He who speaks in a tongue should pray for the power to interpret. (14:13)

Do not be children in your thinking. (14:20) 91

Be babes in evil, but in thinking be mature. ("...in understanding be men." KJV, 14:20) 32, 33, 91

Let all things be done for edification. (14:26) 103, 104
If any one speak in a tongue, let there be only two or at most three, and each in turn; and let one interpret. (14:27)
If there is no one to interpret, let each of them keep silence in church and speak to himself and to God. (14:28)
Let two or three prophets speak, and let the others weigh what is said. (14:29)
If a revelation is made to another sitting by, let the first be silent. (14:30)
The women should keep silent in the churches, for they are not permitted to speak. If there is anything they desire to know, let them ask their husbands at home. For it is shameful for a woman to speak in church. (14:34-35)
If any one thinks that he is a prophet, or spiritual, he should acknowledge that what I am writing to you is a command of the Lord. (14:37)
Earnestly desire to prophesy, and do not forbid speaking in tongues. (14:39)

All things should be done decently and in order. (14:40) 107

Do not be deceived: "Bad company ruins good morals". (15:33) 36, 99

Come to your right mind and sin no more. (15:34) 34

Be steadfast, immovable, always abounding in the work of the Lord, knowing that in the Lord your labor is not in vain. (15:58) 18, 118

On the first day of the week, each of you is to put something aside and store it up, as he may prosper, so that contributions need not be made when I come. (16:2)
When Timothy comes, see that you put him at ease among you...let no one despise him. Speed him on his way in peace. (16:10-11)

Be watchful. (16:13) 17

Stand firm in your faith. (16:13) 18

Be courageous. (16:13) 18

Be strong. (16:13) 18

Let all you do be done in love. (16:14) 22

I urge you to be subject to such men as in the household of Stephanas, and to every fellow worker and laborer. (16:15-16)

Let any one who has no love for our Lord be accursed. (16:22)

2 CORINTHIANS

Direct
    Implied
        Issue Specific
            Incident/Person/Doctrine Specific

Turn to forgive and comfort the one who was punished so that he will not be overwhelmed by excessive sorrow. (2:7) 55

Do not lose heart. (4:16) 16

Look not to the things that are seen, but to the things that are unseen; for the things that are seen are transient, but the things that are unseen are eternal. (4:18) 28, 91

Be always of good courage. (5:6, 8) 16

Walk by faith not by sight. (5:7) 28

Make it your aim to please him. (5:9) 7

Regard no one from a human point of view. (5:16) 85

We entreat you not to accept the grace of God in vain. (6:1) 4

Commend yourself by purity. (6:6) 84

Commend yourself by knowledge. (6:6) 91, 92, 93

Commend yourself by forbearance. (6:6) 25, 89

Commend yourself by kindness. (6:6) 26

Commend yourself by the Holy Spirit. (6:6) 21

Commend yourself by genuine love. (6:6) 22

Commend yourself by truthful speech. (6:7) 65, 94

Commend yourself by the power of God. (6:7)

Commend yourself with the weapons of righteousness. (6:7) 3, 90

Widen your hearts. (6:13) 46, 95

Do not be mismated with unbelievers. (6:14) 42

Come out from them, and be separate from them, says the Lord. (6:17) 32

Let us cleanse ourselves from every defilement of body and spirit, and make holiness perfect in the fear of God. (7:1) 2, 4, 33, 39, 40

Open your hearts to us. (7:2)

COMMANDS SPECIFIC TO THE COLLECTION FROM THE CHURCHES

Excel not only in faith, utterance, knowledge, earnestness, and love, but also in the gracious work of giving. (8:7) 69

Aim at what is honorable, not only in the Lord's sight but also in the sight of men. (8:21) 7, 116, 119

Give proof before the churches of your love and our boasting about you. (8:24)

Do not let our boasting about you be in vain. (9:3)

Be ready with your promised gift. (9:5)

Each one must do as he has made up his mind, not reluctantly or under compulsion. (9:7)

Glorify God by your obedience to this test of service and by your generosity. (9:13)

If you boast, boast in the Lord. (10:17) 87

Let no one think me foolish, but even if you do, accept me as a fool. (11:16)

If you boast, boast in the things that show your weakness. (11:30) 87

Examine yourselves, to see whether you are holding to your faith. (13:5) 14

Test yourselves. (13:5) 14

Mend your ways. (13:11) 31

Heed my appeal. (13:11)

Agree with one another. (13:11) 78, 98, 110, 112

Live in peace. (13:11) 110, 112

Greet one another with a holy kiss. (13:12)

GALATIANS

Direct

Implied

Issue Specific

Incident/Person/Doctrine Specific

Do not turn back again to the weak and beggarly elemental spirits, whose slaves you want to become once more. (4:9) 91, 95, 96

Become as I am, for I have become as you are. (4:12)

Stand fast and do not submit again to a yoke of slavery. (5:1) 18, 91, 95

I have confidence that you will take no other view than mine. (5:10)

Do not use your freedom as an opportunity for the flesh. (5:13) 34, 35

Through love be servants of one another. (5:14) 22, 52

Walk by the Spirit. (5:16) 21

Do not gratify the desires of the flesh. (5:17) 34

IMPLIED COMMANDS AGAINST WORKS OF THE FLESH

191

The work of the flesh is immorality. (5:19) 34
The work of the flesh is impurity. (5:19) 84
The work of the flesh is licentiousness. (5:19) 34
The work of the flesh is idolatry. (5:20) 38
The work of the flesh is sorcery. (5:20) 34
The work of the flesh is enmity. (5:20) 78, 98,112
The work of the flesh is strife. (5:20) 78, 98, 112
The work of the flesh is jealousy. (5:20) 15
The work of the flesh is anger. (5:20) 56
The work of the flesh is selfishness. (5:20) 22, 52, 53
The work of the flesh is dissension. (5:20) 78, 98, 112
The work of the flesh is party spirit. (5:20) 96, 98, 103, 110
The work of the flesh is envy. (5:21) 15
The work of the flesh is drunkenness. (5:21) 34
The work of the flesh is carousing and the like. (5:21) 34
IMPLIED COMMANDS TO LIVE BY THE SPIRIT
The fruit of the Spirit is love. (5:22) 22
The fruit of the Spirit is joy. (5:22) 23
The fruit of the Spirit is peace. (5:22) 24
The fruit of the Spirit is patience. (5:22) 25
The fruit of the Spirit is kindness. (5:22) 26
The fruit of the Spirit is goodness. (5:22) 27
The fruit of the Spirit is faithfulness. (5:22) 28
The fruit of the Spirit is gentleness. (5:23) 29
The fruit of the Spirit is self-control. (5:23) 30
If we live by the Spirit, let us also walk by the Spirit. (5:25) 21
Let us have no self-conceit. (5:26) 87
Let us have no provoking of one another. (5:26) 47, 72, 78
Let us have no envy of one another. (5:26) 15
If a man is overtaken in any sin, the more spiritual should restore him in a spirit of gentleness. (6:1) 29, 105
Look to yourselves, lest you too be tempted. (6:1) 14
Bear one another's burdens, and so fulfill the law of Christ. (6:2) 104
Do not deceive yourself into thinking you are something, when you are nothing. (6:3) 87, 99
Let each one test his own work. (6:4) 14
Bear your own load. (6:5) 117
Let him who is taught the word share all good things with him who teaches. (6:6) 69
Do not be deceived; God is not mocked, for whatever a man sows, that he will also reap. (6:7) 99
Let us not grow weary in well-doing. (6:9) 118, 119
As we have opportunity, let us do good to all men, and especially to those who are of the household of faith. (6:10) 27, 52
Let no man trouble me. (6:17)

EPHESIANS

Direct
: Implied
    Issue Specific
        Incident/Person/Doctrine Specific

Remember that at one time you Gentiles in the flesh were separated from Christ. (2:12)
Do not lose heart over what I am suffering for you, which is your glory. (3:13)
Allow Christ to dwell in your heart through faith; be rooted and grounded in love, so that you may have power to comprehend what is the breadth and length and height and depth of the love of Christ which surpasses knowledge, and so that you will be filled with all the fullness of God. (3:17-19) 6
Lead a life worthy of the calling to which you have been called, with all lowliness and meekness. (4:1-2) 24, 87
Live with patience, forbearing one another in love. (4:2) 22, 25
Be eager to maintain the unity of the Spirit in the bond of peace. (4:3) 103, 110, 112

Use your calling. (apostles, prophets, evangelists, pastors, teachers) for the equipment of the saints, for the work of ministry, for building up the body of Christ, so that we will all attain to the unity of the faith and the knowledge of the Son of God, to mature manhood, to the measure of the stature of the fullness of Christ. (4:11-13) 106

Do not be children any longer, tossed to and fro and carried about with every wind of doctrine. (4:14) 91, 96
Speaking the truth in love, grow up in every way into him who is the head, into Christ, from whom the whole body is joined and knit together. (4:15-16) 74, 93, 94

Do not live any longer as the Gentiles do. (4:17) 32, 34

Put off your old nature which belongs to your former manner of life and is corrupt. (4:22) 34

Be renewed in the spirit of your minds. (4:23) 1, 2, 4

Put on the new nature, created after the likeness of God in true righteousness and holiness. (4:24) 1, 2, 3, 4, 7, 81

Putting away falsehood, let everyone speak the truth with his neighbor. (4:25) 74, 76, 94

Be angry but do not sin. (4:26) 57

Do not let the sun go down on your anger. (4:26) 57

Give no opportunity to the devil. (4:27) 34, 35, 36, 90

Let the thief no longer steal, but rather let him labor, doing honest work with his hands. (4:28) 117

Let no evil talk come out of your mouth, but only such as is good for edifying, as fits the occasion, that it may impart grace to those who hear. (4:29) 75, 76, 77, 78, 79

Do not grieve the Holy Spirit. (4:30) 21

Put away all bitterness. (4:31) 55, 76

Put away all wrath. (4:31) 57

Put away all anger. (4:31) 57

Put away all clamor. (4:31)

Put away all slander. (4:31) 74

Put away all malice. (4:31) 55, 76

Be kind to one another, tenderhearted, forgiving one another. (4:32) 26, 55

Be imitators of God, as beloved children. (5:1) 81

Walk in love, as Christ loved us and gave himself up for us, a fragrant offering and sacrifice to God. (5:2) 2, 22, 81

Immorality, impurity, and covetousness must not even be named among you. (5:3) 34

Let there be no filthiness, nor silly talk, nor levity, which are not fitting; but instead let there be thanksgiving. (5:4) 34, 77

Let no one deceive you with empty words. (5:6) 96, 99

Do not associate with the sons of disobedience. (5:7) 37, 56
Demonstrate the fruit of light, which is found in all that is good and right and true. (5:9) 21

Try to learn what is pleasing to the Lord. (5:10) 7

Take no part in the unfruitful words of darkness, but instead expose them. (5:11) 34

Look carefully how you walk. (5:15) 14, 28

Walk not as unwise men, but as wise. (5:16) 83

Make the most of the time, because the days are evil. (5:16) 118

Do not be foolish, but understand what the will of the Lord is. (5:17) 68, 82

Do not get drunk with wine, but be filled with the Spirit. (5:18) 21, 34
Address one another in psalms and hymns and spiritual songs, singing and making melody to the Lord with all your heart. (5:19). (104)

Always and for everything give thanks in the name of our Lord Jesus Christ to God the Father. (5:20) 19

Be subject to one another out of reverence to Christ. (5:21) 52, 53

COMMANDS SPECIFIC TO FAMILIES

Wives, be subject to your husbands, as to the Lord. (5:22) 44

As the church is subject to Christ, so let wives also be subject in everything to their husbands. (5:24) 44

Husbands, love your wives, as Christ loved the church and gave himself up for her. (5:25) 43

Even so husbands should love their wives as their own bodies. (5:28) 43

Let each one of you love his wife as himself. (5:33) 43

Let the wife see that she respects her husband. (5:33) 44

Children, obey your parents in the Lord, for this is right. (6:1) 45

"Honor your father and mother;" this is the first commandment with a promise, "that it may be well with you and that you may live long on the earth.". (6:2-3) 45

Fathers, do not provoke your children to anger. (6:4) 47

Bring your children up in the discipline and instruction of the Lord. (6:4) 48

COMMANDS SPECIFIC TO SLAVERY

Slaves, be obedient to those who are your earthly masters, in singleness of heart. (6:5) 113

Render service with a good will as to the Lord and not to men. (6:7) 113

Masters, do the same to them, and do not threaten. (6:9)

Be strong in the Lord and in the strength of his might. (6:10) 18

Put on the whole armor of God, that you may be able to stand against the wiles of the devil. (6:11) 18, 90

Take the whole armor of God, that you may be able to withstand in the evil day, and having done all, to stand. (6:13) 18, 90

Stand therefore. (6:14) 18

Gird your loins with truth. (6:14) 94

Put on the breastplate of righteousness. (6:14) 3

Fit your feet with the gospel of peace. (6:15) 24

Take up the shield of faith, with which you can quench all the flaming darts of the evil one. (6:16) 28, 90

Take the helmet of salvation. (6:17) 90

Take up the sword of the Spirit, which is the word of God. (6:17) 90, 92

Pray at all times in the Spirit, with all prayer and supplication. (6:18) 5

Keep alert with perseverance, making supplication for all the saints, and also for me. (6:18-19) 5, 17, 25

PHILIPPIANS

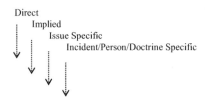

Direct

   Implied

      Issue Specific

         Incident/Person/Doctrine Specific

May your love abound more and more, with knowledge and all discernment, so that you may approve what is excellent, and may be pure and blameless for the day of Christ, filled with the fruits of righteousness. (1:9-11) 22, 84, 92, 97

Let your manner of life be worthy of the gospel of Christ. (1:27) 7

If there is any encouragement in Christ, any incentive of love, any participation in the Spirit, any affection and sympathy, be of the same mind, having the same love, being in full accord and of one mind. (2:1-2) 110, 112

Do nothing from selfishness or conceit. (2:3) 52, 53, 87

In humility count others better than yourself. (2:3) 87

Let each of you look not only to his own interests, but also to the interests of others. (2:4) 52

Have this mind among yourselves, which you have in Christ Jesus, who emptied himself and took the form of a servant. (2:5-7) 52, 81

Work out your own salvation with fear and trembling. (2:12) 93

Do all things without grumbling or questioning, that you may be blameless and innocent, children of God without blemish in the midst of a crooked and perverse generation. (2:14-15) 75

Hold fast to the word of life. (2:16). (6)

      Be glad and rejoice with me. (2:18) 23

      Receive Epaphroditus my brother and fellow worker with all joy; and honor such men. (2:25, 29)

Rejoice in the Lord. (3:1) 23

        Look out for the dogs, look out for the evil-workers, look out for those who mutilate the flesh. (3:2)

   Forget what lies behind and straining forward to what lies ahead, press on toward the goal, for the prize of the upward call of God in Christ Jesus. (3:13-14) 118

Let those who are mature be thus minded. (3:15) 91

Let us hold true to what we have attained. (3:16) 91

Join in imitating me, and mark those who so live as you have an example in us. (3:17)

Stand firm in the Lord. (4:1) 18

      I entreat Euodia and Syntyche to agree in the Lord. (4:2)

      I ask you as true yokefellows to help these women. (4:3)

Rejoice in the Lord always; again I say rejoice. (4:4) 23

Let all men know your forbearance. (4:5) 25, 116, 119

Have no anxiety about anything. (4:6) 20

In everything by prayer and supplication with thanksgiving let your requests be made known to God. (4:6) 5

   Allow the peace of God which passes all understanding to keep your hearts and minds in Christ Jesus. (4:7) 24

Think about whatever is true. (4:8) 8, 88, 94

Think about whatever is honorable. (4:8) 8, 88

Think about whatever is just. (4:8) 8
Think about whatever is pure. (4:8) 8, 84
Think about whatever is lovely. (4:8) 8
Think about whatever is gracious. (4:8) 8, 61, 62
If there is any excellence, if there is anything worthy of praise, think about these things. (4:8) 8, 88
Do what you have learned and received and heard and seen in me. (4:9)
    Like me, be content in whatever state you are in. (4:10)
    Learn the secret of facing plenty and abundance, hunger and want, and knowing how to abound in all circumstances. (4:12)
        Greet every saint in Christ Jesus. (4:21)

COLOSSIANS

Direct
  Implied
      Issue Specific
          Incident/Person/Doctrine Specific

We ask that you may be filled with the knowledge of his will in all spiritual wisdom and understanding. (1:9) 82, 92
    Lead a life worthy of the Lord, fully pleasing to him, bearing fruit in every good work, and increasing in the knowledge of God. (1:10) 7, 92
May you be strengthened with all power, according to his glorious might, for all endurance and patience with joy, giving thanks to the Father. (1:11-12) 18, 25
    Continue in the faith, stable and steadfast, not shifting from the hope of the gospel. (1:23) 18, 28, 91, 96
    Be encouraged of heart, as you are knit together in love, to have all the richness of understanding and knowledge of God's mystery in Christ, in whom are hid all the treasures of wisdom and knowledge. (2:2-3) 92, 104, 110
    Let no one delude you with beguiling speech. (2:4) 96
As you received Christ Jesus the Lord, so live in him. (2:6) 6, 81
Be rooted and built up in Jesus and established in the faith. (2:7) 93
Abound in thanksgiving. (2:7) 19
Do not become prey to philosophy and the empty deceit of human tradition. (2:8) 96
      COMMANDS SPECIFIC TO LEGALISMS
      Do not fall victim to judgments about questions of food or drink. (2:16) 91, 95
      Do not fall victim to judgments about festivals, new moons, or Sabbaths. (2:16) 91, 95
      Do not let yourself be disqualified from insistence on self-abasement or worship of angels. (2:18) 91, 95
    Do not live as if you still belonged to the world. (2:20) 32, 34
      Do not submit to such regulations as, "Do not handle, do not taste, do not touch." (2:21) 91, 95
Seek the things that are above, where Christ is seated at the right hand of God. (3:1) 8
Set your mind on things that are above, not the things of the earth. (3:2) 8
Put to death what is earthly in you. (3:5) 91, 95
Put to death immorality. (3:5) 34
Put to death impurity. (3:5) 34
Put to death passion. (3:5) 34
Put to death evil desire. (3:5) 34
Put to death covetousness, which is idolatry. (3:5) 38
Put away anger. (3:8) 57
Put away wrath. (3:8) 57
Put away malice. (3:8) 55, 57
Put away slander. (3:8) 76
Put away foul talk. (3:8) 77
Do not lie to one another. (3:9) 76
    Put off the practices of the old nature. (3:9) 34
    Put on the new nature, which is being renewed in knowledge after the image of its creator. (3:10) 1, 2, 3, 4, 81
As God's chosen ones, holy and beloved, put on compassion. (3:12) 22

195

Put on kindness. (3:12) 26
Put on lowliness. (3:12) 87
Put on meekness. (3:12) 87
Put on patience. (3:12) 25
Put on forbearance toward one another. (3:13) 25
If you have a complaint against another, forgive each other as the Lord has forgiven you. (3:13) 55
Above all things put on love, which binds everything together in perfect harmony. (3:14) 22
Be thankful. (3:15) 19
Let the word of Christ dwell in you richly. (3:16) 6
    Teach and admonish one another in all wisdom. (3:16) 100
    Sing psalms and hymns and spiritual songs with thankfulness in your hearts to God. (3:16)
Whatever you do, in word or deed, do everything in the name of the Lord Jesus. (3:17) 9
Give thanks to God the Father through Jesus. (3:17) 19
    COMMANDS SPECIFIC TO FAMILIES
    Wives, be subject to your husbands. (3:18) 44
    Husbands, love your wives. (3:19) 43
    Husbands, do not be harsh with your wives. (3:19) 43
    Children, obey your parents in everything, for this pleases the Lord. (3:20) 45
    Fathers, do not provoke your children, lest they become discouraged. (3:21) 47
    Slaves, obey in everything your earthly masters with singleness of heart. (3:22) 113
Whatever your task, work heartily as serving the Lord not men. (3:23) 113, 117, 118
    Masters, treat your slaves justly and fairly. (4:1)
Continue steadfastly in prayer. (4:2) 5, 18
Be watchful in prayer with thanksgiving. (4:2) 5, 17
        Pray for us also. (4:3) 5
Conduct yourself wisely toward outsiders. (4:5)
Make the most of the time. (4:5) 118
Let your speech always be gracious, seasoned with salt. (4:6) 71
        Receive Mark if he comes to you. (4:10)
        Give my greetings to the brethren at Laodicea, and to Nympha and the church in her house. (4:15)
        When this letter has been read among you, have it read also in the church of the Laodiceans. (4:16)
        Read also the letter from Laodicea. (4:16)
        Say to Archippus, "See that you fulfill the ministry which you have received in the Lord.". (4:17)
        Remember my fetters. (4:18)

1 THESSALONIANS

Direct
  Implied
     Issue Specific
        Incident/Person/Doctrine Specific

Speak not to please men, but to please God who tests our hearts. (2:4) 80
    Do not use words of flattery as a cloak for greed. (2:5) 80
    Do not seek glory from men. (2:6) 80
    Lead a life worthy of God, who calls you into his kingdom and glory. (2:12) 7
    Increase and abound in love to one another and to all men, so that he may establish your hearts unblamable in holiness before our God and Father. (3:12-13) 3, 22
Live more and more to please God. (4:1) 7
This is the will of God: that you abstain from immorality. (4:3) 34, 82
Take a wife for yourself in holiness and honor, not in the passion of lust. (4:4-5) 42
Do not wrong your brother in morals. (4:6) 34, 35
Love one another. (4:9) 22
Love the brethren more and more. (4:10) 22
Aspire to live quietly. (4:11) 111

Mind your own affairs. (4:11) 68, 111
Work with your hands. (4:11) 117
Command the respect of outsiders. (4:12) 116, 119
Comfort one another with the words of the Lord's coming. (4:18) 104
Be sober. (5:8) 34
Put on the breastplate of faith and love. (5:8) 22, 28
Put on the helmet of the hope of salvation. (5:8) 100
Encourage and build one another up. (5:11) 104
Respect those who are over you in the Lord and admonish you. (5:12) 51
Highly esteem those over you in love. (5:13) 22, 51
Be at peace among yourselves. (5:13) 24, 110, 112
Admonish the idle. (5:14) 108, 117
Encourage the fainthearted. (5:14) 104, 105
Help the weak. (5:14) 52, 105
Be patient with all. (5:14) 25
Do not repay evil for evil. (5:15) 27
Always seek to do good to all. (5:15) 27, 52, 53
Rejoice always. (5:16) 23
Pray constantly. (5:17) 5
Give thanks in all circumstances, for this is the will of God in Christ Jesus for you. (5:18) 19, 82
Do not quench the spirit. (5:19) 21
Do not despise prophesying. (5:20)
Test everything. (5:21) 97
Hold fast to what is good. (5:21) 27
Abstain from every form of evil. (5:22) 33, 34
        Pray for us. (5:25) 5
        Greet all the brethren with a holy kiss. (5:26)
        Have this letter read to all the brethren. (5:27)

2 THESSALONIANS

Direct
    Implied
        Issue Specific
            Incident/Person/Doctrine Specific

Be steadfast in faith in persecution and affliction. (1:4) 18, 89
    Be worthy of his call, and by his power fulfill every good resolve and work of faith, so that the name of
    the Lord Jesus may be glorified in you. (1:11) 7, 19, 81
        Do not be quickly shaken in mind or excited to the effect that the day of the Lord has
        come. (2:2) 91, 96
        Do not let anyone deceive you; the day of the Lord will not come unless the rebellion
        comes first, and the man of lawlessness is revealed. (2:3) 91, 96, 99
Stand firm and hold to the traditions you were taught by us. (2:15) 18, 91, 93, 100
    Establish eternal comfort and good hope through grace in your hearts in every good work and word.
    (2:16-17) 103
        Pray for us, that the word of the Lord may speed on and triumph. (3:1) 5
        Pray that we will be delivered from wicked and evil men. (3:2) 5, 35, 36
Keep away from any brother who is living in idleness. (3:6) 37, 108, 117
        Imitate us and do not be idle. (3:7) 117
If anyone will not work, let him not eat. (3:10) 117
Do your work in quietness and earn your own living. (3:12) 117
Do not be weary in well-doing. (3:13) 118, 119
        Note anyone who refuses to obey what we say in this letter and have nothing to do with
        him. (3:14) 37, 108
        Do not look upon such a one as an enemy, but warn him as a brother. (3:15) 108

1 TIMOTHY

Direct
: Implied
: : Issue Specific
: : : Incident/Person/Doctrine Specific

> > > Remain at Ephesus. (1:3)
> > > > Charge certain persons not to teach any different doctrine. (1:3) 100
> > Do not be occupied with myths and endless genealogies which promote speculations. (1:4) 91, 96
> > Occupy yourself with the divine training that is faith. (1:4) 28, 100
> > Keep your aim love that issues from a pure heart, a good conscience, and sincere faith. (1:5) 22, 28, 40, 84

Wage the good warfare. (1:18) 90
Hold to faith and a good conscience. (1:19) 28, 40
Make supplications, prayers, intercessions, and thanksgivings for all men, including kings and all in high positions. (2:1-2) 5, 19, 113
Live a quiet and peaceable life, godly and respectful in every way. (2:2) 24, 51, 111, 119
Men should pray in every place, lifting holy hands without anger or quarreling. (2:8) 5, 55, 78

COMMANDS SPECIFIC TO WOMEN

| Women, adorn yourselves modestly and sensibly in seemly apparel. (2:9) 115, 119
| Women, do not adorn yourselves with braids and gold and pearls and expensive clothes, but with good deeds as befits women of faith. (2:9-10) 115, 119
| Let a woman learn in silence with all submissiveness. (2:11)
| I permit no woman to teach or have authority over men. (2:12)
| A woman is to keep silent. (2:12)
| Women are to continue in faith and love and holiness with modesty. (2:15) 115

COMMANDS SPECIFIC TO QUALIFICATIONS OF A BISHOP

| A bishop must be above reproach. (3:2) 41
| A bishop must be the husband of one wife. (3:2) 41, 42
| A bishop must be temperate. (3:2) 34, 41
| A bishop must be sensible. (3:2) 13, 41
| A bishop must be dignified. (3:2) 13, 41, 61
| A bishop must be hospitable. (3:2) 46, 41
| A bishop must be an apt teacher. (3:2) 41, 100
| A bishop must not be a drunkard. (3:3) 34, 41
| A bishop must not be violent. (3:3) 41, 57
| A bishop must be gentle. (3:3) 29, 41
| A bishop must not be quarrelsome. (3:3) 41, 78, 98
| A bishop must not be a lover of money. (3:3) 41, 86
| A bishop must manage his own household well. (3:4) 41, 47
| A bishop must keep his children submissive and respectful in every way. (3:4) 41, 47
| A bishop must not be a recent convert. (3:6) 41, 101
| A bishop must be well thought of by outsiders. (3:7) 41, 116, 19

COMMANDS SPECIFIC TO QUALIFICATIONS OF A DEACON

| A deacon must be serious. (3:8) 13, 41
| A deacon must not be double-minded. (3:8) 41, 96
| A deacon must not be addicted to much wine. (3:8) 34, 41
| A deacon must not be greedy for gain. (3:8) 41, 86
| A deacon must hold the mystery of the faith with clear conscience. (3:9) 40, 41
| A deacon must be tested first and then serve if they prove blameless. (3:10) 41, 101
| The women must be serious. (3:11) 13, 41
| The women must not be slanderers. (3:11) 41, 76
| The women must be temperate. (3:11) 34, 41
| The women must be faithful in all things. (3:11) 28, 41
| A deacon must be the husband of one wife. (3:12) 41, 42
| A deacon must manage their children and households well. (3:12) 41, 47

> Reject no food if it is received with thanksgiving. (4:4) 19, 95
Have nothing to do with godless and silly myths. (4:6) 91, 96
Train yourself in godliness. (4:7) 4
> > > Command and teach these things. (4:11) 41, 100

198

Let no one look down on your youth. (4:12) 41

Set the believers an example in speech and conduct, in love, faith, and purity. (4:12) 100, 116

Till I come, attend to the public reading of scripture, to preaching and teaching. (4:13) 100

Do not neglect the gift you have. (4:14) 106

Practice these duties, devote yourself to them. (4:15) 100

Take heed to yourself and your teaching and hold to it. (4:16) 14 100

COMMANDS SPECIFIC TO TREATMENT OF THE ELDERLY AND WIDOWS

Do not rebuke an older man. (5:1) 51

Exhort an older man as you would a father. (5:1) 51

Treat younger men like brothers. (5:1) 51, 53

Treat older women like mothers. (5:2) 51

Treat younger women like sisters, in all purity. (5:2) 84

Honor widows. (5:3) 50

If a widow has children or grandchildren, let them learn their duty to their own family and make provision for their parents. (5:4) 50

Let a widow be enrolled if she is over sixty, having been the wife of one husband, well attested for her good deeds, who has brought up her children, shown hospitality, washed the feet of the saints, and devoted herself to good in every way. (5:9-10) 50

Refuse to enroll younger widows. (5:11) 50

I would have younger widows remarry, bear children, and rule their households. (5:12) 50

If any believing woman has relatives who are widows, let her assist them so that the church is not burdened. (5:16) 50

Let the church assist those who are real widows. (5:16) 50

Consider elders who rule well worthy of double honor, especially preachers and teachers. (5:17) 51

Never admit a charge against an elder except on the evidence of two or three witnesses. (5:19)

Rebuke those who persist in sin in the presence of all. (5:20) 108

Keep these rules without favor. (5:21)

Do nothing from partiality. (5:21) 59

Do not be hasty in the laying on of hands. (5:22) 101

Do not participate in another man's sins. (5:22) 35

Keep yourself pure. (5:22) 84

Don't drink only water, but use a little wine for your stomach and frequent ailments. (5:23)

COMMANDS SPECIFIC TO SLAVES

Let those under the yoke of slavery regard their masters as worthy of honor. (6:1) 113

Let slaves with believing masters not be disrespectful on the ground that they are brothers. (6:2) 113

Let slaves with believing masters serve them all the better. (6:2) 113

Teach and urge these duties. (6:2) 100

Avoid those who are puffed up with conceit and know nothing. (6:4) 37

Avoid morbid craving for controversy and disputes about words. (6:4) 98

Avoid envy. (6:4) 15

Avoid dissension. (6:4) 98

Avoid slander. (6:4) 76

Avoid base suspicions. (6:4) 64

Avoid wrangling among men who are depraved in mind and bereft of truth. (6:5) 37, 78, 98

Be content if you have food and clothing. (6:8) 24

Do not desire to be rich. (6:9) 86

Do not love money. (6:10) 86

Shun all these evils and distractions. (6:11) 32, 34, 36

Aim at righteousness. (6:11) 3

Aim at godliness. (6:11) 3, 4

Aim at faith. (6:11) 28

Aim at love. (6:11) 22

Aim at steadfastness. (6:11) 18

Aim at gentleness. (6:11) 29

Fight the good fight of the faith. (6:12) 28, 90

Take hold of the eternal life to which you were called. (6:12) 24

Keep the commandment unstained and free from reproach. (6:14) 11, 34

Charge the rich not to be haughty nor to set their hope on uncertain riches. (6:17) 59, 86

If you are rich, do good, be rich in good deeds. (6:18) 27, 59

Timothy, guard what has been entrusted to you. (6:20)

Avoid the godless chatter and contradictions of what is called knowledge 6:20) 91, 92, 98

Do not miss the mark of faith by professing knowledge. (6:21) 28, 92

2 TIMOTHY

Direct
- Implied
  - Issue Specific
    - Incident/Person/Doctrine Specific

Rekindle the gift of God that is within you. (1:6)

Do not be ashamed of testifying to our Lord. (1:8) 18

Follow the pattern of the sound words which you have heard from me. (1:13)

Guard the truth that has been entrusted to you by the Holy Spirit. (1:14) 94

Be strong in the grace that is in Christ Jesus. (2:1) 18

Entrust what you heard from me to faithful men who will be able to teach others. (2:2) 100

Take your share of suffering as a good soldier of Jesus Christ. (2:3) 89

Think over what I say, for the Lord will grant you understanding in everything. (2:7) 91

Remember Jesus Christ. (2:8) 6

Remind others that if we died with Christ, we shall also live with him, that if we endure, we shall reign with him, that if we deny him he will deny us, but that even if we are faithless, he is faithful. (2:14)

Charge others before the Lord to avoid disputing about words. (2:14) 78, 98

Do your best to present yourself to God as one approved, as a workman who need not be ashamed. (2:15) 100

Study to show yourself approved. Rightly handle the word of truth. (2:15) 91, 92

Avoid godless chatter, for it leads people into ungodliness and their talk eats away like gangrene. (2:16) 77

Shun youthful passions. (2:22) 34

Aim at righteousness. (2:22) 3

Aim at faith. (2:22) 28

Aim at love. (2:22) 22

Aim at peace. (2:22) 24

Have nothing to do with stupid, senseless controversies that breed quarrels. (2:23) 98

The Lord's servant must not be quarrelsome. (2:24) 78

The Lord's servant must be kindly to everyone. (2:24) 26

The Lord's servant must be an apt teacher. (2:24) 100

The Lord's servant must be forbearing. (2:24) 25, 89

The Lord's servant must correct his opponents with gentleness. (2:25) 29, 100

Understand that in the last days there will come times of stress. (3:1)

Avoid lovers of self. (3:2) 37

Avoid lovers of money. (3:2) 37, 86

Avoid the proud. (3:2) 37

Avoid the arrogant. (3:2) 37

Avoid the abusive. (3:2) 37

Avoid those who are disobedient to their parents. (3:2) 37

Avoid the ungrateful. (3:2) 37

Avoid the unholy. (3:2) 37

Avoid the inhuman. (3:3) 37

Avoid the implacable. (3:3) 37

Avoid slanderers. (3:3) 37, 75

Avoid profligates. (3:3) 37

Avoid the fierce. (3:3) 37

Avoid haters of good. (3:3) 37

Avoid the treacherous. (3:4) 37

Avoid the reckless. (3:4) 37

Avoid those who are swollen with conceit. (3:4) 37

Avoid lovers of pleasure rather than lovers of God. (3:4) 37

Avoid those who hold to a form of religion but deny its power. (3:5) 37, 54, 65

Avoid those who worm their way into households to influence weak women. (3:6) 37

Avoid those who will listen to anybody but can never arrive at a knowledge of the truth. (3:6) 37, 96

Avoid men of corrupt mind and counterfeit faith. (3:8) 37

Continue in what you have learned and have firmly believed, knowing from whom you learned it. (3:14) 100

As a man of God, be complete and equipped for every good work from the teaching, reproof, correction, and training in righteousness of all scripture. (3:16-17) 100

I charge you to preach the word. (4:2) 100
Be urgent in season and out of season. (4:2)
Convince. (4:2) 100
Rebuke. (4:2) 108
Exhort. (4:2) 104
Be unfailing in patience and in teaching. (4:2) 25
Always be steady. (4:5) 18
Endure suffering. (4:5) 89
Do the work of an evangelist. (4:5)
Fulfill your ministry. (4:5) 100, 106
Do your best to come to me soon. (4:9)
Get Mark and bring him with you, for he is very useful in serving me. (4:11)
When you come, bring the cloak that I left with Carpus at Troas, also the books, and above all the parchments. (4:13)
Beware of Alexander the coppersmith. (4:15)
Greet Priscilla and Aquila and the household of Onesiphorus. (4:19)
Do your best to come before winter. (4:21)

TITUS

Direct
   Implied
      Issue Specific
         Incident/Person/Doctrine Specific

COMMANDS SPECIFIC TO ELDERSHIP
An elder must be blameless. (1:6) 41
An elder must be the husband of one wife. (1:6) 41
An elder's children must be believers. (1:6) 41, 47
An elder's children must not be open to the charge of being profligate or insubordinate. (1:6) 41
COMMANDS SPECIFIC TO QUALIFICATIONS FOR A BISHOP
A bishop must be blameless. (1:7) 41
A bishop must not be arrogant. (1:7) 41, 87
A bishop must not be quick tempered. (1:7) 41, 55
A bishop must not be a drunkard. (1:7) 41, 34
A bishop must not be violent. (1:7) 41
A bishop must not be greedy for gain. (1:7) 41, 67
A bishop must be hospitable. (1:8) 41, 46
A bishop must be a lover of goodness. (1:8) 27, 41
A bishop must be a master of himself. (1:8) 30, 41
A bishop must be upright. (1:8) 3, 41
A bishop must be holy. (1:8) 3, 41
A bishop must be self-controlled. (1:8) 30, 41
A bishop must hold firm to the sure word as taught. (1:9) 41
A bishop must be able to give instruction in sound doctrine and be able to confute those who contradict it. (1:9) 41, 100
Silence the circumcision party. (1:11)
Rebuke the circumcisers sharply, that they may be sound in faith. (1:14)
Teach what befits sound doctrine. (2:1)
COMMANDS SPECIFIC TO OLDER MEN
Bid older men to be temperate. (2:2) 34
Bid older men to be serious. (2:2) 13
Bid older men to be sensible. (2:2) 13
Bid older men to be sound in faith. (2:2) 28
Bid older men to be sound in love. (2:2) 22
Bid older men to be steadfast. (2:2) 18
COMMANDS SPECIFIC TO OLDER WOMEN
Bid older women to be reverent in behavior. (2:3) 61, 62
Bid older women not to slander. (2:3) 75

Bid older women not to be slaves to drink. (2:3) 34
Bid older women to teach what is good. (2:3) 27, 100
COMMANDS SPECIFIC TO YOUNGER WOMEN AND MEN
Bid older women to train younger women to love their husbands and children. (2:4) 44, 49
Bid older women to train younger women to be sensible. (2:5) 13, 49
Bid older women to train younger women to be chaste. (2:5) 49, 84
Bid older women to train younger women to be domestic. (2:5) 49
Bid older women to train younger women to be kind. (2:5) 26, 49
Bid older women to train younger women to be submissive to their husbands. (2:5) 44, 49
Urge younger men to control themselves. (2:6) 30, 49
Show yourself in all respects a model of good deeds. (2:7) 27, 27, 116, 119
In your teaching show integrity. (2:7) 7
In your teaching show gravity. (2:7) 13
In your teaching show sound speech that cannot be censored, so that an opponent may be put to shame. (2:8) 100

COMMANDS SPECIFIC TO SLAVES
Bid slaves to be submissive to their masters. (2:9) 113
Bid slaves to give satisfaction in every respect. (2:9)
Bid slaves not to be refractory. (2:9)
Bid slaves not to pilfer. (2:10)
Bid slaves to show entire and true fidelity. (2:10)
Renounce irreligion and worldly passions. (2:12) 34, 56, 65
Live sober, upright, and godly lives in the world. (2:12) 7, 13, 116, 119
Declare these things. (2:15) 100
Exhort and reprove with all authority. (2:15) 104, 108
Let no one disregard you. (2:15)
Remind them to be submissive to rulers and authorities. (3:1) 113
Be obedient. (3:1) 11
Be ready for any honest work. (3:1) 117
Speak evil of no one. (3:2) 75, 76
Avoid quarreling. (3:2) 78
Be gentle. (3:2) 29
Show perfect courtesy toward all men. (3:2) 61, 62, 71
Insist on these things. (3:8)
Be careful to apply yourselves to good deeds. (3:9) 27
Avoid stupid controversies, genealogies, and quarrels over the law. (3:9) 78, 98
Admonish a factious man once or twice, then have nothing more to do with him. (3:10) 37, 108
When I send Artemas or Tychicus to you, do your best to come to me at Nicopolis. (3:12)
Do your best to speed Zenas the lawyer and Apollos on their way; see that they lack nothing. (3:13)
Let our people learn to apply themselves to good deeds to help cases of urgent need and not be unfruitful. (3:14) 27, 52
Greet those who love us in the faith. (3:15)

PHILEMON

Direct
  Implied
    Issue Specific
      Incident/Person/Doctrine Specific

Do what is required. (8)
Receive Onesimus as you would me. (17)
If he has wronged you in any way or owes you anything, charge it to my account. (18)
Refresh my heart in Christ. (20)
Prepare a guest room for me. (22)

Direct
   Implied
      Issue Specific
         Incident/Person/Doctrine Specific

Pay close attention to what you have heard lest you drift away from it. (2:1) 91, 93, 96
    Do not neglect such a great salvation. (2:3) 4
Consider Jesus, the apostle and high priest of our confession. (3:1) 6
    Hold fast your confidence and your pride in your hope. (3:6) 18
When you hear his voice, do not harden your hearts in rebellion. (3:7-8) 14
Take care lest there be an evil unbelieving heart in any of you. (3:12) 14, 17
Exhort one another every day. (3:13) 104
Fear lest you be judged to have failed to reach God's rest. (4:1)
When you hear his voice, do not harden your hearts. (4:7) 14
Let us strive to enter God's rest, that no one fall by disobedience. (4:11) 118
Let us hold fast our confession. (4:14) 18
Let us with confidence draw near to the throne of grace, that we may receive mercy and find grace to help in time of need. (4:16) 2
Leave the elemental doctrines of Christ and go on to maturity. (6:1) 91
Do not keep laying a foundation of repentance from dead works. (6:1) 91, 93
Show earnestness in realizing the full assurance of hope until the end. (6:11) 118
Do not be sluggish, but imitate those who through faith and patience inherit the promises. (6:12) 118
See how great Melchizedek is. (7:4)
Let us draw near with a true heart in full assurance of faith, with our hearts sprinkled clean from an evil conscience and our bodies washed with pure water. (10:22) 2
Let us hold fast the confession of our hope without wavering. (10:23) 18
Let us consider how to stir up one another to love and good works. (10:24) 27, 104
    Let us not neglect to meet together to encourage one another. (10:25) 104, 109
        Understand that the world was created by the word of God. (11:3) 92
           To draw near to God, one must believe that he exists and that he rewards those who seek him. (11:6) 92
Since we are surrounded by so great a cloud of witnesses, let us lay aside every weight, and sin which clings so closely, and let us run with perseverance the race that is set before us, looking to Jesus the pioneer and perfecter of our faith. (12:1-2) 18, 28, 89
Consider Jesus who endured hostility from sinners, so that you may not grow weary or fainthearted. (12:3) 89
Do not regard lightly the discipline of the Lord, nor lose courage when you are disciplined by him. (12:5) 89
Lift your drooping hands and strengthen your weak knees. (12:12) 18
Make straight paths for your feet, so that what is lame may be healed. (12:13) 10
Strive for peace with all men, and for the holiness without which no one will see the Lord. (12:14) 24, 110, 112, 119
See to it that no one fail to obtain the grace of God. (12:15) 4
See to it that no root of bitterness spring up and cause trouble. (12:15) 57, 66
See to it that no one becomes immoral or irreligious like Esau. (12:16) 34, 65
See that you do not refuse him who is speaking. (12:25)
Let us be grateful for receiving a kingdom that cannot be shaken. (12:28) 19
Let us offer to God acceptable worship, with reverence and awe, for our God is a consuming fire. (12:28-29) 2, 7
Let brotherly love continue. (13:1) 22
Do not neglect to show hospitality to strangers, for thereby some have entertained angels unawares. (13:2) 46
Remember those who are in prison, as though in prison with them; and those who are ill-treated. (13:3)
Hold marriage in honor. (13:4) 42
Let the marriage bed be undefiled. (13:4) 42
Keep your life free from love of money. (13:5) 86
Be content with what you have. (13:5) 15, 24, 86
Remember your leaders; consider their lives and imitate their faith. (13:7) 51, 113
Do not be led away by diverse and strange teachings. (13:9) 96

Strengthen your hearts by grace, not by food. (13:9) 18

Let us go forth to Jesus outside the camp and bear the abuse he endured. (13:13)

Through Jesus, continually offer up a sacrifice of praise to God, as the fruit of lips that acknowledge his name. (13:15) 19

Do not neglect to do good and share what you have, for such sacrifices are pleasing to God. (13:16) 27, 69

Obey your leaders and submit to them; for they are keeping watch over your souls, as men who will have to give account. (13:17) 113

If you are a leader, lead joyfully not sadly. (13:17) 41

      Pray for us. (13:18) 5

      I urge you to pray for us earnestly in order that I may be restored to you the sooner. (13:19) 5

     Equipped by God with everything good, do the Lord's will, which is pleasing in his sight. (13:21-22) 82, 100

      I appeal to you, brethren, bear with my word of exhortation. (13:22)

      Greet all your leaders and all the saints. (13:24)

JAMES

Direct
  Implied
      Issue Specific
          Incident/Person/Doctrine Specific

Count it all joy when you meet various trials, knowing that the testing of your faith produces steadfastness. (1:2-3) 23, 89

Let steadfastness have its full effect, that you may be perfect and complete, lacking in nothing. (1:4) 18, 100

Ask God for wisdom, for he gives to all men generously. (1:5) 83

Ask God for wisdom in faith, with no doubting. (1:6) 83

    Do not be double-minded. (1:8) 97

To show partiality is to commit sin. 59

Let the lowly boast in their exaltation. (1:9) 87

Let the rich boast in their humiliation. (1:10) 59, 87

    Endure trial and be blessed, for when you have stood the test you will receive the crown God has promised. (1:12) 25, 89

Do not say that you are tempted by God. (1:13) 33

Do not be deceived—every good and perfect gift comes from the Father above. (1:16-17) 99

Let every man be quick to hear. (1:19) 73

Let every man be slow to speak. (1:19) 73

Let every man be slow to anger. (1:19) 57

Put away all filthiness and wickedness. (1:21) 34

Receive with meekness the implanted word. (1:21) 87

Be doers of the word, not hearers only. (1:22) 12

Do not deceive yourselves—one who is a hearer of the word and not a doer is like a man who looks in the mirror and quickly forgets what he has seen. (1:23-24) 12, 99

Bridle your tongue. (1:26) 72

    Do not deceive your heart with vain religion. (1:26) 56, 65, 99

Visit orphans and widows in their affliction. (1:27) 50

Keep yourself unstained from the world. (1:27) 32, 34

Show no partiality as you hold the faith of our Lord Jesus Christ. (2:1) 59

    Do not respect the rich over the poor. (2:2-4) 59

Listen, God has chosen those who are poor in the world to be rich in faith and heirs of the kingdom. (2:5) 59

    Do well by loving your neighbor as yourself. (2:8) 22

    To show partiality is to commit sin. (2:9) 59

Speak and act as those who are to be judged under the law of liberty. (2:12)

    Do not pretend to have faith without works. (2:17) 12, 56, 65

Let not many of you become teachers, for teachers shall be judged with greater strictness. (3:1) 101

Look at the rudder of a ship—it is like the tongue, a small member that boasts of great things. (3:4-5) 72

Do not let blessing and cursing come from the same mouth. (3:10) 72
By your good life, show works in the meekness of wisdom. (3:13) 27, 83, 87
Do not boast and be false to the truth if you have bitter jealousy and selfish ambition in your heart. (3:14) 15, 66, 86, 94

Let your lives show the wisdom from above. (3:17) 21, 83
Show God's wisdom by your purity. (3:17) 83, 84
Show God's wisdom by being peaceable. (3:17) 24, 83, 112
Show God's wisdom by being gentle. (3:17) 29, 83
Show God's wisdom by being open to reason. (3:17) 63, 83, 91
Show God's wisdom by being full of mercy. (3:17) 54, 83
Show God's wisdom by demonstrating good fruit. (3:17) 21, 83
Let your lives be without uncertainty or insincerity. (3:17) 65, 74
Sow peace and reap a harvest of righteousness. (3:18) 3, 24, 112
Do not ask God wrongly so as to feed your own covetousness. (4:3) 86
Do not be a friend of the world or you make yourself an enemy of God. (4:4) 32
Submit to God. (4:7) 1
Resist the devil and he will flee from you. (4:7) 33, 90
Draw near to God and he will draw near to you. (4:8) 1, 2
Cleanse your hands and purify your hearts, you of double mind. (4:8) 56, 84, 96
Be wretched and mourn and weep. (4:9)
Let your laughter be turned to mourning, and your joy to dejection. (4:9)
Humble yourself before the Lord and he will exalt you. (4:10) 87
Do not speak evil against one another. (4:11) 75, 76
Do not judge your neighbor. (4:12) 58
Do not make plans when you do not know what tomorrow will bring. (4:13-14)
Rather say, "If the Lord wills, we shall live and shall do this or that". (4:15)
Do not boast in your arrogance. (4:16) 87
If you know what is right and do not do it, for you that is sin. (4:17) 94
You who are rich, weep and howl for the miseries that will come upon you. (5:1)
Be patient until the coming of the Lord. (5:7) 25
Be patient like a farmer awaiting the precious fruit from the earth. (5:7-8) 25
Establish your hearts, for the coming of the Lord is at hand. (5:8) 93
Do not grumble against one another, that you may not be judged. (5:9) 75
Take an example of suffering and patience from the prophets who spoke in the name of the Lord. (5:10) 25, 89
Do not swear, either by heaven or by earth or with any other oath. (5:12) 77
Let your yes be yes and your no be no, that you may not fall under condemnation. (5:12) 74
If you are suffering, pray. (5:13) 5, 89
Are you cheerful, sing praise. (5:13) 23
Are you sick, call for the elders to pray and anoint you with oil in the name of the Lord. (5:14) 5
Confess your sins to one another. (5:16) 39
Pray for one another, that you may be healed. (5:16) 5
Know that anyone who brings a sinner back from the error of his ways will save his soul and cover a multitude of sins. (5:20)

1 PETER

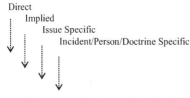

Direct
Implied
Issue Specific
Incident/Person/Doctrine Specific

Rejoice in your inheritance in Christ, though now for a little while you suffer various trials, so that the genuineness of your precious faith may redound to praise and glory and honor at the revelation of Jesus Christ. (1:6-7) 23
Love Christ and believe in him even though you have not seen him. (1:8) 93
Gird up your minds. (1:13) 91
Be sober minded. (1:13) 13

Set your hope fully upon the grace that is coming to you at the revelation of Jesus Christ. (1:13) 18

As obedient children, do not be conformed to the passions of your former ignorance. (1:14) 32

As he who called you is holy, be holy yourselves, for it is written, "You shall be holy as I am holy". (1:15-6) 2, 3

Conduct yourself with fear throughout the time of your exile. (1:17)

> Purify your souls by your obedience. (1:22) 11, 84

Love one another earnestly from the heart. (1:22) 22

Put away all malice. (2:1) 57

Put away all guile. (2:1) 65

Put away all insincerity. (2:1) 65, 74

Put away all envy. (2:1) 15

Put away all slander. (2:1) 76

Long for pure spiritual milk, that by it you may grow up to salvation. (2:2) 91, 93

Come to him, that living stone, rejected by men but in God's sight chosen and precious. (2:4)

Like living stones, be yourselves built into a spiritual house, to be a holy priesthood, to offer spiritual sacrifices acceptable to God. (2:5) 93, 110

> As a chosen race, a royal priesthood, a holy nation, God's own people, declare the wonderful deeds of him who called you out of darkness into his marvelous light. (2:9) 120

As aliens and exiles, abstain from the passions of the flesh. (2:11) 34

Maintain good conduct in the world, so that your good deeds will be seen and God be glorified. (2:12) 7, 116, 119

Be subject for the Lord's sake to every human institution. (2:13) 113

> By doing right, put to silence the ignorance of foolish men. (2:15) 94

Live as free men. (2:16)

Do not use your freedom as a pretext for evil. (2:16) 34

Live as servants of God. (2:16) 9

Honor all men. (2:17) 51, 53

Fear God. (2:17)

Honor the emperor. (2:17) 113

Servants, be submissive to your masters with all respect, even if they are overbearing. (2:18) 114

> Endure pain and injustice patiently. (2:19-20) 25, 89

Follow the example of Christ. (2:21) 81

> > *COMMANDS SPECIFIC TO WIVES AND HUSBANDS*
> >
> > Wives, be submissive to your husbands; you may win them to Christ without a word by your example. (3:1) 44
> >
> > Women, do not be adorned outwardly with braids, robes, and gold jewelry. (3:3) 115
> >
> > Women, let the hidden person of your heart be adorned with the imperishable jewel of a gentle and quiet spirit. (3:4) 115
>
> Thus are holy women adorned who are submissive to their husbands. (3:5) 44, 115
>
> Do right and let nothing terrify you. (3:6) 16, 27
>
> > Husbands, live considerately with your wives. (3:7) 43
> >
> > Husbands, bestow honor on your wives as the weaker sex. (3:7) 43

All of you, have unity of spirit. (3:8) 110

Have sympathy. (3:8) 54

Have a tender heart. (3:8) 54

Have a humble mind. (3:8) 87

Do not return evil for evil. (3:9) 27, 55

Do not return reviling for reviling. (3:9) 27, 54

Bless others. (3:9) 79

Keep your tongue from evil. (3:10) 72, 76

Keep your lips from speaking guile. (3:10) 65, 72

Turn from evil and do right. (3:11) 31, 94

Seek peace and pursue it. (3:12) 24, 110, 112

> Be zealous for right and there will be no one to harm you. (3:13) 118

Have no fear if you suffer for righteousness, nor be troubled, for you will be blessed. (3:14) 16, 89

Reverence Christ as Lord in your heart. (3:15) 6

Always be prepared to make a defense to anyone who calls you to make account for the hope that is in you. (3:15) 94

Keep your conscience clear, so that if you are abused those who revile your good behavior will be put to shame. (3:16) 40

Arm yourself against suffering with thoughts of Christ. (4:1) 6, 89

Live no longer by human passions, but by the will of God. (4:2) 34, 82

Keep your former life in the past, with its drunkenness, revelry, carousing, licentiousness, idolatry, and profligacy. (4:3-4) 34

Keep sane and sober for your prayers. (4:7) 13, 34

Hold unfailing your love for one another. (4:8) 22

Practice hospitality ungrudgingly. (4:9) 46

Employ your gift for one another, whether you speak or give service, as stewards of God's varied grace. (4:10) 106

Do not be surprised at the fiery ordeal that comes upon you to prove you. (4:12) 89

Rejoice when you share Christ's sufferings. (4:13) 23, 89

Consider yourself blessed when you are reproached for the name of Christ. (4:14) 23, 89

Do not be ashamed if you suffer as a Christian. (4:16) 89

Let those who suffer for God do right and entrust their souls to his faithfulness. (4:19) 89

Elders, tend the flock of God that is your charge willingly and eagerly, not by constraint. (5:2) 100

Do not domineer those under your charge, but be an example to them. (5:3) 100, 105

You that are younger, be subject to the elders. (5:5) 51, 113

Clothe yourselves with humility toward one another. (5:5) 89

Humble yourselves before the mighty hand of God, that in due time he may exalt you. (5:6) 89

Cast all your anxieties on him, for he cares for you. (5:7) 20

Be sober. (5:8) 13

Be watchful. (5:8) 17

Resist the devil, firm in your faith. (5:9) 90

Stand fast in the true grace of God. (5:12) 18

      Greet one another with the kiss of love. (5:14)

2 PETER

Direct
   Implied
      Issue Specific
         Incident/Person/Doctrine Specific

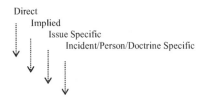

Make every effort to supplement your faith with virtue. (1:5) 7, 27, 28

Supplement faith with knowledge. (1:5) 7, 92

Supplement knowledge with self control. (1:6) 30, 92

Supplement self-control with steadfastness. (1:6) 18, 30

Supplement steadfastness with godliness. (1:6) 3, 4, 18

Supplement godliness with brotherly affection. (1:7) 3, 4, 22

Supplement brotherly affection with love. (1:7) 22

Be zealous to confirm your call. (1:11) 118

Pay attention to the prophetic word as a lamp shining in a dark place. (1:19)

Understand that no prophecy of scripture is of one's own interpretation. (1:20)

Understand that scoffers will come in the last days. (3:3)

Do not ignore this fact, that with the Lord one day is as a thousand years, and a thousand years as one day. (3:8)

    Be persons of holiness and godliness. (3:11) 3, 4

Be zealous to be found at peace, and without spot or blemish. (3:14) 3, 4, 24, 118

Count the forbearance of our Lord as salvation. (3:15) 89

Beware lest you be carried away with the error of lawless men and lose the stability of your faith. (3:17) 14, 35, 36

Grow in the grace and knowledge of our Lord and Savior Jesus Christ. (3:18) 91, 93

1 JOHN

Direct

Implied

    Issue Specific

        Incident/Person/Doctrine Specific

Do not say you have fellowship with God when you are walking in darkness. (1:6) 56, 65

Do not deceive yourself and say that you have no sin. (1:8) 99

Be sure that you know him by keeping his commandments. (2:3) 11

Keep his word so that love for God will be perfected in you. (2:5) 6, 11

If you say you abide in him, walk in the same way in which he walked. (2:6) 6, 21

    Do not say you walk in the light while you hate your brother. (2:9) 56, 65, 99

    Love your brother and walk in the light. (2:10) 22

Do not love the world or the things of the world. (2:15) 32, 33

Let what you heard from the beginning abide in you, and you will abide in the Son and in the Father. (2:24) 6

Abide in him. (2:28) 6

See what love the Father has given us that we should be called children of God. (3:1)

    Hope in him and thereby purify yourself as he is pure. (3:3) 18, 84

Let no one deceive you: He who does right is righteous, as he is righteous. (3:7) 3, 4, 81, 99

Love one another. (3:11) 22

Do not wonder that the world hates you. (3:13) 89

As he loved us, lay your lives down for the brethren. (3:16) 22, 52, 53

    If you have the world's goods, do not close your heart against your brother in need. (3:17) 27, 52

Do not love merely in word and speech, but in deed and in truth. (3:18) 12, 22, 27

    Keep his commandments and do what pleases him, and receive from him whatever you ask. (3:22) 7, 11

This is his commandment, that you should believe in his Son Jesus Christ and love one another. (3:23) 11, 22, 93

    Keep his commandments and abide in him. (3:24) 6, 11

Do not believe every spirit. (4:1) 97

Test the spirits to see whether they are of God. (4:1) 97

    Know the spirit of God by this: every spirit that confesses that Jesus Christ has come in the flesh is of God. (4:2)

    Discern between the spirit of truth and the spirit of error. (4:6) 97

Love one another, for love is of God, and he who loves is born of God and knows God. (4:7) 22

Since God has so loved us, let us love one another. (4:11) 22

    Love one another so that God will abide in you and his love will be perfected in you. (4:12) 6, 22

    Do not say you love God if you hate your brother; you are a liar. (4:20) 12, 56, 65

This commandment we have from him, that he who loves God should love his brother also. (4:21) 11, 22

This is the love of God, that we obey his commandments. (5:3) 11, 22

    Receive the testimony of God that he has borne witness to his son. (5:9)

You who believe in the name of the Son of God, know that you have eternal life. (5:13) 93

Keep yourself from idols. (5:21) 38

2 JOHN

Direct

    Implied

        Issue Specific

            Incident/Person/Doctrine Specific

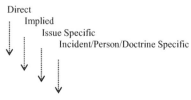

I beg you to love one another. (5) 22

This is love, that we follow his commandments. (6) 11, 22

This is the commandment that you heard from the beginning, that you follow love. (6) 11, 22

Look to yourselves, that you not lose what you have worked for, but may win a full reward. (8) 14

Do not receive anyone who does not bring the doctrine of Christ. (10)

3 John

Render service to the brethren, especially strangers. (5) 52, 53
Support those who are serving the Lord, that you may be fellow workers for the truth. (8) 69
Do not imitate evil, but imitate good. (11) 27, 34
      Greet the friends, every one of them. (15)

Jude

Contend for the faith, which was once delivered to the saints. (3) 100
Remember the predictions of the apostles when they warned against ungodly scoffers in the last days, worldly people who set up divisions. (17-19) 37, 56, 89
Build yourselves up in your holy faith. (20) 28
Pray in the Holy Spirit. (20) 5
Keep yourselves in the love of God. (21) 2, 6
Wait for the mercy of our Lord Jesus Christ unto eternal life. (21)
Convince some who doubt. (22) 100
Save some, by snatching them out of the fire. (23)
On some have mercy with fear, hating even the garment spotted by the flesh. (23) 54

Revelation

Direct
   Implied
      Issue Specific
         Incident/Person/Doctrine Specific
            Of non-Apostolic or divine authority. (spoken in *form* of
               "command" only by miscellaneous persons)

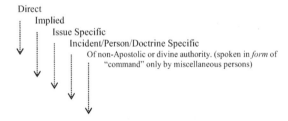

If you read the words of the prophecy and hear it and keep what is written , you will be blessed. (1:3)
    Jesus: Write what you see in a book and send it to the seven churches. (1:11)
    Jesus: Write what you see and what is to take place hereafter. (1:19)
    Jesus: To the church at Ephesus: Remember from what you have fallen, repent, and do the words you did at first. (2:5)
    He who has an ear, let him hear what the Spirit says to the churches. (2:7)
    Jesus: To the church at Smyrna: Do not fear what you about to suffer. Be faithful unto death and I will give you the crown of life. (2:10)
    He who has an ear, let him hear what the Spirit says to the churches. (2:11)
    Jesus: To the church in Pergamum: Repent of the false teachings that are among you. (2:16)
    He who has an ear, let him hear what the Spirit says to the churches. (2:17)
    Jesus: To the church in Thyartira: Hold fast to what you have until I come. (2:25)
    He who has an ear, let him hear what the Spirit says to the churches. (2:29)
    Jesus: To the church in Sardis: Awake, and strengthen what remains and is on the point of death. Remember what you have received and heard. Keep that, and repent. (3:2-3)
    He who has an ear, let him hear what the Spirit says to the churches. (3:6)
    Jesus: To the church in Philadelphia: Hold fast to what you have so that no one may seize your crown. (3:11)

He who has an ear, let him hear what the Spirit says to the churches. (3:13)

Jesus: To the church in Laodicea: Buy from me gold refined by fire, that you may be rich, and white garments to clothe you and keep the shame of your nakedness from being seen, and salve to anoint your eyes that you may see. (3:18)

Jesus: I stand at the door and knock, open the door that I may come in and eat with you. (3:20) 6, 93

He who has an ear, let him hear what the Spirit says to the churches. (3:22)

One of the four living creatures: Come up and I will show you what must take place after this. (4:1)

One of the elders: Weep not, the Lion of the tribe of Judah, the Root of David, has conquered. (5:5)

A second living creature: Come. (6:1,3,5,7)

Kings and great men of the earth: Fall on us. (6:16)

Angel: Do not harm the earth or the sea or the trees until we have sealed the servants of our God upon their foreheads. (7:3)

A voice: Release the four angels who are bound at the great river Euphrates. (9:14)

A voice from heaven: Seal up what the seven thunders have said. (10:4)

The voice from heaven: Go, take the scroll which is open in the hand of the angel. (10:8)

Angel: Take it and eat; it will be bitter to your stomach but sweet as honey in your mouth. (10:9)

You must again prophesy about many peoples and nations and tongues and kings. (10:11)

Rise and measure the temple of God and the altar and those who worship there, but do not measure the court outside the temple; leave that out. (11-1-2)

A loud voice: Come up hither. (11:12)

A loud voice in heaven: Rejoice then, O heaven, and you that dwell therein. (12:12)

If anyone has an ear, let him hear. (13:9)

Angel: Fear God and give him glory, for the hour of his judgment has come; worship him who made heaven and earth. (14:7)

A voice from heaven: Write this. (14:13)

Angel: Put in your sickle, and reap, for the hour to reap has come, for the harvest of the earth is fully ripe. (14:15)

Angel: Put in your sickle and gather the clusters of the vine of the earth, for its grapes are ripe. (14:18)

A loud voice from the temple: Go and pour out on the earth the seven bowls of the wrath of God. (16:1)

One of the seven angels: Come, I will show you the judgment of the great harlot who is seated upon many waters. (17:1)

A voice from heaven: Come out of her, my people, lest you take part in her sins. Render to her as she has rendered, and repay her double for her deeds; mix a double draft for her in the cup she mixed. (18:4, 6)

A voice from the throne: Praise our God, all you his servants. (19:5)

Angel: Write this: Blessed are those who are invited to the marriage supper of the Lamb. (19:9)

Angel: Come, gather for the great supper of God. (19:17)

Write this, for these words are trustworthy and true. (21:5)

One of the seven angels: Come, I will show you the Bride, the wife of the Lamb. (21:9)

Angel: Do not worship me, I am a fellow servant with you and with your brethren and the prophets. Do not seal up the words of the prophecy of this book, for the time is near. (22:9-10)

Come. And let him who hears say, Come. And let him who is thirsty come, let him who desires take the water of life without price. (22:17)

Do not add or take away from the words of the book of this prophecy. (22:18-19)

APPENDIX 3

Omitted and Hard to Categorize Commands

Those readers who study the list in Appendix 2 in detail will readily see many exhortations in the apostolic writings that have not been included in the 120 commands we have considered. Hopefully in most cases, in spirit and intent these will fall generally under the umbrella of one or more of the commands we looked at. An example such as Romans 12:19 comes to mind, in which Paul says, *Never avenge yourselves, but leave it to the wrath of God.* We can see this as indicating the same priority and mindset as Command 55, *Harbor no grievances or animosities.* Some may categorize this and similar commands under different headings, but such is the way I have chosen.

In other cases, the parallels are more difficult to detect. We are often left scratching our heads wondering how we are to actually apply such-and-such a command in daily life. Three examples from *Hebrews* may have great theological implications, yet are difficult to categorize into a practically *live-able* command: "Fear lest you be judged to have failed to reach God's rest," (4:1)..."See how great Melchizedek is," (7:4)..."Let us go forth to him [Jesus] outside the camp." (13:13)

The following list does not identify *every* such problematic passage. Those interested in pursuing the matter further will be able to prosecute their inquiries in the directions that hold most interest to them from the list in Appendix 2. My purpose here is merely to list a few of those seeming "commands," both direct and implied, whose intent and potential universality I particularly struggled with in making this compilation, wondering whether to include them on their own, or, if not, where and how to incorporate them under the heading of another more general command. I have also included a few of my thoughts as I wrestled with these passages.

Make straight paths for your feet. (Hebrews 12:13) This is a wonderful statement of focus and spiritual direction. I loved this command so much that for the first several drafts of the book it occupied a place of its own among the 120. Its ambiguity, however, gave me pause to reflect whether my sense of its meaning, and what it spoke to *me* of remaining single-minded and single-hearted in walking *in* but not *of* the world was indeed an accurate reflection of the author's intent. Though by implication it could be included with many of the commands we considered, it did not seem to fit precisely in any other grouping.

Be baptized. (Acts 10:48). The omission of baptism as an absolute injunction upon believers will surely be controversial. That decision should not imply that baptism is unimportant but only that it did not seem to fit with any of the groupings we considered. Along with this was weighed the fact that baptism is only commanded once, by Peter in *Acts* for a specific situation, though it is also implied by Acts 16:33 and 1 Corinthians 12:13.

Keep your faith between yourself and God. (Romans 14:22) Standing alone, these words would seem to confirm the sentiment of living quiet and peaceably in the world, letting your life be your witness rather than boasting and broadcasting your faith, as well as being quick to hear and slow to speak. Paul may indeed have intended aspects of all these. Yet this verse stands in the midst of a longer passage concerning eating, drinking, and stumbling blocks, raising the question whether Paul was simply speaking to those issues rather than making a broader point.

Run the race that you may obtain the prize. (1 Corinthians 8:24) This passage has always contained special personal meaning for me, as I am sure it does for many readers. It is another instance in which Paul poetically and memorably captures the essence of an important element of the Christian life.

Those who proclaim the gospel should get their living by the gospel. (1 Corinthians 9:14) In my opinion, Paul is taking a liberty with the Lord's words here. A workman worthy of his hire seems to me a thin basis on which to base a paid clergy, and also seems to contradict what Paul says elsewhere about workers paying their own way as he said he did.

Earnestly desire the higher gifts. (1 Corinthians 12:31) If Paul means "love" as the highest of the gifts, which 1 Corinthians 13 and 14:1 ("Make love your aim") implies, then the meaning is clear: Seek love above the public gifts such as speaking in tongues. However, if he intends to say that we should seek certain gifts (such as prophecy) above others, that there is a hierarchy of "greater" and "lesser" gifts given by God, then we may legitimately question the universality of this exhortation that has led many through the years to seek the manifestation of certain gifts more than the Spirit behind the gifts.

Hold true to what you have attained. (Philippians 3:16) This injunction may be implied by building mature beliefs, or being equipped for completeness. Yet it remains ambiguous. Paul may be saying, in different words, what is emphasized elsewhere, "Don't drift away from faith." George MacDonald emphasizes this command as parallel to *Walk in the light you have.* Obey what you know to do, what truth you have been shown, and more understanding will follow. In other words, *Do what you know.*

Do not make plans when you don't know what tomorrow will bring, but say "If the Lord wills." (James 4:13-15) James is here reiterating his brother's command, "Do not be anxious for the morrow," adding the caveat, if you speak of the future, to say, "If the Lord wills."

Live as free men...as servants of God. (1 Peter 2:16) These words are found in the midst of a passage about honoring worldly and governmental authority. It is a puzzling command and the heart of Peter's intent is difficult to plumb. The two enigmatic verses read: "For it is God's will that by doing right you should put to silence the ignorance of foolish men. Live as free men, yet without using your freedom as a pretext for evil; but live as servants of God." (1 Peter 2:15-16)

Hear what the Spirit says to the churches. (Revelation 2 and 3) The repeated use of this phrase in *Revelation* obviously has specialized meaning, which is further individualized in the specific messages to each of the churches. In a general context it may fall under the many injunctions to listen carefully.

Finally, the following is a list of exhortations which I did not think rose to the level of universal applicability, about which I did not feel I had insight to offer, or whose intent and meaning I did not feel I had probed in sufficient depth to comment on.

If you do wrong, be afraid. (Romans 13:4)
Do not let what is good to you be spoken of as evil. (Romans 14:16)
Let those who mourn live as though they were not mourners. (1 Corinthians 7:30)
Let those who rejoice live as though they were not rejoicing. (1 Corinthians 7:30)
Let those who buy live as though they had no goods. (1 Corinthians 7:30)
Let those who deal with the world live as though they had no dealings with the world. (1 Corinthians 7:30)

Do not neglect your salvation, nor accept the grace of God in vain. (2 Corinthians 6:1)

Commend yourself by the Holy Spirit and the power of God. (2 Corinthians 6:6-7)

Do not submit to a yoke of slavery. (Galatians 5:1)

Address one another in psalms and hymns and spiritual songs, singing and making melody to the Lord with all your heart. (Ephesians 5:19, Colossians 3:16)

Do not despise prophesying. (1 Thessalonians 5:20)

Never admit a charge against an elder except on the evidence of two or three witnesses. (1 Timothy 5:19)

Keep these rules without favor. (1 Timothy 5:21)

Rekindle the gift of God that is within you. (2 Timothy 1:6)

Understand that in the last days there will come times of stress. (2 Timothy 3:1)

Be urgent in season and out of season. (2 Timothy 4:2)

Let no one disregard you. (Titus 2:15)

Insist on these things. (Titus 3:8)

Fear lest you be judged to have failed to reach God's rest. (Hebrews 4:1)

See how great Melchizedek is. (Hebrews 7:4)

Draw near to God in assurance of faith. (Hebrews 10:22)

See that you do not refuse him who is speaking. (Hebrews 12:25)

Let us go forth to him outside the camp and bear the abuse he endured. (Hebrews 13:13)

Speak and act as those who are to be judged under the law of liberty. (James 2:12)

Be wretched and mourn and weep. (James 4:9)

Let your laughter be turned to mourning, and your joy to dejection. (James 4:9)

You who are rich, weep and howl for the miseries that will come upon you. (James 5:1)

Conduct yourself with fear throughout the time of your exile. (1 Peter 1:17)

Fear God. (1 Peter 2:17)

Reverence Christ in your heart. (1 Peter 3:5)

Pay attention to the prophetic word as a lamp shining in a dark place. (2 Peter 1:19)

You must understand this, that no prophecy of scripture is a matter of one's own interpretation. (2 Peter 1:20)

Understand that scoffers will come in the last days. (2 Peter 3:3)

Do not ignore this one fact, that with the Lord one day is as a thousand years, and a thousand years as one day. (2 Peter 3:8)

Purify yourself through hope. (1 John 3:3)

Know the spirit of God by this: every spirit that confesses that Jesus Christ has come in the flesh is of God. (1 John 4:2)

Do not receive anyone who does not bring the doctrine of Christ. (2 John 10)

Wait for the mercy of our Lord Jesus Christ unto eternal life. (Jude 21)

Save some, by snatching them out of the fire. (Jude 23)

Do not seal up the words of the prophecy of this book. (Revelation 22:10)

Let him who is thirsty come, let him who desires take the water of life without price. (Revelation 22:17)

Do not add or take away from the words of the book of this prophecy. (Revelation 22:18-19)

Other non-fiction titles from Michael Phillips that readers may enjoy include:

George MacDonald, Scotland's Beloved Storyteller (1987)
A God To Call Father (1994)
Universal Reconciliation (1998)
God A Good Father (2001)
Jesus An Obedient Son (2002)
Make Me Like Jesus (2003)
Is Jesus Coming Back As Soon As We Think? (2004)
The Commands of Jesus (2012)
Bold Thinking Christianity (2013)
Practical Essential Christianity (2013)
The Eyewitness New Testament (2013)
George MacDonald and the Late Great Hell Debate (2013)
George MacDonald's Spiritual Vision: An Overview (2016)
George MacDonald's Transformational Theology of the Christian Faith   (2017)
Finding Fatherhood in the Old Testament (2017)
A Sacrifice of Obedience (2017)
The Will of God (2017)

Made in the USA
Monee, IL
27 February 2022

91992284R00125